NEW ENGLAND
BIKING

NEW ENGLAND
BIKING

100 of the Best Road and Trail Rides

First Edition

Melissa L. Kim

AVALON
TRAVEL

FOGHORN OUTDOORS NEW ENGLAND BIKING
100 of the Best Road and Trail Rides

First Edition

Melissa L. Kim

Printing History
First edition—February 2005
5 4 3 2 1

Avalon Travel Publishing
An Imprint of
Avalon Publishing Group, Inc.

AVALON
publishing group incorporated

ISBN: 1-56691-744-1
ISSN: 1553-5657

Editors: Grace Fujimoto, Elizabeth McCue
Series Manager: Grace Fujimoto
Acquisitions Editor: Rebecca K. Browning
Copy Editor: Karen Gaynor Bleske
Graphics Coordinator: Deb Dutcher
Production Coordinator: Darren Alessi
Cover and Interior Designer: Darren Alessi
Map Editors: Olivia Solís, Kevin Anglin
Cartographers: Kat Kalamaras, Kat Smith, Mike Morgenfeld
Indexer: Laura Welcome

Front cover photo: © John Isch

Printed in the United States of America by Worzalla

About the Author

Melissa L. Kim has been writing about travel and the outdoors for more than a dozen years. Though she's a hiker, sea kayaker, camper, skier, and scuba diver, bicycling is her true outdoor passion. She started biking when she was in grade school in Massachusetts (in fact, one of the routes in this book passes by her former four-room elementary school), graduated to cycle touring in Rhode Island, and evolved into a bike commuter in New York and London. Since then, bicycles have taken her on tours all over the world, though researching, riding, and writing *Foghorn Outdoors New England Biking* took her to exotic and remote places that she never knew, right around the corner from her current home in Portland, Maine.

Regionally, her words and photographs have appeared in the *Portland Press Herald/Maine Sunday Telegram, MaineToday.com, Natural New England* magazine, *Maine: Experience* magazine, and publications of the Maine Audubon Society, The Wilderness Society, the Maine Island Trail Association, the Maine College of Art, and the Children's Museum of Maine. She has also written six children's books, edited two magazines, and contributed to various travel and children's magazines and publications. She holds a bachelor's degree in Environmental Studies from Brown University and a master's degree in Journalism from New York University.

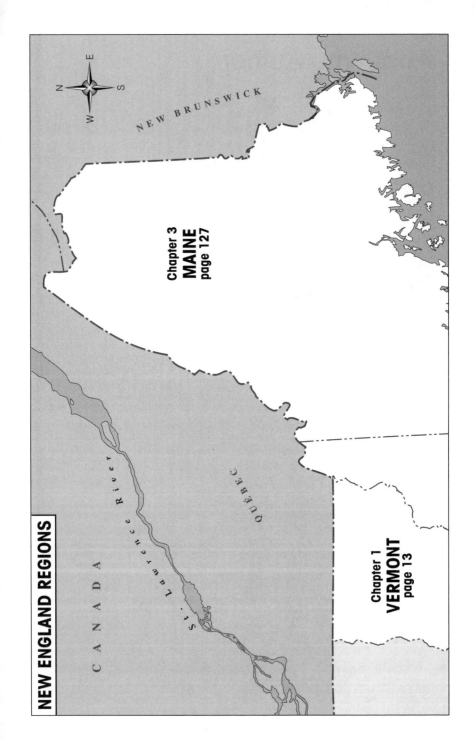

NEW ENGLAND REGIONS

NEW BRUNSWICK

Chapter 3
MAINE
page 127

Chapter 1
VERMONT
page 13

QUÉBEC

CANADA

St. Lawrence River

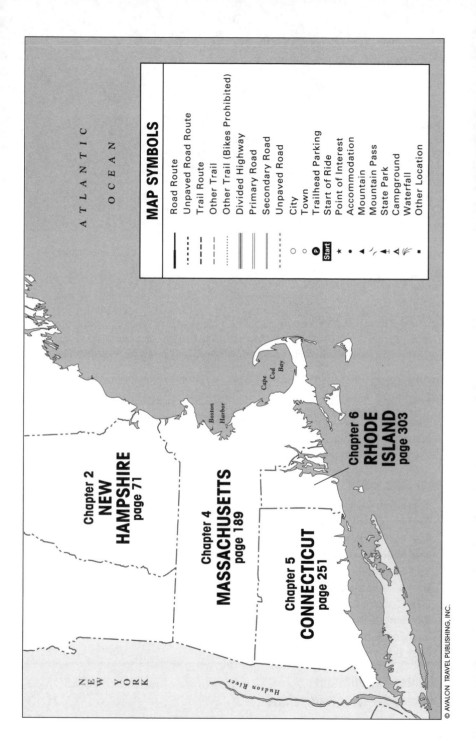

MAP SYMBOLS

———	Road Route
· · · · ·	Unpaved Road Route
– – –	Trail Route
– · –	Other Trail
· · · · · ·	Other Trail (Bikes Prohibited)
═══	Divided Highway
━━━	Primary Road
───	Secondary Road
= = =	Unpaved Road
○	City
○	Town
Ⓟ	Trailhead Parking
Start	Start of Ride
★	Point of Interest
•	Accommodation
◄	Mountain
✓	Mountain Pass
◄	State Park
⩘	Campground
↙	Waterfall
■	Other Location

ATLANTIC OCEAN

Chapter 2
NEW HAMPSHIRE
page 71

Chapter 4
MASSACHUSETTS
page 189

Chapter 5
CONNECTICUT
page 251

Chapter 6
RHODE ISLAND
page 303

Boston Harbor

Cape Cod Bay

NEW YORK

Hudson River

© AVALON TRAVEL PUBLISHING, INC.

Contents

Our Commitment

We are committed to making *Foghorn Outdoors New England Biking* the most accurate and enjoyable biking guide to the region. With this first edition you can rest assured that every ride in this book has been carefully reviewed and accompanied by the most up-to-date information. Be aware that with the passing of time some of the fees listed herein may have changed, and trails or roads may have closed unexpectedly. If you have a specific need or concern, it's best to call the location ahead of time. The authors and publisher of *Foghorn Outdoors New England Biking* are not responsible for injuries that occur to readers using this book.

If you would like to comment on the book, whether it's to suggest a ride we overlooked, or to let us know about any noteworthy experience—good or bad—that occurred while using *Foghorn Outdoors New England Biking* as your guide, we would appreciate hearing from you. Please address correspondence to:

Foghorn Outdoors New England Biking, 1st edition
Avalon Travel Publishing
1400 65th Street, Suite 250
Emeryville, CA 94608

email: atpfeedback@avalonpub.com
If you send us an email, please put "New England Biking" in the subject line.

How to Use This Book

Foghorn Outdoors New England Biking is divided into six chapters: Vermont, New Hampshire, Maine, Massachusetts, Connecticut, and Rhode Island. Navigating this guide can be done easily in two ways:

1. If you know the general area you want to visit within one of the regions, turn to the map at the beginning of that chapter. You can determine which bike routes are in or near your destination by finding their corresponding numbers on the map. Opposite the map is a table of contents listing each route in the chapter by map number and page number. Turn to the corresponding page for the route that interests you.

2. If you know the name of the route—or the name of the surrounding geographical area or nearby feature (town, national or state park or forest, lake, etc.)—look it up in the index and turn to the corresponding page.

About the Ride Number and Name

Each ride in this book has a number and name. The ride's number allows you to find it easily on the corresponding chapter map. The name is either the actual trail or street name (as listed on signposts and maps), or a name I've given to a series of trails or routes. In these cases, the ride's name is taken from the focal point of the route—usually the name of the region or a geographic landmark, such as a river it follows or the destination it reaches.

About the Route Details

At the top of each ride description, you'll find five pieces of key information:

Type of trail—This notes the kind of trail surface or surfaces you'll encounter, plus how much car or other traffic is common along the route. Single-track trails are also noted here. Icons are used to provide at-a-glance information:

 = paved road or bike path; road bikes are appropriate

 = dirt road or trail; mountain bikes are appropriate

If both icons appear, the route is a mix of pavement and dirt; these routes are typically traveled by mountain bikes.

Total distance—This is the total round-trip mileage for the ride.

Riding time—This is the estimated time it will take to complete the ride. Remember that times may vary due to your level of riding experience, the weather, and the number and length of any breaks taken.

Difficulty— Each ride in this book is listed with a difficulty rating. The scale is generally applied as follows:

1 These rides would be suitable for families with young children, novice riders, or those wanting a casual, recreational ride. They include both road rides and mountain bike rides that are nearly level and are usually less than 15 miles or have shorter options. Trail surfaces are smooth, and most are on bike paths where there is no vehicle traffic.

2 These rides are suitable for families with older children and for strong beginners, i.e., novices who are physically fit. Road rides are generally less than 25 miles and have little elevation gain. Off-road rides may involve some varied surfaces but don't require technical mountain biking skills. Bikers should expect to ride on dirt or grassy trails, dirt roads, and a variety of surfaces.

3 These rides are appropriate for people with solid aerobic fitness and some cycling experience. Road rides are generally less than 30 miles and involve moderate hill climbs. Mountain bike rides will require some basic technical skills, such as the ability to ride over and around rough surfaces (rocks, roots, ruts, water obstacles), descend hills, maneuver through tight turns, follow a narrow line with good balance, etc. Bikers should have moderate experience on a variety of trails, including single-track.

4 These rides are suitable for intermediate riders with excellent aerobic fitness. Road rides are generally 20–40 miles long and involve some steep hill-climbing. Mountain bike rides require technical skills, involve some steep hill climbs and descents, and call for good bike handling skills. Bikers should have solid experience on a variety of trails, including single-track.

5 These are challenging rides for experienced cyclists with excellent aerobic fitness. Road rides have several steep or prolonged hill climbs, and some routes are more than 50 miles. Mountain bike rides are technical, on a variety of surfaces and types of trails, require advanced bike handling skills, may have hike-a-bike sections, and generally include steep climbs and descents.

Elevation gain—This conveys the approximate total elevation *climbed.* For example, if there are two peaks in a route, one with an 850-foot climb and the other with a 1,000-foot climb, the total elevation gain would be 1,850 feet. The measurements were taken using topographic maps and other paper sources. They may not be precise, but should be considered very good estimates.

About the Route Description
This narrative section outlines the less measurable elements of the ride. You'll read my observations about the ride in general, plus firsthand experience with other user groups, route conditions, and any technically difficult spots. How rain, wind, and heat can affect your ride is discussed, along with car traffic and any steep grades. I also describe the scenery and outstanding qualities of each ride.

About the Route Directions
With each ride in this book you'll find a mile-by-mile listing of what to expect along the trail or road. Every major junction or turn is noted in the mileage log and recorded to the nearest tenth of a mile. Please note, however, that determining mileage is an inexact science. One bicycle's cyclometer will often disagree with another bicycle's cyclometer. For example, reducing your tire pressure changes the rolling radius of your wheel, which affects what your cyclometer registers as mileage. Putting more weight on your front tire (such as during a descent) affects your cyclometer's reading. Then there is human error: Where you "zero out" your mileage (or where you start the clock) will have a big impact on your mile-by-mile status. Small diversions from

the path (such as riding back 50 yards to check on your riding partner, then turning around and heading back) create noticeable changes in your mileage.

To put it simply, use some perspective when using the mileage logs. If the log notes that a right turn is coming up at mile 4.2 and you can't find it, try riding another quarter mile or so to see if it shows up (or backtrack, to see if you've missed it!). Most importantly, always carry a good map with you.

About the Elevation Profiles

Provided for each ride is an elevation profile, which approximately graphs the hills and dips on the route in height and distance. The scales on each profile are dramatically different, varying from 25-foot to 1,000-foot increments for height (elevation), and varying from a few miles to nearly 100 miles for distance. In addition, not all profiles begin at an elevation of zero feet. For this reason, please pay special attention to the numbers marked on the two axes of the graphs.

About the Maps

Each chapter in this book begins with a map of the region it covers. Every ride's starting point is noted by a number on the map. These points are placed as precisely as possible, but the scale of these maps often makes it difficult to pinpoint a ride's exact starting point. I advise you to purchase a detailed map of the area, especially if it is new to you.

Some of the rides also feature a trail map. However, if the area is new to you, or if you would like to see topographic lines, I recommend obtaining a more detailed map. If you are riding in a national, state, county, or regional park, pick up a park trail map from the visitors center or entrance station. Bike and outdoors shops also carry detailed maps.

Dedicated to the memory of Zachary Robb Gaulkin

1965–2003

© MELISSA L. KIM

Introduction

When I first started researching this book, it became immediately clear that the hardest part would be deciding what *not* to include. Everyone I talked to recommended at least one ride that didn't make the cut. There are so many great places to ride both on- and off-road in New England that choosing only 15 or 18 for each state was a great challenge.

I grew up in New England, and then I left it and the United States for many years. When I was ready to move back, I considered all the corners of North America. But New England drew me in for so many reasons. The four seasons are so distinct here; you could do a ride in spring, come back to the same ride in fall, and have a totally different experience.

The scenery is also rich in diversity, from Maine's dramatic rocky coastline to the sand dunes of Cape Cod, from the lush Green Mountains in Vermont and New Hampshire's rolling hills and valleys to Rhode Island's bays and islands and Connecticut's stone walls and rural corners. History is all around you, in the form of old cemeteries with Civil War graves, Native American trails and place names, town commons and general stores more than 200 years old, and historic houses that were home to some of our nation's founding politicians and artists.

The countryside is so accessible here, and it's easy to get away from the crowds and to get "off the beaten path." New England possesses a seemingly endless supply of back roads, dirt roads, old logging roads, former horse-and-buggy trails, and converted rail trails in a region where trains were once so prevalent. I think I know the area, but I'm always discovering new places to explore and new trails to ride.

For this book, I tried to include a wide range of rides, both in terms of geography and scenery, as well as difficulty, type of riding experience, accessibility, and so on. If you are a New Englander, you may not see your favorite riding spot here. You should be thankful—it's a secret for a little while longer! Some of the most excellent off-road riding spots aren't included because of uncertainty with land access, an issue that continues to challenge mountain bikers everywhere. Thanks to the advocacy and hard work of many cycling groups in New England, there are still plenty of excellent trails and land available, so let's keep it that way.

Many people ask me why the book includes both road and off-road rides. Maybe there was a time when people did only one or the other. But that time is long gone. Plenty of cyclists I know have two bikes, one to take them into the backcountry, stump-jumping and rock-hopping, and one to take them along roads to explore different destinations. Most kids have hybrid or mountain bikes that can just as easily take on a dirt trail as a paved bike path. Families or groups on vacation can have several different biking experiences in one trip.

Even if you're interested in only one type of riding, this book still has plenty to offer. I like to think of the routes in this book as starting points. Each one can lead to another ride in the area, or be adapted or expanded into a different ride. These routes tell you exactly where to go, but that shouldn't limit you. Explore, get lost, discover something new. After all, the best way to experience the many sides of New England is on two wheels.

Biking Tips

Anyone who has ever pedaled a bike knows the feeling of freedom it brings, the breeze on your face and the road flashing by. Cycling, both on- and off-road, is a great way to explore, exercise, and travel, but it also involves certain risks and dangers. Observing the rules of the road or trail, following basic safety guidelines, and knowing how to repair and maintain your bike will ensure you many years of happy, trouble-free biking.

Bike Safety Tips

There are many things you can do to prevent accidents, both to yourself and to others. Bicycling is all about sharing—sharing the road or trail, and sharing information. Above all, prepare and protect yourself.

Wear a helmet. It's like wearing a seat belt when you're in a car. Why wouldn't you? It's your most important piece of safety equipment. Also, make sure it fits correctly. It should be tight enough so that when you open your jaw, you can feel the helmet pulling down on your head, but loose enough so that you can get a few fingers between the strap and your chin. If you're not sure, stop in at a bike shop and ask for help fitting the helmet.

Share the road. If you expect motorists to be courteous, you need to be courteous, too. Obey all traffic laws, ride with traffic, and ride single file in traffic. Ride predictably; don't swerve or dodge between cars, and make sure drivers know what your intentions are by using hand signals to signal turns or stops. In heavy traffic, make eye contact with motorists. Get into the appropriate lane—don't ride in a right-turn-only lane if you are going straight, and move into the straight-through lane early. If you need to pass a pedestrian or cyclist, let him or her know you are coming. Off-road, always yield to hikers or equestrians, and let others know you are coming.

Take care of yourself. Ride within your limits, or at least know your own physical limitations. If you've never ridden more than 20 miles and want to plan a 50-mile trip, factor in rest breaks and a backup plan or route. It's okay to walk, too. You may need to dismount to climb a steep hill, to cross bridges and streams, to climb over rock walls or over a downed tree. You can also walk if the terrain just looks too tough. All mountain bikers spend a lot of time off the bike. Bring plenty of water, and don't wait until you are thirsty to drink. Bring high-energy snacks (energy bars, fruit, nuts) or make sure you stop and get some along the way.

Be observant. You need to be aware of your environment and surroundings, for safety and for fun. Don't wear headphones. On the road, watch for sudden door openings of parked cars, or check to see if people are sitting inside parked cars. Look ahead for changing road conditions, such as sandy shoulders or large potholes. At intersections, look for turning cars. Don't just look ahead; know what's behind you as well, by checking over your shoulder or using a mirror. Off-road, know how to read the trail. Look ahead for obstacles and conditions, so they don't come as a surprise. Don't "trailgate." You want a chance to see trail conditions and hazards and work out how to deal with them. If you are right behind another biker, you won't have a chance to see the trail.

Rules of the Road

Each of the six New England states applies slightly different laws to bicyclists. Most require helmets for children, lights at night, working brakes, and proper child seats. Follow these rules, and you'll be well within the law in any state in New England (this is by no means a comprehensive list of state laws, so check with the state's Department of Transportation or relevant agency if you have any questions; see Resources for contact information):

- Obey all traffic laws, and use hand signals for turning.
- Wear a helmet (in Connecticut, Maine, and Rhode Island, helmets are required by law for youths under 16; in Massachusetts, helmets are required for children under 13).
- Child carriers must offer protection from rear wheel spokes and have a strap to secure the child (in Connecticut, bicyclists riding with child carriers must be 18 years old or older, and a child in a carrier must be no more than 4 years old; in Massachusetts, the child must be between the ages of 1 and 5 years, or be below 40 pounds in weight).
- Ride as far as practicable to the right side of the road.
- If you're riding at night, use a white headlight, a red taillight, pedal reflectors (or, if you have clipless pedals, reflective legbands), and side reflectors.
- Make sure the steering, brakes, tires, and other required equipment are in safe, working condition.
- Ride on regular and permanently attached seats and don't carry extra passengers on your bike.
- Don't hitch a ride or attach your bike to a moving vehicle.
- Don't use earphones and headsets.
- If you ride two abreast, make sure you do not impede traffic and, on a laned roadway, ride single file.
- Carry packages only in or on a basket, rack, or trailer, and keep at least one hand on the handlebars at all times.

Be prepared. Plan your route and make sure you have a good map. Check the weather and dress for the day, or bring along extra clothing or waterproofs if rain is forecast. If you are starting later in the day, bring lights. Wear bright clothing, bring some cash and identification, and make sure your tires are pumped up to the right pressure. If you are riding in a remote area, especially off-road, you'll need a little more preparation. Maps become essential, and you may need a road map as well as a topographic map, a compass, or a GPS device. If you're riding alone, tell someone your trip plans and consider bringing a cell phone. Check the Essential Gear List.

Know your bike. The more you get to know your bike, the more fun you'll have with it. Make sure you know how to do emergency roadside repairs and basic maintenance. If you don't know, or have trouble teaching yourself, take a bike repair or maintenance class. Take a quick safety

Rules of the Trail

New England's off-road riding comes in a variety of places, from trails in state parks and forests to backcountry dirt roads and public rights-of-way and to trails on private property where public access has been granted. In some places, both public and private trails have been, and are being, closed to mountain bikers because of trail erosion, trespassing on closed trails, and conflicts with other users. Mountain bikers have a responsibility, both to landowners and other bikers, to use the land respectfully.

The International Mountain Bicycling Association, an advocacy group that creates, enhances, and preserves trail opportunities, has developed six Rules of the Trail that are recognized around the world as the standard code of conduct for mountain bikers. Follow these rules, be a low-impact rider, and leave no trace, so we can continue to enjoy the thrill of riding off-road.

• Ride on open trails only. Respect trail and road closures (ask if uncertain); avoid trespassing on private land; obtain permits or other authorization as may be required. Federal and state wilderness areas are closed to cycling. The way you ride will influence trail management decisions and policies.

• Leave no trace. Be sensitive to the dirt beneath you. Recognize different types of soils and trail construction; practice low-impact cycling. Wet and muddy trails are more vulnerable to damage. When the trail bed is soft, consider other riding options. This also means staying on existing trails and not creating new ones. Don't cut switchbacks. Be sure to pack out at least as much as you pack in.

• Control your bicycle. Inattention for even a second can cause problems. Obey all bicycle speed regulations and recommendations.

• Always yield trail. Let your fellow trail users know you're coming. A friendly greeting or bell is considerate and works well; don't startle others. Show your respect when passing by slowing to a walking pace or even stopping. Anticipate other trail users around corners or in blind spots. Yielding means slow down, establish communication, be prepared to stop if necessary and pass safely.

• Never scare animals. All animals are startled by an unannounced approach, a sudden movement, or a loud noise. This can be dangerous for you, others, and the animals. Give animals extra room and time to adjust to you. When passing horses, use special care and follow directions from the horseback riders (ask if uncertain). Running cattle and disturbing wildlife are serious offenses. Leave gates as you found them, or as marked.

• Plan ahead. Know your equipment, your ability, and the area in which you are riding—and prepare accordingly. Be self-sufficient at all times, keep your equipment in good repair, and carry necessary supplies for changes in weather or other conditions. A well-executed trip is a satisfaction to you and not a burden to others. Always wear a helmet and appropriate safety gear.

Reprinted with permission from IMBA

check before each ride. Are the wheels fastened tightly and correctly? Make sure the handlebars are tight (push down or pull up on the handlebars). Make sure the stem is tight (facing your bike, straddle the front wheel and try twisting the handlebars from side to side).

Make sure your tires are the right pressure. You'll see the recommended pressures written on the sides of the tires. For mountain biking, if you are going to be on a bumpy, rocky, rooty trail, you'll want less pressure in the tires to get more contact with the ground. If you are riding on a packed gravel bike path, you can put more air in the tires so you'll go a little faster.

Learn some basic riding techniques. Several techniques and tricks will help you improve and make it possible for you to ride safely on a wide range of surfaces. Gears are crucial: If you've never had a bike with 21 gears, get to know how to shift properly and to know what each gear will do for you. Learn from others, practice in an empty parking lot, or take a class.

Use brakes wisely: Most of your braking power comes from the front brakes, but don't use just the front brakes or you'll flip right over the handlebars. Learn to use a combination of front and back brakes. Don't squeeze too hard, or you'll lock up the wheels into a skid. Learn to brake before a curve or corner so you can ride through it at the right speed.

For mountain biking, move your weight back to lift the front wheel slightly to get over rocks and roots. On steep downhills, shift your weight back by sliding well back on the seat, even off the seat and over the rear wheel if possible.

Essential Gear List

It might look like a long list, but you can fit the essentials into a small bag that fits under the saddle of your bike. You may not always carry the other items, depending on how long your ride or how remote the route, but keep them in your car or at home, and know how to use them. Nine times out of 10, you feel stupid for carrying all the gear, but that 1 time in 10, you're a hero. I whipped a bandage out of my handlebar bag to patch up a girl who'd skinned her knee on the Cape Cod Rail Trail, and the relief on her mom's face made me glad I'd carried that little first-aid bag for miles.

Essential:
• Spare inner tube
• Pump
• Tire levers
• Patch kit (make sure it's not 3 years old; the glue can dry out)
• Allen wrench set
• Chain tool (more important if you are mountain biking)
• Small first-aid kit (even if it's just a few bandages and antiseptic cream)
• Water bottles (some riders prefer a hydration bag that you wear on your back; make sure you have at least two bottles full of clean, fresh water)
• Food (high energy snacks are better than candy bars)
• Map
• Lights
• Money and identification

Recommended:
• Biking gloves (for long rides or rides on bumpy, uneven pavement, padded gloves will make your hands and arms so much more comfortable and able to absorb shocks and road vibrations)

- Biking shorts (same as the gloves, but for a different part of your body)
- Spare clothing (and a place to put layers that you remove; even a bungee to strap a jacket onto the back rack is enough)
- Sunglasses and/or eye protection (essential if you wear contact lenses; nothing's worse than dirt, grit, or a piece of glass in your eye)
- Sunscreen and lip balm
- Insect repellent (more important for off-road rides in the woods)
- Bike lock (you never know when you might want or need to leave your bike somewhere)
- More tools (wrenches, and a Swiss Army style knife or multitool with screwdrivers and a blade)
- Duct tape (it holds the universe together; I wrap some around a stub of a pencil, so I've got both a writing tool and all-useful tape)
- Cell phone (as long as you don't rely on it to get you out of a tight spot)
- Waterproof matches (because you just never know)
- Compass (especially useful for off-road riding)

To keep in the car:
- Dry clothes to change into
- Extra water and food
- First-aid kit
- Still more tools
- Oil and chain lubricant
- Rags (if it's raining or muddy, you'll want to wipe off your frame and tires)

Repairs and Maintenance

Have you ever been starting to climb a hill, tried to shift gears, and heard only a clicking sound when the chain won't shift? Or heard that awful squealing as you brake, ineffectively, on a downhill? Don't blame your bike for these noises. You need to take care of your bike so it can take care of you. This means doing some simple upkeep and maintenance. And in case of a real breakdown, every cyclist should know how to do some basic roadside repairs.

Basic Maintenance

According to my favorite bike mechanic, Michael Pappaconstantine of Belmont (MA) Wheelworks, who offered these maintenance tips, cleaning your bike is the best form of basic maintenance. You'll get to know the parts of your bike and spot trouble areas such as worn or misaligned brake pads, cuts in the tires, and fraying or rusting cables. You also get rid of abrasive sand and dirt that causes wear on the bike parts.

To wash your bike, stand it up using a stand or tree or whatever's handy. Don't turn the bike upside down; water may get into bearings that need to stay dry. Rinse the bike first, either with a bucket of water or a garden hose on a gentle setting. Then get a bucket of warm, soapy water (dish soap is fine) and use this to scrub the bike gently with a brush or sponge. Don't forget to scrub the wheel rims, either now or with a rag when the bike is dry. You might want to use a separate sponge for the chain and drive train parts. Rinse the bike off, then dry it with a chamois or soft towel. Then clean and lube the chain.

If there's only one thing you ever do to maintain your bike, make it this one: Clean the chain. This will make riding and shifting so much smoother and efficient; you'll really notice the difference. Wipe the chain off with a clean rag to get at the first layer of grease and grime. Then scrub away at all the parts of the drive train (all the pieces of your bike that the chain comes into contact with)—the chain itself, the crankset, derailleurs, and cassette. Use a citrus degreaser or other biodegradable solvent, and use a rag, small brush (such as an old toothbrush), screwdriver, or whatever tools seem to work. When you're done, apply a small amount of lubricant to the chain. The biggest mistake people make is to overlube the chain. There are several types to choose from, so ask at the bike shop and make sure to mention what type of riding you do.

Roadside Repairs

The more you ride, the more you'll want to learn about how to fix your bike. Every cyclist, beginner or advanced, on- or off-road, needs to know how to fix a flat tire. Mountain bikers in particular should know how to fix a broken chain. From there, you can graduate to replacing broken cables or broken spokes, fixing bent rims, and so on. Many other repairs, adjustments, and fine-tuning can wait until you get home and fix it yourself or take it to a bike shop.

Fixing a flat. If you are 15 miles away from the start of a ride or trailhead and you pop your tire by running over a piece of glass, you need to be able to fix the tire. Don't ride with a flat tire, don't rely on others to know how to fix it for you, and don't rely on a cell phone to get you out of a jam! Fixing a flat can be quick and easy if you practice a few times. Get a bike repair manual, take a class, or have an experienced cyclist show you how to do it. The basic steps: Release the brake and remove the wheel; remove the valve cap, deflate the tire, and use tire levers to remove the tire and tube; inspect the tire, tube, and rim to find and remove the cause of the flat; replace the inner tube with a new one or patch the old one; put the tube and tire back on the wheel; inflate and seat the tire.

Repairing a broken chain. This requires a little more skill and knowledge about what type of chain you have on your bike. You'll also need a chain tool (these are fairly small, inexpensive, and very useful). If you are serious about cleaning your chain, you'll want one anyway, since the most thorough chain cleaning requires removing the chain from the derailleur. For a trailside repair, use the chain tool to push out the damaged pin or link. Use a replacement pin or link to repair the chain; use the chain tool to reconnect the chain. In an emergency, you can reconnect the chain at the next link, though a shorter chain will mean you will probably not have full use of your gears, so ride home cautiously.

Best Bike Rides

Best Family-Friendly Rides

Island Line Rail Trail, Vermont, page 22. This converted railway bed lets you ride from downtown Burlington past parks onto a dramatic causeway sticking right into Lake Champlain.

Franconia Recreational Trail, New Hampshire, page 82. In the heart of the White Mountains, this easy ride gives you some of the best views of the mountains and goes by great picnic spots.

Carriage Roads, Maine, page 160. Choose how long to ride on miles of carriage roads (with no cars to reckon with) that offer views of mountains, lakes, and the ocean.

Peaks Island Loop, Maine, page 179. This short but sweet loop around the island has shoreline views, great picnic spots, and a short ferry ride to get there.

Cape Cod Rail Trail, Massachusetts, page 244. This paved trail is almost totally flat and passes lots of good stopping points, from sandy ocean beaches to trailside food and ice-cream stands.

East Bay Bike Path, Rhode Island, page 318. Though there are a lot of road crossings, this level, smooth bike path rides near two gorgeous state parks, perfect for picnics and side trips.

Best Rides for Wildlife-Viewing

Wells River Rail Trail, Vermont, page 33. This remote rail trail goes through pretty forests and past quiet ponds, all great spots for birders and wildlife enthusiasts.

Kittredge Hill Loop, New Hampshire, page 105. Mud, ruts, and moose are all features of this tough mountain bike ride; we saw three moose during one ride in October.

Baring Division Trail, Maine, page 144. In this remote 17,000-plus-acre national wildlife refuge, you might see leopard frogs, painted turtles, river otters, white-tailed deer, moose, and even black bear—not to mention birds, including American woodcock, osprey, owls, and bald eagles.

Plum Island, Massachusetts, page 194. Something like 300 types of birds come annually to the Parker River National Wildlife Refuge.

Worden Pond Loop, Rhode Island, page 335. Turtles cross the dirt roads in front of you and ospreys nest on poles in the middle of Great Swamp.

Best Butt-Kickers

Kittredge Hill Loop, New Hampshire, page 105. Lots of different obstacles on the trails make this a technically challenging ride.

Grafton Notch Loop, Maine, page 150. Lots of hill-climbing takes you through the beautiful Mahoosuc range on this 67-mile route.

Old Florida Road, Massachusetts, page 200. Depending on the season, this route can have knee-deep mud and ponds to cross, slick rocks to ride both up and down, and steep rocky scrambles in a remote location.

Quabbin East Loop, Massachusetts, page 228. This loop includes endless hills that take you in and out of three lovely villages with great general stores and town greens.

Slick Rock Scramble, Connecticut, page 280. Extremely technical, this loop challenges you with stream crossings, obstacles, and a monster climb up three sections of "slick rock."

The Breakers is one of Newport's grandest mansions. The National Historic Landmark has 70 rooms and sits on 13 prime acres.

Best Historical Rides

Tunbridge Trilogy Loop, Vermont, page 43. Ride this route in the fall and stop by the Tunbridge World's Fair, which has been going continuously since 1867.

Green Mountain Peaks and Hollows, Vermont, page 64. Ride by the Grandma Moses Schoolhouse Museum and circle around the impressive 306-foot-high obelisk dedicated to the Revolutionary War Battle of Bennington.

Cornish Colony Loop, New Hampshire, page 96. An early-20th-century artist's colony, old brick churches, and the country's longest covered bridge are features of this route.

Quabbin East Loop, Massachusetts, page 228. Look for historic markers, stone walls, and old cemeteries as you ride between three charming villages, all with beautiful old town commons anchored by quintessential New England general stores.

Blackstone River Ride, Rhode Island, page 311. Historic mill towns, the Blackstone Canal, built in the 1820s, and a transportation museum give you insight into the Industrial Revolution's birth in this corner of New England.

Ocean Drive, Rhode Island, page 326. Start at a 19th-century fort and ride by the splendors of the Gilded Age mansions.

Cross-Border Ride, Rhode Island, page 329. Stone walls seem to stretch endlessly through fields and hamlets surrounding the lovely 17th-century village of Little Compton.

Best Scenic Rides

Rupert Mountain Loop, Vermont, page 55. Route B of this loop goes from a rail trail into some real backcountry dirt roads with bucolic views of cows grazing in fields near red barns with silver silos.

Carrabassett River Loop, Maine, page 141. You'll get mountains, lakes, and rivers on this wilderness ride; the highlight is the breathtaking Bigelow Preserve, where reflections of mountain peaks shimmer on the surface of beaver ponds.

Schoodic Peninsula, Maine, page 163. Though it's hard to say this is more scenic than riding in the main part of Acadia National Park (with its equally spectacular mountain and ocean views), this loop gets you right next to the rocky coast and you'll see fewer people.

Province Lands Loop, Massachusetts, page 248. You're not just looking at shifting sand dunes, you're riding right through them; try a sunset or sunrise ride to make the most of these great horizons.

Island Loops, Rhode Island, page 341. Though the ocean views are unparalleled, the scenery is also pretty in the island's interior.

Best Bike Paths

Island Line Rail Trail, Vermont, page 22. This converted railway bed lets you ride from downtown Burlington onto a dramatic causeway into Lake Champlain.

Cape Cod Rail Trail, Massachusetts, page 244. This paved trail is almost totally flat and has lots of options for side trips; ride early in the morning to avoid crowds.

Air Line State Park Trail, Connecticut, page 283. A stone dust bike path, this section of the Air Line is level, has few road crossings, and passes some outstanding scenery, including the beautiful Raymond Brook Marsh.

East Bay Bike Path, Rhode Island, page 318. This level, smooth path rides right by two gorgeous state parks and has great views of Narragansett Bay.

Best Coastal Rides

Islesboro Figure Eight, Maine, page 157. Though much of the ride is in the island's interior, you get great ocean exposure on the north and south tips of this lovely island and the ferry ride is fun, too.

Schoodic Peninsula, Maine, page 163. Waves crash on interesting rock formations; on windy days you'll catch the spray as you ride by.

Fortunes Rocks Loop, Maine, page 182. Fortunes Rocks Beach offers tidepools and long sandy stretches, while Biddeford Pool has marshy inlets that open to a rocky coast and pretty summer cottages.

Island Loops, Rhode Island, page 341. So many beaches, so little time—from high rocky cliffs with sandy beaches below to flat pebbly beaches down winding lanes, there's no end to the selection.

Best Single-Track Rides

Lower Nan Out and Back, New Hampshire, page 85. Even though this is an out-and-back trail, this trail is a fun, intermediate ride along the Swift River and is next to one of New England's most scenic roads, the Kancamagus Highway.

Carrabassett River Loop, Maine, page 141. The loop has a variety of trails, from dirt roads to bike paths, but the single-track section is sweet—extremely scenic and challenging without being prohibitively technical.

Trail of Tears, Massachusetts, page 240. A nice change from New England rocks and roots, this Cape Cod ride has endless twisty pine-strewn single-track trails.

Slick Rock Scramble, Connecticut, page 280. Extremely technical, the single-track trail here is tough, with steep rocky ascents and descents.

Breakheart and Shelter Trails, Rhode Island, page 332. Some folks call Arcadia "single-track central" and you could ride there every week and not see all the trails for months.

Best Fall Foliage Rides

Peacham's Twin Peaks Loop, Vermont, page 35. You'll see the colors of fall on the slopes of Roy and Harvey Mountains and reflected in small lakes and ponds.

Green Mountain Peaks and Hollows, Vermont, page 64. This hilly ride gets you great vistas into both Vermont and New York.

Great North Woods Ride, New Hampshire, page 79. Though Berlin itself is dominated by paper mills, it's set against a dramatic backdrop of stone-faced mountains and tree-lined hillsides and you get good views all the way around this loop.

Bradbury Mountain, Maine, page 168. From the top of Bradbury, there's a great 360-degree view, stunning in foliage season; you can see the ocean as well.

Old Egremont Loop, Massachusetts, page 213. Backcountry roads along open farmland give you good views of the rolling hills in the southern part of the Berkshires.

Breakneck Pond Loop, Connecticut, page 266. With its abundant ponds and dense forest cover, this park is magical in fall when the reds and oranges reflect in the water.

Best Rides with Overnight Options

Grand Isle Getaway, Vermont, page 18. This loop is long enough, and there are plenty of places to stop and explore, to merit breaking it in two, and there are several campgrounds and hotels along the way.

Kingdom Trails, Vermont, page 27. If you've come all the way up to this remote spot, it's definitely worth staying for the weekend to ride more of the trails; there's a state park nearby with full camping facilities.

Carriage Roads, Maine, and **Schoodic Peninsula,** Maine, pages 160 and 163. Make this a weekend trip so you can do both rides; take the ferry from Bar Harbor to Winter Harbor to ride the Schoodic loop.

Lake Waramaug Loops, Connecticut, page 273. The two loops of this ride start at the beautifully situated lakeside campground at Lake Waramaug State Park.

riding along the western edge of lovely Lake Waramaug

Chapter 1

© ELLEN KANNER

Vermont

I f forced to choose New England's best state for bicycling, I'd have to pick Vermont. For one thing, Vermont has 55 people per square mile, and only Maine, with much more than twice the land area, is less densely populated. And though it's a dangerous and nebulous thing to try to generalize about the character of a state, the pace of Vermont seems slower and friendlier. New Hampshire has that "Live Free or Die" independent stereotype, and Mainers can often look with suspicion on people "from away." The southern New England states are just too crowded to earn the title.

But it's more than the people and population that make cycling in Vermont so much fun. It's the scenery. The glacial age was good to Vermont, leaving it with beautiful mountains and lush valleys. The jewel in this natural crown is the Green Mountains, filling much of central and southern Vermont. The Green Mountains aren't as high and dramatic as New Hampshire's White Mountains, and this seems to make them more accessible for biking. New Hampshire's got the snow-capped Whites; Vermont has the tree-covered Greens.

Ski areas abound throughout the Greens, and many ski outfitters and centers have diversified into summer mountain biking, creating trails, leading tours, providing rentals, and mapping good off-road routes. These centers are great for intense mountain biking, but there are also plenty of places to get off-road and explore without getting technical. Vermont seems to have more than its fair share of unpaved town roads, which make for great backcountry riding for riders of all skill levels. Many small paved roads seem to dwindle into dirt, especially at town lines, so make sure you put fat tires on your road bikes before heading onto unfamiliar roads.

You can't talk about mountain biking in Vermont, or in New England, without discussing "the kingdom." Vermont's granite-lined Northeast Kingdom has some of the best mountain biking in the country, and any trip to this remote northern area should last at least several days. A model of organization, cooperation, and dedication to recreation, the Kingdom Trails consist of more than 100 miles of beautiful multiuse recreational trails crisscrossing private land that are open to the public.

Between all the granite peaks and tree-lined hills lie lush valleys with broad streams and clear lakes. Along Vermont's northwest border, the vast and beautiful Lake Champlain, in the heart of the Champlain Valley, is a biker's playground. A great two-day ride will take you around the lake or across the islands in the middle. Burlington is the hub for riding in this corner of the state, the most bike-friendly city you could hope to visit on two wheels.

Vermont's valleys were once favored by railways, and as further evidence of the state's general commitment to recreation and alternate transportation, many of these abandoned rail lines are being turned into delightful rail trails.

All these options—rail trails, dirt roads, sparse population—make it easy to get away from commercial areas. Vermont has a plethora of 200-year-old small towns to explore, many of which have retained their own character, not yet eroded by chain stores and suburbs. The general store seems to be alive and well here.

It's a northern New England state, so that means that nights are cold and summers are short. Spring is good for road riding, but muddy for mountain biking. Autumn is glorious, but you may have to share small winding roads with tour buses filled with leaf-peepers.

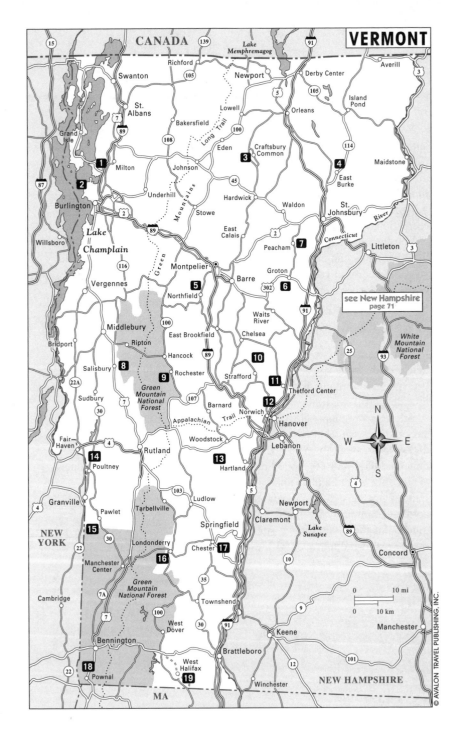

Contents

1 GRAND ISLE GETAWAY

Lake Champlain: Milton, Alburg, and North Hero

 paved roads with minimal traffic

Total distance: 83 miles

Riding time: 9.5 hours, depending on number of days

Difficulty: 5   **Elevation gain:** 692 feet

This classic route circles part of the vast and beautiful Lake Champlain. Comprising quiet country roads and state routes, it wanders through peaceful sections of Vermont's northwest corner and onto islands in the middle of the lake. The terrain is fairly flat but the scenery is unique, you're near water about 70 percent of the way, and the old country back roads make it all the more enjoyable. A wide variety of appealing stopping points lie along the way—picnic spots, nature hikes, convenience stores, farm stands, a bakery on Route 7, the "skillet house" in Swanton, and a winery in South Hero should you be inclined to bike several miles off the main route.

For the most part, the roads have wide shoulders, though in some sections shoulders are narrow to nonexistent. Use care crossing the many causeways, as the wind coming off the lake can be strong. Take particular

A visit to Snowfarm Winery makes a nice side trip off the main route.

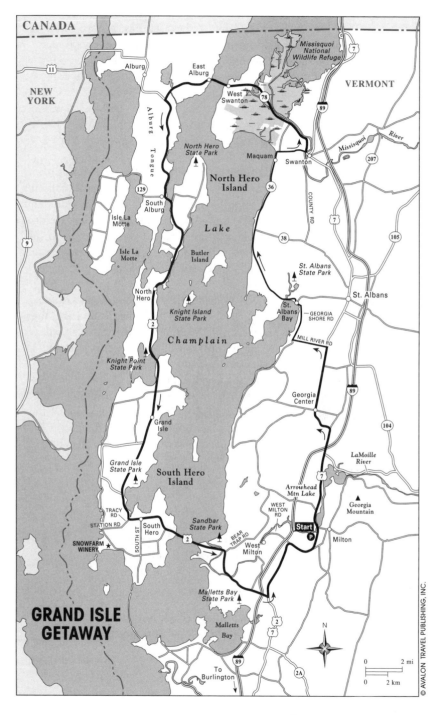

GRAND ISLE GETAWAY

caution crossing the causeway on Route 78 between East Alburg and Swanton. Earplugs or some form of ear protection would also be a good idea.

This long ride can all be done in one day or you can make a two- or even three-day trip out of it (what you decide will determine where you park your car before heading out; see Driving Directions). Should you decide to take more than a day, you'll find a wide range of dining options, inns, motels, and campgrounds along Route 2 south of Alburg and well into North Hero, a charming area teeming with brick buildings. The North Hero Chamber of Commerce office has plenty of helpful information.

Along with the many scenic state parks you pass along the shores of Lake Champlain, which provide facilities, restrooms, picnic spots, camping (Grand Isle State Park has a campground well-placed along this ride), and more, you'll find a nature trail at the Missisquoi National Wildlife Refuge on Route 78 and a Lake Champlain Birding Trail, if you're looking for diversion or doing the ride in two days. Along Route 2 just south of North Hero, the Royal Lipizzan Stallions of Austria have a summer home and perform here in July and August.

At about Mile 64, there's a way to avoid the busy Route 2 and Route 7 junction ahead. After crossing the causeway and Sandbar State Park, turn left onto Bear Trap Road, then left onto West Milton Road, which will take you back to Route 7 and on into Milton. It's a hilly, curvy, narrow alternative that may be worth it to circumvent some traffic.

For more information, contact the Champlain Islands Chamber of Commerce, P.O. Box 213, North Hero, VT 05474, 802/372-8400, website: www.champlainislands.com. For more on bicycling in the area, contact Lake Champlain Bikeways Clearinghouse, 1 Steele Street #103, Burlington, VT 05401, 802/652-BIKE (802/652-2453), website: www.champlainbikeways.org.

Driving Directions
From Burlington, take Route I-89 to Exit 17 and drive east on Route 2. At the Route 2/Route 7 junction, turn left to go north on Route 7. Drive 8 miles to Milton. The Town of Milton Community Park is across from Cherry Street. Day parking is available in this lot. Overnight parking is available by the town offices on Bombardier Road, off Route 7 south of the center of town, or at the School Street Middle School on Cherry Street. The nearest bike shop is in Georgia.

Route Directions for Grand Isle Getaway
0.0 From Milton Community Park, ride north on Route 7.
10.2 LEFT onto Mill River Road.
12.2 RIGHT onto Georgia Shore Road.
14.1 Bear LEFT onto unmarked road.

14.3 LEFT onto Route 36. Pass St. Albans Bay State Park.

23.6 *Restrooms available at Swanton Beach picnic area.*

25.4 LEFT onto South River Street, then LEFT onto Route 78 west.

31.5 Use care crossing causeway; there are strong crosswinds and a minimal shoulder.

35.2 LEFT onto Route 2. *A right turn leads you into Alburg for various lodging, dining, and camping options. A regional information center is about 1 mile north of town.*

40.8 Cross onto North Hero Island.

50.2 *Knight Point State Park has walking trails, sandy beach, swimming, picnic tables, and facilities.*

50.3 Cross onto South Hero Island.

56.2 *Lakefront camping is available at Grand Isle State Park.*

59.6 *You can take an optional side trip by turning right onto Tracy Road (dirt road) and following signs for wine tasting at Snowfarm Winery, about 3.5 miles from Route 2, taking a right on Station Road and then a left on West Shore Road.*

62.8 Cross causeway back to mainland.

68.6 LEFT onto Route 7.

83.0 Return to Milton Community Park.

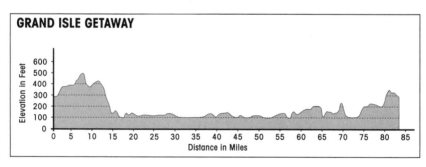

GRAND ISLE GETAWAY

2 ISLAND LINE RAIL TRAIL
Burlington

 rail trail, wooden decking, paved roads

Total distance: 19.6 miles

Riding time: 2.5 hours

Difficulty: 2

Elevation gain: 156 feet

The Island Line Rail Trail offers an adventure for bikers of all abilities looking for a pleasant ride. One can go as far as he or she wishes on this most interesting and scenic of rail trails. The local cycling community has put a lot of thought and hard work into turning a former rail bed into a spectacular bike trail that may once again connect Burlington to Grand Isle.

The trail is well marked all along the route. Though most of the ride is on pavement, there are sections on sand, dirt, and along wooden deck-type boardwalks, so you could take either a road, hybrid, or mountain bike. The Island Line passes through a variety of neighborhoods. For the past few years, there has been a short bike-ferry ride over the Winooski River, at Mile 5.3. However, after years of planning and development, a bridge now connects the Burlington Bike Path directly to the Colchester Causeway Trail with no wait for the ferry and no need to check ferry schedules!

Cyclists used to have to wait and take this bike ferry across the Winooski; a bridge erected in June 2004 changed all that.

The skinny Colchester Causeway sticks out for three dramatic miles into Lake Champlain. Strong winds along these exposed parts of the Island Line are cause to bring a windbreaker in any season.

Beyond the rail trail, Burlington is a great city to explore by bike, with tours marked out for traveling through historic districts. With marked bike routes and racks to park your bike throughout the city, it's no wonder Burlington is said to be one of the most bike-friendly places in the United States.

A stop in the office of Local Motion, a nonprofit organization promoting nonmotorized transportation and travel, is highly recommended. The office is right behind Union Station, and the helpful staff will tell you about ferry developments and bridge crossings and provide you with the colorful Island Line map. The next link in the Island Line Rail Trail will be a bike ferry from the end of the causeway over "The Cut" to Grand Isle; a few experimental ferry trips

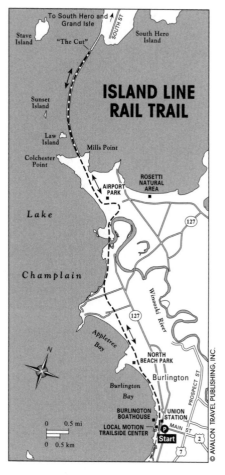

took place in the summer of 2004. For the latest on that, contact Local Motion at 1 Steele Street #103, Burlington, VT 05401, 802/652-BIKE (802/652-2453), website: www.localmotionvt.org.

Driving Directions

Take Exit 14 off Route 89 to Route 2 in Burlington. Follow Route 2 to the very end (it becomes Main Street). Union Station is at the end of Main Street along the waterfront. Parking is available behind Union Station. For the start of the ride, head to the left out of the parking lot along the bike path toward the Local Motion Trailside Center (a galvanized steel building). Supplies and bike shops are available in Burlington.

Route Directions for Island Line Rail Trail

0.0 From Local Motion, head north on the bike path, passing the Burlington Info Center.

1.6 *North Beach park has a campground, beach, and facilities.*

5.3 Arrive at ferry (or ride across the new bridge).

9.8 Arrive at end of causeway. TURN AROUND.

19.6 Arrive back at starting point.

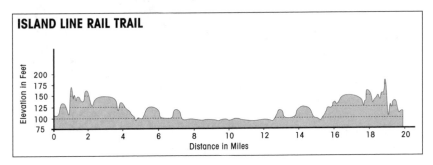

3 CRAFTSBURY COMMON LOOP

Craftsbury

 paved roads with minimal traffic

Total distance: 11.4 miles

Difficulty: 2

Riding time: 1–1.5 hours

Elevation gain: 725 feet

This quick little loop around Craftsbury and Craftsbury Common is a scenic spin and one of the few options for road riding in this remote northern Vermont area that's peppered with dirt roads and grassy trails.

Start in the tiny town of Craftsbury and head straight uphill past a llama farm. You'll soon come to the charming village of Craftsbury Common, where white wooden buildings surround a classic New England common, so well groomed it looks like a British cricket pitch. It has a town hall, inn, bookstore, and occasional farmer's market but no general store. For such a small town, lots of notable things are here: the innovative Sterling College takes over part of town; part of Alfred Hitchcock's *The Trouble with Harry* was filmed here; and just outside of town is the Craftsbury Outdoor Center (more on this attraction later).

You'll see some lovely views of fields and rolling hills as you pass through

The Craftsbury General Store, located at the start and finish of this short route, is the only place for supplies.

town and head down toward the Black River valley. Riding along Route 14, you're no longer on a backcountry road as lots of farm equipment use the road, and what few cars there are tend to move quickly. But it's still a very scenic ride through densely wooded areas with good opportunities for birding and other wildlife-watching. A hybrid bike would allow you to explore the dirt roads that connect Route 14 to South and North Craftsbury Roads.

In the middle of all this nothingness is the Craftsbury Outdoor Center in Craftsbury Common, a mecca for people seeking outdoor recreation and lodging in a remote, beautiful area. Famed for its cross-country skiing, the center also attracts mountain bikers in summer who come to ride on the single-track trails, wider grassy trails, and logging and dirt roads. The center offers bike rentals, on-site and off-site guided tours, and accommodation. For more information, contact the Craftsbury Outdoor Center, 535 Lost Nation Road, Craftsbury Common, VT 05827, 802/586-7767 or 800/729-7751, website: www.craftsbury.com.

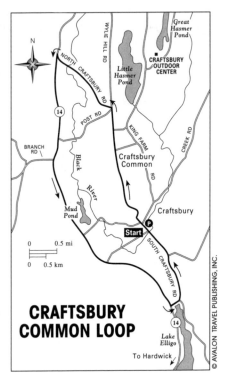

Driving Directions

From St. Johnsbury, take Route 2 west for 10 miles to West Danville. Turn right onto Route 15 and drive 14 miles through Hardwick. Turn right onto Route 14 and drive 7 miles. Turn right onto South Craftsbury Road and drive 1.7 miles to Craftsbury. Parking is available at the General Store and Post Office, in the center of this small town. Supplies are available at the general store.

Route Directions for Craftsbury Common Loop

0.0 From the post office, ride north on South Craftsbury Road.
1.4 Arrive at Craftsbury Common. South Craftsbury Road becomes North Craftsbury Road.
3.9 LEFT onto Route 14.
9.7 LEFT onto South Craftsbury Road.
11.4 Return to Craftsbury.

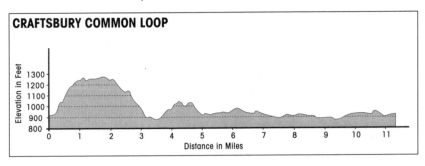

4 KINGDOM TRAILS
East Burke, Northeast Kingdom

single-track, grassy trails

Total distance: 8.7 miles

Difficulty: 3

Riding time: 1.5 hours

Elevation gain: 807 feet

The Northeast Kingdom of Vermont is home to some of the best-maintained mountain biking trails in the Northeast, if not the United States. Thanks in large part to the efforts of the nonprofit Kingdom Trail Association, more than 100 miles of multiuse recreational trails crisscrossing private land are open to the public. There's a price to pay for access to private land on well-groomed and meticulously marked trails, but the $6 day-use fee is nominal when you consider the work that goes into the system.

Marked with purple signs sporting a golden crown in the middle, the trails are all assigned degrees of difficulty comparable to an alpine ski area. The route detailed here is one of many options and is a strong intermediate ride on single-track and wide grassy paths, with some outstanding views and a great picnic spot as well. The scenery is Vermont at its best and the trails vary from grassy to sandy, rocky to rooty, with sections of washout.

More aggressive routes do exist within the trail system and many advanced riders come here for adventure-packed weekends. It is suggested to ride the trails in a counterclockwise direction and there are many options off the route detailed here for further exploration. Trails are open for mountain biking May 1–October 31.

You can order a trail map ahead of time from the Kingdom Trail Association or East Burke Sports, or pick one up when you arrive in East Burke. The map is imperative for full enjoyment of the trails and for direction in this vast trail system. In town, pay the trail fee at the Kingdom Trail Association's new office in the Bailey's and Burke building, upstairs from the general store. On weekends in the summertime, look for an outdoor tent behind the back of the building. Or stop into East Burke Sports to pick up some riding tips, and perhaps some free vegetables. On the day we visited, a box of free veggies waited on the steps outside for anyone interested.

The cross-country ski trails of the local Burke Mountain ski area are also part of the trail system, so plan on making your trip to the Northeast Kingdom a weekend-long visit. Brighton State Park, up Route 114 in Island Pond, offers campsites and shelters with full facilities; you can begin your ride from the campground if you choose.

For more information, contact the Kingdom Trail Association, P.O. Box

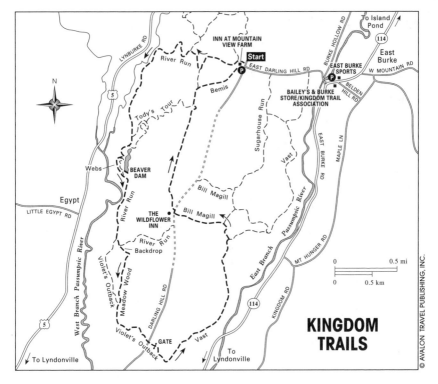

204, East Burke, VT, 05832, 802/626-0737, website: www.kingdomtrails.org;
also East Burke Sports, Route 114, East Burke, VT, 05832, 802/626-3215,
website: www.eastburkesports.com.

Driving Directions

From points south, take Route 91 to Exit 23 north in Lyndon. Take Route
5 north to Route 114, and take Route 114 into East Burke. You can park
in town, behind Bailey's and Burke Store at The Pub Outback, and ride up
East Darling Hill Road to the Inn at Mountain View Farm, where this
ride begins. Otherwise, drive uphill and park in the parking lot at the inn.
The ride starts from the parking lot, heading out to the right behind the
red barn and inn to greener, and well-marked, pastures. Supplies are available in East Burke and there's a pub for postriding eats and brew. The old
general store, Bailey's and Burke, is a treat for trail-ride snacks.

Route Directions for Kingdom Trails

0.0 LEFT out of parking lot, then immediate RIGHT heading behind red
barn (circa 1890).
0.1 Bear LEFT, continuing through field.

0.4 Turn RIGHT at view with yellow farm; pass old barn.

0.5 Bear RIGHT, then immediate LEFT on River Run Trail.

2.3 After bridge, continue to the RIGHT on River Run Trail.

2.6 Bear LEFT.

2.9 Continue STRAIGHT on Violet's Outback Trail. (Watch for the pigs!)

3.0 RIGHT on Violet's Outback Trail.

3.8 Continue STRAIGHT.

3.9 Bear LEFT.

4.0 Continue to RIGHT on Violet's Outback Trail

4.2 *Picnic spot.*

4.3 Cross Darling Hill Road, pass gate, continue on snowmobile trail marked VAST.

6.1 Bear LEFT on Bill Magill Trail.

6.3 Bear LEFT on Bill Magill Trail.

6.6 RIGHT on dirt road by Wildflower Inn.

6.7 LEFT, then behind tennis courts, down hill beyond fence. At bottom of field, bear RIGHT.

8.3 Bear RIGHT on Bemis Trail toward big red barn and parking area.

8.7 Return to starting point.

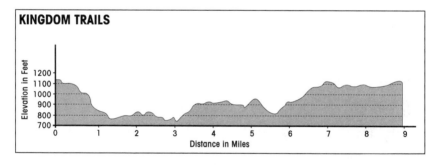

KINGDOM TRAILS

5 DOG RIVER TO MAD RIVER LOOP

Montpelier, Northfield, and Moretown

 dirt roads, paved roads with some deteriorating pavement and moderate traffic

Total distance: 27.9 miles   **Riding time:** 3.5 hours

Difficulty: 4   **Elevation gain:** 1,755 feet

This ride gets its name from the two rivers that run along either side of the Northfield Mountain range just southwest of Montpelier, the state's small, attractive capital. Starting from a Park-and-Ride lot off Route 2 just outside the city, you'll travel mostly along packed-dirt roads and some paved roads. Try riding this route on a dry day when the dirt roads won't be awash in mud. Be prepared for the washboard effect, as the dirt roads can be quite rutted.

The first stretch is along Route 12, a paved road with—for the most part—a nice wide shoulder. Some sections of Route 12, however, have quickly moving traffic and minimal shoulder room. It's fairly flat with a couple of gradual climbs, following and eventually crossing the Dog River. You'll notice some patches or even stretches of pavement that are reddish, a feature unique to this part of the region.

At Northfield Falls, as you turn onto Cox Brook Road, you'll cross several red wooden covered bridges. Travel alongside the Cox Brook against

looking back at the Lower Cox Brook and Northfield Falls covered bridges

the falls, where you'll have both pleasant scenery and an uphill challenge. The route continues through pastoral countryside, replete with red barns and the omnipresent Vermont cow, and accented by babbling brooks and the songs of various field birds.

After the covered bridges in Northfield, the ride continues gradually over rolling hills and then relentlessly uphill through the Moretown Gap for four miles. It's a significant climb, some of it on stretches of dirt road that last for more than two miles. You'll then turn onto Route 100B, which crosses the Mad River several times before connecting to the final section along Backside River Road. Take care as traffic moves a little more quickly here.

For more information, visit the Vermont Department of Travel and Tourism Office in downtown Montpelier or check out the City of Montpelier's website: www.montpelier-vt.org.

Driving Directions

In Montpelier, from Route 89, take Exit 8 marked for Route 2, then an immediate left toward the railroad station and Montpelier Junction on

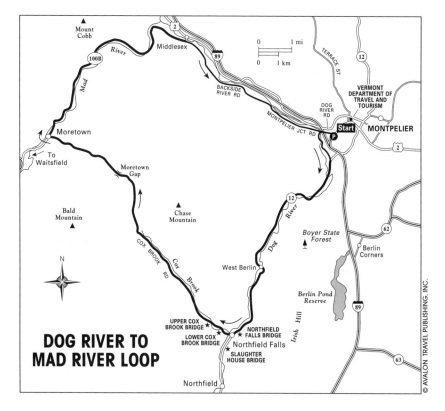

DOG RIVER TO MAD RIVER LOOP

Dog River Road. The Park-and-Ride lot will be on your left before you reach the underpass. The ride leaves from the far end of the parking lot, at the opposite point from where you entered. Supplies are available in Montpelier, and Northfield and Moretown have small general convenience stores. The nearest bike shops are in Waitsfield and Montpelier.

Route Directions for Dog River to Mad River Loop

0.0 LEFT out of parking lot onto Dog River Road. Continue around the pollution control plant, with public works buildings on your left.

0.5 Road turns to packed dirt.

1.5 RIGHT onto Route 12.

5.4 Cross over Dog River.

6.5 Pass Ellie's Farm Market.

7.0 RIGHT onto Cox Brook Road. Continue through three covered bridges.

9.8 Stretches of smooth packed dirt, one for about 2 miles.

13.8 Reach the top of the hill. *You can check out the views; Mount Cobb is to the right.*

15.1 RIGHT onto Route 100B in Moretown. *Supplies available at More-town General Store to the left.*

22.9 RIGHT onto Backside River Road.

26.0 RIGHT on Junction Road (unmarked) toward Montpelier Junction.

27.7 LEFT onto Dog River Road.

27.9 Return to Park-and-Ride lot.

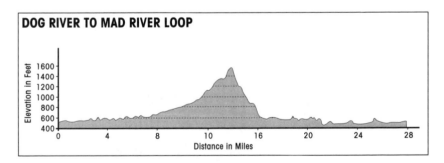

6 WELLS RIVER RAIL TRAIL
Groton

rail trail with ballast

Total distance: 12.4 miles

Difficulty: 2

Riding time: 1.5–2 hours

Elevation gain: 806 feet

This less-trodden (and less-ridden) rail trail takes cyclists through pretty hardwood forests and along quiet ponds. Starting south of Ricker Pond State Park, where the campground provides access to the route, the trail heads northwest past Ricker Pond, follows the edge of Lake Groton up to Kettle Pond and on, for those wishing to explore farther, to Marshfield Pond.

Birders and wildlife enthusiasts will like this trail for its remote location and wildlife-viewing possibilities. Tranquil and colorful in autumn, this trail offers summer riders plenty of swimming options. Incorporate a stay at Ricker Pond Campground for a pleasant weekend getaway.

This route is a straight out-and-back ride, with the total riding distance up to you. The Kettle Pond parking lot makes for a good stopping point at which to turn around and head south again. If you want more, continue to Marshfield Pond about 2.7 miles farther up the trail. A section of the trail beyond Marshfield Pond is more of a walking trail, though long-term plans are to extend this rail trail, officially called the Montpelier and Wells River Rail Trail.

fall foliage across Lake Groton, along the Wells River Rail Trail

For more information on the area, contact Ricker Pond State Park, 526 State Forest Road, Groton, VT, 05046, 802/584-3821, website: www.vtstateparks .com/htm/ricker.cfm.

Driving Directions

From Route 91, take Exit 17, near Woodsville, to Route 302 and drive west to Groton. Drive approximately 2 miles and turn right onto Route 232 north. Drive approximately 1.5 miles to the Ricker Pond Rail Trail terminus (which is approximately .9 miles south of Ricker Pond State Park).

Route Directions for Wells River Rail Trail

0.0 Start from trail terminus at the south end of Ricker Pond.
0.8 Enter state park. *Restrooms and water are available.*
6.2 Pass Kettle Pond parking area and group campground, across Route 232. TURN AROUND and return to starting point. *If you want to extend the ride, you can continue approximately 2.7 more miles to Marshfield Pond.*

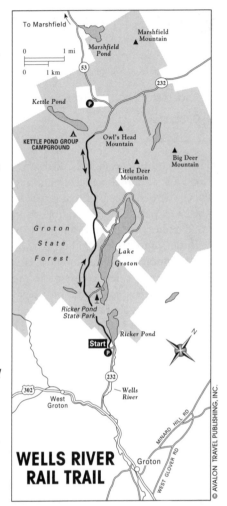

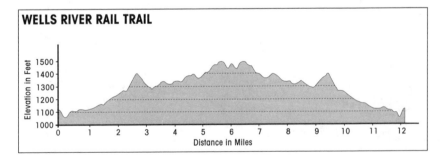

7 PEACHAM'S TWIN PEAKS LOOP
Peacham

 paved and dirt roads with minimal traffic

Total distance: 15.5 miles

Difficulty: 3

Riding time: 1.5 hours

Elevation gain: 1,187 feet

The village of Peacham and the surrounding area can't be equaled for rural charm. Small mountaintops poke out of the landscape, encircling small ponds and lakes, and backcountry roads weave through woodland and farmland. Roads tend to fade from pavement to dirt here, so a road bike with fat tires or even a hybrid is the best choice for this ride.

You'll begin at a Fish and Wildlife pond and take a sharp downhill before turning onto the quiet East Peacham Road. The tiny hamlet of East Peacham is no more than a few houses, a church, a pretty pond, and a fork in the road. Rolling hills and farmlands surround you. There's a 2.5-mile stretch on a dirt road here, which is at first quite bumpy and then very smooth.

Consider that your warm-up for the climbing ahead. Once you turn onto Roy Mountain Road, it's a mile-long climb along the edge of Roy Mountain. At the top, as you ride next to cows penned in by crumbling stone walls, enjoy the outstanding views of Harvey Lake and Harvey Mountain. A long, fun downhill takes you to the southern edge of Harvey Lake, where there's a boat launch and portable toilet if you're desperate.

You'll ride through the summer community of lake-side homes, making your way between the twin peaks of Harvey Mountain on your left and Roy Mountain on your right. As you emerge at the northwest tip of Harvey

no shoulders, but no traffic on this day in late autumn

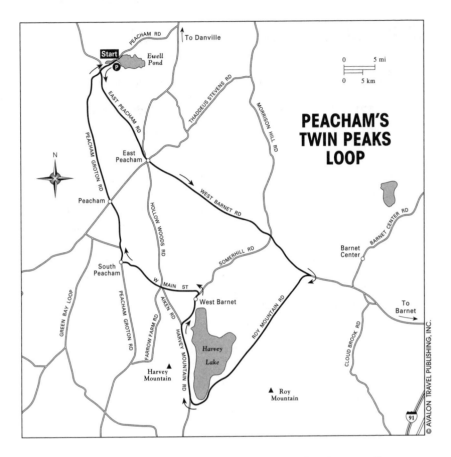

Lake, where there's a public beach, a sign tells you that Jacques Cousteau took his first dive here; apparently he spent summers here as a child.

Some long but gradual uphills will bring you to the historic village of Peacham, with its lovely white church, town hall, post office, and catch-all general store. The town was settled in 1776 and the road signs look as if they were made not long afterward. Some rolling hills past big open fields, and one more long uphill, bring you back to Ewell Pond.

For more information, contact Peacham Town Clerk, P.O. Box 244, 79 Church Street, Peacham, VT, 05862, website: www.peacham.net.

Driving Directions

From St. Johnsbury, take Route 2 west and drive approximately 5 miles to Danville. Turn left onto Peacham Road and drive 4.3 miles. Turn left into the Ewell Pond parking area, a Fish and Wildlife area with ample parking and outhouses, but no drinking water. Supplies are available in Danville and Peacham.

Route Directions for Peacham's Twin Peaks Loop

0.0 LEFT out of Ewell Pond parking lot onto Peacham Road.

0.4 LEFT onto East Peacham Road.

2.0 LEFT at fork, staying on East Peacham Road.

2.5 Pavement turns to dirt road.

5.2 LEFT at junction onto West Barnet Road (unmarked).

5.4 RIGHT onto Roy Mountain Road.

8.5 RIGHT onto Harvey Mountain Road.

10.3 LEFT at stop sign onto West Main Street (unmarked).

11.8 RIGHT onto Peacham Groton Road.

12.8 *Supplies available at general store in Peacham Village.*

15.5 RIGHT into Ewell Pond parking lot.

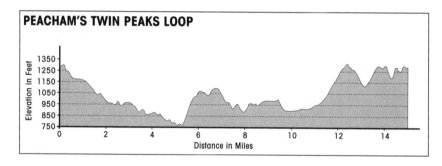

PEACHAM'S TWIN PEAKS LOOP

8 LEICESTER HOLLOW TRAIL
Goshen

 dirt roads, single-track

Total distance: 10.8 miles

Difficulty: 3

Riding time: 2.5 hours

Elevation gain: 1,188 feet

Starting at the town offices in Goshen, this route begins along a dirt road and continues up the Leicester Hollow Trail, a lush, green path bathed in filtered sunlight and lined with stinging wood nettle. Though direct contact with this herb can give you quite a sting or rash, we decided that the temporary discomfort was well worth the adventure, as you are surrounded by verdant underbrush for the majority of the ride. If you tend to react to nettles, wear long tights and sleeves.

The trail surface is mostly dirt single-track and follows along a babbling brook for a long uphill ascent—it's not steep but it's a continuous modest incline. The good news is that since this is an out-and-back ride, you've got it easy on the way back.

After about 5 miles, you'll arrive at pretty Silver Lake, where there's a sweet swimming spot and picnic area. You'll also find water pumps with potable water. For an added adventure, lock up the bikes and hike about 1.5 miles in to the Falls of Lana, where there's an overlook for the dramatic waterfalls.

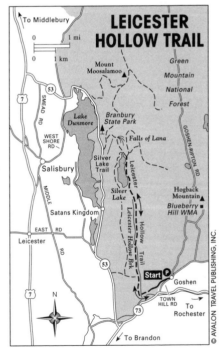

Past Silver Lake, off Route 53, the expansive Lake Dunmore and Branbury State Park have a campground with a sandy swimming beach, hiking trails, boating, and fishing, and you can bike to these spots from the Leicester Hollow Trail.

For more information, contact Branbury State Park, 3570 Lake Dunmore Road, Route 53, Salisbury, VT 05733, 802/247-5925, website: www.vtstateparks.com/

htm/branbury.cfm. For more about the area, contact the Brandon Area Chamber of Commerce, P.O. Box 267, Brandon, VT 05733, 802/247-6401, website: www.brandon.org.

Driving Directions

From Middlebury, take Route 7 south to Brandon, approximately 17 miles. Just past Brandon, take Route 73 East to the tiny town of Goshen, approximately 4 miles. Turn left onto Town Hill Road. Parking is available at the town offices. Supplies are available in Killington, Middlebury, and Brandon, and there are bike shops in Middlebury and nearby Rochester.

Route Directions for Leicester Hollow Trail

0.0 Facing the Goshen town offices, ride LEFT onto Fay Road (dirt road).

1.2 RIGHT onto Leicester Hollow Brook trail.

1.7 Pass Minnie Baker Trail.

4.9 Pass Silver Lake Trail.

5.4 *A left at the dirt campground road will take you to the picnic area, swimming beach, restrooms, and trail to Falls of Lana.* TURN AROUND and retrace route.

10.8 Return to starting point.

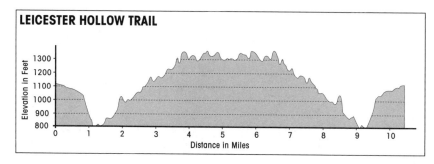

LEICESTER HOLLOW TRAIL

NORTH HOLLOW LOOP

Rochester, Granville, and Hancock

 dirt roads, paved roads with minimal traffic

Total distance: 24.8 miles

Difficulty: 4

Riding time: 4 hours

Elevation gain: 1,913 feet

Why did the chicken cross the road? Perhaps you'll find out on this ride, as I had a run-in with a few of them along these rural roads.

Rochester is a quaint town in central Vermont that gets most of its visitors in the winter because of its central location and proximity to the ski slopes and cross-country ski trails in the Green Mountain National Forest. You'll find a bike shop, plenty of parking, and convenience stores in town as well as a great bakery and café.

The ride starts by the town green and continues up Brook Street to North Hollow Road. Quaint old houses reminiscent of another time mark the beginning of this ride. A hybrid or mountain bike is suggested as North Hollow Road is mostly dirt and can be quite rutted in spots.

The ride out of town heads up a steep hill that goes for about a mile. It then continues past farmland dotted with cows and sheep. Rolling hills, views of distant mountains, and maple-sugar shacks make for traditional

The route starts and ends at the Rochester town green.

Vermont scenery. Make sure you've picked up supplies in Rochester and bring plenty of water for the long hill climbs and the remote trek along North Hollow Road. Scattered along the way, you'll see four or five cemeteries as old as the local hills.

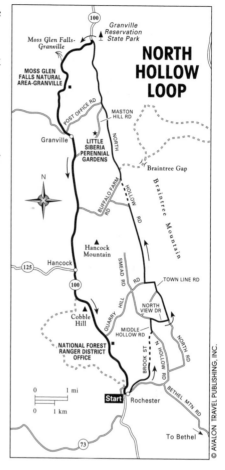

The return route is along Route 100, which has a 2-foot-wide shoulder and a good many options for food and convenience stores, with picnic areas aplenty. Check out Moss Glen Falls on Route 100, refreshing on a hot and humid day. You'll go through the town of Hancock, which has a pizza shop and several convenience stores. The helpful Green Mountain Ranger Information Station is also along the return route between Hancock and Rochester.

If you want to cut about 5 miles off this route, take a left at Mile 10.6 onto Maston Hill Road, and then take a left on Route 100 at the bottom of the hill and follow that back to Rochester. Maston Hill Road is a nice downhill coast with the pretty Little Siberia Perennial Gardens (open during growing season only) about halfway down.

For more information, contact Green Mountain Bicycles, Main Street, Rochester, VT 05767, 802/767-4464, website: www.greenmountainbikes.com.

Driving Directions

From points north or south, take I-89 to Exit 3 and drive west on Route 107 (following signs for 107 through Bethel) approximately 13 miles to the junction with Route 100. Drive north on Route 100 for approximately 7 miles to Rochester. Route 100 becomes South Main Street. Plenty of free parking can be found in the town center and near the town green on South Main Street. The route begins at the corner of South Main Street and Bethel Mountain Road.

Route Directions for North Hollow Loop

0.0 Ride east on Bethel Mountain Road, away from South Main Street.

0.1 LEFT onto Brook Street.

0.3 Bear RIGHT up dirt road, still on Brook Street.

2.2 LEFT at Andrew McQuain marker stone onto Middle Hollow Road.

2.7 RIGHT onto North View Drive.

3.2 LEFT at T-intersection onto North Hollow Road.

4.7 RIGHT onto Town Line Road.

7.6 RIGHT onto North Hollow Road.

8.0 Continue STRAIGHT.

8.2 Pass the cemetery.

10.6 (A left onto Maston Hill Road will take you back to Route 100 for the return trip to Rochester and cut about 5 miles off the route.)

12.8 LEFT onto Route 100 (paved).

24.8 Return to Rochester town green.

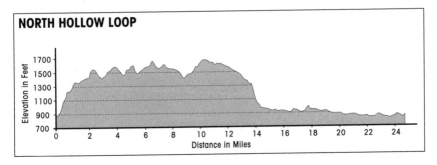

10 TUNBRIDGE TRILOGY LOOP
South Strafford, Tunbridge, and Royalton

 paved roads with some deteriorating pavement and moderate to minimal traffic

Total distance: 27.4 miles

Difficulty: 4

Riding time: 2.5–3 hours

Elevation gain: 2,359 feet

Those familiar with the Tunbridge Trilogy of films produced by Bellwether Films will recognize some of the sights in this region of Vermont. The films, *Nosey Parker, Man with a Plan,* and *Vermont Is for Lovers,* were all produced and filmed in this lovely area, turning colorful local folks (mostly elderly dairy farmers) into movie stars.

Beginning in South Strafford, the ride heads out on Tunbridge Road. Challenging hills and quintessential Vermont farm countryside, including three covered bridges, characterize this ride. What this route lacks in shoulder room, it makes up for in the expansive scenery—horse farms, rolling hills, adorable houses, and fields of green aplenty. A few long hills, offering fantastic mountain-top vistas, are well worth the climb. Bring a water filter as this ride continuously follows flowing brooks and rivers.

In Strafford, you'll ride by the Senator Justin Smith Morrill Homestead, a pink gingerbread-style Gothic Revival house that is now a state historic site. Smith was father of the act that established land-grant colleges, crucial to agricultural states such as Vermont. You face a long gradual climb between Strafford and Tunbridge. If you ride this route in fall, make time to check out the Tunbridge World's Fair, held annually in mid-September. The agricultural fair

The route passes the Strafford green and continues to the right.

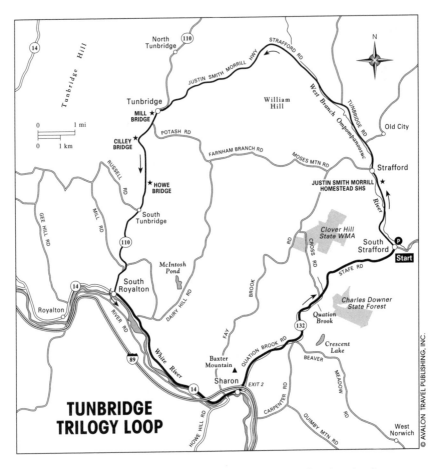

TUNBRIDGE TRILOGY LOOP

has been going continuously since 1867 with only a few breaks for wars and epidemics.

Three covered bridges are fun to check out between Tunbridge and South Royalton. In South Royalton, home to Vermont Law School, you'll find a health-food store and pretty town green if you take a detour across the White River. From there, Route 14 winds along the river on its way to Sharon, where restaurants and ice-cream shops offer refreshment. After you cross under the interstate, there's a big hill to climb before the final leg back to South Strafford.

For more information, contact the Town Clerk, P.O. Box 27, Strafford, VT 05072, 802/765-4411, or visit the Strafford/South Strafford website: www.straffordvt.net.

Driving Directions

From points north or south, take Route 89 to Exit 2 and drive northeast on Route 132 approximately 6 miles to South Strafford. The route begins at the junction of Route 132 and Tunbridge Road. Parking is available at the elementary school or at Baird Memorial Hall, both of which are easily found right in the town center. The nearest bike shop is in Hanover, NH.

Route Directions for Tunbridge Trilogy Loop

0.0 From in front of the Universalist Church, at the junction of Tunbridge Road and Route 132, bear RIGHT and ride north onto Tunbridge Road.
2.2 Pass the post office in Strafford and bear RIGHT (with the town green and town hall on your left) onto Tunbridge Road (unmarked).
5.8 Road becomes Strafford Road.
10.5 LEFT onto Route 110 south.
10.6 Pass Mill Bridge (covered) on right. *Supplies available at village store in Tunbridge.*
11.4. Pass Cilley Bridge (covered).
12.7 Pass Howe Bridge (covered).
16.0 LEFT onto Route 14 south. *Here you can go straight across the bridge for an optional side trip into South Royalton.*
19.9 Pass under Route 89.
20.9 LEFT onto Route 132 east.
23.1 Bear LEFT, staying on Route 132.
27.4 Coast downhill to return to starting point in South Strafford.

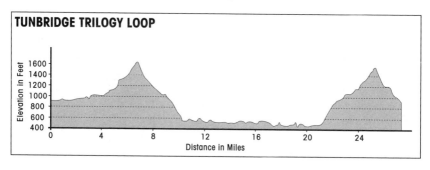

11 UNION VILLAGE DAM
Thetford

🐎 🚵 dirt roads, gravel roads, paved roads

Total distance: 7.6 miles

Riding time: 1.5 hours

Difficulty: 2

Elevation gain: 403 feet

This fun little ride offers a variety of terrain, taking you primarily along an old dirt road that is closed to car traffic through land owned by the Army Corps of Engineers. The Ompompanoosuc River flows along a gorge, culminating in the Union Village Dam, and the Army Corps has created nature trails, picnic tables, and shelters, stocked fishing spots, and other facilities to make this a popular family recreation area.

From the town offices in Thetford Center, head out along Route 113 and turn onto a dirt road lined with a pretty white fence. You'll join Union Village Dam Trail and follow the Ompompanoosuc River, which features many sandy riverside spots where you can take a dip in the cool aqua waters. A marshy area where the branches of the Ompompanoosuc River meet affords excellent bird-watching opportunities. Late spring makes for a great time to ride, as various wildflowers are starting to bloom. The spotting of an occasional lady slipper, trillium, or other wildflower is an added treat along the route.

At the top of a small hill, just before the dam, the route bears left down a dirt road and connects with Academy Road before crossing the Union Village Bridge, a restored wooden covered bridge. As you bear right after the bridge, you'll see an inviting picnic spot before the ride continues back up and across the dam for the return trip.

For more information, contact the U.S. Army Corps of Engineers, Union Village Dam, 2 Main Street, East Thetford, VT 05043, 802/649-1606, website: www.nae.usace.army.mil/recreati/uvd/uvdhome.htm.

Driving Directions
From points north or south, take Route 91 to Exit 14 and drive west on Route 113 approximately 1.8 miles to Thetford Center. Parking is available at the town offices in Thetford Center. Supplies are available at the old general store in Thetford Center and in East Thetford. The nearest bike shop is in Hanover, NH.

Route Directions for Union Village Dam

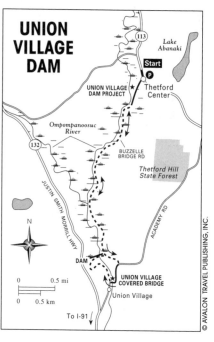

0.0 From the town offices, head LEFT out of the parking lot on Route 113 and take an immediate RIGHT onto Buzzell Bridge Road.

0.4 Go through gated entrance to Union Village Dam trail.

1.0 Pass Mystery Trail. *It's a hiking trail where you might spot red fox, wood ducks, and bullfrogs.*

1.2 Pass Chutes swimming area.

2.9 Bear LEFT down dirt road. Pass dam underground storage tank facility.

3.2 Exit Union Village Dam project area and bear RIGHT onto Academy Road.

3.4 Ride through Union Village Bridge.

3.7 Bear RIGHT on unmarked road after covered bridge. Pass picnic tables and restrooms.

4.2 Bear RIGHT across dam.

4.4 Pass storage tank facility and go LEFT beyond brick building. Retrace route.

7.6 Return to Route 113/Buzzell Bridge Road intersection and go LEFT to return to town offices.

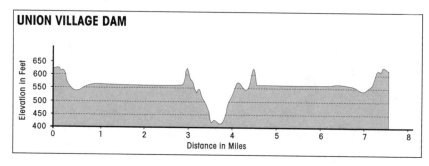

12 OLD NORWICH TURNPIKE LOOP
Norwich

 dirt roads, single-track, paved roads with moderate traffic

Total distance: 20.6 miles

Riding time: 3 hours

Difficulty: 4

Elevation gain: 2,061 feet

This ride takes on a variety of conditions and scenery. From dirt roads to exposed ledges and tricky descents, the ride traverses terrain suitable for a strong intermediate rider. Beautiful scenery is all around, with the colors of autumn making this a perfect ride for viewing foliage. The route takes you from heavily wooded areas to open fields along dirt roads with old country homes. The section along the return route on the Norwich Turnpike Road is fairly isolated and wooded, with few houses to be seen.

Starting in the town of Norwich, the ride along Main Street and onto the Norwich Turnpike Road is one continuous climb with broken pavement, a minimal shoulder, and little traffic. It climbs continuously and relentlessly for the first 6 miles or so. You tackle some rocky, rooty single-track along the Upper Turnpike Road, getting some great views and challenging riding in before the trail turns from an old, gutted jeep road to a even-ground dirt road. You'll come out off the trail right onto the begin-

climbing along Norwich Turnpike Road during fall foliage season ning of Rock Ledge Lane, which is dirt and then quickly turns to a paved road. It's a short road, and you'll feel as if you are going through someone's yard, but it's a public access point for Upper Turnpike Road.

You've then got a few miles of paved roads, on Mine Road and New Boston Road. Along Mine Road, look for some bright orange patches on the ground. These are what's left of the copper mines that used to exist in this area. Turn onto the dirt and heavily rutted Turnpike Road for the return route. Remember the 6-mile climb? Here's the reward—a coast downhill back to your starting point.

For more information, contact the Town Clerk, P.O. Box 376, Norwich, VT 05055, 802/649-1419, website: www.norwich.vt.us.

Driving Directions

From points north or south, take Route 91 to Exit 13 and drive west on Route 5 into Norwich. In Norwich town center, free parking is available near the town green and along the sides of Main Street/Route 5. The ride starts in front of the well-known Dan and Whit's General Store on Main Street, which offers all the supplies one could need in the way of food and beverages. A full range of supplies is available in Norwich; the nearest bike shop is just across the Connecticut River in Hanover, NH.

Route Directions for Old Norwich Turnpike Loop

0.0 From Dan and Whit's General Store, ride north on Main Street (away from Route 91).

0.5 LEFT onto Turnpike Road.

3.5 RIGHT onto Needham Road.

4.2 Continue STRAIGHT. The road is a dead-end (closed to cars). Continue STRAIGHT (bearing slightly to left) onto Upper Turnpike Road.

5.9 Bear LEFT at fork (right and left routes meet later).

6.7 The dirt road becomes Rock Ledge Lane (paved). *Here you can check out the fantastic views.*

7.0 LEFT onto New Boston Road from Rock Ledge Lane.

9.0 New Boston Road becomes Mine Road.

10.7 LEFT onto Turnpike Road (dirt road).

13.3 Road turns to double-track jeep road.

13.6 Bear LEFT.

13.7 Bear LEFT at grassy, open space.

13.8 Continue STRAIGHT at four-way intersection marked with a red dot. Gile Mountain is on your right.

14.9 Rough trail becomes dirt road. Pass Gile Mountain parking area.

17.1 Pass Needham Road. Retrace route to Norwich town center.

20.6 Return to starting point.

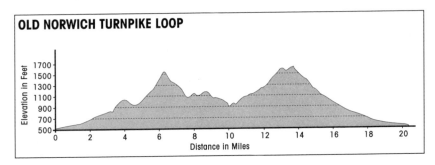

OLD NORWICH TURNPIKE LOOP

13 WOODSTOCK-ASCUTNEY LOOP
Woodstock

 paved roads with moderate to minimal traffic

Total distance: 37.7 miles

Difficulty: 4

Riding time: 3.5 hours

Elevation gain: 1,984 feet

Busy only begins to describe Woodstock on the weekends. It's a good idea to plan to arrive early and beat the crowds, or do this ride during the week, as people come from all over the Northeast to visit this quaint town that was named by *Ladies Home Journal* as the "prettiest small town in America." Once you're out of town, however, the charm comes not from shops but from the rolling green hills and agricultural landscapes that characterize central Vermont.

The first short stretch along Route 4 is rather congested and the shoulder is nonexistent. But the remainder of the ride is incredibly pleasant, along quieter, more secluded roads with decent shoulder room, making it worth putting up with this short section. The scenery varies from open fields with cows grazing to little towns with old houses that sit close to roads, indicative of once-upon-a-time narrower roads.

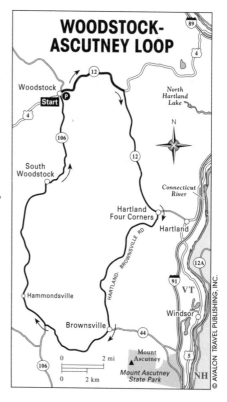

At Hartland Four Corners, if you want a detour or need supplies, ride straight for 2 miles into Hartland. Otherwise, head south on the Hartland-Brownsville Road, where you'll find minimal traffic with good views of Mount Ascutney visible to the south. The dramatic granite peak is a popular launch spot for hang gliders, so keep your eyes to the sky to see if you can spot any. The return route along Route 106 presents a few good long hill climbs, with one killer long hill around South Woodstock, but that makes the decadent dining options in Woodstock all the more well earned.

Woodstock does have all the quaintness you could ask for—brick buildings, a vibrant town green, and a covered bridge right in town. Lodging is plentiful, but make a reservation. The Chamber of Commerce kiosk is right on the town green and public restrooms are available in the town hall on Central Street (Route 4). A bike shop and supplies are available in the town, and the many dining options vary from deli to decadent. A coffeehouse along Central Street serves delicious organic treats and beverages.

For more information, contact the Woodstock Chamber of Commerce, P.O. Box 485, Woodstock, VT 05091, 802/457-3555 or 888/496-6378, website: www.woodstockvt.com.

Driving Directions

Take Exit 1 off Route 89 and drive west on Route 4 approximately 12 miles to Woodstock. Turn right after the post office onto Elm Street; free parking is available at a lot on Elm Street. The ride starts from the head of the town green, heading east along Route 4, the way you drove in.

Route Directions for Woodstock-Ascutney Loop

0.0 With the town green behind you, ride east on Route 4.

4.2 RIGHT onto Route 12 south.

11.0 RIGHT onto Hartland-Brownsville Road in Hartland Four Corners. *Supplies are available in Hartland, 2 miles straight from this intersection.*

18.8 RIGHT onto Route 44. *About .1 mile to the left is a convenience store with sandwiches and locally baked snacks.*

23.6 RIGHT on Route 106 north.

37.5 RIGHT onto Route 4.

37. 7 Return to starting point.

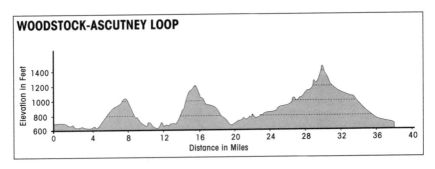

WOODSTOCK-ASCUTNEY LOOP

14 DELAWARE AND
HUDSON RAIL TRAIL NORTH
Castleton to Poultney

rail trail with ballast

Total distance: 15.8 miles

Difficulty: 1

Riding time: 2–2.5 hours

Elevation gain: 165 feet

Part of the longer, not yet fully developed Delaware and Hudson Rail Trail, this northern section of the trail starts in Castleton and travels south to Poultney. The rail trail runs along the rural western border of Vermont, and eventually it's hoped it will be part of a 34.3-mile trail straddling western Vermont and eastern New York. About 15 miles in New York are undeveloped for recreation; the railroad bed then comes back in to Vermont, where about 10 more miles of trail offer more lovely biking (this southern section is described under Route 15, Rupert Mountain Loop). As straight and flat as a railroad bed can get, this northern section is perfect for families with young children or those wanting an easy ride in the rural Vermont countryside.

The route runs almost parallel to Route 30 from Castleton to Poultney, both quaint towns worth exploring by bike. Grapevines and wildflowers line the trail and provide a nice scent on a humid day. Bring sunscreen, as quite a bit of the trail is open to sun exposure. Make bird-watching part of the trip as a variety of field birds and meadow-dwelling species can be spotted in this area.

At the turning point of the ride in Poultney, stop in for a slice of blueberry pie and an iced tea at Perry's. At either end of the ride, Castleton State College in Castleton and Green Mountain College in Poultney are fun to explore by bike.

For more information on the area, contact the Poultney Area Chamber of Commerce, P.O. Box 151, Poultney, VT 05764, 802/287-2010,

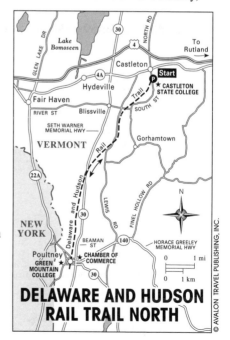

**DELAWARE AND HUDSON
RAIL TRAIL NORTH**

website: www.poultney-vermont.com. For more on the rail trail, visit the New England Rails to Trails website: http://members.tripod.com/Kenyon_Karl/Del-Hud.htm.

Driving Directions

From Rutland, drive west on Route 4 for about 14 miles. Take Exit 5 to Route 4A west toward Castleton State College. From Route 4A, take a left onto South Street. Parking can be found at Castleton State College. Turn left before the Office of Public Safety onto Seminary Street. The visitor parking area is a row of marked parking spaces, on the right side of the lot, for those using the rail trail. The trail is adjacent to this row of parking spaces and starts after you cross South Street. Supplies are available at a convenience store on Route 30 in Castleton and at a supermarket in Poultney. The nearest bike shops are in Rutland.

Route Directions for Delaware and Hudson Rail Trail North

0.0 Begin at intersection of rail trail and South Street.

7.9 Enter Poultney and pass old depot. Explore Poultney, then TURN AROUND and head back.

15.8 Return to starting point.

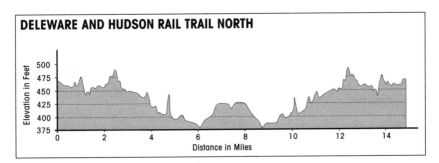

DELEWARE AND HUDSON RAIL TRAIL NORTH

15 RUPERT MOUNTAIN LOOP
West Pawlet

15A (Delaware and Hudson Rail Trail South)

 rail trail with ballast and grass

Total distance: 15.2 miles

Difficulty: 1

Riding time: 2 hours

Elevation gain: 402 feet

15B (Mountain Loop)

  rail trail with ballast and grass, dirt roads, paved roads

Total distance: 19.6 miles

Difficulty: 3

Riding time: 2.5–3 hours

Elevation gain: 1,366 feet

This quiet, scenic slice of Vermont has great off-road riding, which you can tailor to your skill level to ride through cornfields, rolling farmlands, and deep woods. Whether you choose Route A or B, you're sure to get a feeling of remoteness and a real sense of being in the rural countryside.

Both routes start on a well-marked rail trail. The southern section of the Delaware and Hudson Rail Trail is a flat, straight, scenic ride along the Vermont-New York border, running from West Pawlet to West Rupert (the northern section, from Castleton to Poultney, is described in Route 14, Delaware and Hudson Rail Trail North). Route A is an out-and-back ride on the rail trail, perfect for families or beginner riders who want to get off the road and into the countryside. The surface alternates between ballast and grass, and a nearby river creates marshy areas where the occasional great blue heron can be spotted. It's mostly cornfields here, with views of hills rising to the east. Turn around in Rupert; the stretch into West Rupert is more open and less scenic.

Route B begins with the rail trail, and then heads off into those hills on rural dirt roads with jaw-dropping scenery and chance encounters with wildlife. You'll leave the rail trail and ride briefly on the wide, paved Route 315 before heading uphill on a firmly packed dirt road. The road continues to climb the slope of Rupert Mountain. You may share the road with tiny butterflies and chipmunks or larger llamas and wild turkeys. The reward for the climb is spectacular views of the Green Mountains, which crest like wave after wave in the distance. Swaying cornstalks, grazing cows, and red barns with silver silos make it as bucolic a scene as you'd think possible.

Turn onto Chet Clark Road and ride past a lone farm. The road appears to end, but it really just narrows as it enters the woods, turning into a rocky, rutted dirt track for about 1 mile. It's a fun, slightly technical ride, ending in a smoother dirt road with a screaming downhill back to Route 153. You'll join with the rail trail for a tranquil finish to the loop.

For information on the area, contact the Manchester and the Mountains Chamber of Commerce, 5046 Main Street, Suite 1, Manchester Center, VT 05255, 802/362-2100 or 800/362-4144, website: www.manchestervermont.net. For more on the rail trail, visit the New England Rails to Trails website: http://members.tripod.com/Kenyon_Karl/Del-Hud.htm.

Driving Directions

From Manchester, take Route 30 northwest through Dorset and Pawlet for 19 miles. Turn left onto Route 153 and drive 3 miles to West Pawlet. At the triangular intersection, bear right onto Railroad Street and take the first right. Dutchie's General Store is on your left; park in the small parking area on your right. You might want to check in with the folks at the store as you pick up water and supplies. From the parking area, look back across Railroad Street, and you'll see the well-marked trailhead behind the post office and a former freight depot. Supplies are available at the general store here and at the Brick Oven Bakery and Machs General Store in the tiny, charming village of Pawlet. The closest bike shop is in Manchester.

Route Directions for Rupert Mountain Loop 15A (Delaware and Hudson Rail Trail South)

0.0 Begin at rail trail trailhead.

2.3 Road crossing.

3.8 Road crossing.

7.6 At road crossing, TURN AROUND and retrace route. *The rail trail continues for about 2 more miles into West Rupert if you feel like riding farther.*
15.2 Return to trailhead.

Route Directions for 15B (Mountain Loop)
Follow route directions for 15A to mile 7.6.
7.6 LEFT onto Hebron Road and immediate LEFT onto Route 315.
8.3 Continue STRAIGHT at intersection with Route 153.
9.0 LEFT onto Pawlet Mountain Road (dirt road).
12.5 Road becomes Rupert Mountain Road.
14.3 LEFT onto Chet Clark Road.
14.7 Continue STRAIGHT as road narrows into bumpy dirt track.
17.3 RIGHT onto Route 153 and immediate LEFT onto Sawmill Road (dirt road).
17.5 RIGHT onto rail trail.
19.6 Return to trailhead.

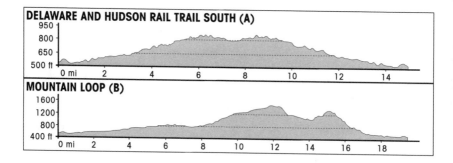

16 WEST RIVER TRAIL

South Londonderry

16A (Rail Trail Out and Back)

 dirt road, single-track, grassy trail, paved road, gravel bike path

Total distance: 12 miles

Difficulty: 2

Riding time: 1.5–2 hours

Elevation gain: 219 feet

16B (Rawsonville Loop)

 dirt road, single-track, grassy trail, paved road, gravel bike path

Total distance: 12.7 miles

Difficulty: 5

Riding time: 2–2.5 hours

Elevation gain: 929 feet

These two routes follow a section of the West River Rail Trail, a 15-mile scenic route along the West River with some sections fully completed, some under development, and some still quite rough. The trail starts in South Londonderry at the new home of the West River Trail Center in the former train depot. You'll ride down a dirt road for almost a mile before getting access to the trail; persevere despite signs marked "Keep Out" and a large, uninviting scrap heap.

Once on the trail, you'll find a bit of easy single-track and then a wide, leafy path. You'll hug the bank of the river, riding on surfaces that bounce from grass to leaves to gravel. It's hard to imagine a train picking its way along this rural, precipitous river's edge and indeed, the narrow gauge rail line was nicknamed "36 Miles of Trouble." You'll ride through the Winhall Brook Camping Area, a large campground run by the Army Corps of Engineers that's open mid-May–mid-October (you could also start your ride here if you are camping here).

Past the campground, the rail trail is marvelous, wide, firmly packed gravel. Across the river, wild, undeveloped hills rise to form a pretty ridge, while on your right, rocks tumble to the trail's edge. After going through a lovely stand of pines, the paved trail ends, and you can either turn back or soldier on.

From here, the West River Trail becomes a hiking trail for the next cou-

riding along the wide, gravel- and leaf-strewn West River Trail

ple of miles. It improves a bit at Ball Mountain Dam and is quite nice for biking for the remaining 3 miles in Jamaica State Park. People do bike (or carry their bikes along) the whole trail; you could also drive to Jamaica State Park and ride the southern end of the trail.

Route B starts up the very hilly, rooty, rocky trail, but soon breaks away to do a loop back to South Londonderry. After a few stream crossings on narrow logs, you'll get to a woodsy, rocky dirt road that gets smoother and smoother until you're out riding on lovely dirt roads past beautiful beaver ponds chock-full of birds and wildlife.

A short stretch on the very busy Route 100 brings you to the remote wooded Goodaleville Road, where you'll have some ups and downs past some lovely houses. Londonderry Memorial Park is a nice picnic spot. A mix of dirt and paved roads will bring you back to the start.

For more information, contact the Friends of the West River Trail, P.O. Box 184, West Townshend, VT 05359, website: www.westrivertrail.org.

Driving Directions

From Brattleboro, take Route 30 west to Rawsonville (approximately 32 miles). Turn north onto Route 100 and drive 4 miles to South Londonderry. Turn right onto West River Road. From Manchester, take Route 11 east to Londonderry (approximately 15 miles). Turn south onto Route 100 and drive 2.8 miles to South Londonderry. Turn left after the bridge onto West River Road. The former train depot is the West River

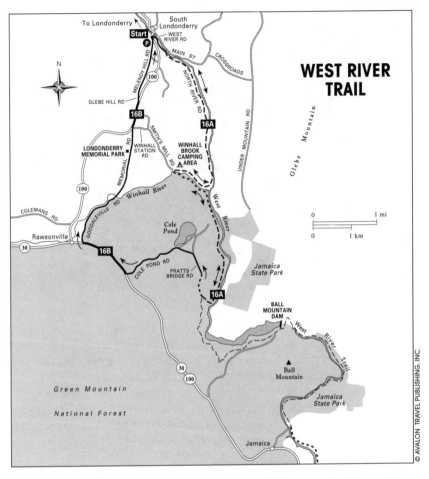

Trail information center and there is a small parking area in front of the depot. Supplies are available at the upscale general store in South Londonderry, and also in Londonderry, Bondville, and Rawsonville (the latter two towns have bike shops).

Route Directions for West River Trail 16A (Rail Trail Out and Back)

0.0 From the depot, ride along dirt road with river on your left.

0.9 Go LEFT through yellow gate following orange blazes.

1.4 Follow narrow grassy trail along edge of field.

2.7 Arrive at Winhall Brook Camping Area and follow main road.

3.4 Pass yellow gate at campground entrance.

3.5 LEFT across bridge, then immediate LEFT back along river, through campground.

4.1 Bear RIGHT.

4.2 STRAIGHT past yellow gate.

6.0 Gravel trail ends. TURN AROUND and retrace route.

12.0 Return to trailhead.

Route Directions for 16B (Rawsonville Loop)

Follow route directions for 16A to Mile 6.0.

6.0 RIGHT onto narrow track marked by purple blazes.

6.3 After major stream crossing, go RIGHT at junction leaving West River Trail (a wooden "Trail" sign and purple blazes point to the left).

6.5 Emerge from woods into clearing, continue STRAIGHT.

6.7 Trail becomes hard-packed dirt road.

7.0 Bear LEFT on Pratts Bridge Road (unmarked).

7.3 LEFT onto Cole Pond Road.

8.2 RIGHT onto Route 30.

9.1 RIGHT onto Goodaleville Road.

10.7 Pass Londonderry Memorial Park.

11.1 At junction, bear LEFT then immediate RIGHT onto Route 100.

11.6 LEFT on Glebe Hill Road and immediate RIGHT onto Melendy Hill Road.

12.6 Cross Route 100 and turn RIGHT onto West River Road.

12.7 Return to depot.

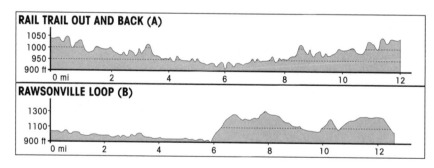

17 CHESTER HILL LOOP

Chester and Grafton

paved roads with some deteriorating pavement and moderate traffic, dirt and gravel road

Total distance: 17 miles

Difficulty: 3

Riding time: 2 hours

Elevation gain: 1,331 feet

If you're looking for a pleasant weekend getaway, plan it for this lovely area in southeastern Vermont. The route starts in the quaint, Victorian village of Chester and makes a counterclockwise loop. It first winds its way along Route 35, climbing hills well worth the effort for the pleasant tree-lined roads on the way to Grafton. A quieter, lesser-known destination, Grafton holds its own for quaintness and charm.

Minimal to wide shoulders exist along the major roads—Route 35 and Route 103—but the middle stretch—along Fisher Hill and Cambridgeport Roads—puts you on a nice packed-dirt surface and wide road with no traffic. A section has loose gravel. Perfect for either a touring bike with beefier tires or a hybrid bike, this ride takes you through scenic farm country between these two pretty towns.

Hilly and winding in spots, this route is a shorter version of the state's suggested Chester-Cambridgeport loop and avoids the broken pavement along one large section of that route on Pleasant Valley Road. If you've got a mountain bike and don't mind the bumps, you can extend this ride by riding past Fisher Hill Road and turning left on Pleasant Valley Road. This takes you north to Route 103, where you turn left and return to Chester, with plenty of good dining options for an after-ride reward.

For more information on the area, contact the Chester Area Chamber of Commerce, P.O. Box 623, Chester, VT 05143, 802/875-2939.

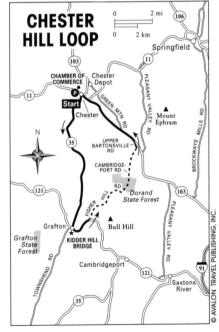

Driving Directions

From points north or south, take Route 91 to Exit 6 and drive west on Route 103 for approximately 10.5 miles to Chester, where Route 11 joins Route 103. Pass the turn, on the left, for Route 35 and look for School Street on the left. The route starts at the intersection of School Street and Route 11 (Main Street), at the southeast corner of the town green. Parking is available along the town green and on Main Street. The Chamber of Commerce office sits across from the town green and has useful information for this area of Vermont. Supplies are available in Grafton and Chester. A bike shop is in nearby Ludlow.

Route Directions for Chester Hill Loop

0.0 From School Street, turn RIGHT onto Route 11 (Main Street), heading southeast.
0.1 RIGHT onto Route 35 south.
7.3 LEFT onto Route 121 east.
8.4 LEFT onto Fisher Hill Road.
9.1 Bear RIGHT, continuing on Fisher Hill Road (packed-dirt road).
10.9 LEFT onto Cambridgeport Road.
13.0 Bear LEFT onto Upper Bartonsville Road (unmarked).
13.6 LEFT onto Route 103.
16.4 Continue on Route 103. (Route 11 joins Route 103.)
16.8 Continue STRAIGHT on Route 11.
17.0 LEFT onto School Street to return to starting point.

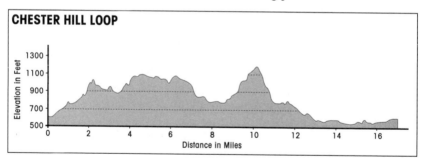

18 GREEN MOUNTAIN PEAKS AND HOLLOWS
Bennington

paved roads with some uneven pavement and minimal traffic

Total distance: 29.5 miles

Riding time: 3 hours

Difficulty: 4

Elevation gain: 1,972 feet

This beautiful ride takes you along the edges of the Green Mountain National Forest, through bucolic farmland and rolling hills with postcard-perfect scenery. It's hilly but fun, and the climbs all have their scenic rewards.

The ride begins in the small, artsy town of Bennington, where there are plenty of places to shop, eat, and stay before or after your ride. After a quick tour past some of the town's historic homes, museums, and its Revolutionary War Monument, you'll be out in the countryside riding through two wooden covered bridges and turning just before a third. That's when the climbing begins, on some lovely backcountry roads. Some of the pavement is uneven as you cross into New York.

The hair-raising crossing of Route 7 (confusingly, this is New York Route 7, which becomes Vermont Route 9) is worth it for the outstanding ride up and over Breese Hollow Road. Cows graze in front of silos in open fields while mountains rise in every direction. Back in Vermont, the 3-mile-long climb out of North Pownal offers similarly spectacular views; it's as though you are in the middle of a sea of mountains as peaks rise and hollows fold all around you.

After carefully crossing Route 7 (the one in Vermont), there's still a bit more climbing to do on Barbers Pond Road. Once you crest the top, you ride along a ridge with more spectacular views of farmland with rolling hills in the foreground and higher ranges in the background.

This is a great ride to do during fall foliage season, but with the brilliant colors come slow-driving leaf-peepers and you'll just have to share the road with them.

For more information, contact the Bennington Area Chamber of Commerce, 800/229-0252, website: www.bennington.com.

Driving Directions
From Manchester and points north, take Route 7 south to Bennington. From Brattleboro and points east, take Route 9 west to Bennington. Routes 9 and 7 meet at an intersection called Four Corners in the center of downtown Bennington. Several free public parking lots are nearby; a large one is at the corner of Pleasant and School Streets, one block off

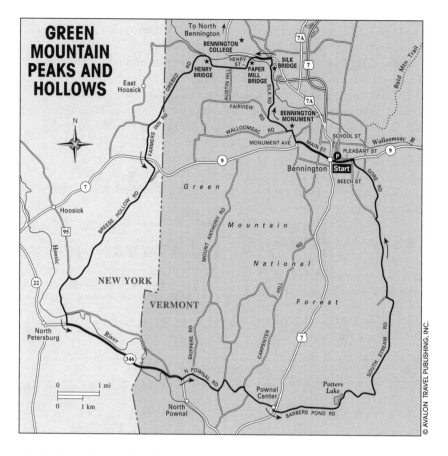

GREEN
MOUNTAIN
PEAKS AND
HOLLOWS

Main Street (Route 9), where this route begins. Supplies and a bike shop are available in Bennington.

Route Directions for Green Mountain Peaks and Hollows

0.0 From the parking lot, turn LEFT onto School Street and RIGHT onto Route 9 (Main Street).

0.1 STRAIGHT through the Four Corners intersection of Route 9 and Route 7.

1.1 RIGHT onto Monument Avenue.

1.5 LEFT at the Monument onto Walloomsac Road.

1.6 RIGHT onto Fairview Road.

2.1 RIGHT onto Silk Road.

3.4 Go through the Silk Road Covered Bridge.

3.6 LEFT onto Route 67A.

4.0 LEFT onto Henry Street. Ride through Paper Mill Covered Bridge.

5.5 Turn LEFT just before the Henry Covered Bridge onto Orebed Road. Cross into New York.

7.9 Bear LEFT at unmarked triangular intersection and take immediate LEFT onto Farmers Inn Road (unmarked).

8.8 Cross Route 7 to Breese Hollow Road, also marked as Rensselaer County Route 100. (Use extreme caution to cross this busy highway.)

12.7 LEFT at triangular intersection onto Rensselaer County Route 95.

13.7 RIGHT over bridge and across railroad tracks.

14.0 LEFT onto Route 346. Cross back into Vermont.

16.4 (Take care over this diagonal railroad track crossing.)

17.2 LEFT at triangular intersection onto North Pownal Road. *Supplies available at general store in North Pownal.*

20.2 Cross Route 7 to Barbers Pond Road, just across the road to the right. (Use extreme caution crossing this busy road.)

22.0 Pass Potters Lake. Road becomes South Stream Road.

27.3 RIGHT at fork staying on South Stream Road.

28.2 LEFT at stop sign onto Gore Road, which becomes Beech Street.

29.0 LEFT at traffic light onto Main Street (Route 9).

29.5 RIGHT onto School Street and RIGHT onto Pleasant Street to return to parking lot.

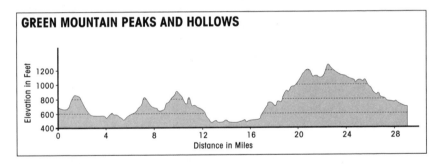

GREEN MOUNTAIN PEAKS AND HOLLOWS

19 GREEN RIVER RIDE

Guilford and Halifax, southwest of Brattleboro

dirt roads with minimal traffic

Total distance: 13.7 miles

Difficulty: 3

Riding time: 2 hours

Elevation gain: 1,558 feet

This loop, traveled exclusively on dirt roads, takes you through a rural corner of southeastern Vermont that seems as if time has passed it by. One indicator is the red wooden covered bridge where the ride begins; it's marked with a sign that reads "Two dollars fine to drive on this bridge faster than a walk." It's easy to put the modern world behind as you ride past flowing rivers and quiet ponds, through dense stands of maples and birches, with occasional patches of crumbling stone walls marking out homes and farms.

Starting in the tiny village of Green River, with just a few beautiful old houses and a bed-and-breakfast, you'll ride alongside the pretty river on a hard-packed flat dirt road. Once you turn onto Deer Park Road, the hill-climbing starts and doesn't quit as you make your way up the heavily wooded side of Jolly Mountain. This dirt road can be potholed and muddy in spring, so wait until the dry season of late summer to ride this route.

walking across the Green River Bridge to avoid the $2 fine

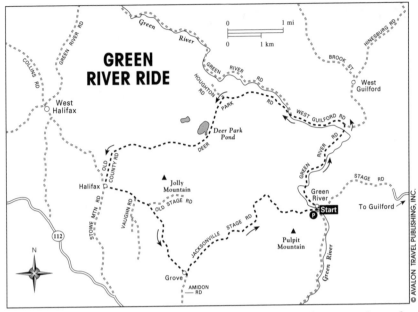

As you get closer to the village of Halifax, there are a few more signs of people: a large horse farm, a few homes, a traditional white church, an old cemetery, and rows of mailboxes. You've got more hill-climbing up the Jacksonville Stage Road, and then suddenly an opening in the woods gives you glorious views of a ridge off to your right. From there it's more or less all downhill. Check your brakes for the last, very steep descent back in to Green River.

For information on the area, contact the Brattleboro Area Chamber of Commerce, 180 Main Street, Brattleboro, VT 05031, 802/254-4565 or 877/254-4565, website: www.brattleborochamber.org.

Driving Directions

From Brattleboro, take Route 91 south to Exit 1, Route 5 south. Drive 1.3 miles to Guilford and turn right on Guilford Center Road. Go 4.6 miles on Guilford Center Road and turn right on Jacksonville Stage Road. This is a hard-packed dirt road that can be narrow and windy at times, but it is fine for driving and gives you an idea of what's to come on the route; it's a very scenic approach to the starting point. Go 2.5 miles on this road until you come to a triangular intersection with Green River Road. Go left and drive carefully across the one-lane covered bridge. There is room for two cars to park on the left. No supplies are along the route; stock up before you leave the Brattleboro area, where there are restaurants, stores, and bike shops.

Route Directions for Green River Ride

0.0 Ride through the covered bridge and turn LEFT on Green River Road.

1.9 LEFT on West Guilford Road (unmarked).

3.0 LEFT on Deer Park Road.

4.2 Bear RIGHT, staying on main road at fork.

4.4 Bear LEFT, staying on main road at fork.

7.1 LEFT on Old County Road.

7.8 LEFT on Jacksonville Stage Road.

8.6 Bear RIGHT, staying on main road at fork.

10.2 LEFT on Jacksonville Stage Road.

13.7 Return to bridge.

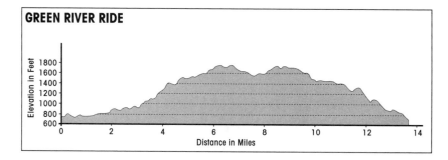

Chapter 2

© MELISSA L. KIM

New Hampshire

New Hampshire

The Granite State lost its most revered icon in May 2003, when the Old Man of the Mountain crumbled. The Old Man, a rock formation in a series of granite ledges that resembled the profile of a man, had captured the imagination of New Hampshire people for hundreds of years. The state's official emblem since 1945, the profile is etched on road signs, on the state quarter, even in maple candy.

Now it's too late to gape at the Old Man, but the forces of nature that created the granite profile also created plenty of other natural wonders. New Hampshire has them all on view, and a bicycle seat makes an excellent vantage point.

The long skinny state separates into three basic geographic sections. In its southeast corner, New Hampshire has a tiny seacoast region, with only 13 miles of coast sticking a toe into the Atlantic between Maine and Massachusetts. These coastal lowlands are mostly flat, with some tidal wetlands, and the cycling is easy and breezy here, though close to heavily populated areas.

The southern half of the state falls into the Eastern New England Upland region, with rolling hills and lakes giving way to two major river valleys, the Merrimack in the center and the Connecticut on the western border. The largest lake, Winnipesaukee, gets busy in the summer, but there are plenty of small lakes, back roads, and quiet villages to explore. You'll see signs of New England's history throughout this southern region as you ride through former mill towns, along converted railway lines, under covered bridges, past crumbling cemeteries, and alongside stone walls. The converted rail trails offer nice family rides, while the hilly regions around Mount Monadnock and in Bear

Brook and Pillsbury State Parks present some nice challenges for mountain bikers.

The northern region is dominated by the White Mountains, where mile-high mountain peaks and narrow valleys and passes make for dramatic scenery and challenging cycling, both on- and off-road. Roads, cars, and tourists get fewer and farther in between the farther north you go, and possibilities for losing yourself in the wilderness increase. Don't expect long horizons and wide open spaces; this is northern forest territory with hardwoods and spruce-fir forests. These heavily forested areas produce spectacular colors during the fall foliage season, making this the best time to visit. However, you'll need to be prepared for unpredictable weather in the Whites. On a sunny September day, clouds can and do sweep in, bringing hail and snow in seconds. Another season to pay attention to is "mud season." In spring, snowmelt creates rivers of mud on the trails and many state parks are closed to mountain biking.

More than 770,000 acres are protected within the boundaries of the White Mountain National Forest, where recreation is paramount. On offer are New England's best hiking trails, fantastic lodging options (rustic mountain huts, public campgrounds, and historic inns), and the world's worst weather on top of Mount Washington, at 6,288 feet New England's highest point. Though you can bike to the top, why would you want to when there's such great riding in the foothills? The bike path in Franconia Notch gives beginners a flavor of the area. For more advanced riders, there's our absolute favorite, the epic Nanamocomuck Trail that parallels the White Mountain Scenic Drive, the breathtaking Kancamagus Highway.

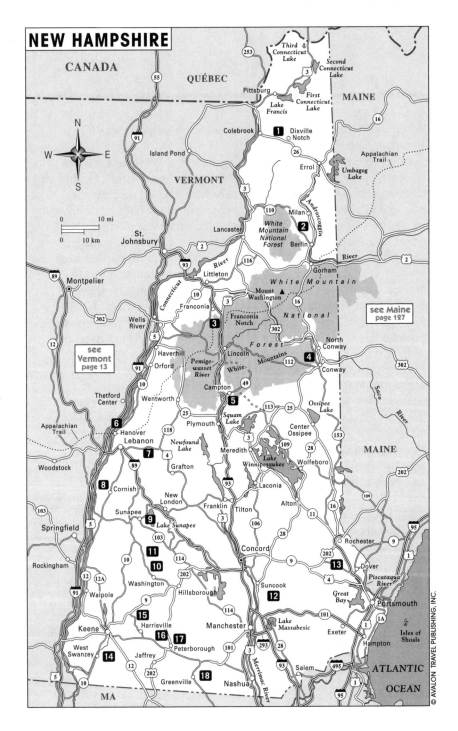

NEW HAMPSHIRE

CANADA

QUÉBEC

MAINE

VERMONT

N W E S

0   10 mi
0   10 km

see Vermont page 13

see Maine page 127

White Mountain National Forest

White Mountain National Forest

Mount Washington ▲

MAINE

ATLANTIC OCEAN

MA

Third Connecticut Lake

Second Connecticut Lake

First Connecticut Lake

Pittsburg

Lake Francis

Colebrook

Dixville Notch

Errol

Umbagog Lake

Appalachian Trail

Island Pond

Milan

Berlin

Androscoggin

Lancaster

Gorham

River

St. Johnsburg

Montpelier

Littleton

Franconia

Franconia Notch

Mountains

North Conway

Conway

Saco River

Wells River

Haverhill

Orford

Lincoln

Pemigewasset River

White

Campton

Squam Lake

Plymouth

Ossipee Lake

Center Ossipee

Thetford Center

Wentworth

Newfound Lake

Meredith

Lake Winnipesaukee

Wolfeboro

Appalachian Trail

Woodstock

Hanover

Lebanon

Grafton

Laconia

Alton

Springfield

Cornish

New London

Franklin

Tilton

Sunapee

Lake Sunapee

Rochester

Dover

Piscataqua River

Rockingham

Washington

Hillsborough

Concord

Suncook

Great Bay

Portsmouth

Walpole

Keene

Harrisville

Manchester

Lake Massabesic

Exeter

Hampton

Isles of Shoals

West Swanzey

Jaffrey

Peterborough

Greenville

Nashua

Salem

Merrimac River

Connecticut

River

Appalachian Trail

Mount Washington

1 2 3 4 5 6 7 8 9 10 11 12 13 14 15 16 17 18

253 55 91 26 16 3 110 116 93 10 302 5 12 89 118 25 4 113 25 153 28 109 202 106 103 114 12A 9 202 101 1A 1 95 495 93 293

© AVALON TRAVEL PUBLISHING, INC.

Contents

MUD POND LOOP
The Balsams, Dixville Notch

paved roads, dirt trails, gravel roads, single-track

Total distance: 8.6 miles

Difficulty: 3

Riding time: 1.5 hours

Elevation gain: 700 feet

Just getting to Dixville Notch can be an adventure as you make your way along winding roads carved through granite cliffs to reach this remote northern New Hampshire village, which has the distinction of being the first to vote in the nation's primaries.

Dixville Notch's other claim to fame is The Balsams. More than 130 years old, The Balsams resort is a grand, alpine-style, historic hotel complete with golf course, tennis courts, pools, an alpine ski slope, hiking trails, and, more to the point, more than 39 miles of biking trails and 34 miles of combined hiking/biking trails. The trails are closed to vehicles, are extremely well marked and maintained, and really get you out into the wilderness in your choice of mountainous or flat terrain.

This route is a mere sampler of the trails, and it includes riding on paved roads, dirt and grassy trails, the lovely Canal Trail, and some single-track trails. The staff at the bike shop will plan a route for you based on how long you can spend exploring. Be sure to get out at least to Mud Pond and beyond. The short single-track trails close to the hotel offer more technical challenges, but the real attractions here are the scenery and wildlife you can spot on the more remote trails.

Winter comes early to northern New Hampshire and the bike shop closes in mid-October. August or September are the best months to ride here.

A signpost at the bottom of Mud Pond. Trails at The Balsams are very well marked and well maintained.

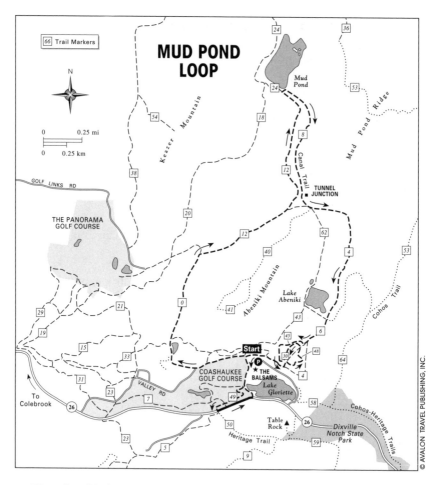

There is a $5 day-use fee to use the mountain biking trails. Trail maps
are available at the bike shop. For more information, contact The Balsams,
Dixville Notch, NH 03576, 800/255-0600, website: www.thebalsams.com.

Driving Directions

From points south, drive north on I-93 past Franconia Notch. Take Exit
35, Route 3, to Colebrook. Drive east on Route 26 for 11 miles to
Dixville Notch. The Balsams main entrance will be on your left. Park at
the main parking lot for the hotel. The bike shop is at the far end of the
parking lot. Limited supplies are available at The Balsams; coffee shops
and restaurants are open to nonguests. Colebrook is the nearest town for
other supplies.

Route Directions for Mud Pond Loop

0.0 From the bike shop, go LEFT on paved road.

0.5 Fork RIGHT onto Trail 0.

1.5 RIGHT onto Trail 12.

3.3 Mud Pond. *Outhouses and a shelter are here. You can do an optional loop around the pond on Trail 24.*

3.4 RIGHT onto Trail 8, Canal Trail.

3.6 STRAIGHT at four-way intersection.

4.5 Bear LEFT and arrive at Tunnel Junction, where several trails meet. Join main trail and go LEFT onto Trail 4.

5.9 RIGHT onto Trail 6.

6.0 RIGHT into single-track trail system onto Trail 30.

6.1 Fork RIGHT onto Trail 45.

6.2 LEFT onto Trail 30 and an immediate LEFT onto main Trail 4.

6.3 LEFT onto Trail 6.

6.5 RIGHT onto Trail 48.

6.7 STRAIGHT across Trail 6, then LEFT onto Trail 30.

6.8 Bear LEFT at fork, then RIGHT onto Trail 4.

6.9 Return to main parking lot.

7.0 Bear LEFT after buildings around back side of golf course.

7.3 RIGHT at stone marker onto Trail 3, then immediate LEFT onto Trail 49.

7.9 LEFT onto grassy road, then LEFT onto paved road (Route 26).

8.1 LEFT at service entrance road.

8.5 Loop RIGHT around buildings.

8.6 Return to parking lot.

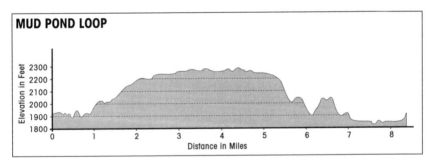

2 GREAT NORTH WOODS RIDE

Berlin

2A (Androscoggin River Loop)

 paved roads with minimal traffic

Total distance: 28.9 miles

Riding time: 2–2.5 hours

Difficulty: 3

Elevation gain: 1,286 feet

2B (Milan Hill Loop)

 paved roads with minimal traffic

Total distance: 27.9 miles

Riding time: 2–2.5 hours

Difficulty: 4

Elevation gain: 1,610 feet

This ride takes you from a northern White Mountain mill town into some pretty, hilly countryside before returning on a long stretch along the mighty Androscoggin River. Though Berlin is dominated by paper mills and billowing smoke stacks, it's set against a dramatic backdrop of stone-faced mountains and tree-lined hillsides. This is a great ride to do during fall foliage season.

The ride starts by going through downtown Berlin and out the other side through a residential neighborhood. Route 110 is industrial at first, but with each passing mile the views of the White Mountains get better and better. Once you turn onto Route 110A, the route also gets steeper and steeper. Route A rolls gently along; Route B, along Route 110B, is the hilly option, with a very steep climb, then some ups and downs, before a steep downhill into the village of Milan.

The return along the river is punctuated by sheep and horse farms, cemeteries, bridges across small streams, and great views of the snow-capped Presidential Mountains. If you're camping at the state park in Milan, you can get to these routes from the campground.

For more information, contact the Northern White Mountain Chamber of Commerce, 164 Main Street, Berlin NH 03570, 603/752-6060 or 800/992-7480, website: www.northernwhitemtnchamber.org.

Driving Directions

From points south, take Route 16 from North Conway through Gorham to Berlin. From points east or west, take Route 2 to Gorham and drive

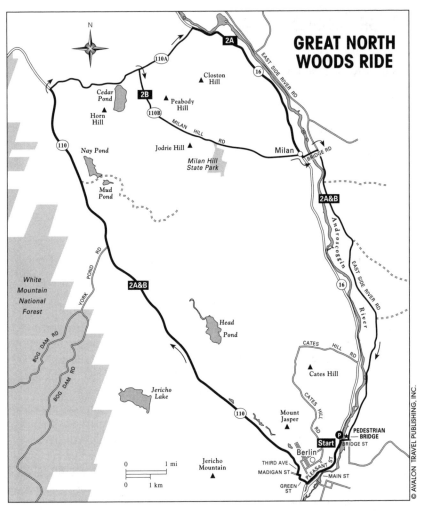

north on Route 16 to Berlin. Go through Berlin, staying on Route 16 through the one-way system. As you leave town, you will pass the Northern Forest Heritage Park, a logging display park with boat tours. Just past the park, look for a pedestrian bridge across the river on the right. A dirt parking lot is just past the bridge on the right. Supplies and a bike shop are available in Berlin.

Route Directions for Great North Woods Ride 2A (Androscoggin River Loop)

0.0 Leave parking area and ride south on Route 16.

0.9 Bear RIGHT on Pleasant Street.

1.2 STRAIGHT at traffic lights.

1.4 RIGHT onto Green Street at traffic lights.

1.5 RIGHT at the end.

1.6 LEFT onto Madigan Street, then immediate RIGHT on 3rd Avenue, which becomes Route 110.

12.8 RIGHT on Route 110A East.

14.7 *Facilities available at Cedar Pond boat launch area.*

16.9 RIGHT at junction onto Route 16 south.

21.0 *Supplies available in Milan.*

21.1 LEFT onto Bridge Street.

21.5 RIGHT onto East Side River Road.

28.3 STRAIGHT through flashing lights. Street becomes Hutchins Street.

28.7 RIGHT onto Bridge Street (a dead-end street).

28.8 Dismount and cross over the river on the pedestrian bridge.

28.9 RIGHT to return to parking area.

Route Directions for 2B (Milan Hill Loop)

Follow directions for 2A to mile 15.2.

15.2 RIGHT onto Milan Hill Road (Route 110B).

18.1 *Facilities available at Milan Hill State Park in summertime.*

19.9 RIGHT at junction onto Route 16.

20.1 LEFT onto Bridge Road.

20.5 RIGHT onto East Side River Road.

27.3 STRAIGHT through flashing lights.

27.7 RIGHT onto Bridge Street (a dead-end street).

27.8 Dismount and cross over the river on the pedestrian bridge.

27.9 RIGHT to return to parking area.

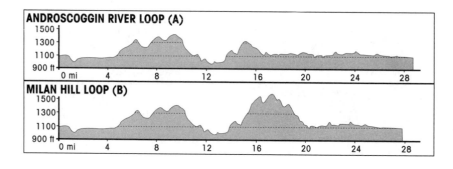

⓷ FRANCONIA RECREATIONAL TRAIL

Franconia Notch State Park, Lincoln

 paved bike path

Total distance: 13.2 miles

Difficulty: 1

Riding time: 2 hours

Elevation gain: 771 feet

The Franconia Notch State Park Recreational Trail is a paved bike trail that parallels Route 3 in the heart of New Hampshire's White Mountain National Forest. It's a pleasant ride, far enough away from the roads so you don't hear the traffic. It's also accessible from the state park campground.

The route begins at the south end of the Franconia Notch State Park Recreational Trail, leaving from the Flume Visitor Center parking lot. If you're staying in North Woodstock or Lincoln, try biking up Route 3 to add approximately 2 miles to your ride. Pick up a trail map during daytime hours at the Flume Visitor Center; the maps have detailed descriptions of all the sights along the way.

The ride out of the Flume parking lot is a continuous uphill ascent with little vertical dips for the majority of the route. Food stops and sights are along the trail, as well as a few designated "walk bike" stretches, signifying sections where you might find pedestrians and car traffic. The route is in-

riding on the Recreational Trail, with the Cannon Balls in the background

tersected by a variety of hiking trails, including the Appalachian and Pemigewasset Trails.

You'll find plenty of places to stop for a picnic, so bring a lunch or pick one up along the way. New Hampshire's crown glory, the Old Man of the Mountain, fell away in 2003, but viewing spots for the former site are still marked. Be sure to bring a bike lock and take the tram up to the Cannon Mountain Ski Area or visit the New England Ski Museum. Once you turn around and head back, it's downhill all the way.

For more information, contact Franconia Notch State Park, 603/745-8391 or 603/823-5563, website: www.nhstateparks.org/ParksPages/franconianotch.

Driving Directions

From points north or south, take Route 93 to Exit 34A for the Flume Gorge and Visitor Center. Park in the Flume Visitor Center parking lot. Supplies are available in Lincoln; there is a sports shop in Franconia where you can rent bikes.

Route Directions for Franconia Recreational Trail

0.0 Ride north out of the Flume Visitor Center parking lot on the paved bike trail.

1.8 Bear LEFT toward the basin. *Here you can lock your bike and walk in to see the basin over the Pemigewasset River.*

4.8 Pass viewing site for former Old Man of the Mountain.

6.6 Pass access to Cannon Mountain

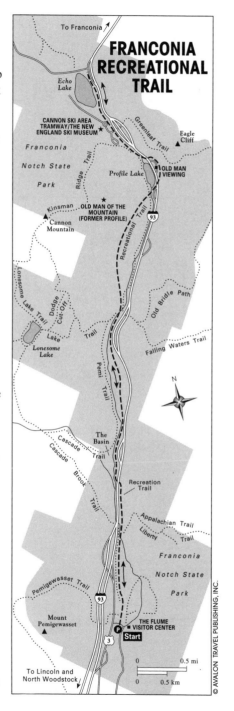

© AVALON TRAVEL PUBLISHING, INC.

Ski Area and Tramway and the New England Ski Museum. TURN
AROUND.
13.2 Return to parking lot.

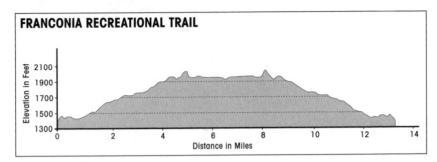

FRANCONIA RECREATIONAL TRAIL

4 LOWER NAN OUT AND BACK
North Conway

dirt roads, single-track

Total distance: 15.6 miles

Difficulty: 3

Riding time: 4 hours

Elevation gain: 1,379 feet

A fun jaunt along the Swift River over single-track and logging roads, the ride on the Lower Nanamocomuck, or the "Nan," cross-country ski trail offers a nice challenge for the intermediate rider. Crossing over log bridges, over tree roots, along beautiful single-track, and through glacial erratic boulder fields, this ride takes you through some wonderful wilderness.

In general, the trails are very well marked and well maintained. Make sure you don't miss the first turn from the wide dirt road onto the narrow Paugus Ski Trail. Nice river views are on your right and there are tempting spots to swim or wade in summer. The trail can get muddy in spring and fall, and the occasional log or wooden bridge can be tricky to navigate. A few technical rocky sections mix with straightforward stretches on pine-strewn trails.

Though this is an out-and-back ride, you have two other options: spot a car at each end of the route, one at the Albany Covered Bridge Campground and the other at the parking area on Bear Notch, and ride it one-way; or head out onto Route 112 from the Albany Covered Bridge and ride back on the twisty, hilly Kancamagus Highway, a National Forest Scenic Byway known fondly to locals as "the Kank."

More trails are here to explore and trail maps are available at bike shops in North Conway or may be obtained at the White Mountain National Forest Saco Ranger

following the bicycle signs to stay on the forested Nanamocomuck Trail

© ELLEN KANNER

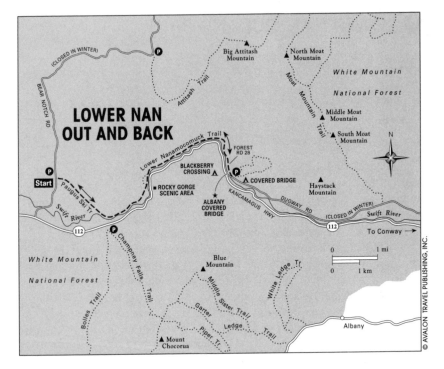

District office in Conway. For more information, contact the Saco Ranger office, 33 Kancamagus Highway, Conway, NH 03818, 603/447-5448, website: www.fs.fed.us/r9/white.

Driving Directions

Take Route 16 to Conway and drive south. Turn right onto Route 112 (Kancamagus Highway) and drive west for approximately 12.5 miles. Turn right onto Bear Notch Road. Drive .9 mile and look for a dirt parking area on the left. An information board and trail map are at this parking area, where Upper and Lower Nanamocomuck Cross-Country Ski Trails and Rob Brook Trails meet. Supplies and bike shops are available in Conway and North Conway.

Route Directions for Lower Nan Out and Back

0.0 Ride north on the Bear Notch Road.

0.1 RIGHT onto Paugus Trail (dirt road with a gate).

1.1 RIGHT following sign for narrow Paugus Ski Trail.

1.3 Bear LEFT onto Nanamocomuck Ski Trail, marked by blue diamond

3.5 Bear LEFT following signs marked for bikes.

4.6 LEFT on Nanamocomuck Trail.

4.7 Bear RIGHT on Nanamocomuck Trail.
6.8 RIGHT onto dirt road (Forest Road 28) toward direction of covered bridge.
6.9 Bear RIGHT.
7.8 RIGHT to cross covered bridge. Arrive at parking lot. TURN AROUND and retrace route.
15.5 Emerge onto Bear Notch Road and turn LEFT.
15.6 Return to parking area.

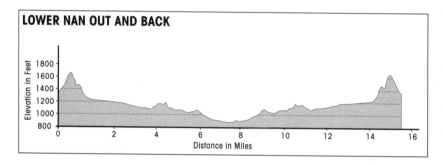

LOWER NAN OUT AND BACK

5 BEEBE RIVER RIDE
Plymouth

dirt roads, single-track

Total distance: 12 miles

Difficulty: 2

Riding time: 1.5 hours

Elevation gain: 573 feet

The Beebe River is the dictionary definition of a babbling brook, and this pleasant ride follows alongside it, making for a good beginner ride with nice river views. From the start of the ride at the gate, a continuous uphill pedal will get the old ticker going. The Beebe River Road, which is closed to all vehicles except White Mountain National Forest ones, is an old, abandoned dirt road, and some sections of it have become single-track, in part because of people using only one track for hiking and snowmobiling. One short section of a boulder field with fist-sized rocks is the most challenging section along this road.

The route meets the Sandwich Notch Road 6 miles out, where you turn around and head back. You've also got a few options to extend the ride. You can continue straight, toward the Guinea and Kiah Ponds. Or you can head to the right down the Sandwich Notch Road, a popular cycling road, toward Center Sandwich. This is a dirt road that is open to vehicles. A left option is an uphill climb without a real destination. Taking along a compass is recommended if you plan to explore beyond the Beebe River Road or on the other side of the Sandwich Notch Road.

For more information on the area, contact the Plymouth Chamber of Commerce, 603/536-6001, website: www.plymouthnh.org.

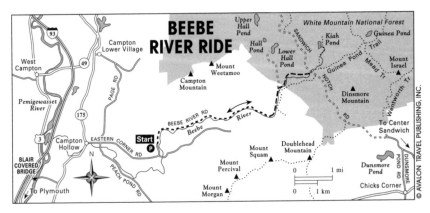

Driving Directions

From Plymouth and points south, take Route 93 to Exit 27. From Exit 27, cross through Blair Covered Bridge onto Route 175 and drive 1.5 miles. Turn right onto Campton Hollow Road, which immediately becomes Eastern Corner Road. Follow Eastern Corner Road for approximately 2 miles, then turn left onto Beebe River Road. In approximately .2 mile, you'll reach a gate; park on the side of the road and do not block the gate. Supplies, restaurants, and a bike shop are available in Plymouth.

Route Directions for Beebe River Ride

0.0 Start at gate.

0.6 Pass power lines.

3.3 Come to logging area.

3.6 Bear RIGHT, following river.

4.2 Bear LEFT onto trail marked for snowmobilers toward Sandwich Notch Road.

5.4 Bear RIGHT.

6.0 Reach intersection with Sandwich Notch Road. TURN AROUND and retrace route.

12.0 Return to gate.

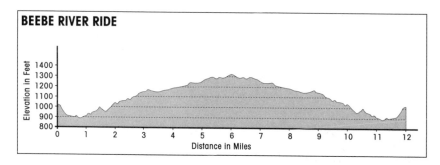

6 CONNECTICUT RIVER RIDE
Hanover, NH, and Thetford, VT

paved roads with some deteriorating pavement and minimal to moderate traffic

Total distance: 21.1 miles

Difficulty: 3

Riding time: 2.5 hours

Elevation gain: 753 feet

If New England country roads and bucolic scenery are on the agenda, then this ride will delight road cyclists of moderate abilities. Following the New Hampshire/Vermont border, the route brings you through old cemeteries, quintessential New England farm land, and rolling hills.

This 21-mile junket begins in the college town of Hanover, NH, home of Dartmouth College. The corner where the ride starts is right on the Appalachian Trail, and there's even a brass plaque on the corner to mark it. After leaving Hanover, the ride continues along the designated state bikeway of Route 10 before heading north on River Road to meander alongside the Connecticut River.

Crossing the river in East Thetford, VT, the ride progresses back along Route 5, a fairly easy ride with rolling hills and views of the river. It crosses Ledyard Bridge before heading back into Hanover. Watch for

Cross the Ledyard Bridge over the Connecticut River to return to your starting point in Hanover.

traffic across the bridge heading back to Hanover.

Hanover is a fun town to explore, and you can pick up foodstuffs and supplies at one of the many shops there. A bike shop is just off Main Street on Allen Street. Along the route, you'll find convenience stores in Lyme or Norwich and you'll also pass a little restaurant just north of the bridge crossing on Route 5 in East Thetford.

For more information, contact the Hanover Area Chamber of Commerce, P.O. Box 5105, Hanover, NH 03755, 603/643-3115, website: www.hanoverchamber.org.

Driving Directions

From points north or south, take I-91 to Exit 13 and drive across Ledyard Bridge into Hanover. Parking is available at any of the municipal lots in town. Parking meters and garages are throughout town. Don't risk parking on the Dartmouth College campus without a permit! This ride starts at the corner of South Main Street and East Wheelock Street in front of the

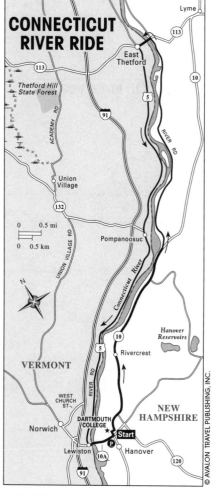

Hanover Inn, across from the Dartmouth College green. Supplies are available in Hanover.

Route Directions for Connecticut River Ride

0.0 RIGHT onto Route 10 (East Wheelock Street). Pass Hanover Inn on right.

0.3 LEFT following Route 10 (also known as North Park Street).

0.4 RIGHT following Route 10 at stoplight, continuing on bikeway.

4.8 LEFT onto River Road along the Connecticut River.

10.1 LEFT onto Route 113 (East Thetford Road). Cross a narrow bridge over the Connecticut River. (Watch for traffic on the bridge.)

10.4 LEFT onto Route 5 south.
19.4 LEFT onto River Road (unmarked).
20.5 LEFT onto Route 10A east. Cross Ledyard Bridge.
21.1 Return to starting point.

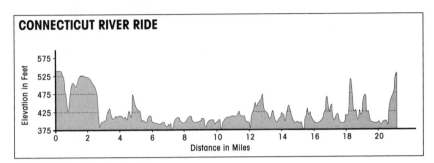

NORTHERN RAIL TRAIL

Lebanon to Grafton, including Mascoma Lake

rail trail with ballast

Total distance: 45.2 miles round-trip, with several access points (turn around whenever you like)

Riding time: 3–5 hours depending on distance

Difficulty: 1   **Elevation gain:** 724 feet

It's all about the journey, not the destination, along this interesting and scenic rail trail that wends its way along the Mascoma River, the shores of Mascoma Lake, and the bed of the former Boston and Maine railroad's Northern Line.

Starting in Lebanon, the trail goes along fairly flat terrain, through the towns of Enfield, Canaan, and Orange, eventually ending in Grafton. Ballast covers most of the trail and provides a fairly even surface. You'll also go under several overpasses and through some large culverts.

You'll pass a dam in East Lebanon that was once the site of a bustling

© ELLEN KANNER

riding through one of the Northern Rail Trail's many oversized culverts

sawmill around the turn of the 18th century. Other features include a covered bridge, a few old train depots (one converted into a laundromat), and seven crossings over the Mascoma River. At about the 4-mile mark, a picnic spot provides quite a vista and nice swimming spot. Riding through the town of Orange on an autumn day, you'll soon discover how the town got its name.

This route is a 22.6-mile out-and-back ride, so if this seems too long, you can turn around at any point, or spot a car at the end in Grafton. Access points and parking areas are also in Enfield and Canaan. A nice short alternative might be to turn around at the end of Mascoma Lake, after about 4 miles, as the trail becomes bumpy and sandy for the last section of the ride.

For up-to-date information on the trail, contact the Friends of the Northern Rail Trail, P.O. Box 206, Enfield, NH 03748, website: www.northernrailtrail.org.

Driving Directions

Parking for the Northern Rail Trail is available at the Carter Community Building Association (CCBA) in Lebanon. From Route I-89, take Exit 18 and drive south on Route 120 toward the center of Lebanon. Drive .3 mile and turn left onto Hanover Street at the stop sign. Follow Hanover Street .5 mile to the town green. Continue around the green on South Park Street and turn left onto School Street. Bear straight down Campbell Street, following signs for the CCBA and Northern Rail Trail. Park in the CCBA lot. The trailhead is on the right; you'll see an information billboard with a trail map. The Grafton trailhead is at the Grafton Recreation field, Prescottt Hill Road, off Route 4 east in Grafton. Services and supplies are available in Lebanon, Enfield, and Canaan; a bike shop is in Lebanon.

Route Directions for Northern Rail Trail

0.0 From the parking lot by the Carter Community Building, ride toward the trailhead on Spencer Street.

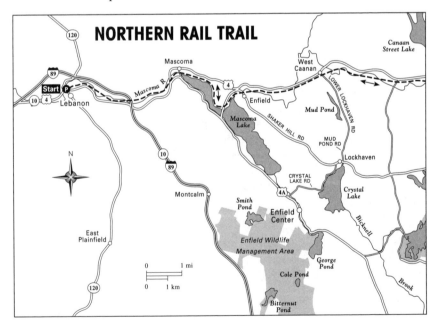

3.6 *Picnic bench.*
4.0 *Picnic spot and swimming area on Mascoma Lake.*
6.7 *Supplies available in Enfield.*
13.5 *Supplies available in Canaan. You can leave your bike at a bike rack along the trail.*
22.6 Enter parking lot for Grafton Recreation Field. TURN AROUND.
45.2 Return to CCBA parking area in Lebanon.

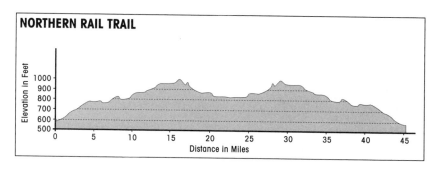

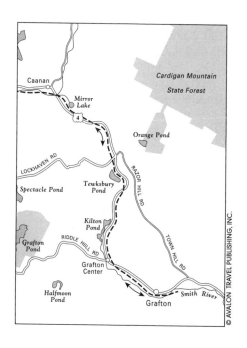

8 CORNISH COLONY LOOP
Cornish, Cornish Flat, and Plainfield

8A (Covered Bridge Loop)

 paved roads with light to moderate traffic

Total distance: 22.2 miles

Difficulty: 2

Riding time: 2.5–3 hours

Elevation gain: 1,070 feet

8B (Plainfield Hills Loop)

 paved roads with light to moderate traffic

Total distance: 30.3 miles

Difficulty: 3

Riding time: 3–3.5 hours

Elevation gain: 1,779 feet

Those familiar with the establishment of artist colonies in the early part of the 20th century will be pleased to find this ride traveling through the once-thriving Cornish Colony of New Hampshire. Established around the turn of the last century by sculptor Augustus Saint-Gaudens, the colony attracted such prominent artists as Maxfield Parrish and Herbert Adams. The area was once considered one of the most beautifully gardened villages in the United States.

This ride begins in Cornish Flat and continues along a variety of paved roads. Use caution and watch for vehicles on the route's one-lane bridges and shady, curvy sections. You'll ride over meadows and rolling hills, passing farm stands and getting glimpses of Vermont's Mount Ascutney to the west. General stores are spaced out along both Routes A and B at stopping points that couldn't have been better planned. A few old brick churches and covered bridges accent this ride, including the longest covered bridge in the country, the 460-foot-long Cornish-Windsor Bridge. Across this bridge to Vermont is Windsor, home to Vermont Crafts and Simon Pearce Glass.

Route A is a shorter route without the challenging, long hill of Route B. On a Sunday afternoon excursion on either route, you can stop at Saint-Gaudens National Historic Site for classical music concerts 2–4 P.M. during July and August.

For more information, contact the Saint-Gaudens National Historic Site, 139 Saint Gaudens Road, Cornish, NH 03745, 603/675-2175, website: www.sgnhs.org/saga.html.

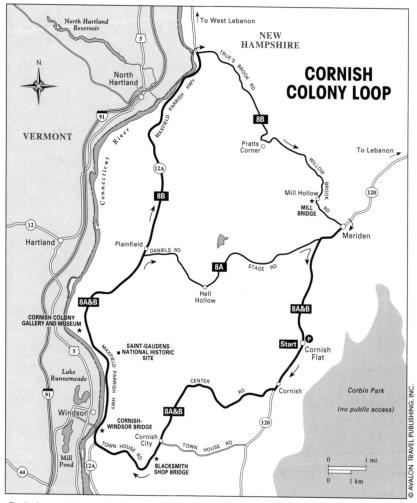

Driving Directions

From Route I-89, take Exit 18 and drive south through Lebanon town center. Continue on Route 120 south for approximately 10 miles to Cornish Flat and look for the Cornish General Store at the intersection with School Street. Supplies are available in Lebanon and West Lebanon; a bike shop is in Lebanon.

Route Directions for Cornish Colony Loop 8A (Covered Bridge Loop)

0.0 From Cornish General Store, ride south on Route 120.
0.9 RIGHT onto Center Road.

2.8 Pass United Church of Cornish on right.

5.3 RIGHT onto Town House Road.

6.8 Pass Blacksmith Shop Bridge.

7.7 RIGHT onto Route 12A north, also known as Maxfield Parrish Highway. *Supplies available at 12% Solution convenience store.*

8.0 Cross Cornish-Windsor Bridge.

9.5 Pass Saint-Gaudens National Historic Site.

10.9 Pass Cornish Colony Gallery and Museum.

13.5 RIGHT onto Daniels Road.

14.3 RIGHT onto Stage Road (unmarked). (Look for Mill Village sign across the road.)

19.2 RIGHT onto Route 120 south toward Claremont.

22.2 Return to Cornish General Store.

Route Directions for 8B (Plainfield Hills Loop)

Follow route directions for 8A to Mile 13.5.

13.5 Continue STRAIGHT (north) on Route 12A.

19.4 RIGHT onto True's Brook Road.

21.0 Road becomes Willow Brook Road.

25.5 Pass Mill Bridge (covered).

26.2 Pass Meriden center and Kimball Union Academy.

26.5 RIGHT onto Route 120 south.

30.3 Return to Cornish General Store.

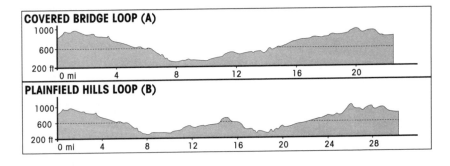

9 SUNAPEE LAKES LOOPS
Sunapee and New London

9A (Lakeside Loop)

 paved roads with light to moderate traffic

Total distance: 20.4 miles

Difficulty: 3

Riding time: 2–2.5 hours

Elevation gain: 1,552 feet

9B (Sunapee to Sutton Loop)

  paved roads with light to moderate traffic, dirt road

Total distance: 25.4 miles

Difficulty: 3

Riding time: 2.5–3 hours

Elevation gain: 1,983 feet

The Sunapee Lakes region is home to a pleasant summer community in this central region of New Hampshire. Not nearly as busy as the better-known Lake Winnipesaukee area, it still bustles and there are plenty of sights, including Sunapee Harbor, several wildlife preserves, a few old cemeteries, and some quaint New England towns.

riding along Route 11 with Otter Pond to the right

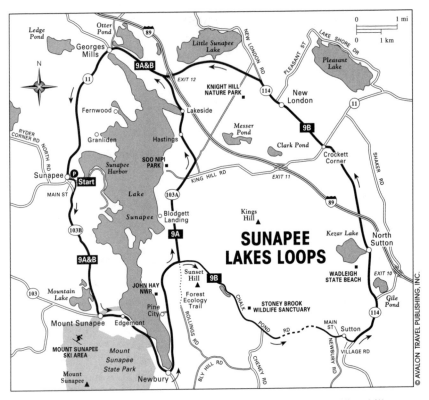

These routes give you two options for loops over gentle rolling hills and along nicely paved roads. Both loops have their long hills and traffic moves quickly on the state routes. The B loop offers more constrained shoulder room and starts with a turn onto Chalk Pond Road with nice views of the pond on the right. A one-mile section is on packed dirt, which often seems to be the case whenever you cross town lines in rural New England.

The Park-and-Ride lot at Mile 14.8 on the A loop makes for a nice connector with the B loop and would be a good meeting point should you and your riding partners decide to do different loops.

Surprisingly for a busy tourist area, only a few convenience stores lie along the way. The charming towns of Sutton, Newbury, and Sunapee offer munching options while New London has more gourmet lunch stops for the connoisseurs.

For more information, contact the Lake Sunapee Region Chamber of Commerce, P.O. Box 532, New London, NH 03257, 603/526-6575 or 877/526-6575, website: www.sunapeevacations.com.

Driving Directions

From points north, take Route I-89 to Exit 12A toward Georges Mills. Turn right onto Springfield Road and drive about .5 mile to Route 11. Turn right onto Route 11 and drive south for about 3.5 miles until you reach the intersection with Route 103B. From points south and east, take Route I-89 to Exit 12 toward Sunapee. Turn left onto Newport Road/Route 11. Drive approximately 5 miles to the intersection with Route 103B. Parking is available in Sunapee Harbor off Route 11. The ride starts at the information booth at the intersection of Routes 103B and 11. The closest bike shop is in Newbury.

Route Directions for Sunapee Lakes Loops 9A (Lakeside Loop)

0.0 Start at information booth on Route 11 and ride south on Route 103B.
0.7 Enter traffic circle. Continue on Route 103 east. Pass Mount Sunapee State Park and beaches.
6.4 LEFT onto Route 103A. Pass Outspokin Bicycle Shop.
14.8 LEFT onto Route 11 west. Pass Park-and-Ride lot.
20.4 Return to starting point.

Route Directions for 9B (Sunapee to Sutton Loop)

Follow route directions for 9A to Mile 9.6.
9.6 RIGHT onto Chalk Pond Road.
10.8 Bear LEFT.
12.8 Road turns to hard-packed dirt for less than 1 mile.
14.5 Bear LEFT on Main Street in town of Sutton.
14.8 LEFT onto Village Road. Pass cemetery on right.
15.0 LEFT onto Route 114.
17.3 LEFT onto Newport Road.
19.8 LEFT onto Route 11 west. Pass under I-89 and pass Park-and-Ride lot.
25.4 Return to starting point.

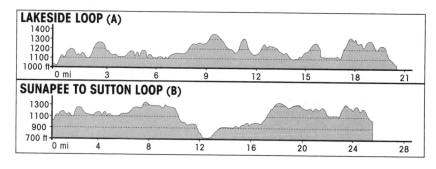

10 LOVEWELL MOUNTAIN RIDE
Washington

dirt roads, double-track, paved roads with moderate traffic

Total distance: 16.7 miles

Difficulty: 4

Riding time: 3.5 hours

Elevation gain: 1,273 feet

Atop a hill in southwest New Hampshire, on Route 31, you'll find the quaint New England town of Washington. This route heads from the center of town, basically circles the base and sides of Lovewell Mountain (or Lovell to the natives), and returns.

The route starts out on old roads and gets progressively more challenging. The trails are well marked by snowmobile signs and the white blaze of the Monadnock-Sunapee Greenway, a long-distance hiking trail. Just before the halfway point, at the turnoff after a small grassy meadow, the trail becomes more challenging because of rocks, mud, and, in the wetter spring months, water.

The final hill, at about the 13th mile, is the toughest section of the route.

A turtle tries to hide from mountain bikers on a dry day in June.

To bypass this incredibly steep climb up Lovewell Mountain Road (an approximately 1.5-mile climb), an optional gentler return route runs along East Washington Road. Once over Lovewell Mountain Road, you'll meet up with your original route and retrace the route back to Washington.

This route is recommended for fit bikers who don't mind bugs that bite. Another suggestion would be to do this ride when mud season (April and May) is long gone.

Driving Directions
From the north, take I-89 to Exit 13 in Grantham. Drive south on Route 10 for approximately 18 miles. Bear

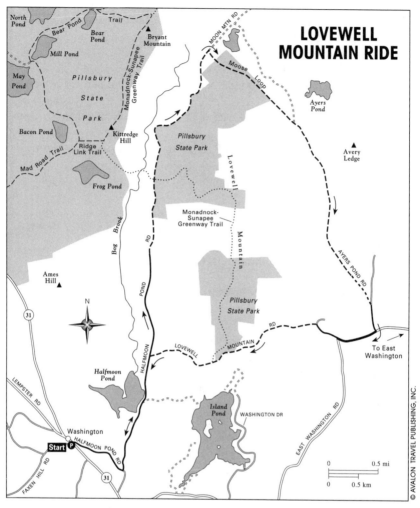

left onto Route 31 and drive 9 miles to Washington. From the south, take I-89 to Exit 5 onto Route 202/9. Follow Route 9 to Route 31 in Hillsborough and drive 8 miles north on Route 31 to Washington. Parking is available behind the large white church meeting house on the hill. The route starts from the tiny green, at the junction of Route 31 (North Main Street) and Halfmoon Pond Road.

Route Directions for Lovewell Mountain Ride

0.0 Ride southeast on Halfmoon Pond Road.

0.7 Bear LEFT on Halfmoon Pond Road at T-intersection.

1.3 Pass Snow Road. Halfmoon Pond is visible through the trees on the left.

2.0 Pass Lovewell Mountain Road on right (you will be returning on this road).

3.5 Pass Martin Road on right.

4.1 Pass Monadnock-Sunapee Greenway Trail on right.

4.7 Bear RIGHT at fork in road, toward bridge.

6.0 Continue STRAIGHT through four-way intersection, marked by snow-mobile trail markers.

6.4 Bear RIGHT onto dirt road with double-track marked as Moose Loop for snowmobilers.

7.4 Come to small grassy area. Go RIGHT onto trail marked as Main Road for snowmobilers.

7.5 Bear LEFT toward East Washington and Smith Pond, marked for snowmobilers.

8.2 Continue STRAIGHT. Pass big yellow gate on left.

8.6 Bear RIGHT on trail marked as Old Trail for snowmobilers, toward Washington.

9.5 Continue STRAIGHT through three-way intersection.

10.4 Pass around cable.

10.9 Bear RIGHT onto Ayers Pond Road (paved).

11.2 Bear RIGHT onto East Washington Road (paved). Pass East Washington School District No. 5 on left.

11.5 (For an optional easier return ride on paved roads with rolling hills, continue on East Washington Road for about 3.1 miles, then take a RIGHT onto Route 31 and continue for about 1.7 miles, back to Washington.)

11.7 Bear RIGHT onto Lovewell Mountain Road (dirt).

12.0 Bear LEFT at MUD sign on Lovewell Mountain Road.

12.5 Bear LEFT at junction after long hill.

13.2 Continue STRAIGHT (pass signs for Island Pond).

14.6 LEFT at intersection with Halfmoon Pond Road. (This is the same route you rode in on.)

15.9 RIGHT continuing on Halfmoon Pond Road.

16.7 Return to starting point.

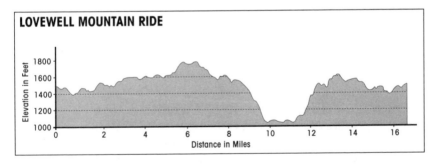

LOVEWELL MOUNTAIN RIDE

KITTREDGE HILL LOOP

Pillsbury State Park, Washington

single-track

Total distance: 5.5 miles

Difficulty: 5

Riding time: 3 hours

Elevation gain: 759 feet

Plenty of options exist in Pillsbury State Park for exploring by mountain bike. This quiet state park is heavily wooded and quite lovely, so it attracts diehard hikers all year long. In fact, you'll need to look out for, and be courteous to, hikers all along this route. For mountain bikers, there are lots of nice trails to explore. The Balanced Rock Trail, Five Summers Trail, and Mad Road all offer good options.

This route, which starts on the Bear Pond Trail, is the most challenging of the options we found, mostly because of the section on the Monadnock-Sunapee Greenway Trail. This section, which goes from a 2,070-foot-high peak to the 2,000-foot-high peak of Kittredge Hill, presents a challenge to cyclists, which puts this ride at a higher level of difficulty. You'll encounter parts where rocks are a real obstacle, and parts where the spacing between rocks may require you to carry your bike.

Overall, it's a rocky, rooty, tough ride, and the trails can be described as old jeep roads with sections deeply rutted from park vehicles. Steep climbs, mud, roots, logs, more mud, ruts, and moose are all features to expect. As we rode down the Ridge Link Trail from the summit of Kittredge Hill on a late October day, we saw three moose.

Though October is a good time to see wildlife, it might not be so great for weather. Fall is normally a good time to ride here, but you can get unexpected snowfalls (as we did), so be prepared for all conditions.

Pillsbury State Park offers camping (with direct access to the trail), hiking, canoeing, and places to picnic, so it's easy to make this into a weekend trip. For more information,

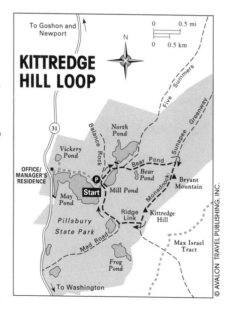

contact Pillsbury State Park, Route 31, Washington, NH 03280, 603/863-2860, website: www.nhstateparks.org/ParksPages/Pillsbury/Pillsbury.html.

Driving Directions

From the south, take I-89 to Exit 5 onto Route 202/9. Follow Route 9 to Route 31 in Hillsborough and drive approximately 10 miles north on Route 31 and look for signs to Pillsbury State Park. The park is just north of the Franklin Pierce Homestead on Route 31. Stop at the manager's office to pay the $3 entry fee and be sure to get a trail map of the park. Follow the entry road to the far end, where you'll find a parking lot. The ride starts on the trail to the left of the parking lot. Supplies are available in Newport, about 9 miles to the north of the park.

Route Directions for Kittredge Hill Loop

0.0 LEFT out of circular parking lot onto trail.
0.1 Continue past gate toward Bear Pond.
0.6 Bear RIGHT onto Bear Pond Trail.
2.0 RIGHT onto Monadnock-Sunapee Greenway Trail (marked with a brown and yellow sign).
3.8 RIGHT onto Ridge Link Trail.
4.5 RIGHT onto Mad Road Trail.
5.4 LEFT after gate and bridge.
5.5 RIGHT onto main road uphill to return to parking lot.

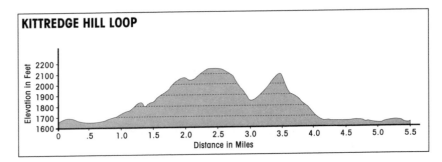

12 KATHY'S BEAR BROOK BOUNDER
Bear Brook State Park, Allenstown

dirt roads, single-track, double-track, paved roads with minimal traffic

Total distance: 8.5 miles

Difficulty: 3

Riding time: 1.5 hours

Elevation gain: 403 feet

In Bear Brook State Park, you'll find a biking trail for every skill level on the 40-plus miles of trails. In fact, you'll find an activity for everyone who loves the outdoors in this 10,000-acre park—camping (the trail is accessible from the campground), hiking, biking, fishing, swimming, horseback riding, and archery. You'll even find a fitness course and for natural history buffs, a museum complex in the park with an antique snowmobile museum, a museum of family camping, and more. You could easily turn a ride here into a weekend vacation.

On a cold day in early November, we found the colors vibrant, the trails empty, and the riding superb. The biking trails, which become cross-country ski trails in winter, are well marked, which makes riding fun and worry-free. You'll find quite a collection of conifers, making for a rocky, rooty ride.

This route is a good intermediate ride, offering terrain varying from wide double-track to steep single-track. Not too technical, most of the route's challenges come in the ascents along the way. This route is mainly on the side of Podunk Road that comprises the conservation area. The other side is open to hunters, so choose your riding routes wisely during hunting season, which runs generally late September–early December.

You can pick up a trail map at the ranger's station

Conifers line many a trail at Bear Brook State Park.

© ELLEN KANNER

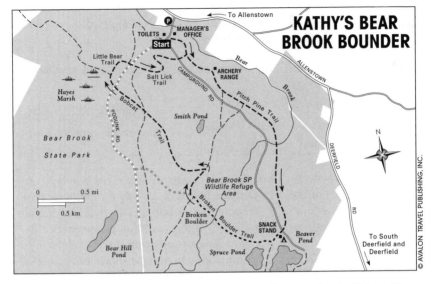

KATHY'S BEAR BROOK BOUNDER

© AVALON TRAVEL PUBLISHING, INC.

May–October. Off-season, it's a good idea to order one ahead of time. For more information or to order a biking trail map, contact Bear Brook State Park, Route 28, Allenstown, NH 03275, 603/485-9874, website: www.nhstateparks.org/ParksPages/BearBrook/BearBrk.html.

Driving Directions

From Concord and points north, or from Manchester and points south, take Route 93 to Routes 3/28 to Suncook. From Suncook, take Route 28 toward Allenstown. Turn right onto the Allenstown-Deerfield Road and drive approximately 3.1 miles. Turn right onto Podunk Road and park in the parking lot immediately to your right. The day-use fee is $3. Supplies are available in Suncook. A campground snack stand in the state park is open in summer. The nearest bike shops are in Hooksett, Concord, and Manchester.

Route Directions for Kathy's Bear Brook Bounder

0.0 On Podunk Road, by manager's house, ride STRAIGHT across from parking lot access road.

0.1 LEFT onto Pitch Pine Trail (also marked XC Ski Trail 1).

0.3 Continue STRAIGHT through sandpit.

0.6 Ride STRAIGHT through archery area, follow paved trail around pond, bear LEFT through parking lot, and continue STRAIGHT on wide trail.

3.2 Enter campground area, bear RIGHT to far side of camp office. Continue on paved road by ponds.

3.4 Bear RIGHT, away from Beaver Pond.

3.5 Bear RIGHT around gate. Continue through former AmeriCorp cabin site.

4.0 Continue STRAIGHT.

4.6 Bear RIGHT on Broken Boulder Trail toward Smith Pond (also marked XC Ski Trail 10).

5.0 LEFT on Bobcat Trail (also marked XC Ski Trail 7).

6.6 RIGHT on Podunk Road (dirt) then immediate LEFT through Hayes Field onto Little Bear Trail.

7.1 Continue on Little Bear Trail, bearing RIGHT.

7.3 At fork, bear RIGHT on XC Ski connector trail, crossing Podunk Road. Bear LEFT onto Salt Lick Trail.

7.8 Cross Campground Road, bearing LEFT twice onto Pitch Pine Trail.

8.2 Follow trail back to paved road.

8.3 Bear RIGHT toward entry gate on paved road.

8.5 Return to parking lot.

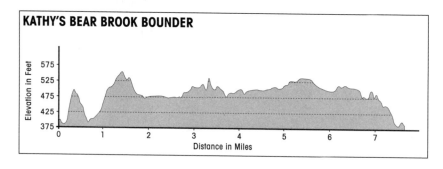

13 COUNTRY STORE RAMBLE

Barrington and Madbury

 paved roads with light to moderate traffic

Total distance: 19.5 miles

Riding time: 2.25 hours

Difficulty: 3

Elevation gain: 652 feet

Away from the hustle and bustle of the seacoast, just west of Dover, this pleasant ride takes you along backroads of Madbury and Barrington past numerous old cemeteries, rolling hills, quaint churches, and pleasant ponds. Most sections of the ride are along mildly traveled roads. Newly paved sections make this ride pleasurable for any cyclist who has had more than his or her share of broken pavement. Routes 155 and 4 have heavy traffic flow but offer plenty of shoulder room. Unfortunately the same can't be said about the short section along Route 9.

You'll also pass farm stands, apple orchards, and an ice-cream stand along the route, so bring some extra change and a bike bag or basket in which you can put some local goodies. A trip inside Calef's Country Store, at the start of the ride in Barrington, is sure to bring back many a child-hood memory. This 150-year-old general store sells New England penny

The McDaniel family plot sits under the power lines along Route 4, a testament to how much has changed since the mid-1800s.

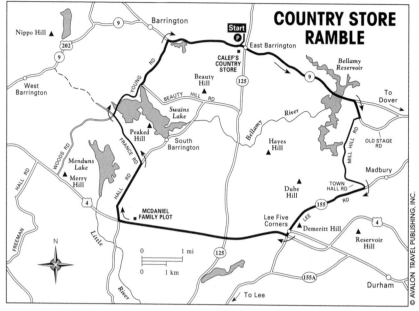

candy such as horehound, Boston baked beans, and molasses puffs, as well as its famous Snappy Old Cheese. There's a deli counter, gifts, and more.

For more information, contact the Barrington Chamber of Commerce, P.O. Box 363, Barrington, NH 03825, 603/664-2200, website: www.barringtonchamber.org. Calef's also has a website: www.calefs.net.

Driving Directions

From Dover, take Route 9 west to East Barrington. Just after the junction of Route 9 and Route 125, turn right into the Park-and-Ride lot, across the street from Calef's Country Store. Supplies are available in Barrington and the nearest bike shop is in Rochester.

Route Directions for Country Store Ramble

0.0 LEFT out of Route 9 Park-and-Ride lot.
0.1 Continue STRAIGHT through intersection on Route 9.
2.6 Cross Bellamy Reservoir.
3.1 RIGHT onto Old Stage Road.
3.5 RIGHT onto Mill Hill Road (unmarked).
4.3 Cross dam for Bellamy River.
4.7 Bear LEFT onto Town Hall Road.
5.4 Pass Madbury Town Hall.
5.7 RIGHT onto Route 155 south/Lee Road.
8.0 RIGHT onto Route 4 west.

9.6 (If you'd like to cut the ride short, a RIGHT onto Route 125 north will take you back to Route 9 and the Park-and-Ride lot.)
12.2 RIGHT onto Hall Road.
13.7 LEFT onto France Road.
15.0 Bear RIGHT onto Young Road (unmarked), pass Swains Lake on right.
15.3 Bear LEFT continuing on Young Road.
17.6 RIGHT onto Route 9.
19.5 Return to Park-and-Ride lot.

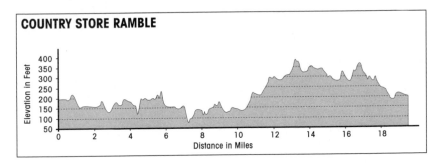

14 **FOUR COVERED BRIDGES RIDE**
Swanzey and Winchester, just south of Keene

paved roads with deteriorating pavement and moderate traffic

Total distance: 14.8 miles

Difficulty: 3

Riding time: 1.5–2 hours

Elevation gain: 241 feet

Starting in Swanzey, a small town south of Keene, this ride follows paved roads through four of the six covered bridges in this area and passes among beautiful stands of pine trees in the Yale-Toumey Forest. At the starting point, explore an old cemetery and the Potash Bowl, a natural amphitheater.

Gradual, low-level hills and shady terrain best describe this mellow ride, perfect for a Sunday afternoon. However, you'll need to pay attention on the two short stretches on Route 10, as the traffic tends to move fast.

The four covered bridges, all wooden, are in scenic settings, giving you lots of visual treats. A note on traversing the bridges: All but the Thompson Bridge in West Swanzey are single-lane only, and you should pay close attention to drivers as you pass through. Be sure to pick up supplies in Keene unless you can wait for the convenience store halfway through the ride. For more information about the area, contact Keene City Hall, 3 Washington Street, Keene, NH 03431, 603/352-0133, website: www.ci.keene.nh.us.

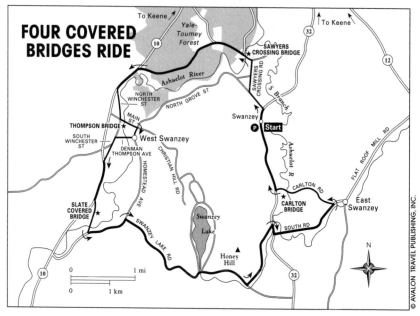

Driving Directions

From Keene, take Route 32 south for approximately 5 miles to Swanzey. The ride begins in Swanzey at the town hall, right on Route 32. Parking is available at the town hall. Supplies and bike shops are available in Keene.

Route Directions for Four Covered Bridges Ride

0.0 RIGHT out of the town hall parking lot onto Route 32 north.

0.1 LEFT onto Sawyers Crossing Road. Pass Potash Bowl on left.

0.4 Follow signs to Sawyers Crossing Bridge.

1.0 Cross bridge. (Take care crossing one-lane bridge.)

1.2 Bear LEFT. Continue through Yale-Toumey Forest.

3.2 LEFT onto Route 10 south.

3.7 LEFT onto North Winchester Street.

4.2 LEFT onto Main Street. Cross Thompson Bridge; two-way traffic.

4.5 RIGHT onto Homestead Avenue.

4.6 RIGHT onto Denman Thompson Avenue.

5.0 RIGHT onto South Winchester Street.

5.0 LEFT onto Route 10 south.

5.7 *Supplies available at a convenience store and ice-cream stand.*

5.8 LEFT in the direction of Westport Station (unmarked road).

6.3 Cross Slate Covered Bridge.

6.4 LEFT just after bridge onto Swanzey Lake Road (unmarked).

7.2 Bear RIGHT on Swanzey Lake Road.

11.1 RIGHT onto Route 32.

11.2 LEFT onto South Road.

12.2 LEFT onto Weber Hill Road.

12.4 LEFT onto Carlton Road.

13.4 Cross Carlton Bridge.

13.6 RIGHT onto Route 32 north.

14.8 Return to Swanzey Town Hall.

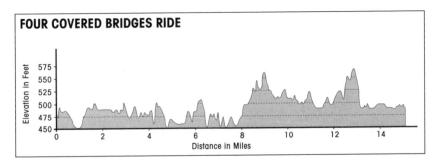

15 CHILD'S BOG LOOP
Harrisville

dirt roads, single-track, paved roads with minimal traffic

Total distance: 6.3 miles

Riding time: 1.5 hours

Difficulty: 3

Elevation gain: 405 feet

Old brick mill buildings and waterfalls punctuate the small town of Harrisville, where the mills are reputed to be the only surviving unaltered examples of a 19th-century industrial community in the whole country. The historic, picturesque village is the starting point for a ride that takes you through thickly wooded terrain, a good jaunt for the advanced beginner or intermediate rider.

The route starts in front of the Harrisville General Store. You'll head down Main Street, then follow a trail varying in width from single-track to a four-wheel-drive road. Cross a paved road, then follow a dirt road before continuing on a rather wide section of the Monadnock-Sunapee Greenway Trail, a long-distance hiking trail. The return ride is on the paved Nelson Road, which takes you by pretty Harrisville Pond.

The scenery along this ride is at its best in summer and fall. Take along

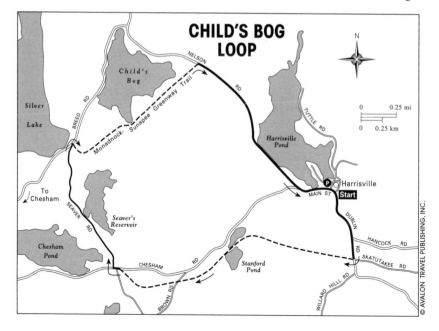

sandwiches and bakery items from the Harrisville General Store for a pleasant picnic lunch at Child's Bog dam.

For more information, contact the Harrisville Town Hall, Chesham Road, Harrisville, NH 03450, 603/827-3431, website: www.keenenh.com/harrisville. For more information on the Monadnock-Sunapee Greenway Trail, contact the Trail Club, P.O. Box 164, Marlow, NH 03456, website: www.msgtc.org.

Driving Directions

From Peterborough, take Route 101 west to Dublin, approximately 7 miles. Turn right onto Dublin Road and follow the signs to Harrisville. Drive approximately 3.5 miles to the center of Harrisville (Dublin Street becomes Main Street). Parking is available throughout this tiny town and supplies are available at the general store. The route begins at Harrisville General Store on the corner of Church and Main Streets. The nearest bike shops are in Keene and Peterborough.

Route Directions for Child's Bog Loop

0.0 From parking lot of general store, take a RIGHT onto Main Street, which becomes Dublin Road.

0.6 RIGHT onto dirt path, across from Skatutakee Road.

2.0 RIGHT onto Brown Road (dirt).

2.1 LEFT onto Chesham Road.

2.6 RIGHT onto Seaver Road. Pass Seaver Reservoir.

3.6 Bear RIGHT at fork in road.

3.7 RIGHT onto Rosemary Trail, a section of the Monadnock-Sunapee Greenway Trail (marked with a white blaze).

4.2 Pass Child's Bog Dam. *A nice picnic spot is on the right side of the dam.*

4.9 RIGHT onto Nelson Road.

6.1 LEFT onto Chesham Road.

6.3 Return to starting point.

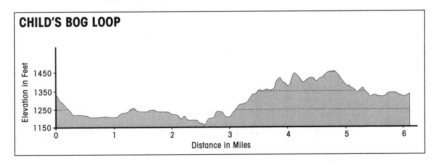

16 HANCOCK HILLS RAMBLE

Peterborough and Hancock

dirt road, paved bike path, paved roads with some deteriorating pavement and moderate to minimal traffic

Total distance: 17.4 miles

Riding time: 2–2.5 hours

Difficulty: 3

Elevation gain: 1,071 feet

Peterborough is probably most famous for the part it played in Thornton Wilder's play, *Our Town.* Wilder modeled Grovers Corners, the town whose characters are the play's main subjects, on Peterborough when he wrote it here in the early 1900s. Peterborough offers arts as well as the outdoors to those wishing to stay for the weekend. The professional theater of the Peterborough Players, which you'll pass on this ride, offers a variety of productions during the summer.

The route starts by following the Contoocook River down Summer Street, and then follows a section of a rail trail bike path. It continues up a long, gradual hill, past farms, and over hilly terrain complete with mountain vistas and erratic boulders. The return route follows similar terrain near the town of Hancock on Route 137, a curvy road with minimal shoulders where vehicles pass at high speeds.

an October snowfall along Middle Hancock Road

A turn onto Sargent Camp Road provides a pleasant respite along a packed-dirt road. As you pass Half-moon Pond, reflective views of Hancock's Skatutakee Mountain appear on the left. After Boston University's Sargent Camp, the route continues past a few horse farms and offers glimpses of Pack Monadnock and Temple Mountain to the east and vistas of Mount Monadnock to the west. On Mac-Dowell Road, you'll come across MacDowell Colony, a private artists' colony founded in 1907 to provide artists with a haven where they could pursue their work without interruption. A pleasant downhill coast at the end of the ride brings you back to the starting point in downtown Peterborough.

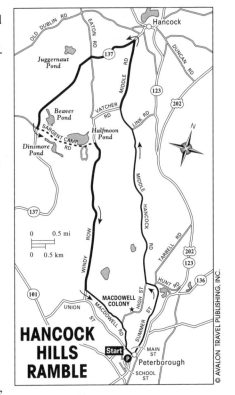

This route could easily be made into a day trip, with a couple of tasty options for lunch in Hancock, about halfway through the ride. For more information about the area, contact the Peterborough Chamber of Commerce, P.O. Box 401, Peterborough, NH 03458, 603/924-7234, website: www.peterboroughchamber.com; or visit the town's website: www.townofpeterborough.com.

Driving Directions

From Manchester and points east, take Route 101 west to Peterborough. After the intersection with Route 202, turn right onto Grove Street. Drive to the end, to the junction with Main Street, and turn right. The route starts at the intersection of Main and Summer Streets. Free parking is available throughout the downtown area, including a municipal parking lot along School Street, just off Grove Street. Supplies are available in Peterborough and a bike shop is on Grove Street.

Route Directions for Hancock Hills Ramble

0.0 Proceed north on Summer Street from intersection with Main Street, across from Roy's Market.

0.8 RIGHT onto marked bike route.

1.6 LEFT onto Hunt Road, then immediate RIGHT onto Summer Street. Summer Street eventually becomes Middle Road.

3.1 Pass Peterborough Players on right.

7.4 LEFT onto Route 137. *A right turn onto Route 137 is a detour to Hancock, where you can find convenience stores and restaurants.*

10.7 LEFT onto Sargent Camp Road (dirt road). Pass Halfmoon Pond.

12.2 RIGHT onto Windy Row (unmarked) at T-intersection. Look for big brown barn on right.

15.4 LEFT onto MacDowell Road. Pass the MacDowell Colony.

15.7 RIGHT onto High Street.

17.1 RIGHT onto Vine Street, then immediate LEFT onto Union Street.

17.4 Return to starting point.

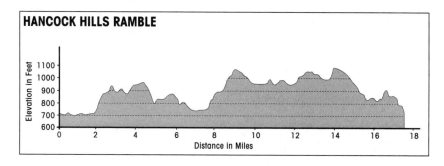

17 NEW COMMON PATHWAY AND OLD RAILROAD TRAIL
Peterborough to Hancock

  rail trail with ballast, paved roads with moderate traffic, paved bike trail

Total distance: 15 miles

Difficulty: 2

Riding time: 2.5 hours

Elevation gain: 259 feet

A ride along the New Common Pathway and the Old Railroad Trail makes for a pleasant trip, whether you start in downtown Peterborough or park in a shopping center lot just south of town and start from there. Suitable for either a mountain or a hybrid bike, the ride begins on paved roads with modest traffic, then continues on the New Common Pathway, a paved bike path. This turns into a packed-dirt bike path, called the Old Railroad Trail, which varies between the usual New England roots and ruts and a ballast surface. More adventurous riders will appreciate the section after crossing Route 202 as this is a more heavily wooded area and an unpaved section is fun to explore all the way up to the Hancock-Bennington town line.

The light at the end of the leafy tunnel leads to Cavendar Road.

Various trail hazards include dips and potholes along the dirt part, so keep alert. Use caution on the short section along Route 202 as shoulder room is minimal and traffic moves along quickly. There are plans to create an underpass underneath Route 202 (as well as a nearby parking lot) in 2005, so you may be spared this hassle altogether!

For more information about the area, contact the Peterborough Chamber of Commerce, P.O. Box 401, Peterborough, NH 03458, 603/924-7234, website:

www.peterboroughchamber.com; or visit the town's website: www.townofpeterborough.com.

Driving Directions

From Manchester and points east, take Route 101 west to Peterborough. After the intersection with Route 202, turn right onto Grove Street. Drive to the end, to the junction with Main Street, and turn right. The route starts at the intersection of Main and Summer Streets. Free parking is available throughout the downtown area, including a municipal parking lot along School Street, just off Grove Street. Supplies are available in Peterborough and a bike shop is on Grove Street. Parking is also available at the Stop and Shop shopping plaza on Route 101. A new, short bike path begins on the far side of that parking lot and takes you into downtown Peterborough, so you could also begin your ride there and add an extra .5 mile, each way, to the trip.

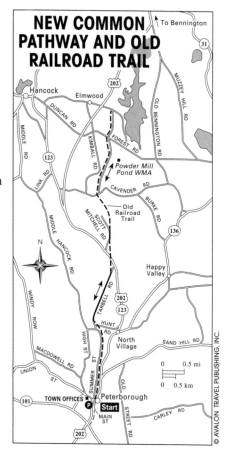

Route Directions for New Common Pathway and Old Railroad Trail

0.0 Proceed north on Summer Street from intersection with Main Street, across from Roy's Market.

0.8 Bear RIGHT onto marked bike route.

1.0 Pass alternate parking lot for bike path.

1.8 Cross Hunt Road and continue on Tarbell Road.

2.1 Bear LEFT onto marked bike path at corner of Tarbell and Nichols Road.

3.0 Continue STRAIGHT through traffic circle to trail on other side.

3.5 Use caution here. Bear RIGHT before gate, between boulders. Walk bike down embankment to the other side of Route 202. Continue on right hand side of road. (On the return route, stay on the opposite side of the road.)

3.8 RIGHT onto Scott Mitchell Road.

4.0 RIGHT onto Old Railroad Trail.
5.3 Intersect with Cavender Road. Continue STRAIGHT (it will seem as if you're riding down someone's driveway)
6.8 Use caution crossing Forest Road. Continue STRAIGHT.
7.4 At intersection with dirt road, TURN AROUND.
15.0 Return to starting point.

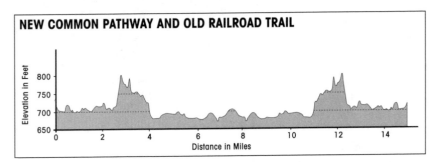

NEW COMMON PATHWAY AND OLD RAILROAD TRAIL

18 ADAMS HILL RAIL TRAIL LOOP
Greenville and Mason

rail trail, dirt roads, paved roads with some deteriorating pavement and minimal traffic

Total distance: 11.4 miles

Riding time: 2 hours

Difficulty: 3

Elevation gain: 839 feet

Half of this ride is on an old railroad bed and the other half is on dirt and paved roads, with one challenging section over an old four-wheel-drive road, making it perfect for a mountain biker or an adventurous hybrid rider.

It starts in the town of Greenville on paved roads, then turns onto an old railroad bed on Adams Hill Road. You'll stay on the rail trail for about 4.5 miles, and then have a short climb up a rocky, rooty, muddy four-wheel-drive road before a coast down Meetinghouse Hill Road into Mason.

In Mason, the ride continues up the dirt Darling Hill Road, which provides a good workout. Route 123 serves as the final leg of the ride, continuing through an orchard and back to Greenville.

Though the ride does not go by the area's favorite tourist attraction, Pickety Place on Netting Hill Road in Mason, it's a nice place to stop on a summer day for lunch or a tour of the herb gardens. Little Red Riding Hood fans may recognize the 18th-century farmhouse; illustrator Elizabeth Orton Jones used it as inspiration for Little Red Riding Hood's grandmother's house. Directional signs are posted throughout Mason.

For more information, contact the Greenville town office, 603/878-2084.

flat and easy riding on the former railway bed

Driving Directions
From Route 101 in Wilton, take Route 31 south for approximately 2.5 miles to

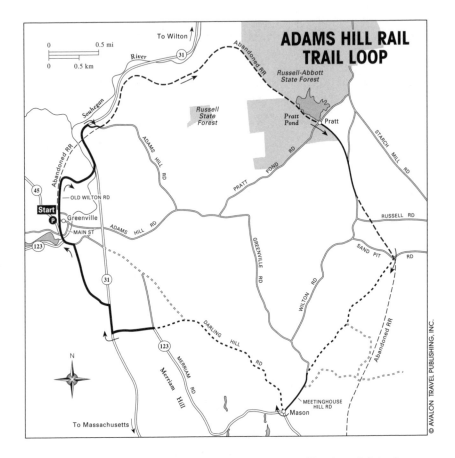

Greenville. Parking is available throughout Greenville along Main Street or behind the old depot in town. The ride starts at the junction of Route 45, Main Street, and Old Wilton Road, heading north on Old Wilton Road out of town. Supplies are available at convenience stores in Greenville. The nearest bike shops are in Rindge and Milford.

Route Directions for Adams Hill Rail Trail Loop

0.0 Start in front of the old depot on Route 45. Turn LEFT onto Old Wilton Road.

0.7 LEFT onto Route 31 north.

1.0 Pass under remains of old railroad bridge.

1.1 RIGHT onto Adams Hill Road.

1.3 LEFT onto old railroad bed.

3.1 Cross under power lines.

4.2 Pass Pratt Pond and Pratt Pond Road.

4.8 *An old quarry on the right has blueberry bushes and perfect picnic rocks.*
5.5 Cross wooden bridge.
5.8 Cross Sand Pit Road. Bear RIGHT up trail beyond road, not on railroad bed.
7.4 LEFT onto Meetinghouse Hill Road (paved).
7.9 Sharp RIGHT onto Darling Hill Road. Pass library.
9.6 Bear RIGHT onto Route 123 north through orchard.
10.0 RIGHT onto Routes 31 and 123 north.
10.2 LEFT onto Route 123 north toward Greenville.
11.0 Bear LEFT.
11.1 Continue across bridge in downtown Greenville.
11.2 Bear RIGHT uphill onto Main Street. Pass Greenville Town Hall on right.
11.4 Return to starting point.

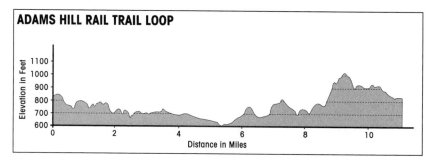

Chapter 3

© MELISSA L. KIM

Maine

Maine

I t might seem a little presumptuous for a state to greet you at the border with a sign that says "Welcome to Vacationland" and the slogan "Maine: the way life should be." But it lives up to its promise. Bicyclists can choose from a full spectrum of places to explore on two wheels—islands and hilltops, logging roads and wildlife refuges.

Maine is almost as large as the other five New England states put together, and with only about 1.3 million people, that leaves plenty of space where there are no houses, no roads, no nothing, just lots of trees and, yes, the iconic moose. Though southern and coastal Maine have all the trappings of an economy based heavily on tourism, the farther north and inland you go, the more you'll find old New England villages with catch-all general stores, graceful colonial buildings, and museums celebrating the state's history and culture, from logging to lighthouses.

Mountain chains punctuate the western side of the state. The Appalachian Trail climbs its way toward its northern terminus at Maine's highest point, Mount Katahdin, in the heart of a backcountry region whose roads and remoteness are not readily accessible to bicyclists. However, the White Mountains also spill into Maine, and cycling along the Maine-New Hampshire border gives you hilly challenges and spectacular vistas as thickly forested mountains meet sparkling lakes. Each season brings a distinctly different look and terrain, from verdant hillsides and muddy trails in spring to fallow farmland and vibrant hues of autumn foliage in the fall. Cycling is good April–November, though the foliage season, which peaks in mid-October, brings hordes of leaf-peepers in cars and buses to this region.

Maine's coast stretches confusingly in an east-west line, giving rise to its famous Down East region. Glaciers helped create these coastal lowlands, where dozens of fingerlike peninsulas reach toward the ocean. Bicycling in this region is a treat, with dramatic rocky cliffs and ocean views, small islands to explore, and sea breezes to moderate even the hottest days. Scenery such as this is not a secret, so tourists can clog roads in August. Try road riding in May and June or September and October, and go just a little beyond the beaten path to find empty roads and quiet harbors.

Maine does tend to have long winters, so don't be fooled when people talk about four-season riding. They usually mean spring, summer, fall, and mud season. Snowmelt and spring runoff can mean a very muddy March or April, and it's better for the trails if you wait to mountain bike until late May or June. Winter is not off-limits, either. Many bike shops sell or make studded snow tires for winter road riding, and winter mountain biking is gaining in popularity. There's a saying in Maine, where they pride themselves on their ruggedness: "There's no such thing as bad weather, only improper outerwear." So dress for the weather and you'll be all set.

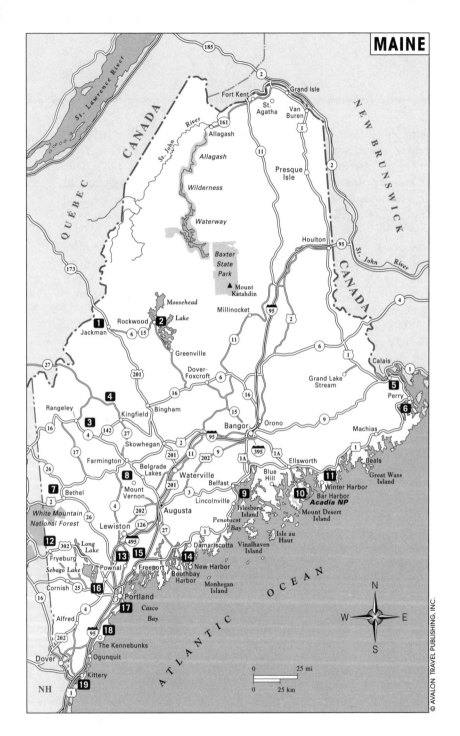

MAINE

St. Lawrence River

QUÉBEC

CANADA

NEW BRUNSWICK

185

Fort Kent

Grand Isle

2

St. Agatha

Van Buren

1

161

Allagash

St. John River

11

Allagash

Wilderness

Presque Isle

2

Waterway

Baxter State Park

173

Houlton

95

St. John River

CANADA

1

Mount Katahdin

4

Moosehead Lake

Millinocket

95

2

27

1

Rockwood

2

1

Jackman

6 15

Greenville

11

6

Calais

1

Dover-Foxcroft

6

Grand Lake Stream

201

201

16

Bingham

16

9

5

Perry

Rangeley

4

Kingfield

15

6

16

3

142

27

Bangor

Orono

Machias

4

17

Skowhegan

2

95

Farmington

201

11

202

9

1

26

Belgrade Lakes

9

Beals

8

Waterville

1A

395

1A

Ellsworth

Great Wass Island

Mount Vernon

201

Belfast

Blue Hill

11

Winter Harbor

7

Bethel

3

Lincolnville

9

10

Bar Harbor

2

202

Augusta

Islesboro Island

Acadia NP

White Mountain National Forest

4

126

Penobscot Bay

Mount Desert Island

26

Lewiston

Isle au Haut

12

302

Long Lake

495

Vinalhaven Island

Fryeburg

13

15

Damariscotta

Sebago Lake

Pownal

14

New Harbor

Cornish

25

Freeport

Boothbay Harbor

Monhegan Island

16

16

4

Portland

17

Casco Bay

Alfred

202

95

18

ATLANTIC OCEAN

Dover

The Kennebunks

Ogunquit

N

W   E

S

NH

Kittery

19

1

0   25 mi

0   25 km

© AVALON TRAVEL PUBLISHING, INC.

Contents

1 RANCOURT POND LOOP

Jackman

 dirt roads with minimal traffic, paved road

Total distance: 10.2 miles

Riding time: 1.5 hours

Difficulty: 2

Elevation gain: 375 feet

Ride down Main Street in Jackman and you'll see restaurants with names such as Lumberjack Steak House and Mama Bear's Den. It's a sure sign that this outpost, close to the Canadian border, is for hearty souls who work and play hard. Snowmobilers have long congregated here, and now mountain bikers are taking notice of the many excellent backcountry trails that begin in Jackman.

There are several ways to get on this short, fun loop around Rancourt Pond. The most convenient place to start is from the Armand Pomerleau Park, formerly the Jackman Recreational Park. Though it means you have to ride on Route 201 for a mile or so, it gives you a good look at Jackman and traffic is not heavy here. You'll cross the Moose River and pass through town. At the left turn on Sandy Stream Road, look for a small blue bicycle route sign.

Ride past a horse farm and then take a right at the fork. The road

Some of the dirt roads are more rock than dirt on this loop.

quickly turns into an overgrown dirt road, then a dirt track. You'll have Sandy Stream on your right as you ride along this narrow, pretty section that passes through woods and fields.

At the next fork, a thin trail goes off to the left, but you'll stay on the main trail to the right. Just .2 mile after that, there's a short steep hill before a T-junction, where you'll head left. From this point on, you'll be traveling on wide dirt roads.

A short incline takes you near the shore of Rancourt Pond, and several little paths will get you right on the banks. Plenty of good picnic spots are here, where the wildlife-watching is excellent.

RANCOURT POND LOOP

© AVALON TRAVEL PUBLISHING, INC.

The next section is a fun, winding stretch with lots of little ups and downs and puddles to hop or avoid. You'll hit a few clearings where butterflies and bees swarm out of the wildflowers. The last stretch of dirt road, rutted though it may be, is also used by trucks, so look out for traffic. It's a series of long but gradual inclines for 1.5 miles, then a long downhill to return to the start of the loop.

For more information, contact the Jackman-Moose River Region Chamber of Commerce, P.O. Box 368, Jackman, ME 04945, 207/668-4171, website: www.jackmanmaine.org.

Driving Directions
From points south, take Route 95 to Exit 133 in Fairfield to Route 201. Drive 88 miles northwest on Route 201 to Jackman. Just before you enter the center of town, look for Armand Pomerleau Park (also called Jackman Recreational Park) on the left. There are picnic tables, a playground, a tennis court, and restrooms with running water. A Chamber of Commerce booth is just past the park on the left. Supplies are available in Jackman.

Route Directions for Rancourt Pond Loop
0.0 Start at Armand Pomerleau Park and turn LEFT on Route 201.
1.4 LEFT on Sandy Stream Road.
1.7 RIGHT at fork onto dirt road.
2.3 Dirt road turns into narrow track.
3.8 Bear RIGHT, staying on main trail, at fork.

4.1 LEFT at T-junction.
4.3 *The small path on right leads to shore of Rancourt Pond.*
6.1 LEFT on dirt road.
8.5 RIGHT at intersection onto Sandy Stream Road.
8.8 RIGHT on Route 201.
10.2 RIGHT to return to Armand Pomerleau Park parking area.

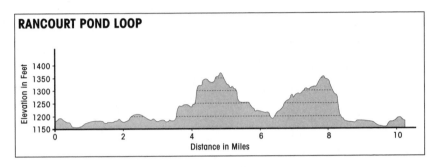

2 MOOSEHEAD LAKE
Mount Kineo, Rockwood

 dirt roads with minimal traffic

Total distance: 21 miles

Riding time: 2.5 hours (not including the ferry ride)

Difficulty: 3   **Elevation gain:** 438 feet

It's difficult to avoid cliché when describing Mount Kineo. This 800-foot-high lump of granite with its sheer cliff faces bursts out of Moosehead Lake with such grandeur that you're sure to feel small and humble as you ride on remote logging roads in its shadow.

The easiest way to reach Kineo and these dirt roads is by a short, scenic boat ride from the opposite side of Moosehead Lake. Three hiking trails go around and up the mountain itself, and though biking these trails is not specifically forbidden, it is not encouraged by the state parks division that oversees this property. If you've got time, leave the bikes at the dock and take a short hike up the peak for panoramic views.

This ride takes you off the Kineo peninsula, across a narrow isthmus, and onto the mainland to make a loop on the logging roads. You will need some map-reading skills (it's not a bad idea to carry a compass) as it's

A wooden bridge goes over the small outlet stream to remote and scenic Lucky Pond.

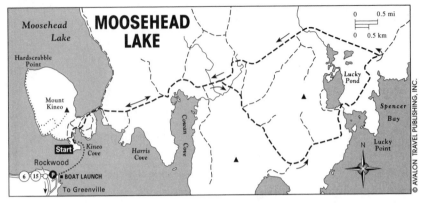

easy to get confused by the unmarked roads. The roads are fairly flat, but the remoteness and length make this a ride for people who are comfortable in the backcountry.

The most scenic section is at the ride's halfway point. On the stretch coming up to Lucky Pond, you'll be riding straight toward the distant peaks of Little and Big Spencer Mountains. The lovely pond is the best picnic spot on the route and a good spot to look for wildlife.

For more information, contact the Moosehead Lake Region Chamber of Commerce, P.O. Box 581, Greenville, ME 04441, 207/695-2702 or 888/876-2778, website: www.mooseheadlake.org.

Driving Directions

From Portland or Bangor, take Route 95 to Exit 157 in Newport. Drive north on Route 7 for 15 miles to Dexter. Take Route 23 for 12 miles to Guilford, and then take Routes 15/6 for approximately 26 miles to Greenville. Go left on Route 15/6 in the center of Greenville. Drive 1.7 miles and bear right in Greenville Junction. Drive approximately 17 miles and turn right at the sign to Rockwood Village and follow signs to the public boat launch. There are a large parking area, picnic tables, and an outhouse, but no water supply. The Kineo Launch shuttle leaves daily from the Rockwood public boat launch on the hour 8 A.M.–4 P.M. and returns on the half hour until 4:30 P.M. The ferry ride lasts about 12 minutes and costs $10 round-trip. Supplies are available in Greenville, at the one general store in Rockwood, and at the golf course snack shop on Mount Kineo. A bike shop and outfitter is in Greenville.

Route Directions for Moosehead Lake

0.0 RIGHT from dock toward golf course.
0.2 RIGHT on dirt road. Pass Kineo Cove on the right.

0.5 Pass by a dirt trail on the left, then take the LEFTMOST dirt road at the three-way intersection.

1.2 Ride across the isthmus. *Boaters come ashore here and you can swim from the pebbly beach.*

1.5 RIGHT and uphill at fork.

1.6 Pass through a gate made of large boulders and continue STRAIGHT.

3.1 LEFT.

3.7 STRAIGHT through four-way intersection.

4.3 LEFT at fork.

4.6 Cross bridge.

5.3 RIGHT at fork.

5.5 Cross bridge.

5.7 RIGHT.

10.1 Cross bridge at Lucky Pond.

12.3 LEFT.

14.2 Cross bridge.

15.4 STRAIGHT at intersection.

15.7 STRAIGHT at intersection.

16.1 LEFT.

16.8 Cross bridge.

17.1 STRAIGHT at fork.

17.7 STRAIGHT through four-way intersection.

18.2 RIGHT.

19.7 Bear LEFT and downhill after stone gate.

20.1 Pass Pebbly Beach.

20.8 LEFT before golf course.

21 Return to dock.

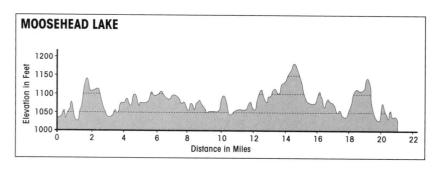

3 RAILROAD LOOP TRAIL

Rangeley

dirt roads, single- and double-track, paved road with minimal traffic

Total distance: 13.6 miles

Difficulty: 4

Riding time: 2.5 hours

Elevation gain: 759 feet

The remote area of Rangeley is recreation central year-round. Hikers, bikers, boaters, anglers, and skiers make the trek to dabble among the pristine lakes and rolling mountains. It seems that everywhere you look, the view is fine. Old logging roads wind in and around this lake-strewn area, so you can always explore those, but this Railroad Loop Trail was developed by local mountain bikers to combine an old railroad bed, former logging road, and some sweet newly created single-track.

The first stretch of the loop starts on the old railroad bed, which can be dry, dusty, and rocky. It's also used by ATVs, so patience and trail manners are essential. Once you're off the railroad bed, the terrain is tougher, with first a rocky section and then a long, steep hill leading to overgrown double-track, a former logging road in a pretty, wild section. Regrowth from clear-cuts has led to thick ground cover, and an abundance of butterflies follows your tires like dolphins leaping at a ship's bow.

taking a break on the Schoolhouse Trail in Rangeley

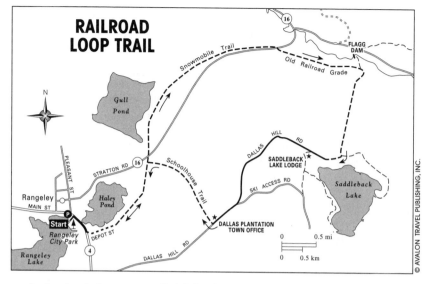

A clearing brings you to Saddleback Lake Lodge and a network of dirt roads. Head right at the tennis courts and soon the smooth dirt road turns into a paved road that becomes Dallas Hill Road. As you churn your way up a killer hill, you can marvel either at the mountain vistas or the golfers playing on what must be the steepest course in the state.

The real gem of this loop is the single-track Schoolhouse Trail, a fun, deep-woods trail full of roots, good-sized rocks, stream crossings, and plank bridges with grooves just wide enough to snag a tire. If you're not up for the single-track, you can continue on Dallas Hill Road back to Route 4, where a right turn will return you to the parking lot.

This well-maintained trail is the result of efforts by the very active Trails for the Rangeley Area Coalition and the Rangeley Recreation Department. Land ownership and access have been a hot topic here, so make sure you ride only on signed trails. TRAC is in the process of creating more off-road trails, so check with the Recreation Department or the folks at Seasonal Cycles, 2593 Main Street, for up-to-the-minute information and maps. For more information, contact the Rangeley Recreation Department, 207/864-3327.

Driving Directions

From Farmington, take Route 4 for 40 miles northwest to Rangeley. This becomes Main Street. Look for signs for the Rangeley City Park on the left. Turn left on Park Road and park in one of the parking areas. A Chamber of Commerce information booth and public restrooms, picnic tables, and a public dock and beach are on this northeastern corner of vast

Rangeley Lake. Rangeley City Park is open 5 A.M.–10 P.M. Parking lots are on both sides of the park. Supplies and a bike shop are available in Rangeley. Stock up since there are no supplies available along the route.

Route Directions for Railroad Loop Trail

0.0 Starting from Rangeley City Park, turn RIGHT onto Main Street.

0.3 LEFT on Depot Street into small gravel parking area just past the Rangeley Inn. The trailhead is to the left of the electrical substation.

1.9 Trail ends. Cross Route 16 and pick up marked trail on other side.

4.6 Trail ends. Cross Route 16 and pick up marked trail on other side.

6.0 RIGHT at junction. *Or you can turn left to explore the remnants of Flagg Dam. This is a good picnic spot and the only potential swimming or wading spot.*

6.9 STRAIGHT around green gate.

7.3 STRAIGHT across clearing.

7.4 RIGHT following the small bike trail sign.

7.5 STRAIGHT around gate.

7.6 RIGHT at Saddleback Lake Lodge tennis courts, on hard-packed dirt road.

9.0 Road becomes Dallas Hill Road (paved).

10.2 RIGHT onto Schoolhouse Trail. The trailhead is marked by a blue bike trail sign just past the parking lot for the town office and plantation office building.

11.8 LEFT onto Railroad Loop Trail.

13.3 Return to trailhead. Turn RIGHT onto Main Street.

13.6 LEFT onto Park Road to return to Rangeley City Park parking lot.

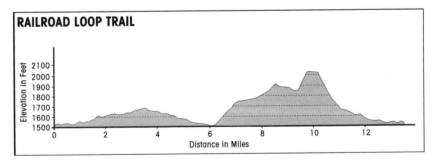

4 CARRABASSETT RIVER LOOP

Carrabassett Valley, Stratton, and Bigelow

dirt trail, single-track, bike path, paved road with minimal traffic

Total distance: 19.6 miles

Riding time: 2.5–3 hours

Difficulty: 3

Elevation gain: 933 feet

This loop is fast becoming a classic ride for Maine's mountain bikers, many of whom consider it one of the best rides in the state. It's easy to see why: You start out in a remote wooded area on former logging roads, enter a beautiful stretch of challenging single-track, then emerge into the breathtaking Bigelow Preserve, where reflections of mountains shimmer on the surface of beaver ponds. One stretch is on a paved road, but the finish is on a smooth bike path along a former narrow gauge railroad bed that runs alongside the pretty rock-strewn Carrabassett River.

The first section of the ride can be a bit confusing, as lots of small dirt roads and trails branch off the main one. Stay on the trail that looks most traveled and you'll be fine. There are several stream crossings and log bridges to cross. The incline is steady for the first third of the ride, so it's not "all play, no work."

The key is not to miss the single-track trail, which begins after about 5 miles. Many local guides call for a left turn at the 5-mile mark, but the right-hand trail has become so overgrown that you're really just staying straight. This twisty trail starts out grassy and turns leafy, with more small stream crossings and nice views of beaver ponds along the way.

When you reach the lovely Stratton Brook Pond, you'll join the trails that crisscross the Bigelow Preserve, 35,000 acres of undeveloped public land that include the peaks of the Bigelow Range. The price you pay for all the beauty is a 2-mile-long climb up Route 16/27, which can be a busy road. Take care as you zoom down the other side, since there's an awkward left turn midway down the steep hill.

This dirt road passes a former train station and some small houses, and then hooks up with the Narrow Gauge Pathway, also marked as "Sugarloaf XC Ski Trail 9," which is for nonmotorized vehicles only. The Sugarloaf Outdoor Center maintains the northern end of this pathway and there is a fee to use the trail in winter.

For more information, contact the Carrabassett Valley town office, 1001 Carriage Road, Carrabassett Valley, ME 04947, 207/235-2645, website: www.carrabassettvalley.org.

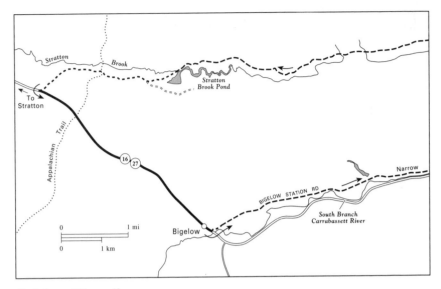

Driving Directions

From Kingfield, drive 9.3 miles north on Routes 16/27 to Carrabassett Valley. Turn right onto Carriage Road and take the first left to the town office, fire department, and recreation department parking lot. You'll find restrooms at the pool, pay phones, and soda machines. There is also a trailhead at Campbell Field, 5 miles farther along Route 16/27, just before the access road to the Sugarloaf Outdoor Center (on the left). Campbell Field is on the right with outhouses and parking for about 20 cars. Take the bridge across the river for access to the Narrow Gauge Pathway. Bike rentals are available in summer at Sugarloaf USA; supplies are available in Carrabassett Valley and Kingfield.

Route Directions for Carrabassett River Loop

0.0 Exit the town office parking lot.

0.1 LEFT onto Carriage Road.

0.5 LEFT onto Huston Brook Road.

1.2 RIGHT up the dirt road, which narrows to a dirt track. (The Narrow Gauge Pathway is straight ahead; you'll be returning on this path.)

1.9 Bear RIGHT, staying on main track.

3.4 Stay on main track curving to the left.

3.6 STRAIGHT through the clearing, past the power lines.

5.4 Stay on main track, branching slightly to the left.

7.7 Bear LEFT as you emerge onto new trail system, just after major stream crossing.

7.9 Major stream crossing. Continue STRAIGHT uphill on the other side.

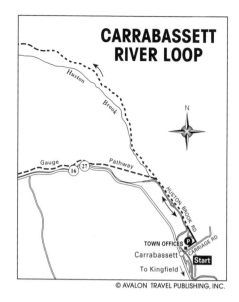

CARRABASSETT RIVER LOOP

8.4 RIGHT on dirt road.
9.2 STRAIGHT at the intersection.
9.9 STRAIGHT at the intersection and go a few hundred yards, then go LEFT on Route 16/27.
13.0 LEFT onto Bigelow Station Road.
13.2 STRAIGHT on dirt trail, start of Narrow Gauge Pathway.
14.2 STRAIGHT at junction.
18.6 Narrow Gauge Pathway ends. Go past gate and go STRAIGHT on dirt road, which becomes Huston Brook Road.
19.1 RIGHT onto Carriage Road.
19.5 RIGHT to town offices.
19.6 Return to parking lot.

© AVALON TRAVEL PUBLISHING, INC.

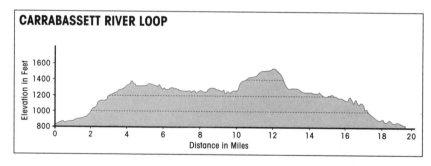

5 BARING DIVISION TRAIL

Moosehorn National Wildlife Refuge, Baring

 dirt roads, paved road with minimal traffic

Total distance: 14.8 miles

Difficulty: 2

Riding time: 2 hours

Elevation gain: 449 feet

Wildlife lovers will delight in this remote, undeveloped corner of Maine. You can explore the 17,000-plus acres of this national wildlife refuge on 50 miles of vehicle-free dirt roads. If you pedal slowly and stop often, you might see leopard frogs, painted turtles, river otters, muskrat, white-tailed deer, moose, and even black bear. The refuge is most famous, however, for the American woodcock. Also known as the timberdoodle, the males of this normally secretive and shy shorebird stage an elaborate courtship ritual that includes a spiraling flight display and complex vocalizations in April and May. The woodcock population is on the decline and studies at Moosehorn are helping to preserve crucial habitat and flyways. Other birds to look for include bald eagles, ospreys, owls, ovenbirds, warblers, and dozens more that use the refuge as a breeding area and migration rest stop.

This wide dirt road, with Otter Pond on its right, is characteristic of the roads in the Baring Division section of the Moosehorn National Wildlife Refuge.

The refute is split in two, with a northern section called Baring and a southern one called Edmunds. This route begins at the Baring Division headquarters, where a well-stocked information kiosk has helpful maps, wildlife checklists, and brochures. The wide dirt roads take you through both woodlands and wetlands, and past several ponds and streams. Most of the area is flat, with one long gradual hill on Youngs Road. An abundance of wildflowers along the pretty Beaver Trail sets a more wild and overgrown tone.

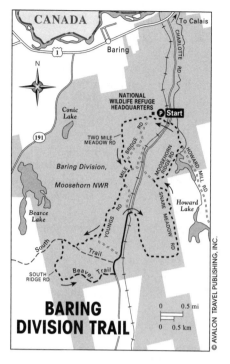

When you turn onto Charlotte Road, ride with care for a few miles as the occasional fast-moving truck barrels along this paved road. At Mile 9, turn right for the second half of the loop around Snare Meadow. This section is much bumpier, on rougher dirt roads, and, in some spots, grassy tracks (so if the first half was enough for you, continue straight on Charlotte Road to return to the headquarters).

Try to visit the refuge early in the morning or late in the afternoon to maximize your wildlife-viewing chances. Nothing stirs in the noonday heat of a summer day—except maybe black flies. Because the refuge is full of swamps and "flowages," the flies can be formidable. Insect repellent is essential.

For more information, contact the Moosehorn National Wildlife Refuge, R.R. 1, Box 202, Suite 1, Baring, ME 04694, 207/454-7161, website: http://moosehorn.fws.gov.

Driving Directions

From Calais, take Route 1 north and Route 9 west for 3.3 miles. Turn left onto Charlotte Road and drive 2.5 miles to the main entrance to the National Wildlife Refuge headquarters on the right. The parking lot is .5 mile in on a bumpy dirt road. You'll find public restrooms, water, and a picnic table. The refuge is open during daylight hours; the office is open 7:30 A.M.–4 P.M. on weekdays. Supplies are available in Calais.

Route Directions for Baring Division Trail

0.0 Start at gated dirt road at far end of parking area. Go STRAIGHT past sign for Mile Bridge Road.

0.7 LEFT onto Two Mile Meadow Road.

1.6 RIGHT onto Mile Bridge Road (unmarked).

1.9 Curve around to right.

2.4 RIGHT onto Youngs Road (unmarked).

3.8 RIGHT at intersection.

4.5 RIGHT at intersection.

4.9 LEFT onto South Ridge Road (unmarked) at pond.

5.9 LEFT onto Beaver Trail (unmarked).

7.5 Trail ends. Pass through a gate and turn LEFT onto Charlotte Road (paved).

9.0 Cross the railroad tracks and turn RIGHT through gate on Snare Meadow Road.

12.8 RIGHT at intersection on Moosehorn Ridge Road (unmarked).

13.6 Trail ends. Go through a gate and turn LEFT on Howard Mill Road.

14.2 Go through a gate and turn LEFT.

14.3 Go across Charlotte Road to headquarters entry road.

14.8 Arrive at headquarters parking lot.

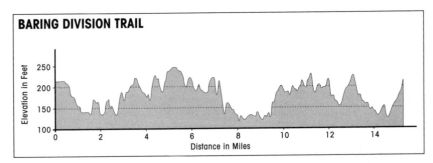

BARING DIVISION TRAIL

Elevation in Feet

Distance in Miles

6 PASSAMAQUODDY BAY

Perry, Pembroke

 paved roads with minimal traffic

Total distance: 27.5 miles

Riding time: 2 hours

Difficulty: 3

Elevation gain: 1,098 feet

Water, water, everywhere, is the theme for this route as you go from the ocean's edge to a quiet lake to a marshy river. With minimal traffic and moderate hills in a remote corner of Maine, this is a nice ride for an advanced beginner looking for a little challenge.

You start at a park that looks across the bay toward Eastport, the United States's easternmost city, which is actually on an island connected to the mainland by a causeway. Turning onto Shore Road, starting with a short steep hill, you'll have some ups and downs as you ride along the western edge of Passamaquoddy Bay, the large bay that separates Maine from Canada here.

Heading inland, cross Route 1 and pass by the northern end of quiet Boyden Lake. A small boat launch and pier give access to the water. A few more ups and downs along Ridge Road take you into a marshy area and the start of the Pennamaquan Wildlife Management Area.

© MELISSA L. KIM

Gleason Cove Park, on Gleason Point, gives views of both American and Canadian islands.

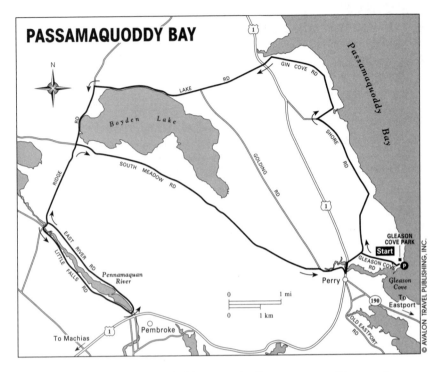

PASSAMAQUODDY BAY

N

Passamaquoddy Bay

GIN COVE RD

LAKE   RD

Boyden   Lake

RD

SOUTH   MEADOW   RD

RIDGE

GOLDING   RD

SHORE   RD

EAST   RIVER   RD

LITTLE   FALLS   RD

Pennamaquan
River

1

GLEASON
COVE PARK

Start

GLEASON COVE
RD

Perry

Gleason
Cove

190   To
Eastport

OLD EASTPORT
RD

1

Pembroke

To Machias

0   1 mi
0   1 km

© AVALON TRAVEL PUBLISHING, INC.

You'll cross an interesting bridge over the Pennamaquan River and reach a 4-way intersection. Now you'll be making a loop around a long narrow stretch of the river with dams at either end that control water levels on Pennamaquan Lake as well as the river's flow into Cobscook Bay. All these controls have created an excellent habitat for waterfowl and a very pretty riverine environment.

At the lower falls and dam, you can stop at Putty Island Park to check out the fish ladder and former iron foundry. Then there's a little backtracking before you head down rural South Meadow Road and cross another interesting bridge, over the Little River, and return to Route 1.

This route is a variation on a bicycle tour recommended by Maine's Department of Transportation. For more information, contact the Eastport Chamber of Commerce, P.O. Box 254, Eastport, ME 04631, 207/853-4644, website: www.eastport.net; or visit the town of Pembroke's website: www.pembroke.maine.org.

Driving Directions

From Machias, drive 40 miles on Route 1 north. Pass the right-hand turn for Route 190 to Eastport. Drive .3 mile and look for a sign for Gleason Cove Park. Turn right onto an unmarked road just before a gift shop and restaurant. Drive .3 mile and turn right onto Gleason Cove Road. Gleason Cove Park is .8 mile ahead; the last .1 mile is a dirt road. The park has grills, picnic tables, a boat launch, and great views of Eastport but no facilities.

Route Directions for Passamaquoddy Bay

0.0 Leave Gleason Cove Park.

0.8 RIGHT onto Shore Road (unmarked).

3.8 Sharp RIGHT onto Gin Cove Road (unmarked).

6.2 Road ends. Go STRAIGHT across Route 1 onto Lake Road. *Supplies available at general store on Route 1.*

9.7 At junction, go LEFT onto Ridge Road (unmarked).

12.8 At four-way intersection, go LEFT onto Little Falls Road.

15.4 LEFT onto East River Road. *A restaurant and ice-cream stand are .1 mile straight ahead, at the corner of Little Falls Road and Route 1.*

15.5 Pass Putty Island Park on the right.

18.0 RIGHT onto Ridge Road.

19.6 RIGHT onto South Meadow Road (unmarked).

26.1 LEFT onto Route 1. *Supplies available.*

26.4 RIGHT onto Shore Road (unmarked).

26.7 RIGHT onto Gleason Cove Road.

27.5 Return to Gleason Cove Park parking lot.

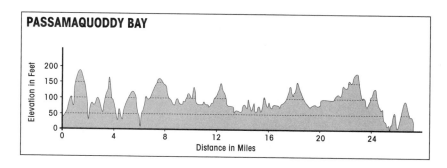

GRAFTON NOTCH LOOP
Bethel, Andover, and Rumford Point

 paved roads with minimal traffic

Total distance: 66.8 miles

Difficulty: 5

Riding time: 5 hours

Elevation gain: 2,665 feet

The Mahoosuc range in western Maine is a dramatic series of high and low points, with the twin peaks of Baldpate and the high point of Old Speck competing with the plunging Screw Auger and Mother Walker waterfalls. Much of the area is protected from development, so the result is untouched wilderness where the chance of seeing a moose is high. Though this is a long, hilly route with few services, the rewards are plentiful: spectacular views, backcountry roads, small villages, and a covered bridge.

At the start of the ride, you'll grit your teeth and endure a few miles of highway cycling; there's a wide shoulder but fast-moving traffic nevertheless. Once you turn onto Route 26, though, rural roads dominate the rest of the way. This is also where the hill-climbing begins. Along this stretch, in Grafton Notch State Park, you'll see signs for Steep Falls, Screw Auger Falls, Mother Walker Falls Gorge, and Moose Cave Gorge. All of them are great spots for a picnic and none are a very long hike in from the road.

the Lovejoy Covered Bridge, built in 1868

A sharp turn puts you onto remote East B Hill, both a joy and a terror. Stretches of the pavement are uneven, so the screaming downhill at the start can be a bit hairy. An uphill climb lasts for about 1.5 miles, but then the pavement improves and you've got a lovely riverside ride to Andover. With a nice town common, a few diners, and an ice-cream stand, this is a good midway rest point.

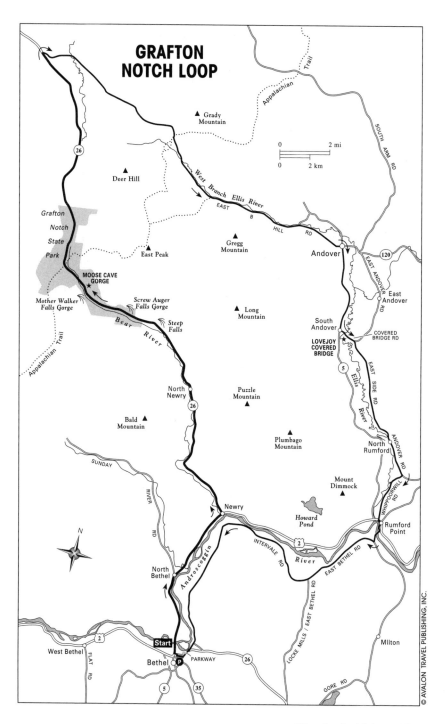

GRAFTON NOTCH LOOP

▲ Grady Mountain

Appalachian Trail

0   2 mi
0   2 km

SOUTH ARM RD

West Branch Ellis River

EAST   B   HILL   RD

Deer Hill ▲

Grafton Notch State Park

East Peak ▲

▲ Gregg Mountain

Andover

120

EAST ANDOVER RD

East Andover

MOOSE CAVE GORGE ★

Mother Walker Falls Gorge

Screw Auger Falls Gorge

Bear River

Steep Falls

▲ Long Mountain

South Andover

COVERED BRIDGE RD

LOVEJOY COVERED BRIDGE ★

5

EAST SIDE RD

Ellis River

Appalachian Trail

North Newry

26

▲ Puzzle Mountain

Bald Mountain ▲

▲ Plumbago Mountain

North Rumford

ANDOVER RD

SUNDAY RIVER RD

▲ Mount Dimmock

WHIPPOORWILL RD

Newry

Howard Pond

Rumford Point

N

INTERVALE RD

2   River

EAST BETHEL RD

North Bethel

Androscoggin

LOCKE MILLS / EAST BETHEL RD

Milton

West Bethel

FLAT RD

2

Start

Bethel P PARKWAY

26

5

35

GORE RD

© AVALON TRAVEL PUBLISHING, INC.

After Andover, you'll follow the Ellis River through the Lovejoy Covered Bridge toward Rumford. Though this is Maine's shortest covered bridge, it's still fun to ride through and look up at the trusses. Take care as you ride along a short stretch on busy Route 2 to get to Route 232 and also on the uneven surface of the bridge.

Rolling hills along the eastern shore of the river bring you back to Bethel, with occasional views of the mountains; look for the shorn slopes of the ski runs at Sunday River and you'll know you are close to the finish line.

For more information, contact the Bethel Area Chamber of Commerce, P.O. Box 1247, Bethel, ME 04217, 207/824-2282 or 800/442-5826, website: www.bethelmaine.com.

Driving Directions

From points north or south on the Maine Turnpike, take Exit 63 in Gray to Route 26. Drive for 50 miles to Bethel. Continue on Route 26 and turn left onto Lincoln Street just before the intersection with Routes 2 and 5. Take an immediate left onto Cross Street and turn right into the Station Place parking lot for the Bethel Area Chamber of Commerce Visitor Information Center. Parking is free. The visitor information center is open 9 A.M.–6 P.M. Monday–Friday, 10 A.M.–6 P.M. Saturday, and noon–5 P.M. Sunday. You'll find toilets, water, and cue sheets for dozens of bicycle rides throughout the area. Supplies are available in Bethel and there's a bike shop in Rumford.

Route Directions for Grafton Notch Loop

0.0 Start from the visitor information center. Turn LEFT onto Cross Street and take an immediate RIGHT onto Lincoln Road.

0.1 LEFT onto Parkway (Route 26).

0.2 RIGHT onto Routes 26/2/5.

6.0 LEFT onto Route 26.

14.2 *Access to Steep Falls, on the right.*

15.8 *Access to Screw Auger Falls Gorge, on the left.*

17.0 *Mother Walker Falls Gorge picnic area is on the right.*

17.8 *Moose Cave Gorge picnic area is on the right.*

27.0 RIGHT onto East B Hill Road.

41.5 RIGHT onto Routes 120/5. *Supplies available in Andover.*

44.8 LEFT onto Covered Bridge Road.

45.5 RIGHT onto East Andover Road.

49.5 LEFT onto Andover Road.

50.9 RIGHT onto Whippoorwill Road.

52.8 LEFT onto Routes 2/5.

53.3 RIGHT onto Route 232 (south) over bridge.

53.8 RIGHT onto East Bethel Road.

56.9 Road curves to the left; go STRAIGHT on Intervale Road.
65.9 RIGHT onto Route 26.
66.3 RIGHT onto Parkway.
66.7 LEFT onto Lincoln Street followed by immediate LEFT onto Cross Street.
66.8 Turn RIGHT to return to parking lot.

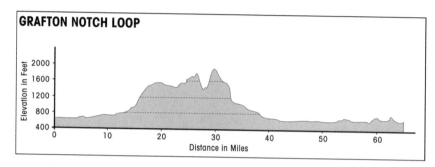

GRAFTON NOTCH LOOP

8 PARKER POND
Mount Vernon

 paved roads with minimal traffic

Total distance: 14.2 miles

Difficulty: 3

Riding time: 1.5–2 hours

Elevation gain: 1,203 feet

This short but steep ride around Parker Pond and other small ponds in the Belgrade Lakes region takes you into truly empty countryside and away from the traffic around the popular larger ponds in the area.

The ride starts in the small village of Mount Vernon. No supplies are along the way so stock up on water at the general store.

You'll climb out of Mount Vernon up a long hill and have a series of ups and downs, passing the boat launch area for Parker Pond, before turning onto a backcountry road. This lovely, woodsy road is totally undeveloped, with only a dirt driveway or two at the edge. You'll pass another boat launch area, and soon woods give way to open fields, stone walls, and old farms.

As you take an easy-to-miss left turn, the pavement becomes more uneven. This makes it harder to fly on the downhills, but you'll want to get up speed to help you up the short steep hills that follow. You'll see the pattern: downhill, pond, uphill.

riding along the shore of Minnehonk Lake with views of Mount Vernon

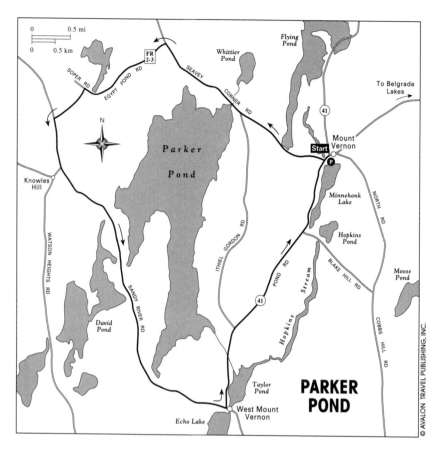

When you reach Route 41, take a moment to explore the dam and boat launch area. The road back, along the shores of Taylor Pond and Minnehonk Lake, is smooth with a wide shoulder and good views of the lake and the village. On a hot day, what better way to end the ride than with a swim in the lake?

For more information, contact Belgrade Lakes Region, P.O. Box 72W, Belgrade, ME 04917, 207/495-2744 or 888/895-2744, website: www.belgradelakesmaine.com.

Driving Directions

From points north or south, take the Maine Turnpike to Augusta. Take Exit 112 to Route 27, the Belgrade Lakes exit. Drive north on Route 27 for 12.4 miles and take a left onto Castle Island Road. Drive 6.5 miles to the town of Mount Vernon. You'll come to an intersection with Pond Road; a fire station is on your left and a lake lies straight ahead. At the lake there is a small park and town beach area with a boat launch and parking for about six cars. There are picnic tables but no facilities. Supplies are available at the Mount Vernon general store. The nearest bike shops are in Winthrop and Augusta.

Route Directions for Parker Pond

0.0 With your back to the lake, go LEFT, past the post office, to the stop sign.

0.1 LEFT at stop sign.

0.2 RIGHT onto Seavey Corner Road.

3.04 LEFT onto road marked FR 2-3 (marked as Egypt Pond Road on most maps).

4.5 Sharp LEFT turn. Stay on unmarked main road; don't go straight on the dirt road, Soper Road.

5.05 LEFT at the junction (unmarked).

5.75 Take the first paved road on the LEFT onto Sandy River Road. (This unmarked road is easy to miss.)

10.4 LEFT onto Route 41.

14.1 RIGHT onto Pond Road.

14.2 RETURN to town beach.

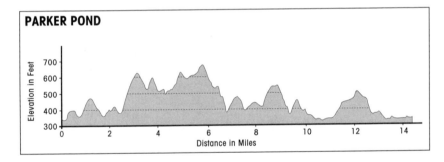

PARKER POND

Elevation in Feet

Distance in Miles

9 ISLESBORO FIGURE EIGHT

Islesboro, an island in Penobscot Bay accessible by ferry
from Lincolnville

paved roads with minimal traffic

Total distance: 29.0 miles

Riding time: 3 hours (not including the ferry ride)

Difficulty: 2   **Elevation gain:** 857 feet

Bicycling on Islesboro is the perfect way to explore a quintessential Maine
island. It's only a 20-minute ferry ride from the mainland, and it's not an
easy island to explore on foot. With a bike you can see the entire island in
an afternoon. Make sure you bring warm clothes for the breezy ferry ride.
The friendly ferry crew will bring out bike racks so you can prop up your
bike. There are two general stores but it's a good idea to bring plenty of
food and water.

Islesboro is popular with tourists and summer residents, including a
celebrity or two, so try to visit in June, September, or on a weekday. Though
there aren't that many cars,
the well-paved roads are narrow and winding.

This ride takes you on
loops both up-island (north)
and down-island (south), so
it's easy to cut it in half if
you've got less time. The
northern end has better ocean
views but the southern end
has a small village and fancier
houses. The first thing you'll
see on the island is the
Grindel Point Lighthouse. A
museum inside is open to the
public during July and August. You'll then loop around
the western edge of the island, where you'll have a few
very gentle hills along with
jaw-dropping views of Penobscot Bay. As you cross The

With your bike parked safely in the bike rack on the
ferry, you can enjoy views of the mainland on the
way to Islesboro.

Narrows onto the northern part of the island, look for great blue herons in the swampy areas to your left. At Seal Harbor, a small unattended public pier and parking area is a fine picnic spot. There's a short hill before the road forks, and again as the road sweeps up and around the northern end. Take a breather at Turtle Head Cove; you could put a toe in water at the beach here before heading up the long hill.

Back on the southern end of the island, you'll have one small hill before the village of Dark Harbor and one just past the village as you make your way to the southern tip. Pendleton Point has a town beach and picnic area complete with barbecue pits. The return loop to the ferry has a few gentle hills and nice views of Broad Cove.

For more information, contact the Maine State Ferry Service in Lincolnville, 207/789-5611 or 800/491-4883, website: www.state .me.us/mdot/opt/ferry/215 -ilseboro.php.

ISLESBORO FIGURE EIGHT

© AVALON TRAVEL PUBLISHING, INC.

Driving Directions

From Camden, take Route 1 north for 5.6 miles to Lincolnville Beach. Turn right onto McKay Road. The Maine State Ferry Service terminal is straight ahead and parking is free in two large parking lots. There are public toilets, water, telephones, and free maps of Islesboro. A round-trip ticket for an adult with a bicycle is $10.25. Supplies are available in Lincolnville Beach, .5 mile north on Route 1, or at the two general stores on the island. The nearest bike shops are on the mainland in Camden and Rockport.

Route Directions for Islesboro Figure Eight

0.0 Start at ferry terminal. STRAIGHT on Ferry Road.
1.1 LEFT onto West Bay Road.

3.3 LEFT onto Main Road.

5.8 *Supplies available.*

6.2 RIGHT at fork, staying on Main Road.

9.7 Turtle Head Cove. Main Road becomes Meadow Road.

12.4 Rejoin Main Road.

16.8 *Supplies available.*

19 Village of Dark Harbor. Main Road becomes Pendleton Point Road.

21.2 Paved road ends. *You may want to walk your bike on the dirt road to the point and back.*

21.5 Pendleton Point and Town Beach. TURN AROUND.

23.4 LEFT onto Derby Road.

24.0 Curve RIGHT onto West Shore Drive (unmarked).

24.5 STRAIGHT through intersection with Babbidge Road.

25.6 LEFT onto Pendleton Point Road.

26.6 LEFT onto Mill Creek Road.

27.9 LEFT onto well-marked Ferry Road.

29.0 Arrive at ferry terminal.

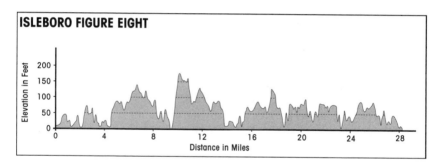

ISLEBORO FIGURE EIGHT

10 CARRIAGE ROADS

Acadia National Park, Mount Desert Island

dirt and gravel roads

Total distance: 18.5 miles

Difficulty: 2

Riding time: 2.5 hours

Elevation gain: 1,874 feet

As you pedal along the spectacular carriage roads of Acadia National Park, give a silent thanks to John D. Rockefeller, Jr. Like modern cyclists, he wanted to travel on roads free of cars, so he turned his wealth and ingenuity to the task of creating scenic roads that wind around Mount Desert Island, where tree-lined mountains drop to smooth lakes and craggy islands pop up from the ocean's sparkling surface.

Forty-five miles of broken stone roads were built between 1913 and 1940. They have been rehabilitated since then, and many of the unique original features, from arching stone-faced bridges to large coping stones that serve as guardrails, look better than ever.

This route starts at the north end of Eagle Lake and makes a big counterclockwise loop to the west and south. The incline is gentle as you begin riding away from the lake, followed by a nice downhill to the shores of the lovely and secluded Aunt Betty Pond. At Signpost 13 (all the roads are marked by brown cedar signposts) you'll face a short, steep climb, but it's well worth it for the outstanding ocean views from the top. (If you just can't face the climb, turn right at Signpost 13 and take the low road above Hadlock Pond to rejoin the route at Signpost 19.)

Another steady incline comes between Signposts 21 and 14, but after that it's fairly smooth with some good downhills to Jordan Pond. The Jordan Pond House is a perfect midway rest stop; sample the scones at the restaurant.

Admire the Gate Lodge as you cross Park Loop Road and head toward Bubble Pond. The road has a few inclines along the way with good views of Cadillac Mountain, the island's highest point, on the right.

It's a smooth flat ride along the shores of Bubble Pond to the parking lot. Take care crossing busy Park Loop Road. (At Eagle Lake, if you want one more hill to climb, take a left at Signpost 7. Otherwise, stay right to take an easy tour of the lake's eastern shore.)

Bicyclists must yield to all other users, and the areas around Jordan Pond, Bubble Pond, and Eagle Lake can get very crowded. A staggering number of people visit Acadia National Park every year, so try to visit in the off-season (spring and fall). If you must go in summer, start your bike

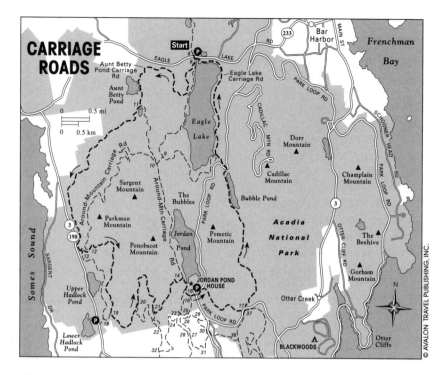

ride as early in the morning as possible. If you are camping in the park at Blackwoods Campground, you can begin the ride from the campground and start at the southern end of the trail system.

Trail maps are available at the visitor center on Route 3. You will want the Carriage Road User's Map, which shows all the signposts and carriage roads. The daily use fee is $10 per vehicle.

For more information, contact the National Park Service, P.O. Box 177, Bar Harbor, ME 04609, 207/288-3388, website: www.nps.gov/acad.

Driving Directions

From Ellsworth, take Route 3 to Mount Desert Island. In Bar Harbor, turn right onto Route 233 and drive 2.5 miles. You will pass the entrance to Park Loop Road. Look for the sign for Eagle Lake Carriage Road. The parking lot is past this sign, on the right. You'll find restrooms and water at the parking area. Supplies and bike shops are available in Bar Harbor.

Route Directions for Carriage Roads

0.0 Take the trail from the rear of the parking lot.

0.1 LEFT under the bridge; pass Signpost 6.

0.2 RIGHT at Signpost 9 toward Aunt Betty Pond.

2.8 RIGHT toward Hadlock Pond.

6.2 LEFT at Signpost 13 (or, turn right to avoid hill and rejoin route at Signpost 19).

6.5 RIGHT at Signpost 12.

8.3 LEFT at Signpost 19.

9.2 LEFT at Signpost 20.

10.5 LEFT at Signpost 21.

11.5 RIGHT at Signpost 14.

11.7 STRAIGHT at Signpost 15.

11.8 LEFT at Signpost 16. *The trail to Jordan Pond House is on the left. It's .1 mile to the restaurant, gift shop, restrooms, and water.*

13.1 STRAIGHT at Signpost 17.

15.8 Enter Bubble Pond Parking lot. *Restrooms available.*

16.0 Cross Park Loop Road.

16.3 RIGHT at Signpost 7.

18.4 RIGHT at Signpost 6.

18.5 RIGHT to return to parking lot.

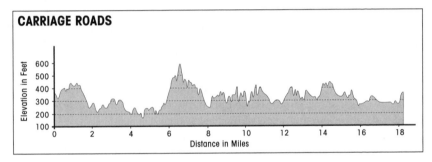

CARRIAGE ROADS

Elevation in Feet

Distance in Miles

11 SCHOODIC PENINSULA

Winter Harbor

 paved roads with minimal traffic

Total distance: 12.8 miles

Difficulty: 2

Riding time: 2 hours

Elevation gain: 402 feet

The views on Mount Desert Island may be lovely but the part of Acadia National Park on the Schoodic Peninsula has ocean vistas that are truly breathtaking. Many of the visitors to the park don't take the hour-long drive down the coast to this section (which is the only part of the national park that's on the mainland) so it's nowhere near as crowded, making it a great place to bike.

This ride starts at Frazer Point Park, a nice place to picnic and stock up on water. Once you leave the park, you'll immediately hit the one-way road system. You'll ride right along the water's edge, and with each bend of the smooth road there are more islands, lighthouses, crashing waves, shorebirds, and seals to look at.

This is a fairly flat ride, so for an optional workout, take the unmarked left turn to climb Schoodic Head. Touring and hybrid bikes will be fine on

Dark green firs contrast with pink granite and rocky beaches along the road leading out of the Schoodic Peninsula.

this bumpy gravel road. It's about a mile to the top of this 440-foot-high mountain, with great views and walking trails as a reward.

The real gem here is Schoodic Point, great slabs of granite ledges that stick like tongues into the salty ocean. Views vary from the microscopic, in the tidepools that form in nooks and crannies in the rocks, to the vast, as you look out over Frenchman Bay and the Atlantic Ocean.

As you continue along the main road, you'll see Little Moose Island and then reach a parking area called Blueberry Hill, giving you a place to stop and enjoy more great views of islands and waves. A short hiking trail, across the road from the parking area, leads up to a knob called The Anvil.

The last stretch of the park road has a gentler beauty to it as you leave the exposed coast for the quieter Schoodic Harbor. Once you leave the park's one-way system, you'll pass Wonsqueak Harbor and Bunker's Harbor, no more than a few houses and lobster boat moorings. After the seclusion, Birch Harbor's convenience stores come as a surprise. Head back on busy Route 186 to return to the entrance road.

For more information, contact the National Park Service, P.O. Box 177, Bar Harbor, ME 04609, 207/288-3388, website: www.nps.gov/acad; or contact the Schoodic Peninsula Chamber of Commerce, P.O. Box 381, Winter Harbor, ME 04693, 207/963-7658, website: www.acadia-schoodic.org.

Driving Directions

From Ellsworth, take Route 1 for 17.2 miles. Turn right on Route 186, signposted for Acadia National Park. Drive 6.5 miles and turn left (a right turn would take you to the village of Winter Harbor). Drive .6 mile and turn right onto Moore Road. Drive 1.6 miles and turn right into Frazer Point Park. The park is open for use 6 A.M.–10 P.M. You'll find restrooms, water, a picnic area, dock, and small beach. Supplies are available in Winter Harbor. The closest bike shops are in Ellsworth or Bar Harbor.

One of the best ways to get to the Schoodic Peninsula is to take the ferry from Bar Harbor to Winter Harbor. The Bar Harbor Ferry company runs at least six trips a day. The ride takes about an hour and costs $24 round-trip plus $5 for a bicycle. Call 207/288-2984 for more information.

Route Directions for Schoodic Peninsula

0.0 Leave the parking lot at Frazer Point Park and turn RIGHT onto the main road. (You immediately enter Acadia National Park and the one-way road system.)

2.4 *Here you can turn left for optional 2.2-mile side trip to the top of Schoodic Head on an unmarked gravel road.*

3.4 RIGHT toward Schoodic Point.

4.0 Schoodic Point. TURN AROUND.

4.6 RIGHT onto main road.

5.1 Pass Blueberry Hill parking area.

7.1 Exit Acadia National Park; road becomes two-way.

9.3 *Supplies available in Birch Harbor.*

9.4 LEFT onto Route 186.

11.2 LEFT onto Moore Road.

12.8 RIGHT to return to Frazer Point Park parking lot.

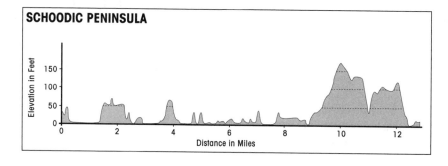

12 COVERED BRIDGE RIDE
Fryeburg

paved roads with minimal traffic, dirt road

Total distance: 22.6 miles

Difficulty: 3

Riding time: 2–2.5 hours

Elevation gain: 603 feet

Riding in this valley with the White Mountains always peeking over your shoulder, you'll go through farmland and along riverbanks, passing classic New England stone walls and one tiny cemetery after another.

The highlight of this ride comes a few miles into the ride, as you turn off Route 5 and make your way down a seldom-traveled dirt lane. This smooth dirt lane, running next to the river, can be muddy, so you'll want to stay to the right side of the lane. At the end, you'll discover what seems like a deserted wooden covered bridge spanning a gently flowing river in a truly idyl-lic setting. The Hemlock Covered Bridge, a 109-foot-long Paddleford truss with wooden arches, built in 1857, spans the upper Saco River. A scenic and remote spot, this is a great place to stop for a picnic.

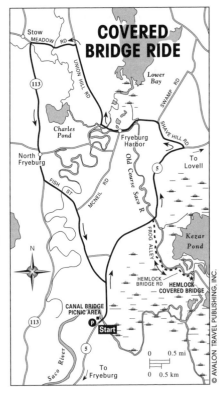

You'll need to endure a few more miles on Route 5, where cars zip by at 50 mph, but once you turn left onto Shave Hill Road you're on small backcountry roads with virtually no traffic, open views of the White Mountains, and, in the fall, spectacular foliage. You'll encounter a few short hills but none steep enough to merit shifting into granny gear.

For more information, contact the Saco Ranger District station of the White Mountain National Forest in Conway, NH, 603/447-5448.

Driving Directions
From Portland, take Route 302 into Fryeburg. Turn right (north)

onto Route 5 and drive 3.3 miles. Turn left into the Canal Bridge picnic area. This picnic area is a canoe launch that is very popular in summertime; an annex parking area is on the opposite site of Route 5. There are covered picnic tables, basic outhouses, and the access road to a private campground. Supplies and lodging are available in Fryeburg. The nearest bike shops are in North Conway, NH.

Route Directions for Covered Bridge Ride
0.0 From the Canal Bridge picnic area parking lot, proceed LEFT (north) on Route 5.

3.1 RIGHT onto Frog Alley.

4.0 LEFT onto Hemlock Bridge Road.

5.1 Hemlock Covered Bridge. TURN AROUND.

7.1 RIGHT onto Route 5.

9.3 LEFT onto Shave Hill Road. *Supplies are available at the Lovell Village Store and Rosie's Restaurant in Lovell, .7 miles north of this turnoff.*

11.0 Pass Fryeburg Harbor.

11.9 RIGHT onto Union Hill Road at the triangular intersection.

14.0 LEFT onto Meadow Road.

15.2 LEFT onto Route 113 at the triangular intersection. *For supplies, you can visit the hamlet of Stow, only .2 miles north of this intersection. The Stow General Store sells sandwiches, pizza, ice cream, and fishing licenses but is most famous for its excellent bakery.*

18.0 North Fryeburg. Continue STRAIGHT (south) on Route 113.

18.4 LEFT onto Fish Street. *Supplies available.*

21.5 RIGHT onto Route 5.

22.6 RIGHT into Canal Bridge picnic area.

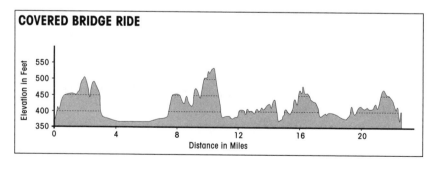

BRADBURY MOUNTAIN
Bradbury Mountain State Park, Pownal

single-track

Total distance: 7.1 miles

Riding time: 2 hours

Difficulty: 4

Elevation gain: 457 feet

Mountain biking at this 590-acre state park proves that you can have a lot of fun in a little space, and all just a short drive from the shopping outlets of Freeport.

The route starts in the main section of the park on multiuse trails; if you stay in the campground, cross Route 9 to pick up these trails. In summer, many families hike the trails, so yield to hikers and to the occasional horseback rider.

The Tote Road Trail leads to the summit with a very gradual climb on a nice, pine-strewn, rooty trail marked by white blazes. (Unofficial mountain bike maps lead you up the steeper Summit Trail but biking on this trail is not allowed by the park.) From the 485-foot-high summit, there are surprisingly good views that stretch all the way to the coast.

The most difficult section is the descent from the summit on the orange-

Glaciers carved out Bradbury Mountain, leaving behind a round top and steep southeast slope

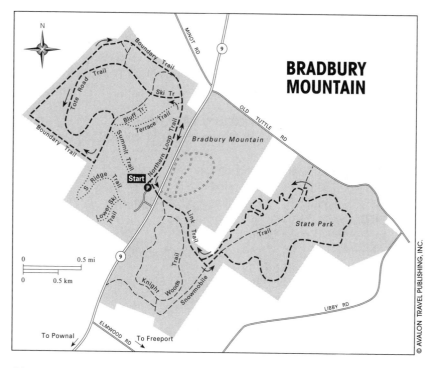

blazed Boundary Trail. Some very steep and technical rocky sections, plus a stream crossing, await you as you descend with a stone wall on your left. There's also one steep rooty, rocky climb just before the trail meets the Tote Road Trail again.

In the eastern half of the park, rangers have created single-track trails for mountain bikers and are adding new trails every year. This route, covering 2.5 miles of this single-track, is nice for advanced beginners because it's not that technical. It can go from very wide to one-tire-width narrow, and it has some fun twists and turns and a few sections of small rock gardens. The leafy, open stands of birch and beech are a nice contrast to the pine-heavy areas on the summit side.

For more information, contact Bradbury Mountain State Park, 528 Hallowell Road, Pownal, ME 04069, 207/688-4712, website: www.state.me.us/doc/parks.

Driving Directions

From Portland, take Route 295 north. Drive approximately 17 miles to Exit 22 for Freeport and Durham. Turn right off the exit toward Route 125/136. At the junction, turn left on Durham Road, then right on Pownal Road (which becomes Elmwood Road). Turn right on Route 9. The entrance to

Bradbury Mountain State Park is .5 mile ahead on the left. The per-car fee is $3. The park is open 9 A.M.–sunset. Ask the rangers for a trail map with the new single-track trails marked. Facilities include outhouses, water, picnic tables, and a campground. Supplies are available in Pownal and Freeport; there are two bike shops in Freeport.

Route Directions for Bradbury Mountain

0.0 Start at the far end of the parking lot on the Northern Loop Trail.
0.4 LEFT on Ski Trail.
0.6 RIGHT at triangular intersection onto Tote Road Trail.
0.8 Intersection with Boundary Trail. Go STRAIGHT on Tote Road Trail.
1.7 Reach the summit. Take the Boundary Trail down from the summit.
2.9 LEFT onto Tote Road Trail.
3.3 LEFT onto Northern Loop Trail.
3.8 Return to parking lot. Turn LEFT and look for sign to Knight Woods Trail leading out the east side of the parking lot.
3.9 Cross Route 9 and go STRAIGHT on the Link Trail past a seating area and trail map sign.
4.3 LEFT on snowmobile trail.
4.4 RIGHT on single-track trail (look for the wooden marker).
5.6 At four-way intersection, go STRAIGHT past seating area and plaque.
6.6 RIGHT on Link Trail
7.0 STRAIGHT across Route 9.
7.1 Return to parking lot.

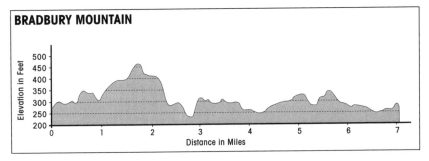

14 PEMAQUID PENINSULA

New Harbor and Round Pond

 paved roads with moderate to minimal traffic

Total distance: 29.4 miles

Difficulty: 3

Riding time: 2.5–3 hours

Elevation gain: 1,126 feet

The Pemaquid peninsula has it all: historic sites, rugged ocean views, quaint villages, and penny candy.

This ride begins at scenic Colonial Pemaquid State Historic Site, which overlooks Pemaquid Harbor. You can get a feel for the harsh life early 17th-century settlers experienced here by touring the reconstructed Fort William Henry, an 18th-century fort commander's home, and a museum with 17th-century artifacts. You'll also find a public boat launch, restaurant, picnic tables, and public restrooms, making it a convenient place to start and end a ride.

Leaving the site and the village of New Harbor, head out along the eastern edge of the peninsula. A ferry to the popular Monhegan Island leaves from New Harbor, so watch out for heavy summer traffic. After the ferry pier, you'll come to the Salt Pond Preserve, where Rachel Carson derived inspiration for her writing. The preserve, owned by The Nature Conservancy,

Both working and pleasure boats moor in Pemaquid Harbor.

has a rocky beach with great views of Monhegan and other islands. Take the steps to the beach or lock your bike and explore the walking trails on the other side of the road. You'll have a few moderate hills on Route 32 on your way to the village of Round Pond. The landmark Granite Hall Store, with ice cream, roasted peanuts, and penny candy, is well worth a stop.

Enjoy the views of Muscongus Sound before tackling a long, steep hill. Leaving the coast, you'll climb a gradual hill before screaming down to a sharp left turn onto Fogler Road. This backcountry road, primarily an access road for cottages fronting Biscay Pond, is fairly well paved and has minimal traffic. Emerge briefly onto Route 130 before turning onto rural Lower Round Pond Road with its two steep hills. Then it's back to Route 32, where you'll retrace your route to New Harbor.

For more information, contact the Colonial Pemaquid State Historic Site at 207/677-2423 between Memorial Day and Labor Day and 207/624-6080 off-season, website: www.state.me.us/doc/parks.

Driving Directions

From Route 1 in Brunswick (to the south) or Camden (to the north), take the Damariscotta exit to Business Route 1. Stay on Business 1 for .9 mile through downtown Damariscotta. Turn right onto Routes 130/129. Drive 11.4 miles on Route 130 and look for signs to Colonial Pemaquid. Turn right onto Huddle Road. Drive 1.2 miles and turn right onto the access road to the state historic site. Parking is free. Fort William Henry, the Fort House, and the museum are open for tours Memorial Day–Labor Day. The fee for tours is $2. Public restrooms are at the museum. Supplies are available in the village of New Harbor.

Route Directions for Pemaquid Peninsula

0.0 Start at Colonial Pemaquid State Historic Site. Proceed from parking lot on the dirt road.

0.1 LEFT onto access road.

0.2 LEFT onto Huddle Road.

1.4 RIGHT onto Route 130 (Bristol Road).

1.8 LEFT onto Route 32.

2.9 Pass Rachel Carson Salt Pond Preserve.

8.8 *Supplies are available in the village of Round Pond.*

8.9 *You can take a side trip by turning right on Back Shore Road to the Granite Hall Store. Taking the next right, marked Shore Access, will get you to the pier bustling with lobstermen and kayakers.*

12.9 LEFT onto Damariscotta Road.

14.9 LEFT onto Fogler Road (this is a poorly marked turn after a steep downhill).

17.7 The road bears sharply to the right.

17.9 LEFT onto Benner Road (unmarked).

19.2 LEFT onto Bristol Road (Route 130).

19.6 LEFT onto Lower Round Pond Road.

22.3 RIGHT onto Route 32.

28.0 LEFT onto Huddle Road.

29.2 RIGHT onto access road.

29.3 RIGHT onto dirt road into Colonial Pemaquid State Historic Site.

29.4 Arrive at parking lot.

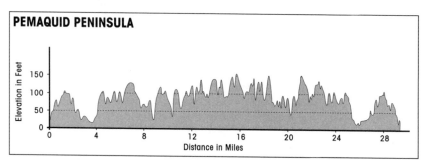

15 FLYING POINT LOOP

Freeport, Brunswick, and South Freeport

 paved roads with minimal to moderate traffic, dirt road

Total distance: 33.5 miles

Difficulty: 3

Riding time: 3–4 hours

Elevation gain: 1,447 feet

Though most people associate Freeport with shopping outlets and the giant retail outfitter L. L. Bean, rolling farmland and coastal vistas await if you stray even a mile from Main Street.

This loop begins with gently rolling hills, then heads down a short, steep hill to picturesque Freeport Town Landing. The public boat launch sits next to the popular Harraseekett Lobster Company restaurant, where you can get fried clams from the walk-up window and sit at the picnic tables—all without having to leave your bike. You'll have one moderate hill and a very short stretch of traffic to contend with as you ride through a busy intersection to cross Route 1 to ride in Freeport's other half. Here, farmlands and rural Maine spread inland as you ride on flat stretches with an occasional long but gradual hill.

Crossing back over Route 1, Highland Road is a cyclist's dream with long rolling ups and downs. You'll get excellent views of the peninsulas and bays that mark the coast here. There's a short ride on a firmly packed dirt road, then a few long hills, especially one killer hill right at the end of the ride. A side trip to Wolfe's Neck Woods State Park is only 2 miles out of the way, and it offers beautiful ocean views, nesting ospreys, 5 miles of hiking trails, and facilities. The first leg of the ride also passes by several excellent places to stop and picnic or sightsee, making this a 3-hour ride that's well worth stretching into a whole-day trip.

For more information, contact the Freeport Merchants Association at 207/ 865-1212 or 800/865-1994, website: www.freeportusa.com.

Driving Directions

From Portland and points south, take Route 295 to Exit 20 for Route 1 to Freeport. Drive north on Route 1 for 1 mile and turn right at the light onto West Street. Take the first left onto Depot Street. You will see a visitor information center shaped like a lighthouse; park in any of the lots near the center. Parking is free. The public restrooms at the visitor information center are open May–December. The visitor information center is open daily, year-round, and has pamphlets and information; the office is staffed 8 A.M.–5 P.M. Monday–Friday. Supplies and bike shops are available in Freeport.

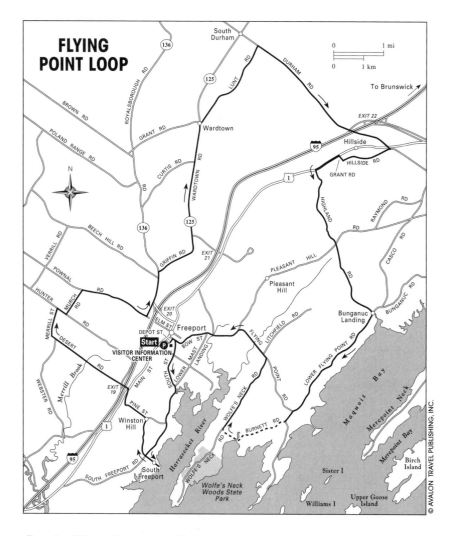

Route Directions for Flying Point Loop

0.0 Begin at visitor information center parking lot. Proceed northeast on Depot Street.

0.1 RIGHT onto Bow Street, then an immediate RIGHT onto South Street.

2.7 LEFT at the stop sign onto Main Street.

3.0 Freeport town landing. TURN AROUND.

3.3 STRAIGHT on Pine Street. *Supplies are available at the Village Deli, to the left.*

5.2 RIGHT onto Route 1. Use extreme caution to get into the left-hand lane.

5.3 LEFT at the light onto Desert Road. Cross over Route 95.

7.2 RIGHT onto Merrill Street.

7.7 RIGHT onto Hunter Street.

7.9 LEFT onto Murch Street.

8.5 RIGHT onto Pownal Street.

9.9 Sharp left curve. Pownal Street becomes Routes 125/136.

11.0 RIGHT onto Route 125 (Griffin Road).

14.4 RIGHT onto Lunt Road. *Supplies are available at the corner store.*

16.2 RIGHT onto Durham Road.

19.8 STRAIGHT at stop sign across Route 1.

19.9 RIGHT onto Hillside Road.

20.9 RIGHT onto Grant Road.

21.0 LEFT onto Route 1.

21.6 LEFT onto Highland Road.

25.0 RIGHT onto Flying Point Road (unmarked).

27.6 LEFT onto Lower Flying Point Road. (This easy-to-miss turn comes after a sharp right-hand curve.)

27.9 RIGHT onto Burnett Road, a well-packed dirt road. *Supplies are available at the Recompense Campground's general store.*

29.4 RIGHT onto Wolfe's Neck Road. *You can go left here for an optional trip to Wolfe's Neck Woods State Park, 1 mile out and back.*

31.0 LEFT onto Flying Point Road. This becomes Bow Street.

33.4 LEFT onto Depot Street.

33.5 Arrive at visitor information center parking lot.

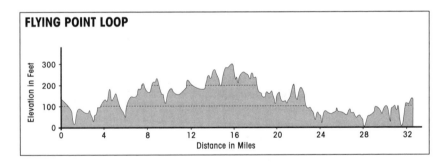

16 MOUNTAIN DIVISION TRAIL

Windham to Standish

 crushed-gravel bike path

Total distance: 7 miles

Difficulty: 1

Riding time: 1 hour

Elevation gain: 258 feet

If you are in either Portland or the Sebago Lakes area and want a nice family bicycling outing in the countryside, look no further than the state's newest rail trail project (actually, this is a Rail-with-Trail project, since the flat, crushed gravel path sits next to, not on top of, the railroad ties).

Officially opened in the summer of 2003, the Mountain Division trail is perfect for families or beginners who want a nice, flat path in the woods with no cars to worry about, though there are four road crossings. It's wide enough to ride side by side, but it is a multiuse trail so be aware of people on foot or on horseback.

The trail lies alongside the former Mountain Division line of the Maine Central Railroad, which was abandoned in 1994 and purchased by the state's Department of Transportation. Trail planners hope one day to turn the whole 45-mile line from Portland to Fryeburg into a multiuse trail, but the first section is a modest 4.7 miles long.

For a nice out-and-back, start at the trailhead in Windham. A kiosk gives information about the culture and natural history of the area, as well as a trail map. Trail markers appear at every quarter mile, so it's impossible to get lost. The trail starts by crossing a bridge over the lovely Presumpscot River and takes you first through woodlands, then through open fields and pasture lands, and back into denser woodlands.

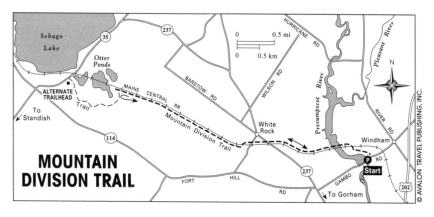

MOUNTAIN
DIVISION TRAIL

After 3.5 miles, you'll reach the Otter Ponds area, home to a YMCA day camp and four small ponds. The Mountain Division Trail leaves the railroad and heads left uphill, following a dirt road for 1.2 miles to the alternate trailhead in Standish on Route 35. Stop for a quick dip or explore the area around the ponds, and turn around and head back on the trail.

Plans are to extend the trail in both directions, so for updated trail information, contact the Mountain Division Alliance, chairman Dave Kinsman, at 207/935-4283, website: www.mountaindivisiontrail.org.

Driving Directions
From the south, take Route 95 to Exit 48 (Portland/Westbrook). Take Route 25 west approximately 5 miles to Gorham. Turn right onto Routes 4/202. Drive 5 miles and turn left at the stoplight onto River Road. Go .5 mile and turn left onto Gambo Road. Go .4 mile and turn right onto the access road; drive .1 mile to the parking lot. From the north, take Route 95 to Exit 63 (Gray). Take Routes 4/202 south approximately 11 miles to South Windham. At the light, turn right onto River Road, then left on Gambo Road as above. Convenience stores are on River Road. Restaurants and supplies are available in Windham, Gorham, and Standish. The closest bike shops are in North Windham and Westbrook.

Route Directions for Mountain Division Trail
0.0 Leave the parking lot and turn LEFT onto the trail.
3.5 Reach Otter Pond Day Camp area. TURN AROUND.
7.0 Return to parking area.

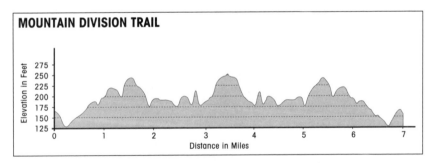

17 PEAKS ISLAND LOOP

Island in Casco Bay accessible by ferry from Portland

 paved roads with minimal traffic

Total distance: 4 miles   **Riding time:** 1 hour (not including ferry ride)

Difficulty: 1   **Elevation gain:** 96 feet

One of Portland's many attractions is its location on the edge of beautiful Casco Bay, which is dotted with islands large and small. Sometimes called the Calendar Islands because in some counts there are 365 of them, the islands are perfect for bicyclists, offering great ocean views, little or no traffic, and a real sense of slow-paced island life. The best biking isles are Great Chebeague Island, Long Island, and Peaks Island.

Peaks is the closest to Portland and has the largest year-round population (about 1,000 people). It's also the most accessible, with the most frequent ferries, and has more services than other islands. This is a great family ride, as there are plenty of things to see, several places to stop, and the bicycling is easy.

Starting from the ferry terminal, you'll ride in a counterclockwise loop around the island. You have a short climb to get up out of the village, but Seashore Avenue is almost totally flat. Take a side trip to Picnic Point or Sandy Beach if you've got time or inclination, or visit the Fifth Maine Regiment museum for a bit of island history. Once you're riding along the ocean's edge, there are plenty of places where you can pull over and explore the rocky beach, have a picnic, or beachcomb. The views are outstanding, as the houses are all on the left and there are only rocks, seagulls, islands, and ocean to your right.

riding along Seashore Avenue with views of Casco Bay's many other islands

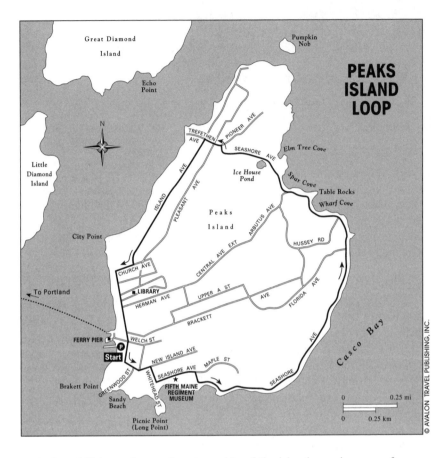

A short hill is on the northeastern side of the island, coming away from the ocean, and then there is a steep downhill to the other side. Island Avenue takes you past summer homes and down into the village, where more of the year-round residents live. You'll find several restaurants, a café, a gift store selling ice cream, and a market where you can get supplies or sandwiches. It can get busy in the middle of summer, so if you hate crowds, try visiting in June or September.

The ferry ride is a short, scenic 20 minutes, giving you great vistas of Portland, South Portland, and the Casco Bay islands. It's always breezy on the ferry, so bring a windbreaker. All tickets are round-trip; it's $6 for passengers plus $5 for your bike. You can also rent bikes on the island. Generally there is one ferry an hour but the schedule changes with the seasons. For updated ferry schedules, rates, and more parking information, contact Casco Bay Lines, P.O. Box 4656, Portland, ME 04112-4656, 207/774-7871, website: www.cascobaylines.com.

Driving Directions

From the south, take the Maine Turnpike (Route 95) to Exit 44, in South Portland, for Route 295. Drive approximately 7 miles and take Exit 7, Franklin Street. From the north, take the Maine Turnpike (Route 95) to Exit 103, in Gardiner, for Route 295. Drive approximately 44 miles and take Exit 7, Franklin Street. Drive to the end of Franklin and go straight through the intersection; the ferry terminal is on your right. A parking garage is adjacent to the terminal, with $1/hour parking. Supplies are available in Portland and on Peaks Island. One bike shop with rentals is on the island and there are several bike shops in Portland.

Route Directions for Peaks Island Loop

0.0 From the ferry pier, walk up a short hill to the main intersection. Turn RIGHT onto Island Avenue.

0.1 Sharp LEFT curve, uphill.

0.25 RIGHT onto Whitehead Street (unmarked). (It's the second paved road on the right.)

0.3 Sharp LEFT curve onto Seashore Avenue. *For an optional side trip, you can turn right onto the next dirt road and ride for about 200 feet. You'll see a narrow grassy path on the left. If you walk out on this path, you'll reach Picnic Point, a spit of land jutting into the bay with pebble beaches on either side.*

0.4 Pass Fifth Maine Regiment Museum.

0.5 RIGHT following Seashore Avenue toward the water.

2.4 Curve LEFT uphill.

2.7 LEFT at T-junction; STRAIGHT through next intersection.

2.8 LEFT at stop sign and junction onto Island Avenue.

3.5 RIGHT at junction (the elementary school is on the left).

3.7 *Public restrooms at library and community center.*

4.0 Return to start, at corner of Island Avenue and Welch Street. Turn RIGHT for ferry pier and parking lot with bike rack.

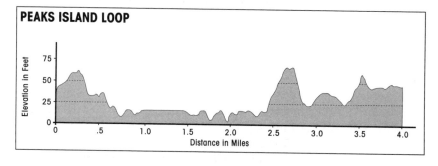

PEAKS ISLAND LOOP

18 FORTUNES ROCKS LOOP

Kennebunkport, Fortunes Rocks, and Biddeford Pool

 paved roads with moderate traffic

Total distance: 29.7 miles

Difficulty: 2

Riding time: 2.5–3 hours

Elevation gain: 217 feet

This ride shows you three very different sides to coastal Maine: Kennebunkport teems with tourists and all the trappings, Fortunes Rocks is all about the beach, and the refreshingly noncommercial Biddeford Pool teems only with rich bird life.

All the parking lots fill up fast, so ride midweek, early morning, or off-season. The ride starts in a satellite parking lot in Kennebunkport and skirts the downtown to put you on Ocean Avenue. Ocean Avenue takes you past marinas, mansions, and the Bush compound, Walkers Point. Though relatively flat, this oceanside road can get windy and foggy, and tour buses may make you uncomfortable in the summer.

Gentle hills take you into the small fishing village of Cape Porpoise. Next, a stretch on Route 9, with smooth pavement and wide shoulders, cuts through land that is remarkably undeveloped, especially through sections of the Rachel Carson National Wildlife Refuge. Two very long but gradual inclines give you a nice workout.

At Fortunes Rocks beach, the road is narrow and the pavement is very rough. Slow down and smell the ocean. The tidal marsh that gives Biddeford Pool its name is on your left as you continue on the flat road out to the end of the peninsula, where the ocean slams against the rocky beach.

The return ride consists of gentle ups and downs, and the scenery gets less residential and more rural as you travel from Biddeford back into Kennebunkport. Though not as scenic as the seaside leg, it's a relaxing traffic-free ride back to the starting point.

For more information, contact the Kennebunk and Kennebunkport Chamber of Commerce, 207/967-0857, website: www.kkcc.maine.org.

Driving Directions

From Portland, take Route 95 to Exit 25 in Kennebunk for Route 35. Follow Route 35 for 1.8 miles into the center of Kennebunk. Turn left to follow Route 35. After 3.7 miles, you'll come into Kennebunkport. Turn left at the traffic light onto Route 9. Drive straight through Dock Square, the heart of Kennebunkport. After .4 mile, turn left onto Maine Street. This

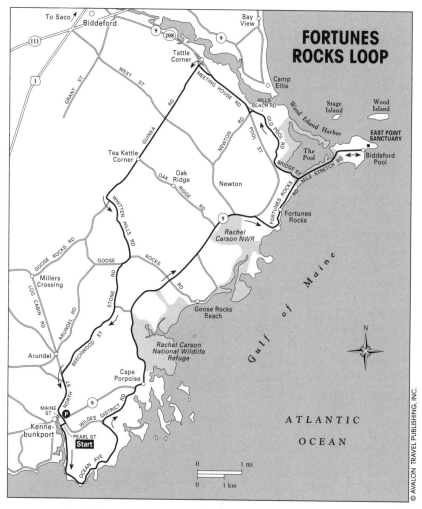

curves to the right and becomes North Street. The parking lot is .3 mile on the left. This public parking lot is free and is for passenger cars only. Supplies and a bike shop are available in Kennebunkport.

Route Directions for Fortunes Rocks Loop

0.0 Start at the parking lot on North Street. Turn RIGHT onto North Street, which turns into Maine Street.

0.5 RIGHT onto Pearl Street.

0.7 LEFT onto Ocean Avenue.

4.2 RIGHT onto Wildes District Road.

5.3 RIGHT onto Route 9 (Main Street).

5.6 Bear LEFT onto Route 9 (Mills Road). *Supplies are available in the village of Cape Porpoise.*

11.3 RIGHT onto Fortunes Rocks Road.

13.0 STRAIGHT on Mile Stretch Road.

14.1 *For an optional side trip, you can turn left on Yates Road to visit Biddeford Pool village, where there are a few markets and restaurants. The road makes a small loop and returns to Mile Stretch Road.*

14.8 TURN AROUND. *The entrance to the East Point Sanctuary is on your left; lock your bike and take a walk on the trails.*

16.6 RIGHT onto Bridge Street (Route 208).

17.2 RIGHT onto Old Pool Road.

18.6 LEFT onto Hills Beach Road past the University of New England campus.

19.0 RIGHT onto Route 9. *Supplies are available at gas station market.*

20.1 LEFT onto Meeting House Road (street sign is hard to spot).

20.4 LEFT onto Guinea Road.

20.9 *Supplies available at West Street Market.*

24.3 Bear LEFT onto Whitten Hills Road.

25.7 RIGHT onto Goose Rocks Road.

25.9 LEFT onto Stone Road.

29.0 LEFT onto North Street.

29.7 LEFT to return to parking lot.

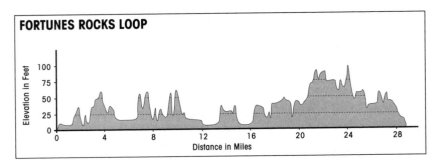

⓵⓽ KITTERY POINT RAMBLE
Kittery Point, Kittery Foreside, York

 paved roads with moderate traffic, dirt road

Total distance: 16.8 miles

Riding time: 2 hours

Difficulty: 3

Elevation gain: 194 feet

Though Kittery is best known for its outlet shopping, the town has another side that adventurers will truly appreciate. Head away from the hubbub and soon seaside views, light breezes, old cemeteries, and grand houses will entice you.

Perfect for a Sunday ramble, the route is primarily along quiet roads through coastal villages. Fort McClary and Fort Foster make interesting stopping points or side tours. Both lie within the first 4 miles of the ride and offer picnic areas and restrooms; both charge a small entry fee in the summertime. Fort Foster also has trails to ride on and rocky shorelines good for beachcombing.

Fast-moving traffic, broken pavement, and shoulders varying between narrow and wide are common in more populated areas. A short section of packed dirt is on the return route on Bartlett Road. The ride has little elevation gain overall with mostly gentle rolling hills.

Docks on Spruce Creek are made to float up and down with the rising and falling tides.

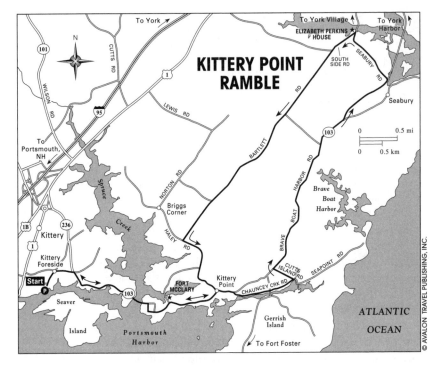

For more information, contact the Greater York Region Chamber of Commerce, 1 Stonewall Lane, York, ME 03909, 207/363-4462, website: www.gatewaytomaine.org.

Driving Directions

From Kittery or points north, take Route 1 to Route 103 east to Kittery Foreside. From Portsmouth, NH, or points south, drive north on Route 1, cross the Piscataqua River and follow Route 103 to Kittery Foreside. The ride starts at the intersection of Government Street, Walker Street, and Route 103. Parking is available throughout Kittery Foreside, and at a municipal lot just northeast of the starting point on Route 103. Restaurants and supplies can be found in Kittery, Kittery Foreside, and York Village. The closest bike shops are in York and in Portsmouth, NH.

Route Directions for Kittery Point Ramble

0.0 From intersection of Government Street and Route 103, go RIGHT on Route 103.
1.6 Cross bridge over Spruce Creek.
2.1 Pass entrance to Fort McClary on the left.
2.9 Continue on Route 103 heading east.

3.2 RIGHT onto Chauncy Creek Road.

3.7 *A right turn onto Pocahontas Road allows for an optional Fort Foster side trip. Then you can follow signs to Fort Foster, bearing right after crossing bridge.*

4.2 LEFT onto Cutts Island Road.

4.6 Bear RIGHT onto Brave Boat Harbor Road/Route 103.

7.1 Bear LEFT onto Route 103.

8.0 LEFT onto Seabury Road (continue uphill). *York Harbor is just north across causeway about 1 mile.*

8.9 LEFT onto South Side Road. Pass Elizabeth Perkins House, circa 1731.

9.3 Bear LEFT on Bartlett Road.

9.5 Road turns to packed dirt for about .5 mile.

12.8 LEFT onto Haley Road.

13.8 Bear RIGHT on Route 103.

16.6 Continue LEFT on Route 103.

16.8 Return to start.

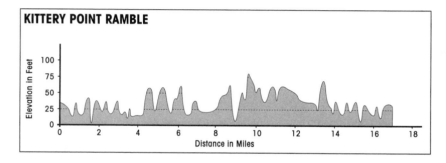

Chapter 4

© MELISSA L. KIM

Massachusetts

Massachusetts

As New England's most populous state, Massachusetts does have a lot of people packed into a relatively small space. So cyclists in the Bay State have learned how to make the most of the green and open spaces, and as a result you'll find some of the region's best mountain biking trails and bike paths.

The state is only about 200 miles wide, but it manages to have at least five distinctly different geographical regions, all of which offer different types of riding. Along the western edge of the state, the Berkshires and the Taconics create long rolling hills and heavily forested peaks and valleys. This rural strip offers the road rider lots of great choices, and mountain bikers can play in the hills too, on rocky, rooty, rough trails.

Adjacent to that, the Western New England Upland is characterized by small hill towns, a mix of agricultural and postindustrial areas, and fast-flowing rivers. Backcountry roads often have stretches of uneven pavement and short steep hills, and the older hill towns and villages may feature gracious town commons, historic buildings, and all-you-could-hope-for general stores. Western Massachusetts has a fall foliage season on par with its northern neighbors.

The mighty Connecticut River bisects the state, creating a river valley rich with agricultural lands, where you'll see tobacco fields and barns, asparagus farms, corn stretching to the sky, and pumpkins nesting on the ground. Denser populations along the river mean biking is best in the state or town parks and on bike paths.

The Eastern New England Upland makes up most of central and

eastern Massachusetts. Though the area around the vast Quabbin Reservoir offers some wonderful opportunities for road riding on backcountry roads, it gets more and more crowded as you near the sprawl of Worcester and Boston. This is where mountain biking organizations and clubs have made a significant impact, led primarily by the New England Mountain Biking Association, a recreational trails advocacy organization. NEMBA, a membership-based group with 17 chapters in New England, advocates for recreational use, gives grants for trail projects, provides volunteers to do trail maintenance and protection, and organizes bicycle patrols. In 2003, NEMBA made history by becoming the first bike advocacy group in the country to buy, own, and manage property, with its purchase of 47 acres in Milford encompassing a trail network known to expert mountain bikers as "Vietnam." In many of the state parks, you'll see signs that NEMBA volunteers have been at work, with a new bridge, trail signage, or a cleared trail. The state parks offer a nice range of off-road riding, too, from wide family-friendly trails to technical single-track.

Coastal lowlands make up the southeast corner and the Cape Cod peninsula, offering a very different type of terrain. Gone are the rocks, roots, and hardwoods of inland riding. Instead, you're more likely to find soft, loamy, or sandy soil, scrubby vegetation, and pine forests. You're also likely to find a lot of tourists, and the bike paths along Cape Cod are an outstanding way to avoid cars and enjoy the sand dunes and ocean views.

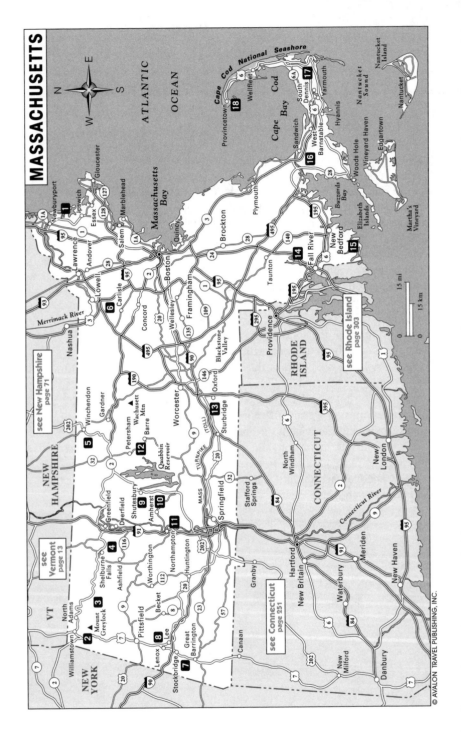

MASSACHUSETTS

Contents

1 PLUM ISLAND

Parker River National Wildlife Refuge, near Newburyport

 dirt roads, paved roads with some deteriorating pavement and moderate traffic

Total distance: 20.6 miles

Difficulty: 2

Riding time: 2 hours

Elevation gain: 10 feet

The special highlight of this ride is the wildlife-viewing at the Parker River National Wildlife Refuge, so be sure to bring binoculars to catch a glimpse of some of the 300 kinds of birds that visit annually. The ride starts in Newburyport, which is chock-full of restaurants, grocery stores, and everything else you could imagine in a New England coastal town.

You'll leave from Market Square in Newburyport and continue out toward Plum Island. Take care when leaving town as there are many parked cars along Water Street. Once you are out of town, the shoulder of the Plum Island Turnpike provides ample riding room. The route, with minimal elevation gain, passes through salt marshes, goes past the Plum Island Airport, and eventually crosses a metal grated bridge before you enter the wildlife refuge.

Bikes are not allowed on the various hiking trails off the main route, but

Market Square in Newburyport marks the start of this ride.

there are plenty of bike racks available throughout the refuge at parking lots, so you can leave your bike and explore the many walking trails. Nice dunes and great wildlife-viewing can be found throughout the refuge, but obey the posted signs as the dunes are fragile. You'll need to observe the noted breeding grounds of the piping plover. Beaches are closed during its breeding season, which begins in April and sometimes goes as late as August. Bring sunscreen, a windbreaker, and warm clothing in the spring and fall as the weather can change pretty quickly.

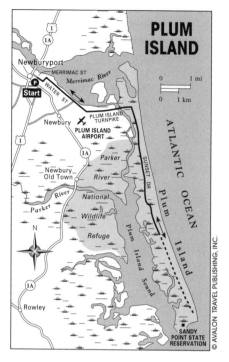

This ride is best for a touring or hybrid bike as the road turns to packed dirt and gravel for about 6 miles at the end of the ride. Cycling is recommended in the morning, before traffic intensifies. The entrance fee is $2 (for bikes and walkers) for the refuge. Maps are available at the gatehouse. Public restrooms are both at the gatehouse and farther along inside Parker River National Wildlife Refuge.

For more information, contact the Newburyport Chamber of Commerce, 38R Merrimac Street, Newburyport, MA 01950, 978/462-6680, website: www.newburyportchamber.org.

Driving Directions

From Route 1, go east on Merrimac Street for about .4 mile into downtown Newburyport. Free parking is available in lots throughout Newburyport, though in summer you'll need to stake your claim early in the day, especially on the weekends. The ride starts downtown at Market Square, at the intersection of Merrimac, State, and Water Streets. Supplies and a bike shop are available in Newburyport.

Route Directions for Plum Island

0.0 Market Square. Proceed east down Water Street.
0.2 Bear LEFT, continuing down Water Street. This eventually turns into the Plum Island Turnpike.

1.4 Pass Massachusetts Audubon Center.
2.9 Cross metal grated bridge.
3.3 RIGHT on Sunset Drive.
3.8 Enter Parker River National Wildlife Refuge. Pay entry fee.
6.3 Bear LEFT.
7.4 Road turns to gravel.
10.3 Enter Sandy Point State Reservation. *Park your bike on the bike rack and walk to the various beaches.* TURN AROUND and retrace your route back to Newburyport.
20.6 Arrive at Market Square.

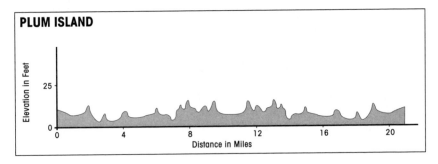

2 IN THE SHADOW OF MOUNT GREYLOCK
Williamstown

 paved roads with moderate traffic

Total distance: 29.1 miles

Difficulty: 3

Riding time: 2.5 hours

Elevation gain: 1,495 feet

This hilly loop takes you into a scenic corner of the Berkshires, giving you great views of the biggest mountain in Massachusetts, Mount Greylock. It starts in the quintessential college town of Williamstown and is a popular ride with cyclists from the Williams College community.

Leaving Williamstown on Route 43, you'll crisscross the Green River as lovely houses and clubs give way to fields and the tree-lined river. Route 43 and Route 7 meet at Five Corners, where the historic Store at Five Corners, which dates to 1762, offers a charming café, eclectic supplies, restrooms, ice cream, homemade fudge, picnic tables, and more.

You'll then have a gradual uphill climb along Route 7. This is a fast and busy road but there is a wide, smooth shoulder where you could easily ride two abreast. However, if riding alongside traffic bothers you, this ride is not for you. It is a very scenic road, making its way between two mountain ranges, with a smooth, rolling range to the west and one punctuated with sharp peaks and ledges and the 3,491-foot-high summit of Greylock to the east.

riding along farms and fields on Route 43

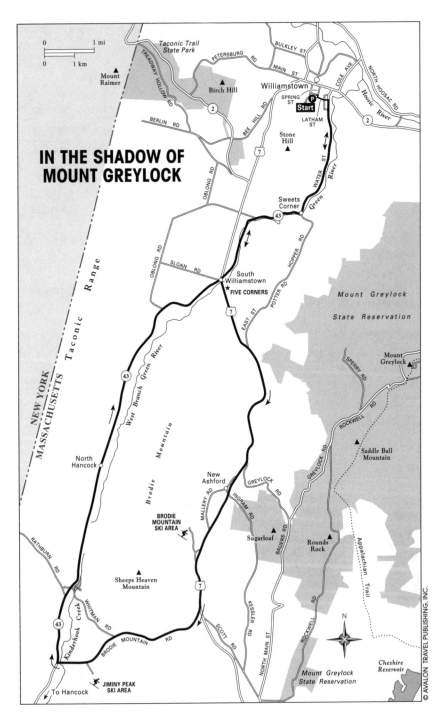

IN THE SHADOW OF MOUNT GREYLOCK

Leaving the traffic behind, you'll face a long, steep climb up the winding Brodie Mountain Road, only to be rewarded by a long screaming downhill to the base of ski resort Jiminy Peak.

The return ride on Route 43 starts with a climb, then turns to a gentle rolling up-and-down ride through farmlands and fields with great mountain views. As you retrace your route alongside the Green River, barely needing to pedal, you'll find you were going uphill without realizing it at the start of the ride.

For more information, contact the Williamstown Chamber of Commerce, P.O. Box 357, Williamstown, MA 01267, 413/458-9077 or 800/214-3799, website: www.williamstownchamber.com.

Driving Directions

From points south, take Route 7 to Williamstown. From points east, take Route 2 to Williamstown. From Route 2 (Main Street), turn south onto the one-way Spring Street, a busy shopping street. Drive .2 mile to the end of Spring Street, where there are several public parking lots. Williamstown has plenty of supplies, lodging options, and bike shops.

Route Directions for In the Shadow of Mount Greylock

0.0 From the Spring Street parking lot, go RIGHT onto Spring Street and bear LEFT onto Latham Street.

0.3 RIGHT onto Water Street (Route 43).

5.0 LEFT onto Route 7. *Supplies available at The Store at Five Corners.*

12.0 RIGHT onto Brodie Mountain Road.

14.8 *Supplies available at Jiminy Peak ski resort.*

15.4 RIGHT onto Route 43.

24.0 Go STRAIGHT across Route 7 staying on Route 43.

28.8 LEFT onto Latham Road.

29.1 RIGHT onto Spring Street and immediate LEFT to return to parking lot.

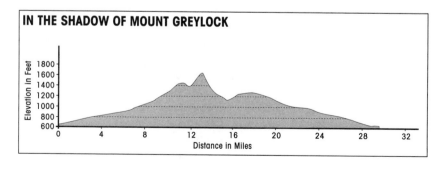

IN THE SHADOW OF MOUNT GREYLOCK

3 OLD FLORIDA ROAD
Savoy Mountain State Forest, Florida

single-track, double-track, dirt roads

Total distance: 7 miles

Difficulty: 5

Riding time: 2 hours

Elevation gain: 763 feet

If the words "state forest" make you think of sculpted woods and nicely groomed trails, put that image right out of your head before you visit Savoy Mountain. This wild and remote state forest is carved out of the Hoosac Range, an extension of the Green Mountains. The vertiginous drive along Route 2 to reach the entrance road gives you an idea of the remoteness of the area.

Some of the forest was originally cleared and used as farmland, and there are a few concrete dams, as well as some stands of apple trees and secondary forests of Norway and blue spruce mixed in with older hardwoods. You'll find a picnic area, campground (from where you can begin the route), camping cabins, two ponds for swimming and fishing, full facilities, and lots of trails to explore.

This route takes you along Old Florida Road, a trail that makes a counterclockwise loop from North Pond. You'll leave the main entrance road and pass through Tower Swamp before heading uphill on a very rocky trail. You'll face a tough series of downs and ups before the trail heads east into slightly less rocky territory. Though most of the trail is technical and rocky, a few late stretches in a pine forest are fun and fast. The trail is remote and not that well marked, so bring a compass.

I waded through endless knee-deep lakes of mud in mid-June here, so it's best to wait until much later in the summer for drier trails and fewer mosquitoes. These are off-road vehicle trails and though they seem impossibly narrow and rocky, I did come across one large group of ORVs and their drivers.

Though some mountain bike guides describe riding on the hiking trails, such as the North Pond Loop, this is very much frowned upon by the forest rangers, so don't be tempted; there are plenty of good trails to explore.

For a slightly less strenuous ride, follow Florida Road south to a large dirt parking lot, where you can pick up the unpaved, rough Tannery Road to check out the natural features of Balanced Rock and Tannery Falls, a dramatic plunging waterfall. It's not too bad to reach the rock, but it's a hilly ride to Tannery Falls. You'll have to leave your bike and hike in a short distance to see the falls.

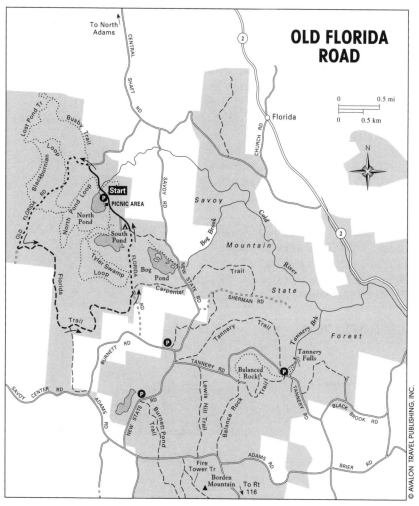

For more information, contact Savoy Mountain State Forest, Central Shaft Road, Savoy, MA 413/663-8469, website: www.state.ma.us/dem/parks/svym.htm.

Driving Directions

From North Adams and points west, take Route 2 east to the small town of Florida. Turn right onto Central Shaft Road. From the east, take Route 2 through Charlemont and drive 14 miles to Florida. Turn left onto Central Shaft Road (watch for the brown signs for Savoy Mountain State Forest). Drive 3.7 miles to the park's North Pond parking area, just past the boat launch. The parking fee is $5. North Pond has fishing, swimming, and full facilities with water and restrooms. Supplies and a bike shop are available in North Adams.

Route Directions for Old Florida Road

0.0 From North Pond parking lot, go LEFT on Central Shaft Road (toward park exit).

0.5 LEFT onto Old Florida Road.

0.6 RIGHT at fork.

0.8 Stream crossing on rock slabs.

2.9 Bear LEFT, following snowmobile signs, into rocky clearing. Trail continues to right of clearing, then takes immediate LEFT.

4.1 LEFT following main trail.

5.6 Cross clearing to row of boulders, LEFT onto dirt road (Florida Road, unmarked). (To check out Balanced Rock and Tannery Falls, turn RIGHT instead of left onto the unmarked Florida Road. Head south for about one mile to a large dirt parking lot and pick up the unpaved, rough Tannery Road that leads to these natural features.)

7.0 Return to North Pond parking area.

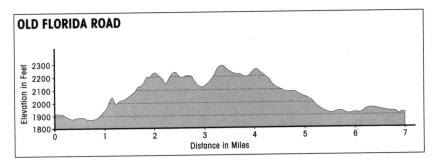

4 BARDWELLS FERRY LOOP
Shelburne Falls

 paved roads with minimal to moderate traffic, dirt road

Total distance: 27.5 miles

Riding time: 3 hours

Difficulty: 5

Elevation gain: 2,440 feet

The interesting hill town of Shelburne Falls is worth a visit on its own merits, even if you aren't drawn there by the fantastic on- and off-road riding nearby. Coffee roasters, art galleries, a glass-blowing studio, trolley museum, and more line the main streets on both the Shelburne and Buckland sides of the Deerfield River. Two bridges span the river—the Iron Bridge and the pedestrian-only Bridge of Flowers, reputed to be the only one of its kind in the world. A former trolley bridge, the concrete span is now completely taken over by gardens and flowers that bloom continuously thanks to volunteer efforts. Before or after your ride, stroll across this unique landmark.

This route gets you into the hills of the Berkshires on some beautiful backcountry roads where seeing a house or car seems out of place. There's a long climb out of Shelburne Falls and then a steep downhill with a sharp backhand turn at the bottom to get you to the Bardwells Ferry Road. A few steep hills and some uneven pavement take you from woodlands into more open farmlands, and as you crest the last hill you get outstanding rural views of the river valley. Zip down toward the river and cross high above the water under the red spans of the Bardwells Ferry Bridge, a Massachusetts Historic Civil Engineering Landmark constructed in 1882.

A very steep switchback hill gets you out of the river valley as you pedal by the expansive grounds of a large, very well-manicured estate belonging to comedian Bill Cosby. More open fields and pretty farmlands line the rural Zerah Fiske Road, though some of the pavement is uneven here too. Climbing another hill here gets you nice views of the whole area.

You'll ride a very short stretch on a dirt road before you reach Route 2. A seasonal farm stand, just to the right, might provide some supplies. Cross with care and head up the very steep but short Frank Williams Road. You'll reach the fast-moving Colrain-Shelburne Road, with a decent shoulder and moderate traffic. Agriculture provides the scenery, with fields of cows, horses, and goats, as well as duck ponds and a winery to check out. After a long gradual climb, this road makes a very steep descent, so check your brakes before you scream into the tiny village of Colrain.

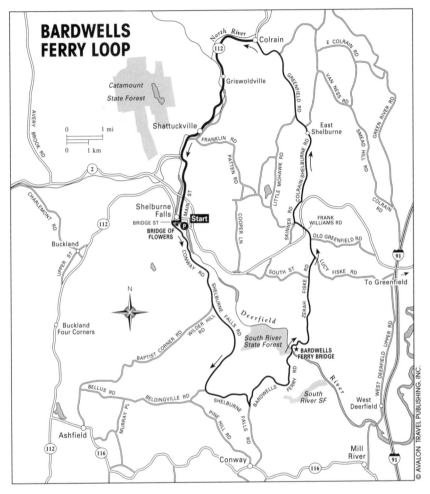

BARDWELLS
FERRY LOOP

Catamount
State Forest

Colrain

North River

E COLRAIN RD

VAN NESS RD

112

Griswoldville

Greenfield Rd

East
Shelburne

Smead Hill Rd

Green River Rd

Shattuckville

FRANKLIN RD

0   1 mi

0   1 km

2

Patten Rd

Little Mohawk Rd

Skinner Rd

Colrain-Shelburne Rd

Colrain Rd

Charlemont Rd

Shelburne
Falls

BRIDGE ST

Start

Main St

Cooper Ln

Frank Williams Rd

Old Greenfield Rd

91

112

**BRIDGE OF
FLOWERS**

Conway Rd

South St

Zerah Fiske Rd

Lucy Fiske Rd

To Greenfield

Buckland

Upper St

N

Deerfield

*South River
State Forest*

★ **BARDWELLS
FERRY BRIDGE**

River

West Deerfield Upper Rd

Buckland
Four Corners

Baptist Corner Rd

Wilder Hill Rd

Shelburne Falls Rd

Bellus Rd

Beldingville Rd

Murray Pl

Shelburne Falls Rd

Bardwells Ferry Rd

Pine Hill Rd

South
River SF

West
Deerfield

Ashfield

112

116

Conway

116

Mill
River

91

© AVALON TRAVEL PUBLISHING, INC.

The route follows the North River all the way back, with a mountain looming on your left and heavy industry (hydropower plants and factories) along the river on your right. You'll cross the river twice before going underneath Route 2 and riding back into Shelburne Falls.

The village information center is at 75 Bridge Street; you can get an area map and use the public restrooms. Make sure you walk across the Bridge of Flowers and look at the Glacial Potholes, with access from Deerfield Avenue, that have been carved out by the river. For more information, contact the Shelburne Falls Area Business Association and Village Information Center, 75 Bridge Street, Shelburne Falls, MA 01370, 413/625-2544, website: www.shelburnefalls.com.

Driving Directions

From points north and south, take Route 91 to Greenfield and take Route 2 west (Exit 26). Drive 9 miles and take Route 2A (at the Sweetheart Restaurant) to Shelburne Falls. Route 2A becomes Bridge Street. Drive .3 mile and turn right onto Main Street. A public parking lot is on the left, where this route begins. Supplies are available in Shelburne Falls. The closest bike shops are in Greenfield.

Route Directions for Bardwells Ferry Loop

0.0 From the public parking lot, turn RIGHT onto Main Street.

0.1 RIGHT onto Bridge Street; go across the Iron Bridge.

0.3 LEFT along river onto Conway Road (this becomes Shelburne Falls Road).

7.5 Sharp LEFT onto Bardwells Ferry Road.

10.4 Cross Bardwells Ferry Bridge.

11.8 RIGHT at fork onto Zerah Fiske Road.

13.1 Go STRAIGHT through intersection, continuing on Zerah Fiske Road.

14.1 STRAIGHT at a four-way intersection onto a dirt road.

14.5 Go across Route 2 (use extreme care) onto Frank Williams Road.

14.7 RIGHT onto Skinner Road (unmarked).

15.5 LEFT onto Colrain-Shelburne Road.

20.8 LEFT onto Route 112. *Supplies available at general store in Colrain.*

21.8 *Supplies available at general store in Griswoldville.*

26.8 Go under Route 2. Continue on Route 112, which becomes Main Street.

27.5 RIGHT into public parking lot just before Bridge Street.

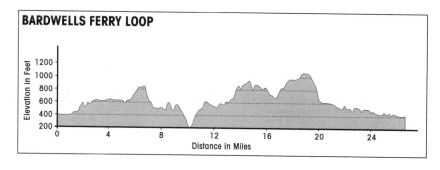

BEAVER POND LOOP
Otter River State Forest, Winchendon

dirt roads, double-track

Total distance: 8.7 miles

Difficulty: 2

Riding time: 1.5–2 hours

Elevation gain: 156 feet

In an unlikely pocket of central Massachusetts, this state forest offers some great mountain biking trails that make you think you are actually in the wilderness. Trails vary from wide dirt roads to narrow single-track so riders of all levels will find something to their liking.

This ride begins on the wide, smooth, unpaved New Boston Road. (You can also camp here and begin your ride from the campground.) The first turn onto Burgess Road leads you farther into the woods on a slightly bumpier road. The next turn, onto unmarked Swamp Road, moves you into nice double-track territory on a snowmobile trail.

As you near Birch Hill Dam, the road improves again. You'll pass a large pond and come out on some rock slabs before turning left and heading toward the dam itself. The narrow path winds through an open field, uphill into the woods, then alongside a chain-link fence with the dam on your right. After that, the loop on River Road is a delight as the trail narrows into a fun, nontechnical meander along Millers River.

a wide smooth trail near Beaver Pond

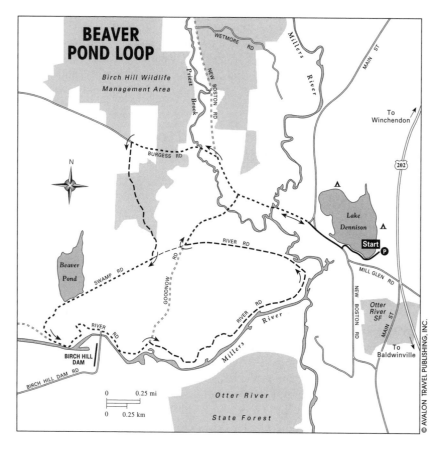

The swampy areas and ponds make mosquitoes a real problem so don't forget the bug repellent. The trails are not all marked, many small tempting single-track trails shoot off the main ones, and it's quite possible to get lost even with a trail map, available from the ranger station. For a more challenging ride, try the well-marked Wetmore Road trail off the New Boston Road.

For more information, contact Otter River State Forest, New Winchendon Road, Baldwinville, MA 01436, 978/939-8962, website: www.state.ma .us/dem/parks/ottr.htm.

Driving Directions

From points east or west, take Route 2 to Exit 20 (Baldwinville Road). Drive 2.5 miles to a flashing red light. Turn right on Maple Street and pass through Baldwinville. Maple Street becomes Route 202. After 1.2 miles you'll see the main entrance to Otter River State Forest; pass this entrance and take the second entrance 1 mile farther down the road. Take the winding access road to Lake Dennison and park in the large parking lot on the right. The $5 day-use fee gets you access to a swimming beach at the lake, a campground, many picnic areas, and restrooms with flush toilets and water. The park hours are 10 A.M.–8 P.M. Supplies are available in Baldwinville and the nearest bike shop is in Gardner.

Route Directions for Beaver Pond Loop

Start from the parking lot along the paved road with the lake on your right.
0.3 LEFT onto wide dirt road.
0.9 RIGHT onto New Boston Road at the intersection.
1.2 LEFT onto Burgess Road.
1.8 Cross the town line into Baldwinville. The road becomes a paved road.
1.9 LEFT onto trail. Follow orange blazes onto Swamp Road (unmarked).
2.2 STRAIGHT on main trail at fork in path.
2.8 RIGHT at intersection following blue trail markers.
3.3 Pass Beaver Pond on right.
3.8 LEFT at the junction.
4.3 The trail comes to an L-shaped junction. Turn LEFT through the yellow gate into a field.
4.4 Follow trail along a chain-link fence; the dam is on the right.
4.7 RIGHT at intersection on River Road (unmarked) through an orange gate. There is a yellow gate to the left.
6.8 STRAIGHT at four-way intersection.
7.2 RIGHT at junction with Goodnow Road (unmarked).
7.8 RIGHT at intersection on New Boston Road.
8.4 RIGHT onto paved road.
8.7 Return to parking lot.

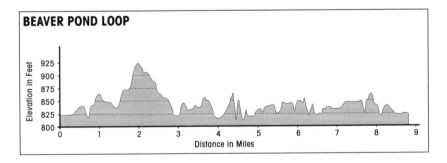

6 GREAT BROOK FARM TOUR

Great Brook Farm State Park, Carlisle

 single-track, double-track, dirt and gravel roads

Total distance: 9 miles

Riding time: 1.5–2 hours

Difficulty: 3

Elevation gain: 226 feet

This family-friendly state park, within easy driving distance from Boston, is popular for a host of reasons, one being its well-maintained and fun mountain biking trails. On the grounds of an old dairy farm, the park still has a small working dairy farm, duck ponds, an ice-cream stand, picnic areas, a cross-country ski touring center, a canoe launch, and more. All in all, it means that you'll share the trails with walkers and horseback riders, so if you want to ride hard and fast, come on a weekday or choose a different spot. This is a great place for beginner mountain bikers.

This route takes you all over the park, through fields and meadows, through pine forests and woodlands, past swamps and cornfields. You'll start in the fields, do a little rocky, hilly stretch along the Indian Hill Trail, and ride along some gentle hills on the Woodchuck Trail. It's mostly double- and single-track, but not technical, on this northern side. Across the road, in the south side of the park, you'll find some really fun single-track,

conveniently placed bike racks near the ice cream stand

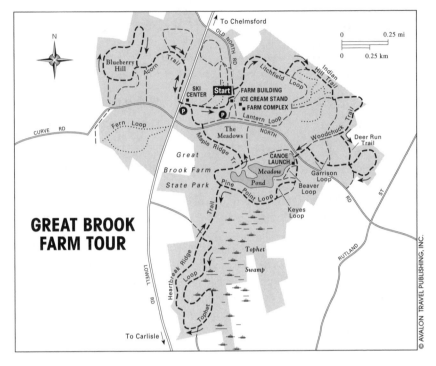

To Chelsmford

GREAT BROOK
FARM TOUR

© AVALON TRAVEL PUBLISHING, INC.

including the new Keyes Loop, which is a half mile of twisty, rocky trail with some stone walls to pass over and an occasional view of Beaver Pond to boot.

Heartbreak Ridge and Tophet Loop offer some nice wide single-track in the woods as you ride along a ridge and past a swamp. The trails are banked nicely so you can pick up some speed; a beautiful new bridge makes it passable even in wetter seasons. The swamp means mosquitoes are always present.

Head back around the pond through several meadows and along a gravel trail to return to North Road. An easy ride next to cornfields will bring you to the ski center, where you can cross Lowell Road and take a loop around Blueberry Hill. It's mostly dirt roads and double-track, with a small, more challenging section of single-track that's hilly and rooty just around the base of the hill.

The route directions may seem to be lots of stops, starts, twists, and turns. Don't worry if you miss a turn; most of the loops seem to meet and the loops are short so you can never get lost. If you're going to do only one section of the park, I'd recommend the southern side, around Meadow Pond. The Pine Point Loop, Heartbreak Ridge, and Tophet Loop are longer, more fun trails in the woods.

The Greater Boston chapter of the New England Mountain Biking Association is very active in this park, maintaining trails, creating trails, building bridges, and even doing a patrol (look for patrollers in red jerseys). One of the newest single-track trails, the Keyes Loop, is named after NEMBA's executive director, Philip Keyes.

For more information, contact Great Brook Farm State Park, 984 Lowell Street, Carlisle, MA 01741, 978/369-6312, website: www.state.ma.us/dem/parks/gbfm.htm.

Driving Directions

From Lowell, take Route 495 to Exit 34 and follow Route 110 south for 2.5 miles to the center of Chelmsford. Follow signs through the one-way system to Route 4 south. Drive 1 mile and bear right onto Concord Road (which becomes Lowell Road). Drive approximately 2.5 miles and turn left onto North Road; look for signs to Great Brook Farm State Park. Turn left into the first parking lot. At the end of this lot, there's a small park building with full facilities, restrooms, water, and trail maps (the main farm building and ice-cream stand are past the pond at the next parking area). The parking fee is $2. The route begins behind this farm building. Supplies and a bike shop are available in Chelmsford.

Route Directions for Great Brook Farm Tour

0.0 Start at rear of park building on Litchfield Loop.
0.2 LEFT at fork onto single-track.
0.6 LEFT at edge of field.
0.8 Take LEFTMOST trail at three-way intersection onto Indian Hill Trail.
0.9 LEFT onto main trail.
1.2 STRAIGHT through two four-way intersections.
1.3 Cross first bridge and take LEFTMOST trail.
1.6 LEFT at three-way intersection.
1.9 LEFT at four-way intersection.
2.2 Bear RIGHT at junction.
2.3 LEFT at four-way intersection.
2.4 Cross bridge.
2.5 Bear RIGHT on Garrison Loop.
2.8 LEFT onto wide dirt road (Woodchuck Trail, unmarked).
2.9 Cross North Road and pick up Pine Point Loop trail to left of pond.
3.0 *Here you can take an optional side loop left on the Beaver Loop trail.*
3.1 LEFT onto Keyes Loop.
3.6 RIGHT back onto Pine Point Loop.
3.9 LEFT onto Heartbreak Ridge trail.

4.2 LEFT at triangular intersection, then immediate LEFT onto Tophet Loop trail.

5.0 RIGHT back onto Heartbreak Ridge trail.

5.6 RIGHT at triangular intersection.

5.9 LEFT onto Pine Point Loop.

6.2 LEFT onto Maple Ridge trail.

6.4 LEFT at fork.

6.5 Cross North Road and pick up trail just to the left.

6.7 Arrive at ski touring center parking lot. Cross Lowell Road.

6.8 Pick up Acorn Trail.

7.0 LEFT at fork.

7.3 LEFT at junction on narrow trail.

7.4 STRAIGHT (Acorn South trail goes off to left).

8.2 LEFT at junction onto trail between fields

8.3 Bear LEFT.

8.7 Cross North Road.

8.8 Go through the parking lot and pick up dirt road to left of kiosk.

9.0 Return to parking lot.

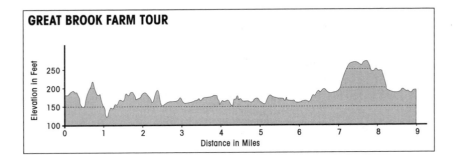

OLD EGREMONT LOOP

West Stockbridge, Alford, North Egremont

 paved roads with some uneven pavement and minimal traffic

Total distance: 27.4 miles

Riding time: 2.5 hours

Difficulty: 4

Elevation gain: 1,580 feet

This lovely ride through the heart of the Berkshires gets you away from the Tanglewood tourist routes and onto less-traveled rural roads for a real glimpse of the beauty of the hills.

The route begins in West Stockbridge, a happening town split by the Williams River, with plenty of shops, restaurants, cafés, and supplies. You'll have a short stretch on a busy, major road and some very uneven pavement on Route 102, but you're soon riding through open farmland and big fields with nice views of the hills. There's hill climbing to be done here but for every climb there seems to be a downhill reward. As you fork onto East Alford Road, you'll pass several nice stands of mountain laurel; in late springtime the fresh smell is intoxicating. The gently rolling road passes more large farms and heads into a more thickly forested area where the understory is carpeted with ferns.

A long downhill followed by a small climb gets you into the charming

Sheep graze in a field along Egremont Plain Road.

village of Alford, more a concentration of well-maintained historic houses than a town. Uneven pavement during a steep downhill marks the end of Seekonk Crossing Road, and then you've got a long steep hill, the route's biggest climb, on Seekonk Road. Pass a big sheep farm as you cruise into the village of North Egremont and take a break in front of the country store to study the historic Revolutionary War marker.

The second half of the loop gives you nice views of the ridge you rode along during the first half. More in forest than in open fields, the roads pass by many lovely, sprawling houses with sculptured gardens and grounds. On many of the older houses, look for the distinctive, decorative, overhanging trim on the porches. Farther along, houses give way to farms, ponds, and a few swampy, marshy areas. Turn onto West Center Road and retrace the route back into West Stockbridge.

For information on the area, contact the Stockbridge Chamber of Commerce, 6 Elm Street, Stockbridge, MA 01262, 413/298-5200, website: www.stockbridgechamber.org.

Driving Directions

From points east or west, take the Massachusetts Turnpike to Exit 1 and drive north on Route 41. Drive .3 mile and turn left onto Routes 41/102. Go about .5 mile into the center of West Stockbridge. You'll be on Main Street; turn left onto Center Street and drive 2 blocks to the end, where there is a public parking lot and public restrooms. Farther along Main Street is a tourist information booth if you need advice on the area. Supplies are available in West Stockbridge. The closest bike shops are in Great Barrington and Lenox.

Route Directions for Old Egremont Loop

0.0 Proceed LEFT out of the public parking area onto Depot Street.

0.1 LEFT onto Albany Road (Routes 102/41).

0.2 LEFT onto Route 102.

1.6 LEFT onto West Center Road.

5.1 STRAIGHT (Willson Road intersects from right).

5.7 RIGHT onto East Alford Road.

10.1 LEFT at stop sign onto East Road.

10.3 RIGHT at triangle onto Old Barrington Road (becomes Seekonk Crossing Road).

11.5 RIGHT onto Seekonk Road.

11.9 LEFT onto Boice Road.

13.6 RIGHT onto Egremont Plain Road. *Supplies available at Old Egremont Country store, with picnic tables in front.*

14.1 RIGHT onto Rowe Road.

15.4 LEFT at triangle onto Green River Road (unmarked).

15.6 RIGHT onto North Egremont Road.

16.9 LEFT at triangle onto West Road (becomes Willson Road).

22.2 LEFT onto West Center Road.

25.8 RIGHT onto Route 102.

27.2 RIGHT onto Albany Road (Routes 102/41).

27.3 RIGHT onto Depot Street.

27.4 RIGHT into parking lot.

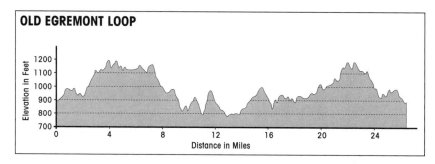

8 OCTOBER MOUNTAIN LOOP

October Mountain State Forest, Lee

 dirt roads, paved roads

Total distance: 17.1 miles

Difficulty: 3

Riding time: 2.5 hours

Elevation gain: 1,554 feet

Fun riding for all abilities is to be found here in the largest state forest in Massachusetts. Wide dirt roads, narrow and rocky dirt tracks, rocky single-track, and paved roads wind up, over, and around October Mountain. Thick woodlands, lakes and reservoirs, a gorge, and scenic lookouts give you plenty to look at. A pleasant campground lies at the base (it provides access to the trail), and the proximity to popular destinations in Lenox and Stockbridge means it can get crowded on a summer weekend, so you may be sharing trails with ATVs, horses, birders, and of course, other mountain bikers.

Start on the wide dirt road with Woods Pond and the Housatonic River on your left. You'll leave the state forest briefly, and the dirt road turns into uneven pavement as you ride by houses in this rural neighborhood. As you leave the pavement behind to reenter the state forest, there's a very steep but short hill as the rocky trail crisscrosses the pretty Mill Brook.

Back in the state forest, you'll pass an old dam house, dam remains, and beaver ponds as the trail narrows and becomes rockier. Turning onto the Whitney Place Road, climb a short steep hill in the midst of a pine forest and come out alongside the scenic Farnham Reservoir. There's more rocky climbing to do and the trail becomes a bit more challenging and technical. Once you take the wide turn onto the Aqueduct Trail, you'll make a broad loop on three trails that are all fairly flat, wide, and rocky. All have deep ruts, which means the trails can get very muddy in spring. Since you're in deep woods most of the time, the mosquitoes can also be fierce, so bring insect repellent.

A clearing at the Sandwash Reservoir is a good place for a break or picnic. After that it's back into the woods for a steep rocky climb. You'll come out onto a very wide and smooth dirt road—look out for four-wheel-drive vehicles. This route continues to the right, but if you're eager for more, turn left. You'll soon reach a large open clearing where four trails meet. One option is to turn left onto West Branch Road and make a clockwise loop, turning right at every intersection, to come back to the four-way intersection.

To complete this route, turn right and ride along the wide road to a junction, where you'll turn left onto Schermerhorn Road. A scenic vista

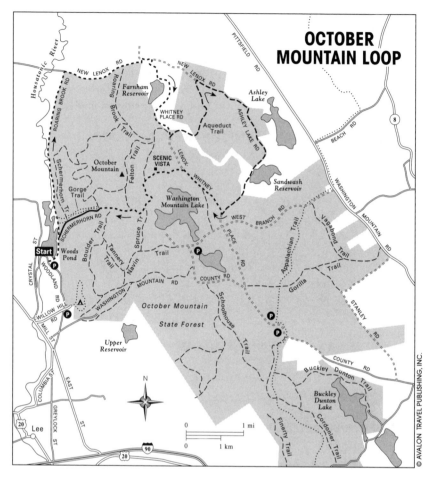

OCTOBER MOUNTAIN LOOP

on the right offers an outstanding view of the roll of hills to the north. You can also lock your bike to a tree and hike in to see Schermerhorn Gorge. After some twists and turns, check your brakes and watch for cars: the dirt road turns to uneven pavement and becomes a very, very steep downhill ride back to Roaring Brook Road.

For more information, contact October Mountain State Forest, 317 Woodland Road, Lee, MA 01238, 413/243-1778, website: www.state.ma.us/dem/parks/octm.htm.

Driving Directions

From points east or west, take the Massachusetts Turnpike to Exit 2 in Lee. Take Route 20 east for 1.1 miles. Turn left on Maple Street in East Lee. Cross over the turnpike. Drive .8 mile and bear right at the fork onto

East Street. Go 1.5 miles and turn right just before hitting the main road onto Woodland Road. Follow signs for .5 mile to October Mountain State Forest. You'll come to the main entrance for the campground, where there are restrooms and water. Continue on Woodland Road (a dirt road) for about 1 mile. Park at the large clearing before the pond. Supplies are available in Lee. The closest bike shops are in Great Barrington and Lenox.

Route Directions for October Mountain Loop

0.0 Start from the parking area on Woodland Road. Go RIGHT on Roaring Brook Road (unmarked) with the pond on your left.

3.4 RIGHT on New Lenox Road.

5.0 Go past a gate and trailhead on the right. The road curves to the left and comes to a T-junction. Go RIGHT at the T-junction.

5.2 RIGHT at the fork in the trail onto Whitney Place Road (unmarked).

7.1 LEFT onto Aqueduct Trail (unmarked).

8.9 RIGHT onto New Lenox Road (unmarked).

10.0 RIGHT at fork onto Ashley Lake Road.

10.9 RIGHT at junction onto unmarked road (left trail marked as Pittsfield Road).

12.3 RIGHT onto Lenox-Whitney Place Road (unmarked).

13.3 LEFT onto Schermerhorn Road (unmarked) which becomes paved for a mile.

16.6 LEFT onto Roaring Brook Road (unmarked).

17.1 Return to parking area.

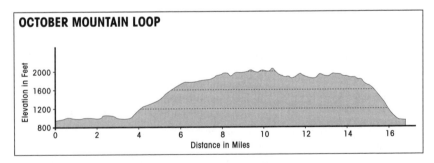

9 LAKE WYOLA LOOP
Shutesbury and Leverett

paved roads with minimal traffic

Total distance: 18.3 miles

Difficulty: 3

Riding time: 2 hours

Elevation gain: 1,325 feet

This rural area is popular with bicyclists from the Amherst-Northampton Five College area who come out to this sparsely populated spot for a workout on the hills. It offers some steady hill climbs and pretty riverside roads.

The ride starts at the Carroll A. Holmes Recreation Area, also known as Lake Wyola State Park. The lake has a sandy beach, a campground (with direct access to the route), and day-use facilities including toilets and water. You'll have to climb a few good hills to get from the lake to Shutesbury center with horse farms, stone walls, and little else but trees for scenery. From the village center, with its classic New England church, town hall (my old elementary school), and post office, it's a curvaceous 4-mile downhill as you chase a roadside brook the whole way.

A small uphill brings you into tiny Leverett center, distinguished by a crafts and artists center that might tempt you to stop. Once out of Leverett, you're faced with a mile-long climb up Cave Hill Road. If you need a rest, there's a peace pagoda at the top, an interesting and unexpected spectacle. The New England Peace Pagoda was built by Americans and Japanese of the Nipponzan Myohoji order of Buddhism.

Smaller, rolling hills get you to Moore's Corner, marked by an ultrahip, bike-friendly Village Co-op. This is the only place along the ride to get supplies, so fortunately there's great food as well as outdoor picnic tables, a pay phone, restrooms, and friendly folk.

A decent hill rises out of Moore's Corner, followed by a lovely smooth ride on this backcountry road that winds along next to a brook all the way to Lake Wyola. To make this ride more challenging, ride it in a counterclockwise loop. You won't be alone; it's a fairly common sight to see Lycra-clad road racers toiling up the 4-mile-long Shutesbury hill.

For more information, contact the Carroll A. Holmes Recreation Area, Lake Wyola State Park, Lakeview Road, Shutesbury, MA 01072, 413/367-0317.

Driving Directions
From Greenfield, take Route 2 to Exit 12 and drive south on Route 63 through Montague for approximately 5 miles. At the junction with Route

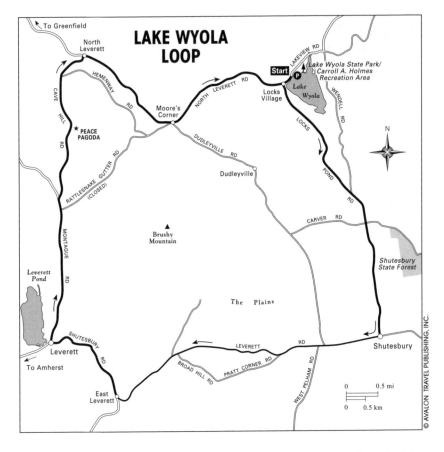

47, bear left onto North Leverett Road and follow it for approximately 5.5 miles. The lake will be on your right; parking for the Carroll A. Holmes Recreation Area will be on the left. The parking fee is $5. The closest bike shops are in Greenfield and Amherst.

Route Directions for Lake Wyola Loop

0.0 Exit the parking lot and turn RIGHT.

0.1 LEFT onto Locks Pond Road.

4.3 Arrive at Shutesbury center. RIGHT onto Leverett Road.

8.6 RIGHT at the triangle onto Shutesbury Road.

10.0 Arrive at Leverett center. RIGHT onto Montague Road.

12.1 RIGHT onto Cave Hill Road.

13.4 *The peace pagoda is up a dirt entrance road on the right.*

14.4 RIGHT at the junction onto North Leverett Road.

16.1 Arrive at Moore's Corner. *Supplies available.* Take the LEFT fork, staying on North Leverett Road (not the right fork onto Dudleyville Road).

17.8 Road becomes Lakeview Road.

18.3 LEFT back into Lake Wyola State Park.

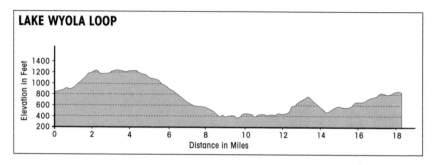

10 MOUNT ORIENT LOOP
Amethyst Brook Conservation Area, Amherst

 dirt trails, double-track, single-track

Total distance: 6.7 miles

Difficulty: 4

Riding time: 2 hours

Elevation gain: 750 feet

The small western Massachusetts town of Amherst serves as the hub of the Five College area that includes a 24,000-strong student population, and somehow you know that where there are this many college students, there are bound to be good mountain biking trails.

The gem of the region is the Robert Frost Trail, named after the great poet who spent time teaching at Amherst College in the earlier part of the 20th century. The 40-mile multiuse trail stretches from the Holyoke Range in the south, up through Amherst and on through Mount Toby State Park to finish at Wendell State Forest—hitting four great mountain biking spots.

The sweet spot in Amherst is the Amethyst Brook Conservation Area, an area popular with local mountain bike clubs, horseback riders, dog walkers, and families alike. In this multiuse area, don't expect to own the trail. While a small percentage of the trails are on public land, many more are on private land and signs repeatedly urge you to respect private property.

Amethyst Brook is a warren of trails and you could easily lose yourself for a full day; it's not a bad idea to bring a compass. For your first ride here, you'd do well to stick to the best-marked and clearest trails. Take the Robert Frost Trail, marked consistently with orange blazes, on your way out and return via the Conservation Commission trails, marked with yellow diamonds. There are stretches of fine narrow trail, not quite single-track but too narrow to ride two abreast. You pass through stands of birches, ever-present pines, oaks, and vast stands of mountain laurel that are a treat to the eyes and nose in early summer.

This is the kind of trail you could ride again and again, trying to improve your riding skills each time. The rocky, steep trail up to the wooded summit of Mount Orient and down the other side is technical because of the boulders, roots, rocks, stream crossings, and the occasional downed tree, but it's doable.

There's one major obstacle—a short steep section of the ascent that is totally vertical, taking you up and across vast slabs of rock. If you are a beginner mountain biker, you will look at the orange blazes going straight up and think it's just not possible to bike it, when all of a sudden a biker passes you and somehow scrambles up. To say it's technical is an under-

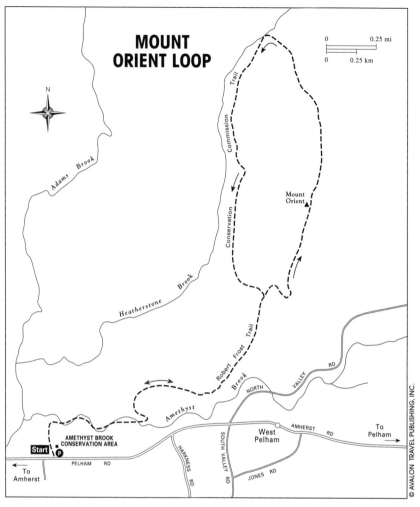

MOUNT ORIENT LOOP

Commission Trail

Conservation Trail

Robert Frost Trail

Adams Brook

Heatherstone Brook

Mount Orient

Amethyst Brook

Brook

NORTH

VALLEY RD

N

AMETHYST BROOK CONSERVATION AREA

Start P

PELHAM RD

To Amherst

HARKNESS RD

SOUTH VALLEY RD

JONES RD

West Pelham

AMHERST RD

To Pelham

0   0.25 mi

0   0.25 km

© AVALON TRAVEL PUBLISHING, INC.

statement; most bikers carry their bikes up this section. The reward is a great 180-degree view of the Holyoke Range to the south.

The best time to ride is in midsummer. Bikers are asked not to ride when trails are wet or muddy and to stay off the trails completely November 1–April 30.

For more information, contact the Amherst Trails Committee at the Amherst Conservation Department, 413/256-4045, or visit the recreation section of the local community website: www.amherstcommom.com. You can pick up the "Guide to the Robert Frost Trail" trail map at A. J. Hastings Newsdealers and Stationers on Pleasant Street in the center of Amherst. Hastings has an exhaustive selection of maps and guides to the region.

Driving Directions

From Boston and points east, take Route 2 to Route 202, Exit 16 for Belchertown/Amherst. Drive on Route 202 for approximately 15 miles to a blinking yellow light. Turn right onto Amherst Road (which turns into Pelham Road) and drive 5.7 miles. The Amethyst Brook Conservation Area parking lot will be on the right side of Pelham Road. If you are coming from the center of Amherst, drive east on Main Street, which parallels Route 9, for 1.3 miles. Main Street becomes Pelham Road. The Amethyst Brook Conservation Area parking lot is on the left-hand side of Pelham Road. Supplies and bike shops are available in Amherst.

Route Directions for Mount Orient Loop

0.0 From the Amethyst Brook parking area, take the Robert Frost Trail marked with orange blazes, bearing LEFT through hay field. Pass community gardens on your right.

0.6 Cross over Amethyst Brook on footbridge. Follow orange-blazed trail on north side of brook. At third footbridge, turn LEFT following orange-blazed trail, continuing through trail junctions. Pass "Leaving Conservation Area" sign.

1.6 Continue STRAIGHT on orange-blazed trail up sheer slabs of rock. (The trail intersects with a yellow diamond-blazed Conservation Commission Trail on your left; that will be your return route.)

2.5 Summit of Mount Orient at 957 feet.

3.6 After steep, technical downhill, take sharp LEFT on yellow diamond-blazed Conservation Commission Trail heading south. (If you reach the brook, you've gone too far.)

5.0 Turn RIGHT at junction onto orange-blazed Robert Frost Trail and retrace your route.

6.7 Return to parking area.

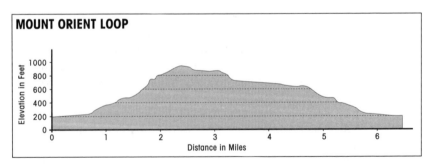

MOUNT ORIENT LOOP

#
Northampton, Hadley, and Amherst

 paved bike path

Total distance: 17 miles

Difficulty: 1

Riding time: 2 hours

Elevation gain: 300 feet

The Norwottuck Rail Trail is one of the best maintained, best serviced, and user-friendly bike paths in all of New England. It's a perfect ride for families or beginner bikers as it's mostly flat, has plenty of places to stop along the way, and has several access points so you can make the ride as long or short as you like.

The trail begins by taking you over the mighty Connecticut River on an impressive iron bridge. The historic bridge, which dates from 1887, takes you over Elwell Island, a river island with a grassy interior inhabited once by grazing cattle and now by migratory birds. The eastern side of the island is lush with trees that spill leaves and shade over the bridge, giving it quite a magical feel.

You'll then ride through the fields of Hadley. On your left, farmland and pumpkin, tobacco, or cornfields stretch away. On your right, you see the backs of stores that line the busy commercial strip of Route 9. The route is extremely well marked, with mileage markers, signs that tell you where you can get air and water, trailside ice-cream stands and burger bars, a bike shop, and well-posted road crossings. It's also a multiuse trail, heavily used by walkers, roller bladers, and families, so be courteous and observe the rules of the trail posted at the trailhead.

At Mile 3, there's a small downhill curve to go through

riding along an 1887 iron bridge that spans the Connecticut River and is now part of the Norwottuck Rail Trail

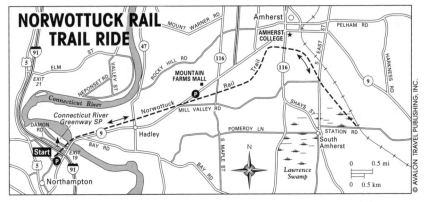

a tunnel underneath Route 9, and the scenery reverses. On your right, fields stretch to the foothills of the Holyoke Range. On the left, it's the backside of several shopping malls. As you get past the commercial strip, you'll have a very small and gradual incline, the only one on the whole path. If you can't cope with a hill, plan your route to avoid this section.

Once you cross into Amherst, the landscape changes first to sculpted greens—a golf course, Amherst College athletic fields—and then to wild and pretty conservation lands. The trail passes through Lawrence Swamp; slow down to see and hear all the wildlife chirping and croaking away. At the Station Road parking area, there is a short 1.2 mile extension into Belchertown if you want to ride on before turning around and heading back.

For more information, contact the Connecticut River Greenway State Park, 136 Damon Road, Northampton, MA 01060, 413/586-8706, ext. 12, website: www.state.ma.us/dem/parks/nwrt.htm; also check this community website: www.hadleyonline.com/railtrail.

Driving Directions

From points north or south, take Route 91 to Exit 19, Amherst and Northampton. Come off the exit ramp and go across Route 9 onto Damon Road. The parking area for the Connecticut River Greenway State Park (also called Elwell State Park) is about .1 mile ahead on the right. At the trailhead are restrooms, an information kiosk, picnic tables, bike rentals, and an ice-cream stand. Supplies and bike shops are available all along the trail in Northampton, Hadley, and Amherst.

Route Directions for Norwottuck Rail Trail Ride

0.0 From the parking area, start on the rail trail.

0.9 *Air and water are available at Saturn car dealer.*

1.7 *Food, ice cream, supplies, and bike rentals at Valley Bicycles are all available trailside. This is an alternative access point to the trail.*

3.1 Pass through tunnel.

3.6 *There is another alternative access point to the trail here, behind the Bread and Circus supermarket at the Mountain Farms Mall.*

6.0 Pass through tunnel.

7.3 Pass the Fort River Loop Trail, a walking trail. *There is a small parking area, making this an alternative access point to the trail.*

8.5 Arrive at Station Road parking area. TURN AROUND.

17.0 Return to trailhead.

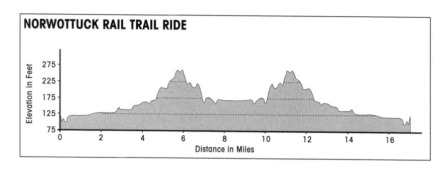

12 QUABBIN EAST LOOP
Barre, Hardwick, and Petersham

 paved roads with some uneven pavement and minimal traffic

Total distance: 45.7 miles

Riding time: 3.5 hours

Difficulty: 5

Elevation gain: 3,260 feet

In the heart of central Massachusetts, the Quabbin Reservoir constitutes the state's largest inland body of water, and in fact it is one of the largest man-made public water supplies in the nation. Four towns were flooded to create the 18-mile-long reservoir in the 1930s. This hilly route explores the largely undeveloped eastern shores of the Quabbin and the towns circling the Ware River Reservation, another watershed area protected and managed by the state's Metropolitan District Commission.

It's a popular area for road racers who are attracted by pretty, hilly, backcountry roads with minimal traffic. Riders taking their time will appreciate the small villages along the way. They seem untouched by time and commercialism, and all feature beautiful town commons and wonderful general stores that provide just about anything either a cyclist or a community could need.

Barre is the starting point for the route. The expansive town common has a gazebo and benches and is surrounded by diners, ice-cream shops, a bike store, and a tourist center. A very steep downhill out of town takes you into a rural, wooded area. You'll pass the entrance to Barre Falls Dam, an Army Corps of Engineer site. It's worth the mile out and back for great vistas, a look at the impressive dam, and the recreation area where there are picnic areas, disc golf, and facilities.

After a short stretch on the fast-moving Route 68, you'll be on some lovely, smooth backcountry roads at the edge of the Ware River Reservation. Every now and then, between hill-climbing, you'll spot historic markers, stone walls, and old cemeteries. There are a few miles to ride on busy Routes 122A and 122, but the shoulder is nice and wide. Expect some major hill-climbing on Old Turnpike Road as you pass from woodlands into open pasturelands.

The ride's steepest climb comes on the way to Hardwick, but the scenery is sweet. As you get closer to town, the views change from farms and pastures to historic white houses with picket fences, fancy porches, impressive gardens, and well-kept stone walls. Hardwick's town common is a great meeting or stopping point, and the general store and post office has rest-

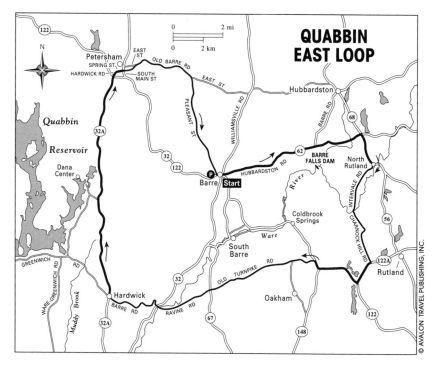

rooms, a great deli counter where you can get sandwiches, and a porch where bikers tend to hang out.

The next stretch, on Route 32A, takes you along the eastern edge of the Quabbin, and the rolling hills give you occasional views of the water. You'll encounter some stretches of very uneven pavement and more lovely stone walls and houses on this backcountry road that takes you into Petersham. Yet another lovely town common, with gazebo and benches, and another fantastic country store, give you another excuse to stop and rest before the last leg, which features some more hill-climbing through rural farmlands before finishing with a nice downhill into Barre.

For more information, contact the Central Quabbin Area Tourism Association, P.O. Box 95, Barre, MA 01005, website: www.centralquabbinarea.org.

Driving Directions

From Worcester, take Route 122 west for approximately 20 miles to Barre. As you enter the center of town, bear right around the large town common onto Exchange Street. You'll find free parking lots around the common and a large lot on the eastern edge. Supplies and a bike shop are available in Barre.

Route Directions for Quabbin East Loop

0.0 From Exchange Street in the center of Barre, turn RIGHT onto Mechanic Street (this becomes Hubbardston Road/Route 62).

2.5 *A right turn will take you on an optional side trip to Barre Falls Dam.*

6.8 RIGHT onto Route 68.

8.2 RIGHT onto Intervale Road.

10.6 Bear LEFT onto Charnock Hill Road.

13.1 RIGHT onto Route 122A.

14.1 RIGHT onto Route 122. *Small roadside picnic area.*

16.6 LEFT onto Old Turnpike Road.

21.7 STRAIGHT through intersection onto Ravine Road.

24.3 STRAIGHT through intersection onto Barre Road. *Supplies available at Cloverhill Country Store farm stand.*

27.0 RIGHT onto Route 32A at Hardwick common. *Supplies and restrooms available at Hardwick General Store.*

37.1 STRAIGHT through intersection onto Hardwick Road.

37.3 Bear RIGHT at triangle onto Spring Street.

37.6 LEFT onto South Main Street.

37.8 RIGHT onto East Street. *Supplies available at Petersham Country Store.*

41.0 East Street becomes Old Barre Road.

42.3 Old Barre Road becomes Pleasant Street.

45.6 LEFT at stop sign onto Route 32/122.

45.7 Return to Barre town center.

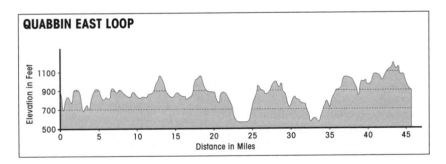

QUABBIN EAST LOOP

13 HODGES VILLAGE DAM LOOP
Oxford

dirt roads, single-track, double-track

Total distance: 6.5 miles

Difficulty: 2

Riding time: 1–1.5 hours

Elevation gain: 37 feet

This south-central corner of Massachusetts, despite being a densely populated and developed area, has a lot of fun places to mountain bike, thanks
in large part to the efforts of the New England Mountain Biking Association. In 2003, NEMBA made history by becoming the first bike advocacy
group to buy, own, and manage property, with its purchase of 47 acres in
Milford encompassing a trail network known to local mountain bikers as

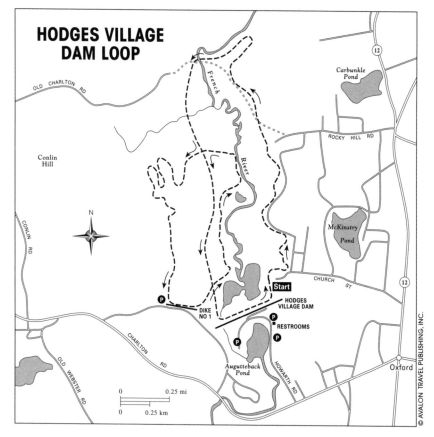

"Vietnam." Within a stone's throw from Worcester and Boston, you can also choose from trails at Douglas State Forest, Upton State Forest, Buffumville Park, Callahan State Park, and Hodges Village.

Advanced beginners would do well to choose Hodges Village, an Army Corps of Engineers site with 15 miles of trails that twist and turn on either side of the French River. The trail designers have made a lot out of a little space here, and though each section of trail is short and you'll be taking lots of turns, it's a fun place to ride. You're always in the middle of thick forests that line freshwater wetlands. The western side has some nice oak hardwoods and the eastern side features an Atlantic white cedar swamp.

This route is a sampler of the trails along the southern end. Start at the dam and ride along the east side of the river, starting on a wide dirt road. You'll leave the road and pass through some meadows before getting onto some fun single-track edging the wildlife-filled cedar swamp. After you cross the river, you'll ride on a dirt road again before turning onto a system of single-track trails that are rooty, rocky, and just a little bit hilly, but not too technical.

The trails are blazed with blue, yellow, red, and pink marks but I found the blazes confusing. Blazes with a black dot in the center mean you are headed toward the dam. But even if you lose your way, the trail system is relatively short, so you can't go too far wrong. You can pick up a trail map at a kiosk in the parking lot.

For more information, contact Hodges Village Dam, P.O. Box 155, Oxford, MA 01540, 508/248-5697, website: www.nae.usace.army.mil/recreati/hvd/hvdhome.htm.

Driving Directions
From Worcester, take Route 395 south to Exit 4B. Drive west through Oxford Center and continue straight for .5 mile to Howarth Road. Turn right and follow the access road all the way to the parking lot at the end, near the top of the dam. There are restrooms and water, a kiosk with trail maps, picnic areas, disc golf, and more. Supplies are available in Oxford. The nearest bike shops are in Worcester.

Route Directions for Hodges Village Dam Loop
0.0 From parking lot, cross road to right of office building, go down stone steps, and look for hiking trail sign at edge of woods. Fork LEFT at two immediate forks in path and turn RIGHT onto dirt road.
0.8 LEFT at fork.
0.9 LEFT at four-way intersection.
1.1 Pass around yellow gate.
1.2 At three-way intersection, go RIGHT then LEFT.
1.4 STRAIGHT through intersection.

1.6 LEFT at crossroads.
2.0 LEFT at junction, then immediate RIGHT at next junction and across a bridge.
2.1 LEFT after bridge. Trail swings to right and meets dirt road.
2.6 RIGHT.
2.7 LEFT onto single-track trail.
2.9 RIGHT.
3.2 RIGHT at crossroads.
3.3 LEFT at junction.
3.8 LEFT at junction, ride on trail alongside dike.
4.1 LEFT at end of dike onto dirt road.
4.2 LEFT past yellow gate.
4.3 RIGHT on pink-blazed trail.
4.6 Cross plank bridge.
4.8 RIGHT at intersection.
5.4 LEFT away from river, then STRAIGHT at crossroads staying on red-blazed trail.
5.5 LEFT onto woods road.
6.1 Return to yellow gate. LEFT onto dirt road.
6.2 Cross the dam.
6.3 LEFT at fork by gate.
6.4 Pass wildlife blind on left. Take hard RIGHT up trail.
6.5 A log across trail marks the trailhead. Return to parking lot.

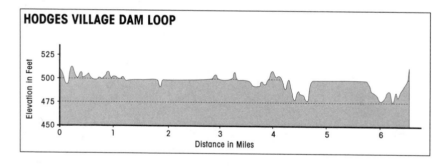

14 FREETOWN SAMPLER
Freetown/Fall River State Forest, Assonet

 dirt roads, gravel roads, single-track

Total distance: 7 miles

Difficulty: 3

Riding time: 1.5 hours

Elevation gain: 80 feet

This vast state forest just outside of Fall River gives riders from southern and eastern Massachusetts a chance to play in a coastal lowland environment without having to cross the bridge to Cape Cod. Low, scrubby bushes and gravelly soil with traces of sand make you feel as if you're near the coast. This doesn't mean you're free from the rocky New England single-track, though. You'll find 20-plus miles of single-track trails here, some of which are extremely rocky. It's a popular spot for mountain bikers, and you might see races or group rides. It's also popular with equestrians and, in certain seasons, dog sled teams in training, so be a courteous rider.

This route, which starts at the forest headquarters, is about two-thirds dirt road and one-third single-track (if you are looking for more challenging single-track, you might try parking on Bell Rock Road and hitting the trails to the southwest of Copicut Road). From the trailhead, you'll begin on a wide track that's a mix of sand and gravel, and then ride on a wider

A rocky single-track trail cuts through the dense shrubby vegetation.

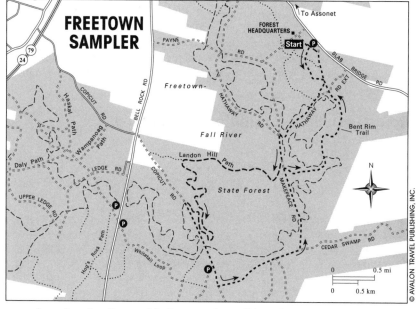

gravel road and a dirt road before turning off into the single-track system. Look for the short wooden post marking the trail.

Though the soil generally drains quickly here, this first stretch can get muddy and you may have some stream crossings or muddy rutted sections to negotiate. Once you curve to the south, you'll be in a twisty section of dry, rocky, narrow trail with the occasional rock slabs. There's no real elevation gain, so the fun—and the challenge—is in taking tight turns and maneuvering around rocks. After the single-track, it's dirt roads all the way back. A nice stretch runs through a lovely leafy section on the narrower Bent Rim Trail at the end.

Freetown is a place to come back to again and again to explore the many trails. In many sections, the single-track is marked by short wooden posts with a mountain bike symbol inside a yellow triangle. Bring a compass, a map, and plenty of mosquito repellent.

For more information, contact Freetown/Fall River State Forest, Slab Bridge Road, Assonet, MA 02702, 508/644-5522, website: www.mass.gov/dem/parks/free.htm.

Driving Directions

From points north, take Route 24 south to Exit 10. Bear left onto South Main Street. Turn left at four-way intersection onto Route 79 north and take an immediate right at the fork onto Elm Street (which turns into Slab Bridge Road). Drive 1.5 miles to the forest entrance on the right. From the access road, the main parking area is on the left. You'll find picnic tables, restrooms, water, a wading pool, and pay phones. Parking is free. The trailhead is on the right at the far end of the parking lot. Pass around a gate; playing fields and the group picnic area will be on the right. Supplies are available in Assonet. The nearest bike shops are in Swansea and New Bedford.

Route Directions for Freetown Sampler

0.0 Begin at trailhead.
0.3 Bear RIGHT.
0.5 RIGHT onto Hathaway Road Extension.
1.0 LEFT onto Makepeace Road at four-way intersection.
1.2 RIGHT onto unmarked single-track trail.
2.1 Continue STRAIGHT.
2.3 LEFT at fork.
3.6 STRAIGHT at intersection.
3.7 LEFT onto paved road (which quickly becomes dirt road).
4.0 LEFT onto Cedar Swamp Road.
4.8 LEFT onto Makepeace Road at circle.
5.4 RIGHT onto Bent Rim Trail.
6.6 STRAIGHT at intersection.
6.7 Continue STRAIGHT.
6.9 LEFT before paved road.
7.0 Return to parking lot.

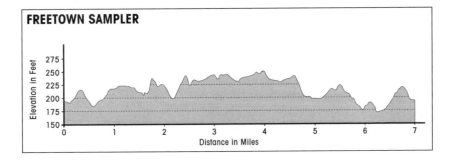

15 LITTLE RIVER LOOP
South Dartmouth

 paved roads with minimal to moderate traffic

Total distance: 23.3 miles

Difficulty: 2

Riding time: 2–2.5 hours

Elevation gain: 575 feet

Below the former whaling and mill towns of Fall River and New Bedford lies a lovely coastal corner of New England, partly in Massachusetts and partly in Rhode Island, where small peninsulas and river inlets add watery charm to historic villages. Though the coast attracts tourists and sailors, the back roads still have a feel of unspoiled countryside and long, open, quiet stretches.

The route begins just across the bridge from South Dartmouth, or, as the central village is also called, Padanaram. The small village bustles with cafés, shops, ice-cream stands, fishermen, and sailors, so it's a fun place to explore after a ride. Leaving from the town park, you spend a few miles riding through a residential area before getting into tiny Russells Mills and the remote roads beyond. Leafy and pleasant, the area has few major hills and only the gentlest of ups and downs.

Cruise down Gidley Town Road and arrive at a four-way intersection in South Westport (if you want a longer ride, go straight across Hix Bridge to connect to the Little Compton ride, described in the Rhode Island chapter as Route 8, Cross-Border Ride). Turn south onto Horseneck Road onto a more open stretch of land, with expansive fields and farmlands and nice views of the Westport River on your right. If you want to brave the crowds, you can ride a few miles farther to reach Horseneck Beach State Park. Otherwise turn east and ride up a small incline past more open fields and farmlands.

Now your views are of Slocums River, which at the top gets quite marshy and attracts a wide range of birdlife. Russells Mills Landing is the perfect picnic spot with a boat launch, small playground, toilets, and picnic tables overlooking the river. Leave Russells Mills behind for the backcountry ride on Potomska Road. Although some of the pavement is uneven, it's a sweet stretch through forested land that suddenly opens to the tranquil inlets of the Little River.

Smith Neck Road, your last leg, takes you past grassy lawns, gray clapboard houses, golf courses, and Salvador Dairy and Ice Cream, an ice-cream stand in the shape of an old milk bottle. Who can resist? Then it's back to the shores of Padanaram with a few sandy beaches and lots of boats moored in the harbor making for a picturesque end to the ride.

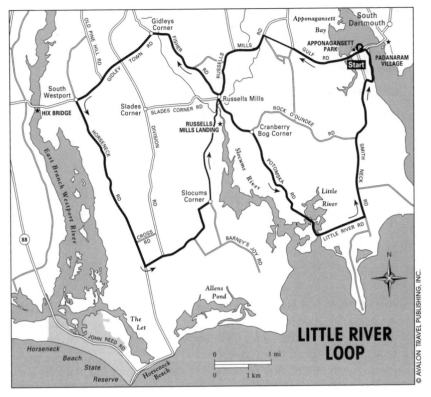

For more information, contact the Coastal Villages Cooperative, email: info@coastalvillages.com, website: www.coastalvillages.com.

Driving Directions

From points east or west, take Route 195 to Exit 12 for Faunce Corner Road. Drive south on Faunce Corner Road for about 1 mile. Cross Route 6 onto Chase Road and drive approximately 4.3 miles. Turn left onto Russells Mills Road, drive .6 mile and turn right onto Gulf Road. Drive 1.4 miles and turn left into Apponagansett Park, just before the bridge to Padanaram Village. Toilets, water, a playground, and small sandy beach are at the park. Parking costs $3 on weekends and $2 on weekdays for nonresidents. Supplies are available in Padanaram. The nearest bike shops are in Westport and New Bedford.

Route Directions for Little River Loop

0.0 From Apponagansett Park, turn RIGHT out of parking lot onto Gulf Road.
1.4 STRAIGHT through intersection.

2.0 LEFT onto Russells Mills Road.

3.8 RIGHT onto Fisher Road.

4.5 LEFT at stop sign.

5.6 LEFT onto Gidley Town Road.

7.6 LEFT at four-way intersection onto Horseneck Road.

8.5 (Don't be fooled by this intersection with another, older Horseneck Road!)

11.1 LEFT on Horseneck Road (unmarked).

13.1 LEFT at stop sign.

14.9 Pass Russells Mills Landing.

15.1 RIGHT onto Rock O'Dundee Road. *Supplies available at general store in Russells Mills.*

16.2 STRAIGHT onto Potomska Road. Road becomes Little River Road.

18.9 Cross Little River Bridge.

19.7 LEFT onto Smith Neck Road.

23.1 LEFT onto Gulf Road.

23.3 RIGHT to return to Apponagansett Park.

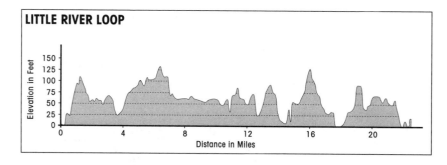

TRAIL OF TEARS
West Barnstable Conservation Area, West Barnstable

🚵 single-track

Total distance: 12 miles   **Riding time:** 2.5 hours

Difficulty: 4   **Elevation gain:** 302 feet

Though you'd never guess it when you're stuck in summer Cape Cod traffic on Route 6, just a stone's throw from the highway is a 1,000-plus-acre conservation area that offers some of the best mountain biking trails in the state. The West Barnstable Conservation Area has miles of fun, twisty single-track winding its way through deep scrub pine and oak forest.

The trails aren't all that technical, but they do require a lot of aerobic fitness as there are a lot of short steep ascents and descents. One minute you're in low gear puffing up a hill, and the next minute you're maneuvering down a steep rocky slope. Most of the time, though, you are twisting through soft pine-covered trails, sliding your handlebars between slender tree trunks and wondering which way to turn at the upcoming fork in the trail. This is really fun riding, great for intermediate riders who want a break from the rocky, muddy trails of New England's interior.

A designated 16-mile single-track Trail of Tears is signposted with red

taking a tight turn on the Trail of Tears

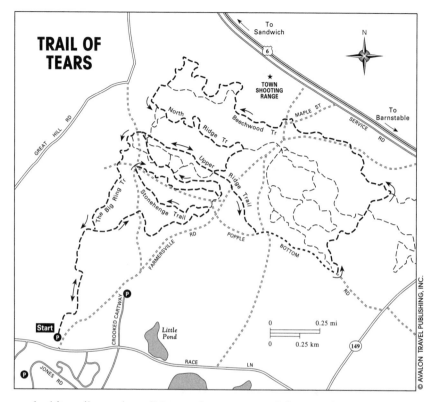

and white mile markers. It's not always easy to follow, and up-to-date trail maps are hard to come by. It seems as if new paths are being created all the time, and it's very easy to get lost. You'll see three types of markers—the red and white Trail of Tears signs, brown signs with white arrows, and small circular patches with reflective arrows. In general, the best bet is to follow what appears to be the main trail—it is usually a little sandier and more packed down. Newer trails are more loamy and have more pine coverage.

This route follows most of the Trail of Tears, starting on some tight single-track with some fun downs and ups on the way to the Walker Point lookout platform. A few rocky patches mix in with the pine trails as you work your way east. The northeast corner is more sandy and you'll ride parallel to the power lines until returning to deeper, leafier forested areas in the northwest corner. Bring a compass, be prepared to get lost, and oil your chain before riding as you'll be shifting gears a lot.

For more information and to obtain a trail map, contact the Barnstable Conservation Commission, 200 Main Street, Hyannis, MA 02601, 508/862-4093, website: www.town.barnstable.ma.us.

Driving Directions

From points east and west, take Route 6 to Exit 5, Route 149. Drive south on Route 149 for about 1.5 miles; at the intersection, turn right onto Race Lane. Drive 1.8 miles and turn right onto Farmersville Road. Look for the sign for West Barnstable Conservation Area. A gravel parking lot is large enough for about a dozen cars. A trail map is posted at the trailhead, and there is a white Trail of Tears marker. There are no facilities here or at the other two parking lots for the conservation area. Supplies can be found in West Barnstable, Barnstable, and Hyannis; the closest bike shops are in Hyannis.

Route Directions for Trail of Tears

0.0 START from parking lot.
0.7 RIGHT at the T-junction.
0.8 RIGHT at the fork.
1.0 STRAIGHT across intersection (with wider dirt track) onto single-track.
1.7 LEFT at intersection.
2.2 Come to a five-way intersection. Look for the single-track going STRAIGHT across the intersection, across a dirt road.
2.8 LEFT at junction.
3.2 Continue STRAIGHT past Spur 2 and Spur 1.
3.4 Arrive at Walker Point lookout platform (you'll see a 3.4-mile marker).
3.4 Continue STRAIGHT at next marker (ignore two trails on left).
3.48 Cross a paved road and turn LEFT and immediate RIGHT.
3.5 Come to a four-way intersection and go RIGHT (this is marked as a three-way intersection on most trail maps; the newest trail is the one straight ahead). At the next intersection, go RIGHT (ignore small trail on left).
3.66 Continue STRAIGHT at marker, uphill.
4.1 Come to five-way intersection and go STRAIGHT across (ignore one trail on left and two trails on right; this is marked as a four-way intersection on most trail maps).
4.25 Turn RIGHT onto road then immediate LEFT onto single-track trail.
4.54 Cross road, go STRAIGHT.
4.7 Cross road, go STRAIGHT.
4.9 LEFT at fork and continue STRAIGHT on main trail, ignoring side trails.
5.25 RIGHT onto wide trail.
5.3 LEFT onto dirt road.
6.0 LEFT off wide path onto single-track.
6.2 Go under power lines.
6.36 STRAIGHT across dirt road.
6.7 RIGHT at fork in trail, follow signs.
7.1 LEFT at Trail of Tears sign marked 11.8.

7.8 LEFT at intersection.

7.86 LEFT at fork.

8.0 RIGHT at intersection.

8.56 LEFT at intersection.

8.78 Trail loops to RIGHT following trail marker.

8.8 LEFT at intersection with wider trail.

8.9 Go STRAIGHT under power lines.

8.94 LEFT back onto single-track trail.

9.0 LEFT at fork.

9.1 LEFT (carrying on main trail).

9.8 RIGHT at fork.

10.0 RIGHT at the five-way intersection.

10.5 STRAIGHT at the four-way intersection, then RIGHT at fork.

10.6 LEFT uphill at fork.

10.8 STRAIGHT across dirt road.

10.9 Follow arrow to RIGHT.

11.2 RIGHT at intersection, then LEFT at unmarked trail to go back to parking lot. (Don't miss this turn!)

12.0 Return to parking lot.

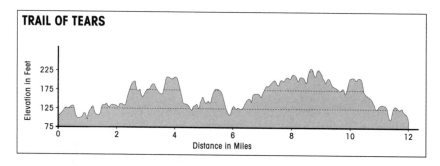

TRAIL OF TEARS

paved bike path

Total distance: 11–28.2 miles one-way, with options for shorter rides

Riding time: 1–5 hours

Difficulty: 1   **Elevation gain:** 398 feet

Anyone who's been to Cape Cod in the summertime knows that along with the beauty of the beaches and the dunes comes the hassle of the crowds and traffic. A ride along the wonderful Cape Cod Rail Trail can get you away from all the cars and bring you to some of the Cape's best beaches and parks. The trail is not immune to crowds and can get busy with walkers, riders, joggers, and strollers. Your best bet is to start very early in the morning for maximum privacy.

You've got lots of options depending on the type of ride and outing you want. This 28-mile one-way route includes a side trip to Nauset and Coast Guard Beach. If you ride the whole trail from South Dennis to Wellfleet and back with no side trips, you'll cover about 48 easy, flat, smooth miles. You can turn around whenever you like, or start at one of the many access

Along the Nauset Bike Trail, a wooden boardwalk crosses over a piece of Nauset Bay before bringing you to the dramatic sand dunes of Coast Guard Beach.

points along the way. Nickerson State Park is a good starting point about midway along the trail. Bike rental shops are at many points along the route if you don't have your own bike with you. Make sure you build in time for stops, since there are so many parks, ponds, beaches, and ice-cream stands along the way. Any type of bike is suitable for the 8-foot-wide asphalt trail. It's mainly flat with just a few gradual inclines. There are lots of road crossings, so be prepared to stop frequently.

Starting in South Dennis, you'll ride 1 mile or so before it starts to get prettier and you'll see swans and ducks in Swan Pond. You'll have road crossings and a tunnel before you reach a string of pretty ponds, all of which look suitable for swimming. After some suburban scenery, there's a scenic stretch of typical Cape lowland scrub pine forest, interrupted briefly by the town of Brewster. About halfway through, Nickerson State Park is leafy and offers shade as well as a nice stopping or starting point. Marshlands with birding opportunities come on either side of Orleans, the next town you'll ride through. A salt-marsh restoration project is under way along the peaceful Boat Meadow River, just past Orleans.

Take a side trip to ride the Nauset Trail, a bike path going from the Salt Pond Visitor Center to Coast Guard Beach. The trail is a little more challenging and hilly than the rail trail, but still quite easy. You wind through lovely undeveloped scrub pine forest before emerging onto a boardwalk across part of Nauset Bay. The wind picks up and you arrive at Coast Guard Beach.

Back on the rail trail, the vegetation gets a little flatter, there's not as much shade, and it can get hot in the midday sun. You'll pass a possible side trip to Marconi National Seashore before reaching the trailhead off LeCount Hollow Road in Wellfleet, where there are picnic tables, restrooms, supplies, a general store, a bike shop, and free parking.

For more information, contact the Cape Cod Rail Trail at the Massachusetts Division of State Parks and Recreation, 508/896-3491, website: www.mass.gov/dem/parks/ccrt.htm. For more information about the Cape Cod National Seashore, contact the National Park Service, 99 Marconi Station Site Road, Wellfleet, MA 02667, 508/349-3785, website: www.nps.gov/caco.

Driving Directions

From anywhere on Cape Cod, take Route 6 to Exit 9 (West Harwich and Dennisport). Drive .5 mile on Route 134 south. You will go through two traffic lights. Look carefully for the trailhead sign on the left, just past the Cranberry Square shopping plaza. You'll find a parking lot and trail sign but no facilities here. Bike rentals are available at Barbara's Bike and Sport shop, just past the parking lot. Supplies are available all along Route 134 and along the bike path. Bike shops can be found in Brewster, Eastham, North Eastham, North Harwich, Orleans, South Dennis, and South Wellfleet.

Route Directions for Cape Cod Rail Trail

0.0 Start at Dennis trailhead.

3.2 *Harwich-Chatham side route.*

4.4 Gentle incline on bridge over Route 6.

4.7 *Access point and parking lot at Headwaters Drive on the shore of Hinckleys Pond.*

5.2. *Supplies and ice cream available at Pleasant Lake General Store, with bike racks, picnic tables, and portable toilets.*

8.0 *Access point and parking lot along Route 137 in South Brewster. Here there are picnic tables, bike rentals and shops, restaurants, and ice-cream stands.*

10.7 *Parking lot with bike rentals, restaurants, and ice-cream stand.*

11.0 Nickerson State Park. *Free parking, picnic tables, lots of side bike trails, campground, facilities.*

12.7 Come off bike path onto town road.

12.8 Turn RIGHT onto West Road, cross bridge over Route 6, and turn LEFT to return to rail trail.

13.7 Cross Main Street, Orleans. *Access point with free parking, supplies, restaurants, ice-cream shops, and Orleans Cycles.*

14.1 Bridge over Route 6. (Beginner riders may want to dismount and walk across the bridge, which has a gentle incline.)

17.1 Turn RIGHT onto Locust Road.

17.5 LEFT onto Salt Pond Road.

17.6 Cross Route 6 with caution at traffic lights and enter the Cape Cod National Seashore Salt Pond Visitor Center parking area. *Free parking, information, maps, restrooms are available at the visitor center.*
17.9 Continue on the Nauset Bike Trail from far end of parking lot.
19.9 Reach Coast Guard Beach parking area. TURN AROUND.
21.9 Return to the visitor center, cross Route 6, and resume on Salt Pond Road.
22.1 RIGHT onto Locust Road.
22.5 RIGHT onto bike trail.
27.4 *Optional side trip to Marconi Station and Marconi Beach.*
28.2 Arrive at Wellfleet trailhead on LeCount Hollow Road. TURN AROUND and retrace route, skipping the side trip to Nauset.
51.0 Return to South Dennis trailhead.

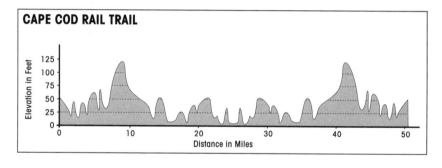

CAPE COD RAIL TRAIL

18 PROVINCE LANDS LOOP
Provincetown

 paved bike path

Total distance: 8.9 miles

Difficulty: 3

Riding time: 1–2 hours

Elevation gain: 260 feet

While the Cape Cod Rail Trail offers a scenic and simple way to get from one place to another, the Province Lands bike trail is a fun biking experience in a truly unique and spectacular natural setting. At the very tip of Cape Cod, the trail winds its way in, around, up, and over sand dunes, scrub pine forest, and a beech forest surrounding a pond, giving riders great views of the ocean and horizon.

There are sharp hills to climb, and signs warn riders of the difficulties of the trail, but any intermediate or experienced cyclist will find them to be no problem. More tricky is the shifting sand, blown onto the trail by the wind, especially when rain or ocean spray gets the sand wet. The National Park Service can and will close sections of the trail if it thinks conditions are too dangerous.

Starting from the Province Lands Visitor Center, take the bike trail downhill toward Race Point. It's worth making a side trip to Race Point,

All the hills are clearly marked on the Province Lands bike trail.

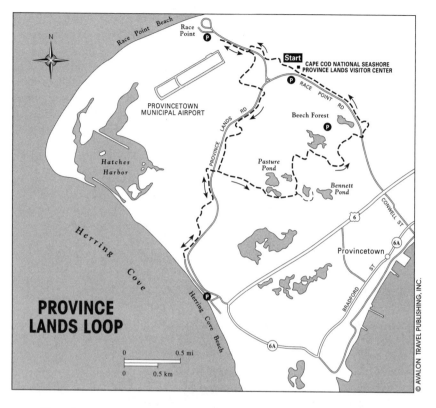

PROVINCE LANDS LOOP

even if you're not going to visit the beach, just to see the high sand dunes. Back on the trail, you'll ride through low scrubby pines and bushes in sandy soil, getting some ocean breezes. A low tunnel and a little incline are at the other side.

At the junction, take the right turn to head toward Herring Cove Beach. You'll face a fairly short, steep incline before you arrive at the beach parking area. The trail comes out at the far end of the parking lot; seasonal restrooms are at the other end of the parking lot. This is a lovely beach, with beach roses and other low-lying shrubs lining the sand dunes.

When you return to the main bike trail, you'll find a steep, curvy section followed by a winding downhill on the way past Pasture Pond. You're in the shade for the first time as you enter Beech Forest and a totally different ecosystem of trees, swamp, and marshland. Pass through the Beech Forest parking area, cross the road you drove in on, and resume on the bike trail. Some twisty, fun S-curves are on this stretch along with a short steep hill, where you get great panoramic views of the dunes and ocean, just before you reach the visitor center.

The Province Lands Visitor Center is open 9 A.M.–5 P.M. daily, May 1–October 31, and offers programs, information, an observation deck, amphitheater, exhibits, restrooms, a pay phone, small book and gift store, and trail maps. Parking is free. Restrooms with flush toilets and sinks are available in the parking area year round. For more information about the Cape Cod National Seashore and the Province Lands Visitor Center, contact the National Park Service, 99 Marconi Station Site Road, Wellfleet, MA 02667, 508/349-3785 or 508/487-1256 May 1–October 31, website: www.nps.gov/caco.

Driving Directions

From anywhere on Cape Cod, take Route 6 toward Provincetown. You'll pass the intersection with Route 6A. Drive 1.5 miles farther and turn right at the traffic light onto Race Point Road. You'll see signs for Province Lands Visitor Center. Drive 1.4 miles and arrive at the visitor center and parking area. Supplies and bike shops are available in Provincetown.

Route Directions for Province Lands Loop

0.0 Start at the trailhead in front of the visitor center.

0.5 Cross the road and come to a T-junction. Go RIGHT.

0.9 Arrive at Race Point Beach parking area. *Restrooms available. There is a $3 beach entrance fee for bicyclists.* TURN AROUND.

3.0 RIGHT at intersection toward Herring Cove.

4.1 Arrive at Herring Cove Beach parking area. *Restrooms available. There is a $3 beach entrance fee for bicyclists.* TURN AROUND.

5.3 STRAIGHT at intersection toward Beech Forest.

6.1 *Optional .5-mile side trip to Bennett Pond.*

7.4 Arrive at Beech Forest parking lot. *Picnic area, restrooms.* Go LEFT, following signs for Province Lands Visitor Center, and cross Race Point Road to continue on bike path.

8.9 Return to visitor center parking lot and trailhead.

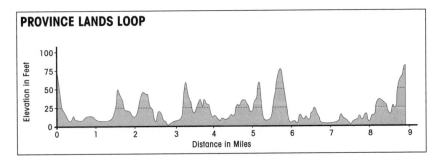

Chapter 5

© MARC FLEISHER

Connecticut

Connecticut

New England's second-smallest state, Connecticut sometimes suffers from its proximity to Manhattan, and the crowded southwestern corner is linked more to New York than New England. But just an hour's drive or so from there, rural country lanes, rolling hills, sharp ridges, and cows grazing in fields put you in something more like a Vermont state of mind. Both the northwest and northeast offer excellent road riding, and scenic, challenging mountain biking can be found just about anywhere in the Nutmeg State.

Connecticut is split almost exactly in half by the Connecticut River as it makes its way to Long Island Sound, having traveled from its source in northern New Hampshire. The western half of the state is the hilliest, as the Western New England Upland, which continues into Massachusetts and Vermont, provides lovely ridges and valleys. The Litchfield Hills area is popular for cycling, with its green hills, small lakes, and fast rivers. It's also prep-school land and the wealth shows in lakes dotted with sailboats and rowing crews, and in fancy houses with landscaped gardens. Summer homes and tourist attractions mean that roads can get a little crowded in summer; fall foliage season might be a better season for cycling.

As you head east of the Connecticut River and the capital city of Hartford, things quiet down a bit. The Eastern New England Upland features low hills, river valleys, and heavily forested areas, especially in the northeast. This northeast corner, dubbed the Quiet Corner, is the state's least developed area, and small villages display their historic homes, monuments, and industry with quiet pride.

The southeast corner, however, is packed with tourist attractions, with two major casinos and the busy seaport towns of New London and Mystic. The best bet for mountain biking in the south and east is in state forests and town parks or conservation areas. Off-road trails in Bluff Point State Park offer nice views of Long Island Sound. Inland, miles of trails in the sprawling Pachaug and Natchaug State Forests are a world away from the dice at Foxwoods.

The state takes its role in the history of American bicycling seriously. In the late 1800s, a Civil War colonel-turned-businessman named Albert Pope became excited by the newfangled two-wheeled contraptions coming from England. He created the country's first manufacturing plant for the modern bicycle in Hartford and later went on to become the founder of the Good Roads Movement. More than 100 years later, various state agencies are committed to maintaining and creating pathways, multiuse trails, and greenways of open spaces that preserve natural corridors. Pope, a champion of motorized vehicles, might not have liked it, but the wonderful Air Line rail trail is a prime example, providing an easily accessible wilderness experience for people of all abilities.

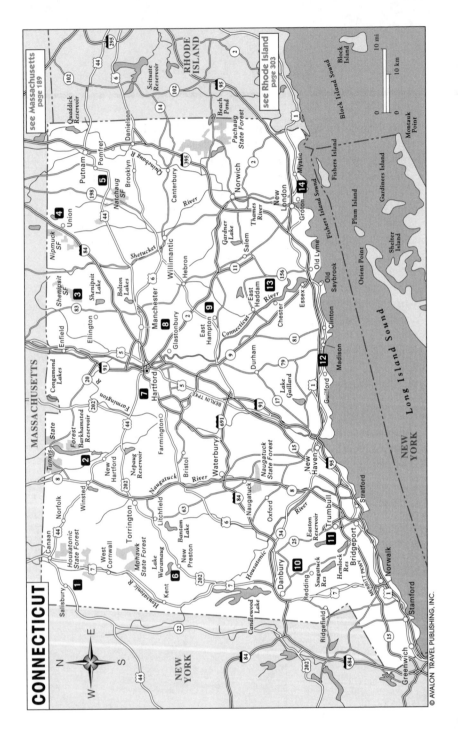

Contents

SALISBURY HILLS AND HOLLOWS
Salisbury

 paved roads with minimal to moderate traffic

Total distance: 20.2 miles

Riding time: 2 hours

Difficulty: 4

Elevation gain: 1,360 feet

The green rolling hills of the Berkshires extend attractive fingers into this lovely corner of northwestern Connecticut, and lots of quiet backcountry roads through pastoral farmland make for nice bike outings. The starting point is the preppy, pretty town of Salisbury, where there are cafés, markets, ice-cream shops, and tea rooms.

The first stretch, along Salmon Kill Road, takes you through gently rolling hills with nice views of the ridges that extend on either side. You'll pass nicely landscaped lawns, stone walls, split rail fences, babbling brooks, and the occasional farm on this well-contoured road.

Use caution as you ride a .2-mile stretch on Route 112, as traffic moves faster here. Turning onto White Hollow Road takes you past Lime Rock Park, and you definitely want to check the race schedule (website: www.limerock.com), because roads around this race track can get very

a flat stretch along the shores of Mudge Pond

© MELISSA L. KIM

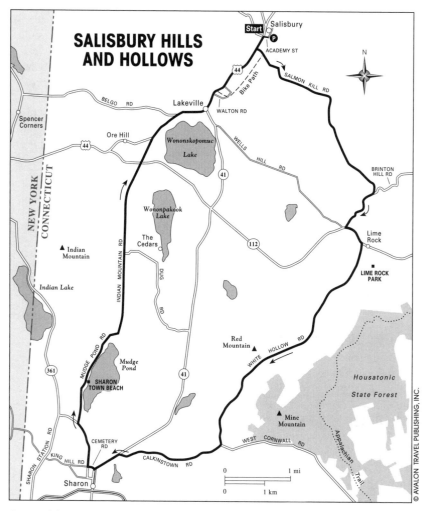

SALISBURY HILLS
AND HOLLOWS

busy with people pouring in to camp on the fields and watch the
NASCAR and Grand Prix races at the "Road Racing Center of the East."

Past the track, White Hollow Road is a lovely rural road with more gently rolling hills. You'll go up and down on evenly spaced quarter-mile inter-
vals, with a steeper climb to get you up to and along the start of
Calkinstown Road. Then there's a glorious long downhill taking you from a
rural to more residential area with some tight curves as you enter the outskirts of Sharon. There's some fast traffic on Route 41, and then a sharp
right onto the steep descent on uneven pavement past a pretty cemetery.

It's downhill all the way on Route 361 before the poorly marked turn to
Mudge Pond Road. After some nice views of the pond, and an opportunity

to stop and swim, you face a good-sized climb up Indian Hill with more pastoral scenes and nice mountain views. As you approach Lakeville, you'll get some good views of Wononskopomuc Lake from Route 44. Traffic can get heavier along Route 44 so use caution through Lakeville and into Salisbury. If you've got thick tires or a hybrid, consider taking the bike path on an old railroad bed back to Salisbury.

For more information, contact the Litchfield Hills Visitors Bureau, P.O. Box 968, Litchfield, CT 06759-0968, 860/567-4506, website: www.litchfieldhills.com.

Driving Directions

From Hartford, take Route 44 west approximately 47 miles to Salisbury. From Danbury and points south, take Route 7 to Kent. Continue on Route 7 for approximately 18 miles, past West Cornwall, and turn left onto Route 112 (Lime Rock Road). Drive approximately 7 miles and turn right onto Route 41. Drive 2.5 miles and turn right onto Route 44. Drive 2.5 miles into Salisbury. Turn right onto Academy Street opposite the town hall and park at Salisbury Marketplace. The route begins at the corner of Main Street and Academy Street, opposite Salisbury Town Hall. Supplies are available in Salisbury.

Route Directions for Salisbury Hills and Hollows

0.0 Ride south on Main Street (Route 44).
0.3 LEFT onto Salmon Kill Road.
3.7 At fork, bear RIGHT on Salmon Kill Road.
4.0 Curve RIGHT and cross bridge.
4.5 LEFT onto Route 112 (Lime Rock Road).
4.8 RIGHT onto White Hollow Road.
5.1 Pass entrance to Lime Rock Park.
9.2 RIGHT at triangle onto Calkinstown Road.
10.3 Sharp right, then left, curve.
11.1 LEFT onto Route 41. *Supplies available in Sharon.*
11.6 RIGHT onto Cemetery Road.
11.7 RIGHT onto Route 361.
12.4 RIGHT onto Mudge Pond Road (caution: poorly marked).
13.8 Bear RIGHT at fork.
13.9 *Entrance to Sharon Town Beach on right, with small sandy beach, pay phone, changing rooms, restrooms, picnic tables, and playground.*
17.0 STRAIGHT across Route 112, staying on Indian Mountain Road.
17.5 RIGHT onto Route 44 (Millerton Road).
18.5 STRAIGHT at fork with Route 41 in Lakeville. *Supplies available in Lakeville.*
18.8 (Optional return route: Turn RIGHT onto Walton Road, ride to the

end, and look for the signs for the bike path on the LEFT. It starts paved but turns into a grassy narrow single-track, suitable for hybrid or mountain bikes. You come out onto Salmon Kill Road; turn LEFT, then RIGHT onto Main Street to return to Salisbury.)

19.1 STRAIGHT through traffic light.

20.2 Return to corner of Main Street and Academy Street.

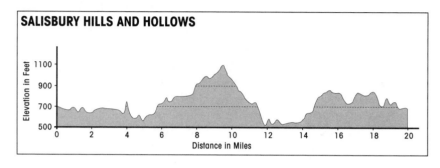

SALISBURY HILLS AND HOLLOWS

2 BARKHAMSTED RESERVOIR LOOP
Barkhamsted

 paved roads with minimal to moderate traffic

Total distance: 23.6 miles

Riding time: 2–2.5 hours

Difficulty: 5

Elevation gain: 2,200 feet

Northwest of Hartford, just south of the Massachusetts border, lies the state's largest water supply reservoir in the middle of unspoiled, undeveloped, leafy countryside. Much of the property surrounding Barkhamstead Reservoir is state forest land, especially to the north and west, which lets you leave urban concerns far behind as you tackle the tough hills. This is a ride for experienced cyclists who want a fun, challenging workout along quiet, pretty rural roads. Most of the route is under heavy foliage, which provides nice shade in summer and beautiful colors in autumn.

The route begins at the Lake McDonough Recreation Area, a great spot to cool off after you're through riding. It's a tricky start; you'll turn uphill onto Route 219, then left to get across the dam. Some nice vantage points lie along Saville Dam, with views of the reservoir on the right and Lake McDonough on the left.

Turn right after the reservoir up a steep, bumpy, uneven side road to

toiling up the steep hill at the northern end of the reservoir

start the circuit around the reservoir. The hill-climbing begins with one big one and then a series of smaller ones, as you ride along this leafy, largely undeveloped road. As you reach the small residential village of West Hartland, you get a break with rolling hills, before one more big climb at Mile 5. Still more rolling hills take you along the northwest shore, where you'll get occasional views of the ridges to the east and the water below. You'll reach a small layby at Mile 11, where you can sneak a peek at the reservoir and take a break.

Two miles downhill are followed by two miles uphill at the northern end of the reservoir, bringing you into East Hartland. There's a bit more traffic along this eastern side of the reservoir, especially on Route 219. The road has a wide, smooth shoulder, but in late spring when we did the route it was quite sandy. The finish is a very steep long downhill with a dangerous left turn at the end, so check your brakes and don't get carried away with the downhill.

For more information, contact the Metropolitan District Barkhamsted Headquarters, 39 Beach Rock Road, Pleasant Valley, CT 06063, 860/379-3036, website: www.themdc.com/lakemcdonough.htm.

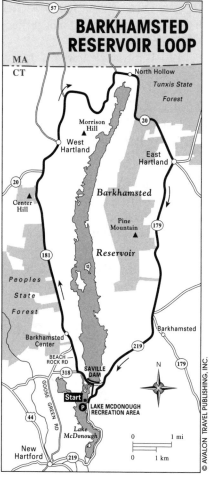

Driving Directions

From Hartford, take Route 44 west for approximately 18 miles to New Hartford. Turn right onto Route 219 and drive 3.6 miles along the shores of Lake McDonough. Turn left into the recreation area. The parking fee is $4; you can park at the boat launch or at the beach, in season. You'll find several beaches with changing rooms and lifeguards, row boat and paddle boat rentals, picnic sites, and nature trails. Supplies are available in New Hartford, but not at any point along the ride. Bike shops are nearby in Canton, Granby, and Simsbury.

Route Directions for Barkhamsted Reservoir Loop

0.0 From the Lake McDonough Recreation Area entrance road, turn LEFT onto Route 219.

0.4 LEFT at triangle toward dam, and immediate LEFT onto Route 318 to go across dam.

1.3 RIGHT onto Beach Rock Road (unmarked).

2.0 Bear RIGHT onto Route 181.

7.2 Continue STRAIGHT through intersection onto Route 20.

15.9 At stop sign, take a RIGHT and an immediate LEFT onto Route 179 (South Street) in East Hartland.

20.4 Stay to the RIGHT at intersection to continue on Route 219 (Route 179 veers to left).

23.0 LEFT turn at junction to stay on Route 219. (Caution: This is an extremely difficult intersection and turn. Come to a complete stop before turning.)

23.6 RIGHT to return to Lake McDonough Recreation Area.

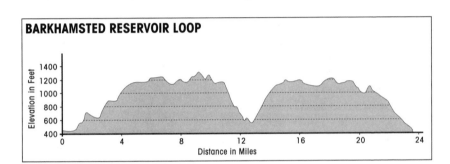

3 SOAPSTONE MOUNTAIN RIDE-AROUND

Shenipsit State Forest, Ellington

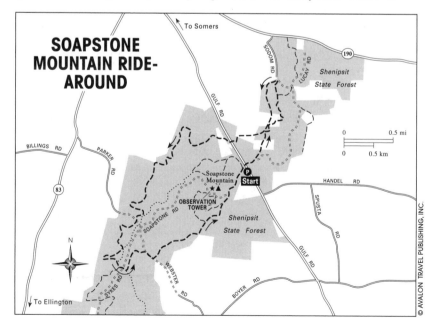

dirt and fire roads, single-track, double-track

Total distance: 7.5 miles   **Riding time:** 1.5–2 hours

Difficulty: 4   **Elevation gain:** 1,030 feet

Shenipsit State Forest has long been a favorite of mountain bike riders in northeastern Connecticut because of its well-developed trail system and extremely technical trail surface. The 6,000-acre forest lies within three towns, Somers, Ellington, and Stafford Springs. Overall the trails within the park are very hilly, rocky, and rooty—making for some fairly difficult riding.

The forest is closely identified with Soapstone Mountain, which is in the southwestern section and peaks at just over 1,000 feet. Some trails lead to the top, but all are too steep to be ridden up; riding down the trails from the top is best left to expert riders. Useful for orientation, Gulf Road splits the forest in two sections—most of the forest is southwest of Gulf Road; the rest is to the northeast.

One nice feature at Shenipsit is the abundant dirt roads for convenient exit points if necessary. It may be easy to get lost on the many trails within the

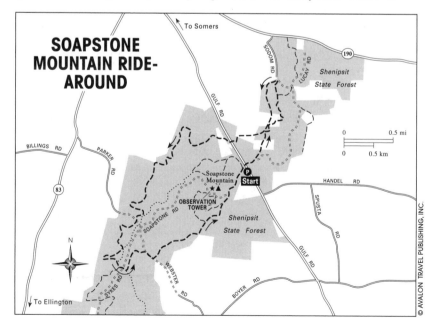

park, but the dirt roads provide frequent reminders of where you are. The map available from the Connecticut Department of Environmental Protection has been recently updated and now includes many of the trails within the park. As in all Connecticut State Parks and Forests, riding mountain bikes is prohibited on single-track blue-blazed trails. Mountain biking is allowed on certain parts of the blue trail only where it converges with other trails.

The route starts off by crossing Gulf Road; you'll ride down a dirt road, passing a scenic pond on the right. It is not uncommon to see blue herons fishing in the pond. The fun begins as you climb and descend some excellent single-track and double-track trails through the white pine stands on the northeast side of the forest.

After crossing Gulf Road again, back into the mainly hardwood-forested southwestern side, you travel along the yellow diamond trial. The trail is mainly a fire road with some double- and single-track sections. Don't be fooled by the width of the trail; it is a very hilly, technical ride with a lot of rocks, roots, and trees for which Shenipsit is famous.

The route continues with the rolling single-track of the white trail, again littered with rocks, roots, and logs. It ends with a fast ride down the paved road to drop you back at the parking lot. For an added challenge try taking a left on the paved road up to the observation deck on top of Soapstone Mountain.

Trails can be very muddy in the early spring, so it's best to avoid riding before the first week of May. In the fall, be aware that hunting is allowed in the park, though not on Sunday. For more information, contact Shenipsit State Forest, 166 Chestnut Hill Road, Stafford Springs, CT 06076, 860/684-3430, website: www.dep.state.ct.us/stateparks/forests/ctforests .htm#Shenipsit.

Driving Directions
From points west and south, take Route 84 east to Exit 67 and take a left off the exit onto Route 31. From points east and north, take Route 84 west to Exit 67 and take a right off the exit onto Route 31. At the first light, turn right onto Route 30. At the second stoplight, turn left to stay on Route 30/Crystal Lake Road. Drive 3.5 miles and turn left onto Burbank Road, which becomes Gulf Road. Drive 2.8 miles and look for the parking lot on your left. There are outhouses but no other facilities at the state forest. Supplies are available in Rockville. Bike shops can be found in South Windsor, Vernon, and Manchester.

Route Directions for Soapstone Mountain Ride-Around
0.0 Start from parking lot, cross Gulf Road, and ride on dirt road.
0.1 LEFT onto blue trail.

0.5 RIGHT onto yellow diamond trail.
1.2 LEFT U-turn onto blue/white trail.
1.9 RIGHT onto yellow diamond trail.
2.2 RIGHT onto unmarked trail that leads to Gulf Road. After crossing Gulf Road, follow yellow diamond trail.
5.1 (Caution! Dangerous descent on washed-out trail.)
5.3 Yellow diamond trail goes right; follow blue trail STRAIGHT ahead to the dirt road and cross dirt road.
5.4 LEFT after climbing large rock.
5.5 LEFT onto white trail.
5.6 RIGHT at the end of white trail onto dirt road.
5.7 LEFT onto white trail (you'll see some yellow diamond markers).
6.1 White trail goes left; go STRAIGHT onto unmarked trail.
6.4 LEFT to continue climbing.
6.6 RIGHT onto paved road.
7.5 Return to parking lot.

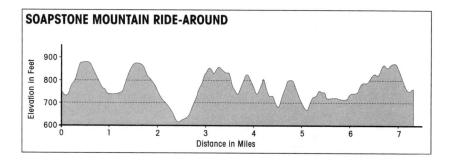

SOAPSTONE MOUNTAIN RIDE-AROUND

4 BREAKNECK POND LOOP

Bigelow Hollow State Park, Union

dirt and fire roads

Total distance: 7 miles

Difficulty: 2

Riding time: 1–1.5 hours

Elevation gain: 365 feet

Bigelow Hollow State Park, along with adjacent Nipmuck State Forest, encompasses more than 9,000 acres, all lying entirely within Union, the state's smallest town. The beauty of Bigelow Hollow is hard to overstate. The park is forested largely by hemlock and white pine, so there is a dense and low canopy year-round. Plenty of hilly, very technical single-track trails will require even the best biker to spend some time pushing his or her bike because of the steep technical climbs.

Bigelow is perhaps best known in the area as a place where people get lost. In the past, it was not uncommon to read of hikers and bikers spending the night in the woods after getting turned around on one of the many similar-looking dirt roads. The state has taken strides to reduce this problem by clearly marking trails and developing a detailed map of the area.

riding the rocks on the shores of Breakneck Pond

The park, as evidenced by its abundant ponds, has a very high water table. Riding there means you are definitely going to have to ride through, or walk around, some water and mud. Through the years, some alternatives have been built with materials at hand (mostly logs), making for some interesting water crossings. The abundant water means that in the summer there are plenty of mosquitoes and deer flies—bring your bug spray!

This route follows the dirt and fire roads around the shoreline of Breakneck Pond. While it is a relatively easy ride, there are some difficult parts where the road is washed out and covered in rolling rocks. As you ride along the roads there are many opportunities to take short side trips to the pond's edge. It is truly a magical ride in the fall when the leaves are showing off their brightest colors and reflecting in the water.

Start off at the dirt parking lot overlooking Bigelow Pond and continue around Breakneck Pond. The ride out to the turning point is mostly flat on dirt roads. At the apex of the ride, the trail dips briefly into Massachusetts (look for the stone monument on the right-hand side of the trail).

The return route is somewhat more hilly and technical, though it is still fairly easy. Several water crossings can be 2 or 3 feet deep at times, especially in spring. The logs across the water give another option for those who don't want to get wet. Finish the ride along the same dirt roads you came in on.

BREAKNECK POND LOOP

If you're riding in the fall, remember that hunting is allowed in the park, though Connecticut state law prohibits hunting on Sunday. In the summer, a dip in crystal-clear Mashapaug Pond is an excellent way to end a warm ride. On summer weekends the park can get quite busy with boaters and swimmers, though once you leave the parking and swimming areas, it's likely you will encounter very few, if any, other people.

For more information, contact Bigelow Hollow State Park, c/o Shenipsit State Forest, 166 Chestnut Hill Road, Stafford Springs, CT 06076, 860/684-3430, website: http://dep.state.ct.us/stateparks/parks/bigelow.htm.

Driving Directions

From points west and south, take Route 84 east to Exit 73 and take a right onto Route 190. From points east and north, take Route 84 west to Exit 73 and take a left off the exit onto Route 190. Follow 190 east for 3 miles, and turn right onto Route 171. Drive 1.4 miles to Bigelow Hollow State Park; the entrance is on the left. Follow the access road .6 mile to the parking lot on the left. A parking fee, on weekends only, is $10 for nonresidents and $7 for Connecticut residents. The park has picnic tables and outhouses. Bike shops can be found in Putnam.

Route Directions for Breakneck Pond Loop

0.0 Take a LEFT out of the parking lot on the paved road and take the first RIGHT onto the dirt road behind the park building onto Chateau Road.

0.3 LEFT onto Park Road.

1.3 RIGHT onto Snowsled Trail.

2.8 Stay to the LEFT at junction.

3.3 At the end of Breakneck Pond, turn LEFT onto Cat Rocks Road.

4.7 Go LEFT.

5.0 Go LEFT onto Breakneck Hill Road.

5.2 Stay LEFT at fork to remain on Breakneck Hill Road. (Danger—washed out road.)

5.7 RIGHT to return to Park Road.

6.7 RIGHT onto Chateau Road.

7.0 Take LEFT onto paved road. The parking lot is on the right.

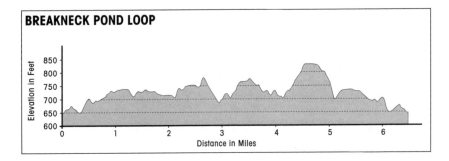

BREAKNECK POND LOOP

5 QUIET CORNER LOOP

Eastford and Pomfret

 paved roads with moderate to minimal traffic

Total distance: 29.3 miles

Difficulty: 4

Riding time: 2.5–3 hours

Elevation gain: 1,900 feet

Dubbed "the Quiet Corner," the northeast section of Connecticut is said to be the least developed and most rural part of the state, the only dark spot in nighttime satellite images from Washington, D.C. to Boston. There are plenty of backcountry roads and small villages to explore. This route, with one killer hill and lots of smaller ones, is a challenging road ride with nice scenery and a few great stopping points along the way.

Starting from Natchaug State Forest, where you can begin the ride right from the campground here, there's a short stretch on busy Route 198. Once you cross Route 44, reach Eastford, and turn right, you'll be on smooth, wide empty roads passing big open fields and farmlands. A short stretch on Route 171 can also see fast-moving cars before you turn uphill to ride along a ridge above Wappaquasset Pond. Passing some modest lakeside houses, you'll soon return to the big open fields and farmlands, with some long, lovely vistas of the Pomfret hills. As you cross Route 244,

riding past a sheep farm on Quasset Road in Pomfret

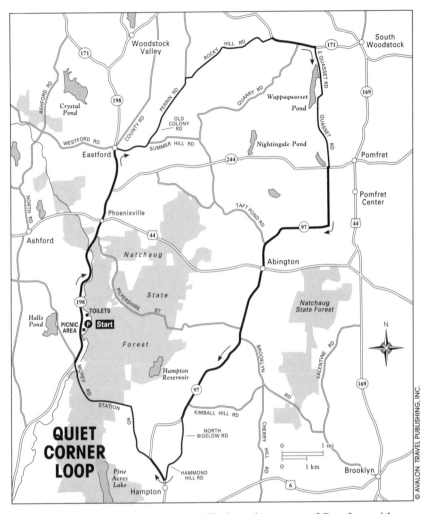

if you want a side trip, ride left—uphill—into the center of Pomfret, with two private schools, a few restaurants including the atmospheric Vanilla Bean Cafe (serving lunch, dinner, desserts, and beverages, as well as inviting outdoor picnic tables), and an interesting herb shop.

Route 97 is hilly, horsy countryside. As you pass Abington, you'll see a lovely meetinghouse, erected in 1751, which claims to be the oldest standing meetinghouse in the country. The next attraction is the We-Li-Kit farm, where the milking center is a stone's throw from the ice-cream stand; rich ice cream is made fresh daily in ordinary as well as custom flavors such as Holstein, Guernsey Cookie, and Road Kill Ripple. You might want to fortify yourself, because the route's killer hill is coming up. Hammond Hill Road might be called Hammer Hill as it's a half mile of a sharp, steep climb.

Station Road has a few hills of its own, but it's a narrow, pretty country lane with some interesting houses and cemeteries to look at. Grit your teeth for the last 2 miles along busy Route 198, past several riverside campgrounds, to return to Natchaug State Forest.

For more information, contact Natchaug State Forest, c/o Mashamoquet Brook State Park, RFD #1, Wolf Den Road, Pomfret Center, CT 06259, 860/ 928-6121, website: www.dep.state.ct.us/stateparks/forests/ natchaug.htm. For information on the region, contact the Quiet Corner tourist office, 107 Providence Street, Putnam, CT 06260, 860/779-6383 or 888/628-1228, website: www.ctquietcorner.org.

Driving Directions

From Putnam and points east, take Route 44 west to Route 198 in Phoenixville. Take a left onto Route 198 and drive approximately 2.5 miles. Turn left at the forest entrance. From Hartford and points west, take Route 84 east to Exit 69 and turn right onto Route 74. Go east on Route 74 until it ends, then go left onto Route 44 east. Drive approximately 5 miles and turn right onto Route 198 south. Drive 2.5 miles and turn left at the forest entrance. Natchaug State Forest, popular with those troutfishing the Natchaug River, has free parking, riverside picnic tables, and portable toilets. Supplies are available in Phoenixville, Pomfret, and Putnam, and the nearest bike shops are in Putnam.

Route Directions for Quiet Corner Loop

0.0 From parking area, ride out the access road and turn RIGHT onto Route 198.

2.5 At flashing red lights and intersection with Route 44, go STRAIGHT, bearing slightly to the left, to continue on Route 198. *Supplies available at Corner Market general store.*

4.0 RIGHT on Old Colony Road in Eastford.

5.0 Continue STRAIGHT on Old Colony Road (which becomes Perrin Road).

7.0 RIGHT onto Rocky Hill Road at four-way intersection.

9.7 RIGHT onto Route 171.

10.8 RIGHT onto East Quasset Road (which becomes Quasset Road).

14.0 RIGHT then immediate LEFT onto Route 97. *An optional side trip is to turn left onto Route 244/97 and ride .7 miles into the pretty center of Pomfret. The excellent Vanilla Bean Cafe, on the left, has outdoor picnic tables and is a popular meeting spot for bicyclists and motorcyclists.*

15.4 RIGHT at stop sign and T-junction, staying on Route 97.

17.7 STRAIGHT at traffic light and intersection with Route 44.

18.8 *The popular We-Li-Kit Farm Ice Cream Stand, on the left, is open April–November.*

22.1 LEFT onto North Bigelow Road.

22.9 RIGHT onto Hammond Hill Road.

23.8 RIGHT onto Route 97.

24.5 LEFT onto Station Road (which becomes Morey Road).

27.8 Bear LEFT and cross river.

28.1 RIGHT onto Route 198.

29.3 RIGHT to return to Natchaug State Forest parking area.

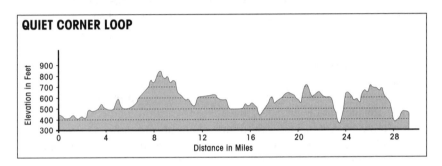

6 LAKE WARAMAUG LOOPS
New Preston

6A (Lakeside Loop)

 paved roads with minimal traffic

Total distance: 8 miles

Difficulty: 2

Riding time: 1 hour

Elevation gain: 160 feet

6B (Hills and Hollows Loop)

 paved roads with minimal traffic

Total distance: 20.2 miles

Difficulty: 3

Riding time: 2 hours

Elevation gain: 1,195 feet

This lovely little lake makes a great biking spot for riders of all abilities. Beginners can do a scenic loop around the tree-lined lake, admiring the gracious summer homes with landscaped lawns and the smooth surface of the lake, interrupted only by the dip of a rowing oar (nearby prep schools practice here). Those who want a longer, hillier ride can explore the backcountry roads to the northwest, where farm roads give views of the ridges that rise from this basin.

The routes begin in Lake Waramaug State Park at the northwest tip of the lake. If you're camping at the state park, you can begin the routes from the campground. Riding clockwise gives you the best views of the lake for Route A. Both West Shore Road and North Shore Road are twisty and narrow, and a biker definitely impedes traffic, so be aware of cars. Though the lake is lined mainly with tasteful residences, there are a golf course, a vineyard, and a few inns as well.

Route B takes you away from the lake on Route 45. There's a tricky intersection to get onto Route 341, where traffic can be moderate and fast-moving. Ride in the smooth, wide shoulder past marshland and some fine open views. The left turn onto Kent Hollow Road is easy to miss; the road narrows at the top of a hill and the left is on the way down.

Once you're on Kent Hollow Road, the traffic fades to nothing. Some of the pavement is uneven along the next few miles, but the scenery is beautiful—some rolling hills, some open fields and farmlands, a stretch of wild, undeveloped land, and views of mountains and valleys in the distance.

You face a long hill to climb as you head up the New Preston Hill Road, with a sweet little river valley running on the left. The hilltop is graced with a distinctive stone church, marking the start of a long, smooth, gorgeous 2-mile downhill past horse farms into the village of New Preston. Check out the waterfall and antique shops in this former grist mill town before heading up Route 45 back to the lake.

For more information, contact Lake Waramaug State Park, 30 Lake Waramaug Road, New Preston, CT 06777, 860/868-0220, website: www.dep.state .ct.us/stateparks/parks/lake-waramaug.htm.

the distinctive stone Hill Church atop New Preston Hill Road

Driving Directions

From Litchfield and points east, take Route 202 west to New Preston. From New Milford and points west, take Route 202 east to New Preston. Once in New Preston, turn north onto Route 45 and drive .5 mile. Turn left at the intersection onto West Shore Road and drive 3.9 miles. Turn left into Lake Waramaug State Park. Supplies are available in Kent, Bantam, or New Milford. New Preston has one restaurant, but no other supplies are available there or along the route. The state park has a summer-only campground with showers and a concession stand, pay phones, picnic areas, restrooms, and a small sandy beach. On weekends and holidays, the parking fee is $7 for residents and $10 for nonresidents. The nearest bike shop is in New Milford.

Route Directions for Lake Waramaug Loops 6A (Lakeside Loop)

0.0 From state park entrance road, turn LEFT onto West Shore Road.
0.2 Bear RIGHT onto North Shore Road.
2.5 RIGHT onto Route 45.

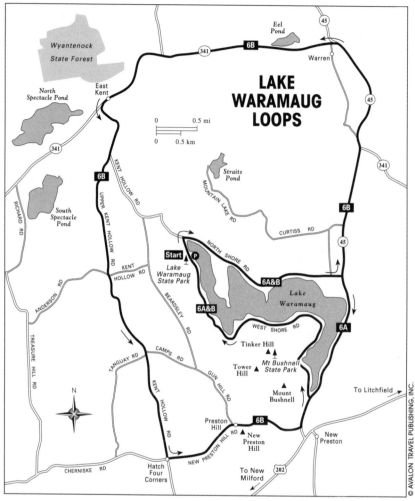

LAKE
WARAMAUG
LOOPS

4.1 RIGHT onto West Shore Road.

8.0 LEFT to return to Lake Waramaug State Park.

Route Directions for 6B (Hills and Hollows Loop)

0.0 From state park entrance road, turn LEFT onto West Shore Road.

0.2 Bear RIGHT onto North Shore Road.

2.5 LEFT onto Route 45.

4.1 LEFT at stop sign onto Route 341.

5.6 Continue STRAIGHT on Route 341 in Warren.

9.0 LEFT onto Kent Hollow Road.

9.8 RIGHT at fork onto Upper Kent Hollow Road.

11.4 At intersection, take a LEFT then immediate RIGHT onto Kent Hollow Road.
13.9 LEFT onto New Preston Hill Road.
15.9 LEFT at junction onto Route 45 in New Preston.
16.3 LEFT onto West Shore Road at intersection.
20.2 LEFT to return to Lake Waramaug State Park.

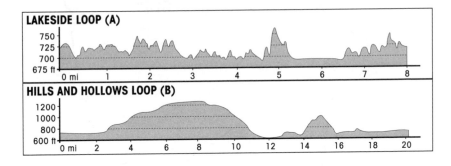

7 WEST HARTFORD RESERVOIRS LOOP

West Hartford

 paved bike paths, fire roads, single-track

Total distance: 8.6 miles

Difficulty: 2

Riding time: 1.5–2 hours

Elevation gain: 560 feet

Right smack in the middle of the state, next to the busy capital of Hartford, a fun trail system offers a quick getaway from the city. The West Hartford Reservoirs, which is actually four active reservoirs and two water-treatment facilities all in one spot, is run by the Metropolitan District Commission (MDC), which manages the water supply for Hartford and the surrounding towns.

This is the place to bring the family as there is a mix of roads and paths both paved and gravel, as well as a good amount of single-track.

The single-track here is twisty, turny, and fun, and it is perfect for novice to intermediate mountain bikers. It has no huge drops and nothing extremely technical, but it's interesting enough to be fun, and more advanced riders can still get a great workout.

The route starts out on a paved path that has clearly marked pedestrian and bike lanes. You will be heading out on a clockwise circuit around the reservoirs. A notice board at the trailhead has a map posted; sometimes trail maps are available there, sometimes not (there are free brochures and $2 trail maps). The bike path is one-way and is clearly marked with signs and arrows. You will pass some grass-covered earthen dikes on your left and soon come to a yellow gate. Pass through the gate and the path begins to climb to the reservoirs.

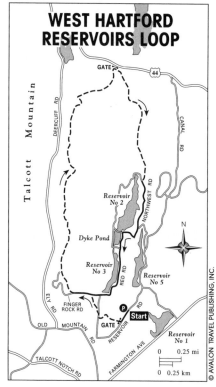

WEST HARTFORD RESERVOIRS LOOP

You'll come to a dam at the south end of Reservoir 3. There you want to take a sharp left, leaving the main path. Take a right onto the powder-blue-blazed trail. Follow the blue arrow left after the steepest part of the hill. Take a left-hand fork, still following the blue. Look sharp for an unmarked trail on your left. Take this for some sweet, fun single-track. You are on the very edge of the MDC land and will see boundary signs on some of the trees. Eventually the trail joins back with the blue-blazed trail and heads downhill. You cross a stream at a point where the trail turns right, and when you reach the bottom of the hill, the trail turns left (north). After a shortish flat blast you will come to a major road and a green gate. Another reservoir and many more miles of trails lie across that road, but for this ride we're not going to cross it.

Follow the trail right here through a grassy area and along the top of a dike. It soon turns back into the woods and begins to climb. The trail finds the eastern border and plays around in the woods behind some houses. Just as the trail seems to be about to lead you into someone's backyard, take a sharp right onto a paved path. In another minute you will be riding along the edge of the reservoir headed south. Follow the bike lane back to the parking area.

For more information, contact the West Hartford Reservoirs, 1420 Farmington Avenue, West Hartford, CT 06107 860/313-0031, website: www.themdc.com.

Driving Directions

From points east or west, take Route 84 to Exit 39. Turn right at the first light onto Route 4 (Farmington Avenue). Drive 2.2 miles and turn left into the MDC entrance. Follow the access road to a large gravel parking lot; parking is free. There are portable toilets at the parking lot. Supplies are available in West Hartford and Farmington; there are bike shops in Farmington and Bloomfield.

Route Directions for West Hartford Reservoirs Loop

0.0 Leave parking area and follow paved bike lane to yellow gate.
0.4 STRAIGHT through gate.
1.1 LEFT at dam at south end of reservoir.
1.5 RIGHT onto blue trail, leaving pavement.
1.8 LEFT at top of steep hill.
2.0 LEFT at fork.
2.3 LEFT onto single-track (unmarked).
4.5 RIGHT on trail, at main road.
6.8 RIGHT onto paved path.

7.5 LEFT at dam at south end of reservoir; retrace route.
8.6 Return to parking lot.

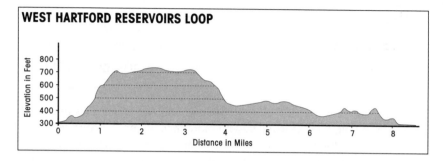

WEST HARTFORD RESERVOIRS LOOP

SLICK ROCK SCRAMBLE
Case Mountain, Glastonbury

single-track, double-track, fire roads

Total distance: 11.4 miles

Difficulty: 5

Riding time: 2–2.5 hours

Elevation gain: 780 feet

Case Mountain is one of the most popular mountain biking sites in central Connecticut, and it's no wonder, with more than 20 miles of very technical, mostly single-track trails to choose from. Because of the popularity of Case, it can get quite busy on weekends with nice weather. It's also a popular hiking spot, and as always a little courtesy toward other trail users goes a long way to keep multiuse trails open.

Case Mountain, as local riders call it, is actually land from three different areas—Birch Mountain, Case Mountain, and Manchester Water Company land. The Case Mountain area is managed by the town of Manchester and all trails are open to mountain biking. From the top of Case Mountain on the Manchester side, at an elevation of 774 feet, there is a spectacular view of downtown Hartford and the surrounding area. Trail maintenance by the mountain bike community here has kept most trails within the system in pretty good shape, and some of the trails have been built specifically with mountain biking in mind. Once you are on Case Mountain proper, there is a seemingly unending network of trails.

a rocky descent at Case Mountain

Having a guide familiar with the area is a definite advantage to get to the best trails.

The trails at Case are extremely technical, littered with rocks small and large. The terrain is very hilly with some lung-busting climbs and nice long descents. A beginner rider will be able to walk the more difficult sections, but this is a place best enjoyed by intermediate and above riders. The streams crossed along the way are fed largely by runoff, so their intensity varies wildly throughout the year. During the early spring the streams can be quite challenging to cross—even if you walk them. In the late summer, however, most of the streams are barely running at all and are very easy to cross.

The route starts with an almost 3-mile-long descent on classic swoopy New England single-track, eventually landing on the shores of scenic Buckingham Reservoir. Although the water company is tolerant of mountain bike usage on its property, it would not take much to change its mind, so tread lightly to ensure continued access to this section.

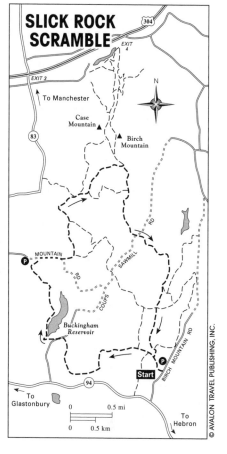

The trail progresses through hardwood forest, crossing the power-line access road several times. After doing some moderate climbing through the woods you come upon a monster climb of three sections of "slick rock." Making it to the top without dabbing is a goal that many in the area strive to hit. After climbing the third section of slick rock you will be at a spectacular lookout spot under a canopy of white pines. The ride finishes with a roller-coaster ride out to the power lines, an incredibly steep and technical descent, and finally a climb back up the trail you started on.

Driving Directions

From Hartford, take Route 84 to Exit 4 and take Route 2 east. Drive approximately 8 miles and take Exit 8. Take a left off the exit onto Hebron Avenue, Route 94. Drive 6.8 miles on Hebron Avenue and turn left onto

Birch Mountain Road at the top of the hill. Drive about .25 mile and look for the parking lot on the right, next to the radio towers. There are several other places to park to start a ride at Case Mountain. Many riders start at the abandoned Girl Scout camp parking lot in Manchester. Supplies and bike shops are available in Glastonbury and Manchester.

Route Directions for Slick Rock Scramble

0.0 RIGHT out of dirt parking lot.
0.1 LEFT onto blue/red single-track.
0.4 LEFT onto fire road after crossing under power lines.
0.7 LEFT onto single-track.
1.7 Take the RIGHT fork in the trail.
2.6 LEFT onto dirt road, then immediate RIGHT onto single-track.
2.9 Cross log bridge, STRAIGHT across at top of the hill.
3.4 At four-way intersection go STRAIGHT.
3.8 LEFT at T in the trail.
4.3 RIGHT onto fire road, under power lines.
4.6 LEFT onto single-track (easy to miss).
4.9 RIGHT onto single-track.
5.4 LEFT at three-way intersection.
6.2 RIGHT onto fire road.
6.5 RIGHT onto hairpin to fire road.
6.9 RIGHT onto yellow single-track.
7.6 RIGHT onto blue single-track. (To get to the summit take a LEFT on blue here, then a LEFT on yellow.)
10.0 *Scenic lookout spot.*
10.7 Blue veers RIGHT.
10.8 LEFT at the power lines.
11.0 RIGHT onto blue/red single-track (crossing back under power lines).
11.3 RIGHT onto road.
11.4 Return to parking lot on left.

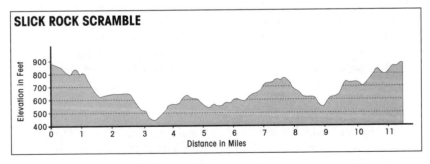

9 AIR LINE STATE PARK TRAIL

East Hampton to Hebron

  stone dust bike path

Total distance: 21.4 miles round-trip with shorter options

Riding time: 2–2.5 hours

Difficulty: 1   **Elevation gain:** 1,315 feet

Once upon a time, a railway ran from Boston to New York in almost a straight line. In the years 1873–1959, trains carried passengers along the Air Line at high speeds through Massachusetts and Connecticut. But the trains ceased to run, the railway bed was abandoned, and eventually the line was deeded to the state's Department of Environmental Protection. The story has a happy ending, because now it is one of the region's loveliest multiuse trails, crossing high over rivers, giving dramatic views of lush countryside, and passing through areas rich with wildlife.

The state is developing the trail into two state parks, the Air Line North (from Putnam to Windham) and Air Line South (from Windham to East Hampton). Not all the sections are completed, and the best-developed stretch is about 10 miles between East Hampton and Hebron. Here, the level trail is covered with stone dust and is suitable for road or mountain

starting at the Air Line Rail Trail in East Hampton

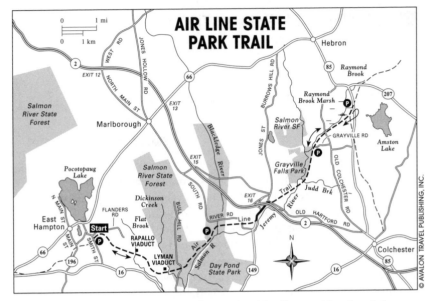

bikes, wheelchairs, horses, and walkers. It's wide, flat, and level and there are benches and picnic tables along the way as well as lots of interesting sights—adding up to a great family outing. Don't let the elevation gain fool you; the climbing is so gradual that you will hardly notice it.

Starting in East Hampton, you'll quickly come to two viaducts, first Rapallo and then Lyman. These former viaducts drop off steeply on either side and give you great unobstructed views of rolling hills and lush green valleys. Built in 1873, the Lyman Viaduct was once a 1,000-plus-foot-long iron trestle bridge that loomed 137 feet above Dickinson Creek.

You'll pass through Salmon River State Forest, where the terrain drops steeply off to the right to a river bed. The total lack of development makes you feel you are deep in the woods. A new wooden bridge takes you high above Blackledge River. A short unfinished section means a .2-mile detour on the road, passing underneath Route 2, to return to the trail. Next you'll cross a beautiful bridge over the Jeremy River and then over the fast-flowing, waterfall-forming Judd Brook before coming to Grayville Road. To view waterfalls and have a picnic, take a side trip into Grayville Falls Park by turning left onto Grayville Road and riding about .2 mile to the park entrance.

After crossing Old Colchester Road, you'll come to wonderful Raymond Brook Marsh, a veritable trove of flora and fauna. In late spring, for example, you might see lady slipper orchids or dwarf ginseng, orioles or warblers, Canada geese, beavers, deer, or painted turtles.

Air Line trail maps and brochures can be picked up at the Town Office buildings in East Hampton and Hebron. The map boxes at the trailheads may be empty. For more information, contact the Department of Environmental Protection Eastern District Headquarters, 209 Hebron Road, Marlborough, CT 06447, 860/295-9523. The best website for trail information is http://pages.cthome.net/mbartel/ARRhome.htm.

Driving Directions
From Hartford and points west, or Norwich and points east, take Route 2 to Marlborough and take Exit 13 to Route 66 west. Follow Route 66 through East Hampton and turn left onto Lakeview Street (Route 196). Turn left onto Flanders Road, then right onto Smith Street. Drive .2 mile on Smith Street and turn left into the trailhead parking lot. No facilities are along the trail. Supplies are available in East Hampton, Hebron, and Colchester, and you'll find bike shops in Hebron and Colchester.

Route Directions for Air Line State Park Trail
0.0 Start at trailhead in East Hampton.
1.4 Cross Rapallo Viaduct.
2.5 Cross Lyman Viaduct.
3.0 Cross Bull Hill Road. *Access to trail and parking lot on Bull Hill Road.*
5.4 Cross River Road.
5.9 Cross Route 149.
6.5 Arrive at Park-and-Ride parking lot. RIGHT out of lot onto Route 149. (If you are on a mountain bike, you can ride along the short unfinished section of the trail.)
6.6 RIGHT onto Old Hartford Road. *Access to trail and parking lots on Old Hartford Road.*
6.7 LEFT at parking area to resume on trail.
8.9 Cross Grayville Road.
9.5 Cross Old Colchester Road.
10.0 Pass Raymond Brook Marsh.
10.7 Arrive at Route 85 parking lot and trailhead. TURN AROUND.
21.4 Return to East Hampton trailhead parking lot.

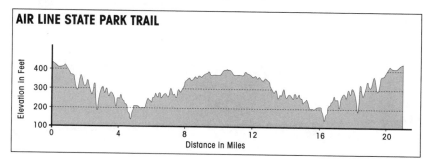

AIR LINE STATE PARK TRAIL

HUNTINGTON SAMPLER
Collis P. Huntington State Park, Redding

carriage roads, single-track

Total distance: 7.9 miles

Difficulty: 3

Riding time: 1–1.5 hours

Elevation gain: 615 feet

A little more than an hour's drive from New York City, the quiet green woods and pristine ponds of southwestern Connecticut's Huntington Park are a welcome escape and a great place to ride.

Following the route laid out here, you will be riding an almost equal mix of single-track and carriage roads. From the main parking area off Sunset Hill Road, the ride begins with a blast down a grassy hill. At the bottom of the hill go left for about 50 yards and take a right onto the single-track at the blue blaze. This short but challenging and fun section dumps you on a dirt carriage road, where you continue up a slight incline for about .5 mile.

Look for the next section of single-track opening on your right. Eventually you will end up back on the carriage road. Stay right and hang on for a bumpy descent on the blue perimeter road. The road winds downhill, following a stream on the right while several granite outcroppings crowd the trail to the left. Then it's time to pay for your fun with a long climb up the side of the ridge.

Mountain bikers use these teeter-totters and bridges for fun stunts.

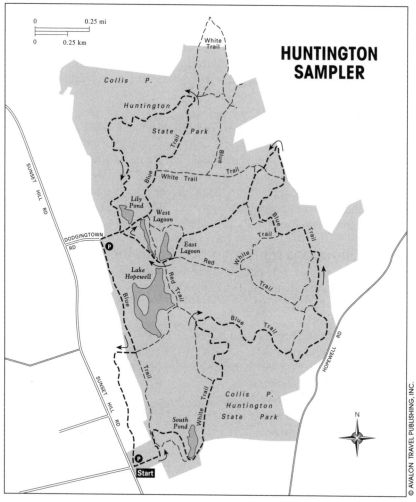

At the top of the climb you will snake between two ponds. Go straight across the wooden bridge and up just a bit more. Go right on a broken up, paved track called Dodgintown Road. The road is very short and at its end is an extensive network of single-track, where a little exploration will pay off with plenty of tight, twisty, rocky, and rooty fun. There are trails with some fairly sketchy drops, ramps, a teeter-totter, and at least one bridge across which all but the best riders will dismount and walk. Some trails lead to private property, so when you see the No Trespassing signs, turn around.

All trails eventually lead back to Dodgintown Road. At the top of the road go left through a small dirt parking area and follow the carriage road past some stables. Look to the right for a mile-long stretch of smooth, rolling single-track through a beautiful meadow that will take you right back to where you began the ride.

For more information, contact Collis P. Huntington State Park, c/o Putnam Memorial State Park, 492 Black Rock Turnpike, Redding, CT 06896, 203/938-2285, website: www.dep.state.ct.us/stateparks/parks/huntington.htm.

Driving Directions

From Danbury and Route 84, take Exit 5 to Route 53 south. Drive 3.4 miles. At the junction of Route 53 and Route 302, take Route 302 east, through Bethel, for 1.6 miles. Turn right onto Route 58 south and drive 4.6 miles. Turn left onto Sunset Hill Road. Collis P. Huntington State Park is .8 mile on the right. There is no fee, the park is open 8 A.M.–sunset, and there are outhouses but no other facilities. Supplies are available in Bethel, and there are bike shops in Bethel and Danbury.

Route Directions for Huntington Sampler

0.0 From parking lot, ride past notice board onto trail.
0.1 LEFT and immediate RIGHT at blue blaze.
0.7 RIGHT onto single-track.
1.3 RIGHT at fork.
1.4 RIGHT onto carriage road and immediate RIGHT at fork in carriage road.
2.0 RIGHT at blue blaze.
2.4 LEFT at fork. (You will be riding straight between two ponds, Lake Hopewell and East Lagoon.)
3.8 RIGHT at Dodgintown Road.
4.1 LEFT on blue trail at the end of the road.
4.7 LEFT onto single-track.
6.5 RIGHT onto Dodgintown Road.
6.8 LEFT onto carriage road at parking area.
7.3 RIGHT on trail through meadow.
7.9 Return to main parking lot.

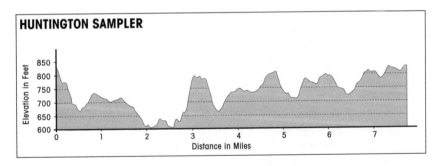

11 PEQUONNOCK RIVER VALLEY RIDE

Trumbull

11A (Rail Trail Out and Back)

unpaved rail trail

Total distance: 5.8 miles

Difficulty: 2

Riding time: 1.5–2 hours

Elevation gain: 195 feet

11B (Indian Ledge Loop)

unpaved rail trail, single-track

Total distance: 7.2 miles

Difficulty: 4

Riding time: 1.5–2 hours

Elevation gain: 355 feet

Mountain bikers in this crowded corner of southwest Connecticut know how to find great spots tucked in where you might not expect them. Just north of busy Bridgeport, a trail system along the Pequonnock River is confined to a scenic, narrow river valley and gorge. An unpaved but fairly smooth rail trail runs along the west side of the river, while the east side hides a warren of single-track that can be as technical as any diehard freerider could want.

The old rail bed climbs north along the river gradually for 2.6 uninterrupted miles. The gorge falls away short and steep to your right and along the way are plenty of places to stop and take in views of the river below. You'll come to a gate and the trail briefly becomes a road. Then you cross a major road (Whitney Avenue) and the rail trail picks up again. A sign there tells you that you're in Parlor Rock Park, a former amusement park with not much left to show for it today. The rail trail soon ends at the divided highway, Route 25. For Route A and an easy ride, turn around and retrace your route to the beginning.

For Route B and some challenging single-track, retrace your route to Whitney Avenue. Go left on the road for approximately 50 yards, just across the river, and take the single-track trail to your right (if the road starts climbing you've gone too far). Now you are in for some fun riding. Keep to the double blue- and single blue-blazed trails here, staying as close to the river as possible. There are more side trails than you can shake your water bottle at here, but don't worry about getting lost, because in this relatively narrow, confined area between the highway and the river you can't really lose your bearings for too long. Warning: Some of these trails feature drops and stunts that only expert riders should attempt. Parts of the trails are technical and rugged so you may have to carry for a short section or two.

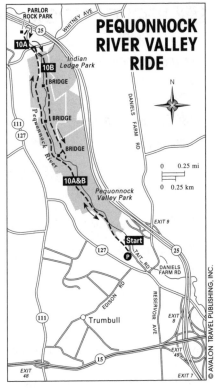

Soon you will come to yet another Trumbull park called Indian Ledge Park. A stream crossing on a wooden bridge is just before the parking area. The trail continues to your right here and works back toward the river. Look for the double blue blaze and follow it left. This is a fun trail that stays close as possible to the riverbank. Typical of Connecticut, it is rocky and rooty—the exact opposite of smooth. You will soon come to another bridge crossing the river so if you've had enough bouncing around this is your chance to escape back to the rail bed.

Persevere and you will find a beautiful rock outcropping overlooking the river. This is the place to take a break, eat your lunch, or just enjoy the rocks and the river. Continuing brings you to a three-way fork in the trail. Stay on the blue blaze, which is the middle trail in the fork. You are now in the bottom of the river valley and it is fairly flat and smooth. After crossing a couple of small streams, the blue trail becmes too rugged to ride; you'll know it because it happens quite suddenly. Backtrack to the three-way fork and follow the left branch to a bridge crossing back to the rail trail. There's a fast blast down the rail trail and your ride is complete.

For more information about the area, visit the Trumbull Historical Society's website: www.trumbullhistory.org/written/prv.shtml; or contact the Trumbull Parks Department, Highway Garage, 366 Church Hill Road, Trumbull, CT 06611, 203/452-5075, website: www.trumbullct.com.

Driving Directions
From points east or west, take Route 15 (the Merrit Parkway) to Exit 49 onto Route 25 north. From Route 95, take Exit 27 to Route 25 north.

From Route 25, take Exit 9 onto Daniels Farm Road. Drive .5 mile and turn right onto Route 127. Drive about 100 yards and turn right onto Tait Road. A small parking area is on the right and the trailhead is just a few yards down Tait Road on your left. Supplies are available in Trumbull and there are bike shops in Monroe and Bridgeport.

Route Directions for Pequonnock River Valley Ride 11A (Rail Trail Out and Back)

0.0 From parking area, start at trailhead on left side of Tait Road and go LEFT through gate onto rail trail.

2.7 Cross Whitney Avenue.

2.9 TURN AROUND and retrace back to start.

5.8 Return to parking area.

Route Directions for 11B (Indian Ledge Loop)

0.0 From parking area, start at trailhead on left side of Tait Road and go LEFT through gate onto rail trail.

2.7 Cross Whitney Avenue.

2.9 TURN AROUND and retrace back to Whitney Avenue.

3.1 LEFT on Whitney Avenue, and take immediate RIGHT onto single-track just across river.

3.5 RIGHT after bridge.

3.8 LEFT at double blue blaze.

4.8 STRAIGHT at three-way fork.

5.4 TURN AROUND where trail deteriorates.

6.0 LEFT at three-way fork to bridge trail and cross bridge.

6.1 LEFT onto rail trail.

7.2 Return to parking area.

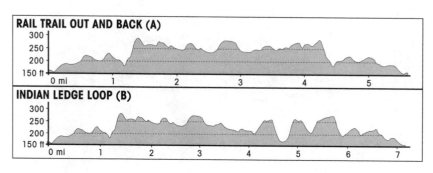

12 WESTWOODS TRAILS
Guilford

double-track, single-track

Total distance: 4.5 miles

Difficulty: 4

Riding time: 1.5–2 hours

Elevation gain: 345 feet

Close to the Connecticut coast, just off I-95, lies a technical maze of trails that many riders call the best technical riding in the state. The Westwoods Trails are full of granite-spined ridges creating lots of steep up-and-down riding, along with some unavoidable hike-a-bike sections. This is not a place for an aerobic, endurance workout, but it is a great opportunity to work on your technical mountain biking skills. It has a mix of single- and double-track; however, much of the double-track is technical and does not ride like a leisurely fire road.

All the trails here are marked by shapes and colors—green rectangle, yellow circle, red triangle, violet circle, and so on, a bit like a game of Twister. This route begins on Green Rectangle trail, which goes from single to double back to single-track with some fun riding and one small stream crossing along the way. The trail has a long climb that is fairly steep and then becomes more gradual as it tops out, eventually leading you to the Moose Hill Road entrance to the trail system.

A blight has forced trail crews to cut down some pine trees at Westwoods.

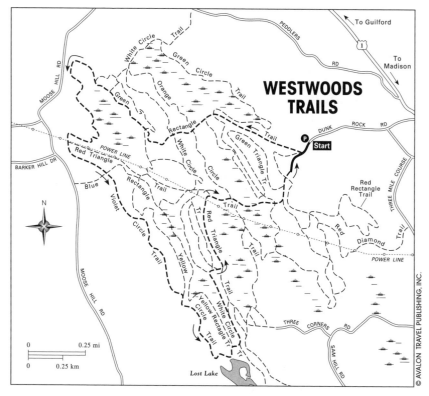

Look to your left here for Violet Circle Trail, a really nice single-track. Though not extremely difficult, it has enough in the way of obstacles to remain interesting. At the bottom of a steep, technical descent, you come to a fork in the trail. Take a right here onto Yellow Circle Trail. You've descended into a gully and now you have to climb back out. Go left up a steep, rocky hike-a-bike section on Yellow Rectangle Trail. You have two more options to climb out if you keep straight, but each is harder than the last.

You will top out on a granite ridge that is great fun to play around on, with a view of Lost Lake below. Several trails intersect here. Take White Circle to a left on Red Triangle. Stay left and it will work you back toward Dunk Rock Road. Just after you cross under a power line, you will come to Blue Rectangle Trail. Go right here and before you know it you're back where you started.

Westwoods covers 1,200 acres with 39 miles of trails crossing and recrossing, and it can get confusing. Trails marked with an X are connectors, so a red X, for example, will connect you to a red trail. Several trailheads touch on area roads, so if you become disoriented, you can always bail out and ride the road back to your starting point.

The Westwoods Trails area is owned in part by the state, the city of Guilford, the Guilford Land Conservation Trust, and private owners. For more information, contact the Guilford Land Conservation Trust, Box 200, Guilford, CT 06437, 203/457-9253, website: www.westwoodstrails.org.

Driving Directions
From points east and west, take Route 95 to Exit 57 and follow Route 1 toward Guilford for .6 mile. Turn right onto Dunk Rock Road and drive .5 mile to the parking area across from Bishop's Pond, where you'll see a trailhead and sign. Several different parking areas allow access to the trails; this ride starts from the Dunk Rock Road area, which is the closest and easiest to find from the interstate. Supplies are available in Guilford; bike shops are in Branford and Clinton.

Route Directions for Westwoods Trails
0.0 From Dunk Rock Road parking lot, ride up Dunk Rock Road.
0.2 RIGHT onto Green Rectangle Trail.
1.5 LEFT onto Violet Circle Trail at Moose Hill Road entrance.
2.4 RIGHT onto Yellow Circle Trail.
2.7 LEFT up Hike-a-Bike onto Yellow Rectangle Trail.
2.8 LEFT onto White Circle Trail.
3.1 LEFT onto Red Triangle.
3.8 RIGHT onto Blue Rectangle Trail.
4.3 LEFT onto Dunk Rock Road.
4.5 Return to parking area.

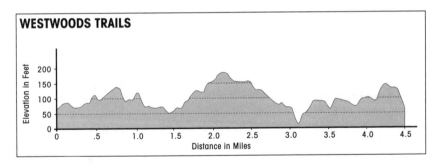

DEVIL'S HOPYARD LOOP

East Haddam

 paved roads with minimal to moderate traffic

Total distance: 27.1 miles
Difficulty: 3

Riding time: 2.5 hours
Elevation gain: 1,680 feet

This ride takes you through a pocket of southern Connecticut that's rich with backcountry roads, rolling hills, brooks, and crumbling stone walls. This might be called an exurban community, far from suburbs but not entirely rural. Whatever you call it, it's lovely road riding with just two major hills to tackle.

The route leaves from Devil's Hopyard State Park (it's worth spending some time at the park, especially to see Chapmans Falls and the curious stone pothole formations; you can also begin the ride right from the campground if you are camping here). You'll begin by exploring some rural, thickly wooded, hilly roads to the north, then head down to do a loop around the southern end of Lake Hayward. You'll encounter some uneven pavement along the lake and then one killer half-mile hill as you climb away from the lake onto Mill Lane.

© MELISSA L. KIM

Chapmans Falls drops about 60 feet over a series of steps. Nearby, perfectly round potholes are a wonder of nature and a testament to the power of streams.

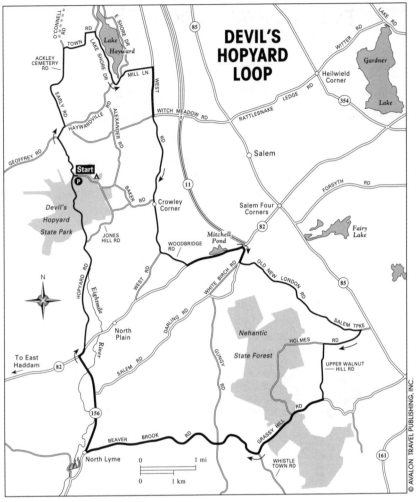

After crossing Route 82, turn onto Darling Road and you'll see Salem Valley Farms. This popular ice-cream stand, open in spring and summer only, makes a great regrouping or rest stop, with picnic tables, a pay phone, large parking area, and, of course, great ice cream. The next stretch is along another rural road. You'll have a nice downhill just before making a sharp right-hand turn onto Holmes Road where there's another tough half-mile hill. The next 5 or 6 miles are a joy, on lovely lanes with smooth surfaces and downhill grades. The bike hugs the curves as you pass stone walls, horses in fields, old cemeteries, and pretty houses.

Turn onto Route 156 and you'll see the library and school in Lyme. Traffic moves a little faster on this scenic highway, taking you through more open countryside with expansive fields and still more horse farms. For the finish, the narrow, winding Hopyard Road mimics the curves and bends of the lovely Eightmile River as you ride in deep shade back to the state park.

For more information, contact Devil's Hopyard State Park, 366 Hopyard Road, East Haddam, CT 06423, 860/873-8566, website: www.dep.state .ct.us/stateparks/parks/devilshopyard.htm

Driving Directions

From the south, take Route 95 to Exit 70 and drive north on Route 156 for approximately 9.5 miles. Turn right onto Route 82 and take the first left onto Hopyard Road, following signs for Devil's Hopyard State Park. Drive 3.5 miles and turn right into the Chapman Falls parking area. From the east, take Route 395 to Norwich and take Exit 80 to Route 82. Drive approximately 13.5 miles and turn right onto Hopyard Road, following signs for Devil's Hopyard State Park. Drive 3.5 miles and turn right into the Chapman Falls parking area (the second entrance to the park). Devil's Hopyard State Park offers picnic areas, outhouses, a campground, pay phone, and free parking. Supplies are available in Salem and East Haddam, but not along the route. A bike shop is nearby in Essex.

Route Directions for Devil's Hopyard Loop

0.0 From parking lot, turn RIGHT onto access road and RIGHT onto Hopyard Road.

0.8 RIGHT onto Haywardville Road.

1.1 LEFT onto Early Road.

1.9 RIGHT onto Ackley Cemetery Road (unmarked).

2.8 Bear RIGHT staying on Ackley Cemetery Road (becomes Town Road).

3.2 Bear LEFT.

3.7 RIGHT onto Lake Shore Drive.

4.7 LEFT at junction onto Haywardville Road.

5.1 Continue STRAIGHT on Haywardville (becomes Mill Lane).

5.8 RIGHT at stop sign onto West Road.

6.7 STRAIGHT at stop sign, continuing on West Road.

9.3 West Road becomes Woodbridge Road.

10.0 LEFT onto Route 82 at junction. (Caution: steep downhill just before the junction.)

11.1 RIGHT onto Darling Road at flashing yellow light.

11.2 *Salem Valley Farms ice-cream stand.*

11.4 LEFT onto Old New London Road at four-way intersection.

13.8 Old New London Road becomes Salem Turnpike.

14.3 Sharp RIGHT onto Holmes Road.

15.1 LEFT onto Upper Walnut Hill Road.

16.2 RIGHT at junction onto Grassy Hill Road.

17.8 RIGHT at three-way intersection onto Beaver Brook Road (unmarked).

18.8 STRAIGHT at stop sign, staying on Beaver Brook Road

21.5 RIGHT onto Route 156 at junction.

23.4 RIGHT onto Route 82 at junction.

23.6 LEFT onto Hopyard Road.

26.8 Pass first main entrance to state park.

27.1 RIGHT into Devil's Hopyard State Park Chapman Falls entrance to return to start.

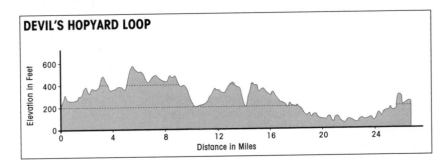

14 BLUFF POINT LOOP

Bluff Point State Park, Groton

dirt roads, single-track

Total distance: 7.5 miles

Difficulty: 3

Riding time: 1.5–2 hours

Elevation gain: 425 feet

Near the Groton-New London airport, Bluff Point State Park is a beautiful gem along the Connecticut shore. Conveniently just minutes from I-95, this coastal preserve is used by hikers, bikers, anglers, and equestrians. In addition, Bluff Point is a nice launching point for kayak trips around the southeast Connecticut shoreline. The park is big enough, however, that on any typical day you still are likely to spend most of your riding time alone in the woods.

The mountain biking trails at Bluff Point include many miles of single-track and one main dirt-road loop. The dirt-road loop is about 3.3 miles long and can be a nice ride for families, with a stop at the beach. The single-track is mostly nontechnical, suitable for beginners taking it slowly or more advanced riders going faster.

The route roughly circumnavigates the park, going south along the west side and returning north on the east side. The trails are completely unmarked, and there are many more trails besides those described in this route. Because the park is essentially on a peninsula and you are surrounded by water on three sides, it's hard to stay lost for long. At the end of the route, you will be at the northeast corner of the park. If you want still more, you can turn left and enter the single-track switchbacks that climb over the center ridge of the park to return the way you entered.

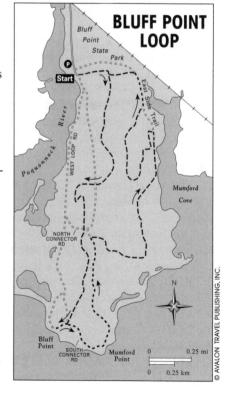

The park contains some protected research areas, so please stay on the trails. Bugs can be a problem, so repellent is advised, and check for ticks after you ride. For more information, contact Bluff Point State Park, c/o Fort Trumbull State Park, 90 Walbach Street, New London, CT 06320, 860/444-7591, website: www.dep.state.ct.us/stateparks/parks/bluffpoint.htm.

Driving Directions
From points east or west, take Route 95 to Exit 87, Route 117. Southbound, turn left at the exit; northbound, turn right. Drive approximately 2 miles to Route 1, just past the Groton Public Library, and turn right at the stoplight. Drive approximately 1 mile to North Street. Turn left and go approximately 1 mile, then turn right under the railroad overpass to enter the park. It's about .25 mile on a dirt road to the parking lot. Parking is free; there are picnic tables and outhouses but no other facilities at the park. Supplies and bike shops are available in Groton or Mystic.

Route Directions for Bluff Point Loop
0.0 Start from the Bluff Point sign at the south end of the parking lot, ride 50 feet and go LEFT on first narrow trail. Ride STRAIGHT through intersections to rocky hill and turn RIGHT at the Y at the top of hill.
0.3 RIGHT at the T, then LEFT after 50 feet.
0.4 STRAIGHT at intersection.
0.5 Bear RIGHT at Y-intersection, then stay LEFT.
0.7 LEFT, then veer RIGHT.
0.9 Veer RIGHT at the big rock at Y-intersection.
1.1 STRAIGHT across at Upper Road intersection.
1.3 LEFT at intersection.
1.4 RIGHT at intersection, going through gap in stone wall.
1.6 LEFT as the trail divides.
1.7 STRAIGHT across at North Connector intersection.
1.8 RIGHT at junction.
2.4 South Connector double-track intersection. Go RIGHT for .1 mile and take the trail on the LEFT to Bluff Point. *This is the perfect place to sit on the bench, eat a snack, and enjoy the view.* Retrace your route to the South Connector road, and head back up the hill on the double-track road.
3.7 RIGHT at trail entrance on right side of road (at meadow).
4.0 STRAIGHT across the muddy river bottom.
4.3 LEFT at Y-intersection, then another immediate LEFT.
4.5 LEFT at Y-intersection, then another immediate LEFT.
4.7 RIGHT downhill.
4.9 LEFT on East Side trail at the big rock.
5.0 RIGHT at Y-intersection.

5.2 LEFT entrance to a .3-mile stretch of challenging single-track. Enter, go 50 feet, then take a sharp LEFT (south) and wind your way up to the top of the hill.

5.5 RIGHT at intersection. The trail winds uphill back to the center of the park.

6.2 LEFT, then immediate RIGHT.

6.3 RIGHT downhill.

6.4 Pass through stone wall and turn RIGHT on East Side trail.

6.7 LEFT, then STRAIGHT for 50 feet, and turn LEFT onto the road.

7.5 Return to parking lot.

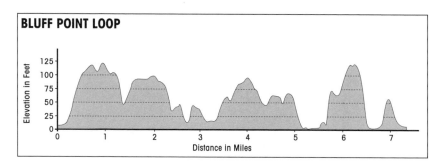

Chapter 6

© MELISSA L. KIM

Rhode Island

Rhode Island

People tend to overlook Rhode Island. After all, it's the smallest state in the nation—only 40 miles long and 30 miles wide. With about a million people, it does not have a lot of wide open space or wilderness. But it would be a big mistake to dismiss the Ocean State as a bicycling destination.

The state's Atlantic coastline is spectacular and diverse. It has some heavily developed tourists spots but there are also quaint coastal villages surrounded by stone walls, wonderful island day trips, and opulent Newport. Newport is a microcosm of the rest of the state—very posh, trendy areas suitable for millionaires shoulder to shoulder with working class neighborhoods that look as if they haven't changed since the '50s, with remnants of colonial architecture thrown in for good measure. All along the beautiful coastline, you can find nice, relatively flat, scenic rides. Rhode Island has its fair share of tourism, so go in spring or fall to have minimal traffic. Nothing matches the beauty of a sunny autumn day on Block Island.

Inland, the terrain turns to gentle rolling hills and though there aren't any real mountains to speak of, mountain bikers still have plenty of places to explore. Some of the best off-road rides can be found in the state's Wilderness Management Areas (WMAs), and while you may long for real, unbounded wilderness, be thankful that the state has had the foresight to preserve these places. Far from being manicured, tamed parks, the WMAs still feel quite wild, chances of seeing wildlife are high, and it's very easy to get lost on the trails. Arcadia, with its miles of single-track, attracts serious riders from all over New England. In fact, its popularity has made trail maintenance and courteous off-road riding a major issue in all the WMAs, so make sure you ride respectfully.

The state's small size may also be the reason for another nice bicycling feature: bike paths. Rhode Island has some of New England's best bike paths, and they cover almost every corner of the state. The East Bay Bike Path, which runs north to south along the edge of Narragansett Bay, is a model path allowing people to escape urban Providence to the breezy shores of Bristol. There are several other excellent paths in various stages of development, a long-range plan to link several of the paths, and links to the East Coast Greenway, the planned bike path from Florida to Maine. The paths are great for family rides or for anyone who wants to avoid riding with cars and traffic.

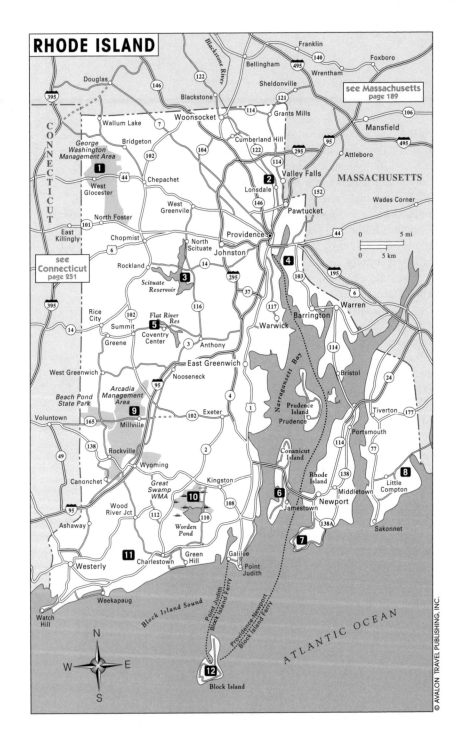

Contents

1 WALKABOUT TRAIL

George Washington Management Area, Burrillville

1A (Wilbur Pond Scramble)

 single-track, dirt roads

Total distance: 9.5 miles   **Riding time:** 3 hours

Difficulty: 5   **Elevation gain:** 410 feet

1B (Northern Loop)

 single-track, dirt roads

Total distance: 7.9 miles   **Riding time:** 2 hours

Difficulty: 3   **Elevation gain:** 415 feet

Though it seems unlikely in this quiet corner of Rhode Island, the Walkabout Trail was created by Australian sailors in 1965 while they were waiting for their ship, the H.M.A.S. *Perth,* to be ready for them. They had six weeks to wait, so the forestry division of Rhode Island suggested they help clear an 8-mile walking trail. The sailors apparently had a great time, throwing barbecues on Saturday nights for the locals.

The trail winds its way in and around this densely forested wildlife management area. These two bike routes travel only on small sections of the narrow Walkabout Trail, but the goal is for visitors to "go walkabout" and explore, so with a trail map you can easily find more routes of your own.

Both rides start out on the Walkabout Trail, with a fairly challenging stretch of single-track through some wet, swampy areas, then leave it behind in favor of wide dirt roads. At 5.5 miles, the rides split, with Route B heading straight and then left, taking dirt roads all the way back to the start.

Ride A makes a loop, first through a sweet little covered bridge and then on some lovely woodsy single-track before heading back on those same dirt roads. The real challenge lies in one last side trip on the Walkabout Trail. It's narrow, rooty, swampy, steep, and extremely rocky in places, and you need to be prepared to carry your bike in spots. The payback is views of the beautiful and secluded Wilbur Pond.

You can end either ride with a swim at the lovely beach on the edge of the Bowdish Reservoir. You can also camp here and begin your ride from

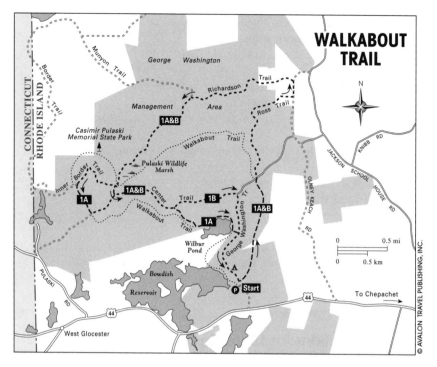

the campground. For more information, contact the George Washington Management Area, 401/568-2248.

Driving Directions

From Providence and points east, take Route 295 to Route 44 west (Exit 7B). Drive approximately 14 miles and look for the sign for the George Washington Camping Area. Turn right into the camping area and follow the main road for about .3 mile. Turn left into the parking area for the beach. There is a beach house with facilities, water fountains, and a pay phone. Trail maps are available in a box by the information kiosk. There is a small day use fee in summer. The campground offers primitive campsites and a few camping shelters for a modest fee. Supplies are available in Chepachet or West Glocester. The closest bike shop is in Putnam, CT.

Route Directions for Walkabout Trail 1A
(Wilbur Pond Scramble)

0.0 Directly across the road from parking lot, begin on the trail marked with blue, orange, and red blazes.

0.6 STRAIGHT following orange and red blazes.

1.5 RIGHT onto Center Trail (unmarked).

1.6 LEFT onto Ross Trail (unmarked) through red gate marked GW7.

2.6 STRAIGHT across clearing.

2.7 STRAIGHT through gate marked GW8.

2.8 LEFT onto dirt road.

3.0 LEFT onto Richardson Trail (unmarked) following red arrows.

4.1 LEFT at three-way intersection.

5.3 *A left turn onto the orange-blazed trail makes for a side trip to the lovely Pulaski Wildlife Marsh.*

5.5 RIGHT onto Inner Border Trail (unmarked) through red gate marked GW10.

5.6 STRAIGHT through covered bridge.

6.0 LEFT onto Walkabout Trail marked by orange blazes.

6.5 LEFT onto orange-blazed trail.

6.9 LEFT onto dirt road.

7.1 RIGHT onto Center Trail (unmarked).

7.7 RIGHT onto Cut Across Trail (unmarked) following red blazes.

7.8 LEFT onto Walkabout Trail following red and orange blazes.

9.0 RIGHT onto dirt road.

9.5 RIGHT into parking area.

Route Directions for 1B (Northern Loop)

0.0 Same as Route 1A for first 5.4 miles.

5.4 LEFT onto Center Trail (unmarked).

6.9 RIGHT onto dirt road.

7.9 RIGHT into parking area.

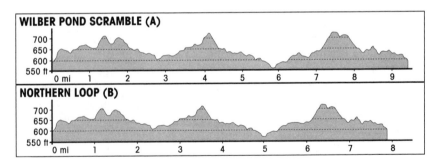

2 BLACKSTONE RIVER RIDE
Lincoln and Cumberland

2A (Riverside Ride)

 paved bike path

Total distance: 11.6 miles

Difficulty: 1

Riding time: 1.5 hours

Elevation gain: 100 feet

2B (Mill Town Tour)

 paved bike path, paved roads with moderate traffic

Total distance: 15.9 miles

Difficulty: 3

Riding time: 2 hours

Elevation gain: 470 feet

Route A follows the Blackstone River Bikeway, a multiuse path alongside the Blackstone Canal and railway, and considering that this area used to be a major cog in the wheels of the Industrial Revolution, it's quite a pretty ride with lush vegetation, tasteful stone markers, and even good wildlife-viewing. It has only one road crossing and the smooth, flat pavement

© MELISSA L. KIM

the canal alongside the well-kept Blackstone River Bikeway

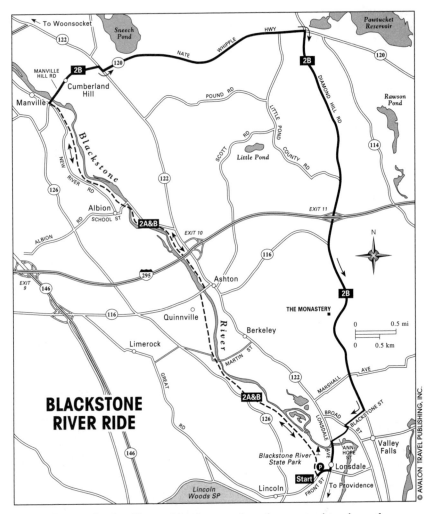

makes it ideal for families and beginners, though you need to share the path with roller bladers, stroller pushers, and walkers.

Route B leaves the tranquility of the path for the roads of suburban Rhode Island. A long, steep hill takes you into the village of Cumberland. Once you're on Route 120, you'll have some nice views of Sneech Pond. Diamond Hill Road gives you a taste of the rural as you pass a vineyard and farm stand, but then you're back into a 3-mile-long commercial stretch and the historic mill towns of Lonsdale and Valley Falls. This ride is for you only if you don't mind riding in traffic; definitely avoid rush-hour riding.

The Blackstone River Bikeway is the promising first step in a bike path that will run for 48 miles from Providence, RI to Worcester, MA. It also serves as a section of the East Coast Greenway, the proposed bike trail from Florida to Maine. To check on the progress of the bikeway, contact the Blackstone Valley Chamber of Commerce, 110 Church Street, Whitinsville MA, 01588, 508/234-9090, website: www.blackstoneriverbikeway.com.

Driving Directions

From points north, take Route 295 to Exit 9A, Route 146 south toward Lincoln. Drive 3.2 miles and take the Breakneck Hill Road/Route 123 exit. Turn left off the exit ramp onto Route 123 east. Drive 2.9 miles and turn left into Blackstone River State Park. From Providence, take Route 95 to Exit 23, Route 146 north. Drive 5 miles and take the Breakneck Hill Road/Route 123 exit. Turn right off the exit ramp onto Route 123 east. Drive approximately 2.8 miles and turn left into Blackstone River State Park. Supplies are available in Lincoln and Lonsdale. The state park has no facilities, only parking lots and an information kiosk. The nearest bike shops are in Providence and East Providence.

Route Directions for Blackstone River Ride 2A (Riverside Ride)

0.0 Leave parking lot and start on bike path.

0.2 Bear right over bridge following bike path.

2.5 *The Kelly House Museum is a transportation history museum with pretty gardens.*

5.8 Bike path ends. TURN AROUND.

11.6 RETURN to parking area.

Route Directions for 2B (Mill Town Tour)

0.0 Follow route directions for 1A to Mile 5.8.

5.8 Bike path ends. Bear left out of parking area and turn RIGHT onto New River Road.

6.0 RIGHT onto Manville Hill Road.

6.8 RIGHT onto Route 120. Get immediately into left lane.

6.9 LEFT onto Nate Whipple Highway (Route 120).

9.6 RIGHT onto Diamond Hill Road (Route 114).

10.3 *The lovely grounds of the Diamond Hill Vineyards make a nice optional side trip; the winery is open for tastings in the afternoons.*

12.3 Pass a busy entrance ramp for Route 295; take extreme care.

13.4 *A right turn leads to a side trip to The Monastery, the grounds of a Cistercian monastery dating from the early 1900s with a cemetery, walking trails, picnic tables, playground, and a public library.*

14.6 RIGHT onto Blackstone Street.

14.9 LEFT onto Broad Street (unmarked).

15.0 RIGHT onto Ann-Hope Street. Get into left lane.

15.2 LEFT onto Lonsdale Avenue.

15.6 RIGHT onto Front Street.

15.8 RIGHT into Blackstone River State Park.

15.9 Return to parking area.

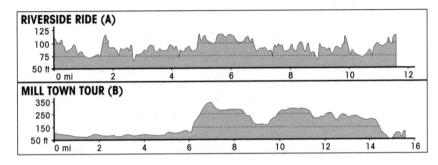

3 SCITUATE RESERVOIR RIDE
Scituate

 paved roads with moderate traffic

Total distance: 18 miles

Riding time: 1.5–2 hours

Difficulty: 4

Elevation gain: 1,170 feet

Lots of cyclists zip out from the Providence area to enjoy the water views and sweat the hills on this fun ride around the Scituate Reservoir. The construction of the reservoir in 1915 created 66 miles of scenic shoreline, though 300 homes, farms, schools, and churches were flooded in the process. The traffic moves fast on these roads, but there's almost always a nice wide, smooth shoulder and the property along the reservoir is largely undeveloped, especially on the southern pine-lined shore.

You start by crossing a bridge over one of the reservoir's inlets and navigating a bizarre three-way intersection (called Crazy Corners on some maps). Stay right and start a climb up Route 14. You'll have a few uphills and downhills before coming down to the reservoir and crossing a lovely causeway across the water.

You face a long uphill before you turn off Route 14 onto a residential road dotted with farm stands and lined with a wide smooth shoulder (the

riding along Gainer Memorial Dam at the southeast corner of the Scituate Reservoir

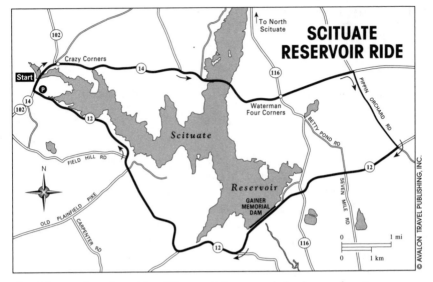

shoulder on the other side of the road, however, is broken and uneven, a reason not to ride this route counterclockwise). Turn right onto Route 12, and you'll soon come to Confreda's Greenhouses. Complete with café, store, and farm stand, it's a good place to make a pit stop.

Don't get too carried away by the following long, steep downhill—it ends abruptly at a busy four-way intersection, so check your brakes. You'll have a very scenic stretch over the dam and then a challenging finish with a few good hills to climb before returning to Route 14.

For more information, contact Scituate Town Hall, 401/647-2822, website: www.scituateri.org.

Driving Directions
From Providence and points east, take Route 295 to Exit 4 and drive west on Route 14. In approximately 8.8 miles, bear left at a three-way intersection onto Routes 14/102. After crossing a bridge, you'll see two small dirt parking bays, one on either side of the road. Supplies are available in North Scituate and the nearest bike shop is in Warwick.

Route Directions for Scituate Reservoir Ride
0.0 Start from parking area and ride north on Routes 14/102.
0.4 Bear RIGHT at three-way intersection, staying on Route 14.
5.0 STRAIGHT through four-way intersection. *Ice cream and a pay phone available at Suzy Q's ice-cream shop.*
6.6 RIGHT onto Pippin Orchard Road.
8.2 RIGHT onto Route 12.

8.9 *Supplies available at Confreda's Greenhouses farm stand.*

10.4 STRAIGHT through four-way intersection.

10.9 Cross the causeway of Gainer Memorial Dam.

17.8 RIGHT onto Routes 14/102.

18.0 Return to parking area.

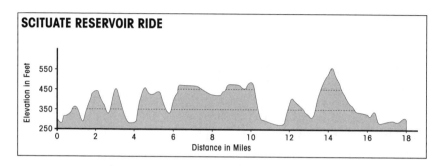

Bristol, Warren, Barrington, and East Providence

 paved bike path

Total distance: 17.6–27.2 miles

Difficulty: 1

Riding time: 2–3 hours

Elevation gain: 17 feet

This model rails-to-trails bike path is a pleasure to ride. It somehow manages to slip through urban industrial areas while giving you a sense of being in the countryside as you ride along the shore of Narragansett Bay and the Providence River, watching egrets fish in small marshy ponds on one side and waves crash on rocky islands capped by lighthouses on the other.

There are many access points to the wide, flat, smooth path, and plenty of spots along the way for good side trips and picnics, making this a great ride to do with the kids. If you're in Providence, start in East Providence (don't start at the trailhead in India Point Park; it's no fun to cross the bridge over Route 195 and climb the hill to Veteran's Memorial Park-

Who can resist a side trip to Colt State Park with waterfront paths like these?

way). You'll get a great breath of fresh air as you ride into the prevailing headwinds toward Bristol. It's a great city escape.

If you're just visiting the Ocean State, start in the charming historic village of Bristol. This route makes an out-and-back from Bristol to Veteran's Memorial Parkway in East Providence and returns (a shorter alternative, 17.6 miles round-trip, is to ride from Bristol to Haines Memorial Park).

You'll encounter many road crossings and two bridge crossings with uneven surfaces, but otherwise the only traffic you'll need to mind are dog walkers, roller bladers, and pedestrians. The path goes through leafy, lush, undeveloped areas and the villages of Warren and Barrington.

For more information on the bike path, visit the Rhode Island Department of Transportation's website: www.dot.state.ri.us/WebTran/bikeri.html. For information on visiting the area, contact the East Bay Tourism Council, 654 Metacom Avenue, Warren, RI 02885, 401/245-0750 or 888/278-9948, website: www.eastbayritourism.com.

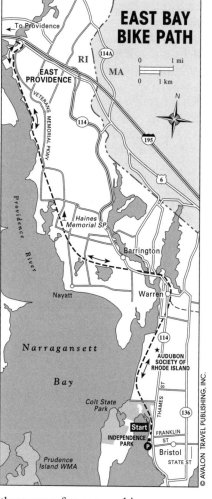

Driving Directions

From Providence and points north, take Route 195 for about 7.5 miles to Exit 2, Route 136. Follow Route 136 through Warren for 7.2 miles. In Bristol, turn right onto State Street, and right at the end onto Thames Street. From Newport, take Route 114 for approximately 13 miles to Bristol. In the center of Bristol, turn left onto State Street, and right at the end onto Thames Street. Independence Park is at the corner of Thames and Franklin. A large parking lot is at the harborside park. Supplies are available in Bristol, Warren, and Barrington, and there are a few seasonal ice-cream stands along the bike path. You'll find bike shops and rentals in Providence, East Providence, Riverside, and Warren.

Route Directions for East Bay Bike Path

0.0 Start on bike path from Independence Park.

1.0 *A left turn here leads to a highly recommended optional 3.5-mile side trip to Colt State Park, a beautiful, vast oceanside park with bike trails, facilities, and picnic tables.*

2.8 *A right turn makes for an optional side trip through a wildlife refuge and environmental center belonging to the Audubon Society of Rhode Island;*

there is a bike rack next to the path where you can leave your bike and walk the trails.

3.9 *Supplies available as you go through Warren.*

4.3 Cross bridge over Warren River.

5.5 Cross bridge over Barrington River.

6.0 *Supplies available as you go through Barrington.*

8.8 *A left turn leads to an optional side trip to Haines Memorial State Park, with picnic tables and restrooms.*

13.6 Arrive at second of two bike path parking lots along Veterans Memorial Parkway. TURN AROUND.

27.2 Return to Independence Park parking area.

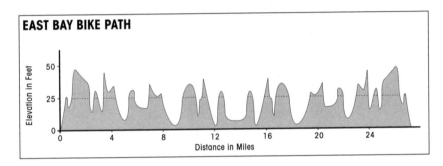

5 TRESTLE TRAIL
Coventry Center

unpaved rail trail

Total distance: 14.4 miles

Difficulty: 3

Riding time: 2.5–3 hours

Elevation gain: 400 feet

This trail follows a former railway bed that bisects the state. While there are plans to pave sections of it to extend the Coventry Greenway, a bike path to its east, it's a rough-and-tumble ride in fair to poor conditions that offers a fun ride through some scenic, remote areas.

Start from the eastern end of the Trestle Trail in Coventry Center. You'll have lovely views of Stump Pond and a pretty trestle bridge to cross before you hit the humps. Much of this trail is like a dragon's back, with stretches of countless little hillocks that take one or two pedal strokes to go up, and one or two to go down. This roller-coaster effect is fun except in the sections where the trail is extremely dry and sandy and your tires have nothing to grab. Since the trail is mostly flat, this is what makes it a challenge instead of a family ride.

After 1.6 miles, you'll probably need to portage over a small stream where the bridge has been washed out and pass around a gate on the other side. You'll face a few tricky road crossings, and a section where you'll need to be creative if the trail is washed out, until you get to a very pretty marshy stretch.

You will need to walk your bike across another elevated trestle bridge (giving great views) before you reach the dirt trails around Carbuncle Pond. Explore the shores of this popular fishing spot before turning around and heading back.

For more information, contact the Greenways Alliance of Rhode Island, 31 Stanchion Street, Jamestown, RI 02835, website: www.rigreenways.org.

Driving Directions

From points east or west, take Route 95 to Exit 6, Route 3 north. Drive 1 mile and turn left at the traffic light onto Harkney Hill Road. Drive .1 mile and turn right onto Hill Farm Road. After approximately 3 miles, you will reach a junction with Phillips Hill Road. The small dirt parking area is across Phillips Hill Road. Supplies are available in the small village of Coventry Center and at the general store in Summit, and there's a bike shop in Coventry.

Route Directions for Trestle Trail

0.0 Start at the trailhead from the parking area.
1.6 Portage around washed-out bridge.
3.2 Cross Route 102 and pick up trail on other side.
3.6 Go STRAIGHT on paved road.
3.7 Pick up dirt trail STRAIGHT ahead.
5.8 Walk your bike across trestle bridge.
6.1 Cross Hollow Road (unmarked dirt road).
6.8 Cross unmarked dirt road.
7.2 *A right turn onto a wide dirt trail will take you there if you want to explore the Carbuncle Pond area.* TURN AROUND.
14.4 Return to parking area.

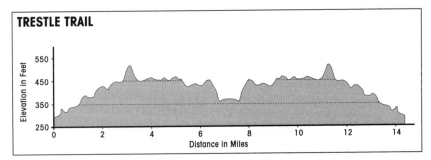

6 CONANICUT ISLAND LOOP
Jamestown

paved roads with minimal traffic

Total distance: 21.6 miles

Difficulty: 3

Riding time: 2–2.5 hours

Elevation gain: 1,070 feet

This beautiful island in the mouth of Narragansett Bay is the perfect place for a half-day trip. With spectacular ocean views, very little traffic, moderate hills, a pretty beach, a historic lighthouse, and a nice village to explore, it's easy to see why it's a popular destination for cyclists.

This route begins at Fort Wetherill State Park and makes a counterclockwise loop around the island. Cafés and ice-cream shops will tempt you as you ride through the village. Once you go past the highway and bridge access roads, the traffic and noise subside. Though you have only occasional ocean views on the northern part of the island, and there's not much of a shoulder on the road, it's peaceful and fairly flat.

Round the tip of the island and head south, pedaling up a slight incline, and stop to admire the creek and marsh at Mile 11. Somehow the marsh and its teeming bird life manage to make the cables and uprights of the Pell Bridge, rising in the background, seem beautiful as well.

You'll go past the outskirts of town again before riding along a narrow strip of land called Town Beach. Only residents are allowed to park here, but bikers can stop and beachcomb on either side. You'll face a steep hill

The long thin cables of the Pell Bridge mirror the long legs of wading birds in the marsh.

up Beavertail Road and some prevailing headwinds before you arrive at Beavertail State Park, home to America's third-oldest lighthouse, perched right at the island's dramatic rocky edge next to the pounding surf. There are picnic tables, walking trails, and a museum that's open during the summer.

Retrace your route past Town Beach and then climb a few small hills, through a pretty residential area, to return to Fort Wetherill State Park. The park, a popular launching spot for scuba clubs, has picnic tables, seasonal restrooms, a boat ramp, and nice views from its granite cliffs.

For more information and an excellent street map of the island, contact the Jamestown Chamber of Commerce, P.O. Box 35, Jamestown, RI 02835, 401/423-3650, website: www.jamestownri.com. For more information on the state parks, contact Fort Wetherill State Park, 401/423-1771, website: www.riparks.com/fortweth.htm; and Beavertail State Park, 401/423-9941, website: www.riparks.com/beaverta.htm.

Driving Directions

Bikes are not allowed on either of the bridges to Conanicut Island, so you have to drive. From Newport, take Route 138 across the Newport Bridge (also called Pell Bridge). The toll is $2 each way. Take the first exit for Jamestown. Turn right off the exit, then left at the stop sign toward Jamestown village.

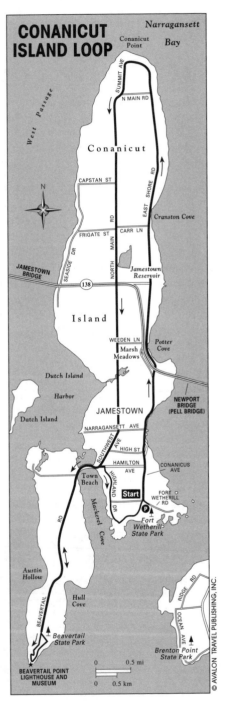

CONANICUT ISLAND LOOP

© AVALON TRAVEL PUBLISHING, INC.

Drive through town, on Conanicus Avenue, and go 1 mile. Turn left at a triangular intersection onto Fort Wetherill Road. Turn right into the first parking area for Fort Wetherill State Park. Parking is free and the park is open sunrise–sunset. From points west, take the Jamestown Bridge (Route 138) and take the Jamestown village exit as above. Supplies are available in Jamestown. The nearest bike shops are in Newport or North Kingston.

Route Directions for Conanicut Island Loop

0.0 From parking area at Fort Wetherill State Park, go LEFT onto Fort Wetherill Road.

0.2 RIGHT at triangle onto unmarked road (this becomes Conanicus Avenue).

1.1 Jamestown village. *Supplies available throughout town. Public restrooms are at the recreation center on the corner of Union Street and Conanicus Avenue.*

1.6 LEFT at fork.

2.1 RIGHT at fork to go under the bridge approach.

2.5 STRAIGHT at stop sign on East Shore Road (unmarked).

7.0 LEFT at stop sign onto Summit Avenue (unmarked).

7.5 RIGHT at stop sign onto North Main Road (unmarked).

12.3 *Supplies available in Jamestown.*

12.5 STRAIGHT at intersection onto Southwest Avenue.

13.0 Stay on Southwest Avenue as road curves to the right.

13.2 Town Beach. Proceed STRAIGHT on Beavertail Road (unmarked).

15.8 Enter Beavertail State Park.

16.3 Pass Beavertail Point and Lighthouse Museum.

17.0 Exit the state park.

19.0 Pass Town Beach.

19.8 RIGHT onto Hamilton Avenue.

19.9 RIGHT onto Highland Drive (unmarked).

21.3 RIGHT at triangle followed by an immediate RIGHT onto Fort Wetherill Road.

21.6 RIGHT into parking area.

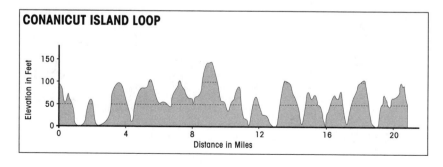

🄷 OCEAN DRIVE
Newport

paved roads with moderate traffic

Total distance: 10.6 miles

Difficulty: 2

Riding time: 1–1.5 hours

Elevation gain: 140 feet

Don't be fooled into dismissing Newport as a tourist destination too crowded for good cycling. The millionaires had a reason to build their mansions here at the turn of last century. The peninsula juts into the turbulent Atlantic Ocean with an end-of-the-earth quality and has a rugged, natural beauty that can still be found if you look in the right place at the right time. This route takes in the splendors of both man and nature, cruising past the most magnificent mansions and the ocean's edge. To avoid crowds and traffic, try doing this short ride very early on a summer morning, or wait until late fall to visit.

Starting from Fort Adams State Park, you'll make a loop on Ocean Drive, getting sprayed by the surf as you go past Brenton Point State Park, then passing by quiet landscapes of ponds, coves, and beaches.

Then it's on to the opulence of Bellevue Avenue, the main avenue of the Gilded Age mansions. Turning off Bellevue onto Ruggles Avenue, you'll go through the lovely campus of Salve Regina University and ride to the end, where you'll get a good look at The Breakers mansion (built for Cor-

riding along Ocean Drive near Brenton Point State Park

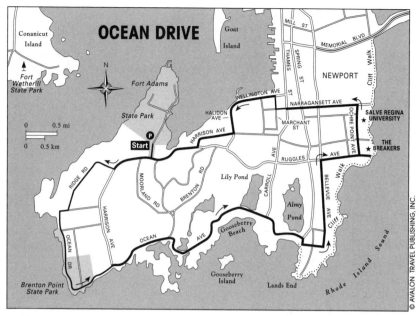

nelius Vanderbilt in 1895) and have access to the Cliff Walk, a 3.5-mile National Recreation Trail. You could lock up your bike and do a .75-mile stretch of the walk, from Ruggles to Narragansett Avenue, for the best mansion views and a taste of the spectacular path with its sheer drop-offs and breaking surf.

Leaving mansions behind, you'll pass through a residential neighborhood with modest houses and come out onto Newport Harbor and the waterside King Park. A small incline goes up Halidon Avenue before you head back to Fort Adams.

For more information, contact the Newport County Convention and Visitor's Bureau, 23 America's Cup Avenue, Newport, RI 02840, 800/976-5122, website: www.gonewport.com. Also, for more on Fort Adams State Park, contact Fort Adams State Park, Harrison Avenue, Newport RI 02840, 401/847-2400, website: www.riparks.com/fortadams.htm.

Driving Directions

From the center of Newport, drive south on Thames Street and turn right onto Wellington Avenue. The road bends left and becomes Halidon Avenue. Turn right at the stop sign onto Harrison Avenue, left at the next stop sign, and right onto Ridge Road (unmarked). Drive .5 mile and turn right into Fort Adams State Park. Go past the entry booth and park in one of the large lots on the left. Parking is free and the park is open sunrise–sunset. Supplies, bike rentals, and bike shops are available in Newport.

Route Directions for Ocean Drive

0.0 Leave main parking lot of Fort Adams State Park. *The park has free parking, restrooms, pay phone, a visitor center and gift shop, boating center, and museum. Tours of the 19th-century fort are available during the summer for a small fee.*

0.2 RIGHT onto Ridge Road.

0.5 Bear RIGHT at fork, staying on Ridge Road.

1.3 Road bends LEFT and becomes Ocean Drive.

1.9 *Brenton Point State Park has picnic tables, pay phone, concession stand, and restrooms, open May–October.*

3.4 Bear RIGHT at the fork.

4.6 Pass Gooseberry Beach. *Of the three beaches along Ocean Drive, this is the only public one. There are no facilities.*

5.3 RIGHT at the junction.

5.4 LEFT at the end onto Bellevue Avenue. *A short cul-de-sac on the right gives access to the Cliff Walk and nice views.*

6.6 RIGHT onto Ruggles Avenue.

7.1 Road ends. *The Breakers is on the left; you can get to the Cliff Walk from here.* TURN AROUND.

7.2 RIGHT onto Ochre Point Avenue.

7.7 LEFT onto Narragansett Avenue.

8.1 STRAIGHT through traffic lights across Bellevue Avenue.

8.6 RIGHT onto Marchant Street.

8.7 LEFT onto Wellington Avenue. *Facilities available at King Park.* Wellington Avenue curves to the left and becomes Halidon Avenue.

9.5 RIGHT at stop sign onto Harrison Avenue.

9.8 LEFT at stop sign.

9.9 RIGHT onto Ridge Road (unmarked).

10.4 RIGHT to Fort Adams State Park.

10.6 Return to parking lot.

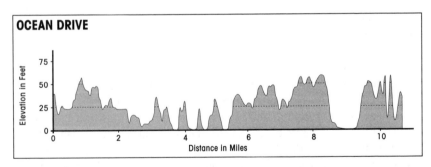

8 CROSS-BORDER RIDE

Little Compton, RI and Acoaxet, MA

paved roads with minimal traffic

Total distance: 17 miles

Difficulty: 2

Riding time: 1.5–2 hours

Elevation gain: 575 feet

The lovely 17th-century village of Little Compton makes a nice starting point to explore the coastal hamlets of Rhode Island and Massachusett's southern shore. This route takes you on a clockwise loop from Little Compton to the beach community of Acoaxet and back; crisscrossing roads make it easy to either expand or decrease the length of the ride with the help of a good map.

Start by heading north from the village, also called The Commons. You'll ride past fields and farmlands divided by picture-perfect stone walls, as well as elegant houses and the occasional farm stand. There's a short uphill before a descent into the charming village of Adamsville. (Go straight through Adamsville to Westport and you can join the South Dartmouth ride, described in the Massachusetts chapter under Route 15, Little River Loop.)

You'll need a cloudy fall day to find Atlantic Avenue, in Acoaxet, free of walkers, joggers, or cyclists.

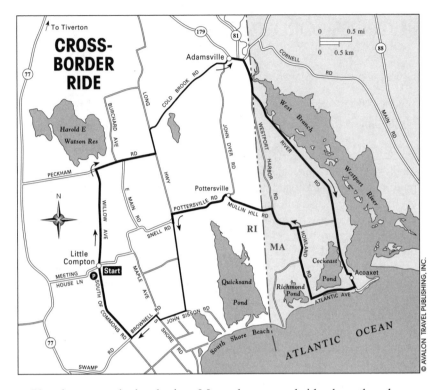

You then cross the border into Massachusetts and ride along the edge of the west branch of the Westport River. Small islands dot the pretty river, which teems with bird life and bird-watchers. After a few small hills, you'll come to the summer beach community of Acoaxet, with its quaint inns, gray clapboard houses, and beach and tennis clubs. Pedal down Atlantic Avenue with beach clubs on your left and aromatic beach rose shrubs and showy hydrangeas on your right. In summer, expect to share the road with joggers, walkers, and slow-driving tourists.

The steepest hill of the ride comes after the tiny crossroads village of Pottersville. Otherwise it's more fields bounded by stone walls and bucolic scenery as you return to The Commons.

For more information, contact the Little Compton Community Center, P.O. Box 926, Little Compton, RI 02837, 401/635-2400, website: www.lc-center.com; or visit the Coastal Villages website: www.coastalvillages.com.

Driving Directions

From the north (Massachusetts), take Route 24 south to Exit 5 (Route 77 south) in Tiverton. Take Route 77 for 10.2 miles to an intersection; turn left onto Meeting House Lane, following signs to The Commons (as the center of Little Compton is known). Drive about .8 mile to the village center, marked by a large common, cemetery, and church. Parking is available along the common and behind the post office. Supplies are available in Little Compton. The closest bike shop is in Westport, MA.

Route Directions for Cross-Border Ride

0.0 Start from the common and ride north on Willow Avenue.

1.5 RIGHT onto Peckham Road (unmarked).

2.0 STRAIGHT at stop sign (left-hand branch of triangular intersection).

2.5 LEFT at stop sign onto Long Highway (unmarked).

2.9 Bear RIGHT onto Cold Brook Road (unmarked).

4.7 RIGHT at stop sign. *Supplies are available in Adamsville.*

4.9 RIGHT onto Westport Harbor Road.

5.4 LEFT at fork onto River Road.

9.0 RIGHT onto Atlantic Avenue.

9.7 RIGHT at the end onto Howland Avenue.

10.8 LEFT at junction onto Mullin Hill Road.

11.4 LEFT, continuing on Mullin Hill Road.

12.2 Bear LEFT on the main road at triangular intersection in Pottersville.

13.1 Bear LEFT at the triangle.

13.2 LEFT at the stop sign onto Long Highway (unmarked), then STRAIGHT at the intersection immediately after that.

14.7 Follow main road, taking sharp curve to the RIGHT onto John Sisson Road (unmarked).

15.2 RIGHT at the junction onto South Shore Road (unmarked). *You can make a left turn here for an optional side trip to South Shore Beach.*

15.3 LEFT at the stop sign onto Brownell Road (unmarked).

15.8 RIGHT onto South of Commons Road.

17.0 Enter village of Little Compton.

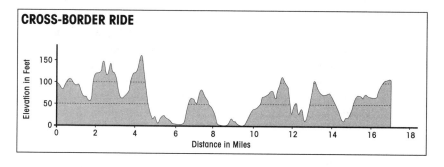

9 BREAKHEART AND SHELTER TRAILS
Arcadia Management Area, Millville

dirt roads, dirt trails, single-track

Total distance: 8.7 miles

Difficulty: 4

Riding time: 2 hours

Elevation gain: 515 feet

Mountain bikers from all over New England travel to this otherwise unremarkable area of south-central Rhode Island to test their skills in a place that's been dubbed "Single-track Central." As many as 50 miles of single-track trails wander around Arcadia Management Area's 15,000 acres.

This route is a small sample of the trails, combining technical single-track, easy single-track, and dirt roads. You'll start by warming up on the Deion Trail, a wide, overgrown trail strewn with pine needles. You'll then take dirt roads to go around the Frosty Hollow fishing area. Once you pick up the J. B. Hudson Trail, you'll be on some fun, tight, twisty, rooty trails that bring you to Breakheart Pond. Follow an easy, wide woodland trail along the western shore of the pond, and then turn onto Yellow Dot, or Breakheart, Trail.

The next 1.5 miles are rocky and technical, the hardest stretch of this route. Follow the double yellow blazes through deep woods until you reach an AMC-built bridge; make sure you don't miss the left turn right after the bridge. You'll face a tricky climb and a few log bridges before you reach Shelter Trail, which starts with a very narrow, twisty, fun stretch. After that it's dirt roads and Midway Trail, a wide path through an area where hunters train their bird dogs, to return to the parking area.

With so many trails, it's hard to know where to ride, and easy to get lost, so make sure you carry a trail map and a topo map, or join a group ride. The trail map boxes at the parking lot were empty when I visited. You can also get maps at local bike shops (try Victory Cycles in Wyoming, RI), or online from the state at: www.state.ri.us/dem/maps/wma.htm.

RINEMBA, the Rhode Island chapter of the New England Mountain Biking Association, does trail maintenance and bike patrol and leads group rides in Arcadia. Contact Tina Hopkins, RINEMBA secretary, by email at vcycles@mindspring.com. For information on Arcadia itself, contact the Department of Environmental Management, Arcadia Management Area, 401/539-1052.

Driving Directions

From points east or west, take Exit 5 off Route 95 to Route 102 east. Drive .7 mile and make a sharp right turn onto Route 3 south. Drive approximately 1

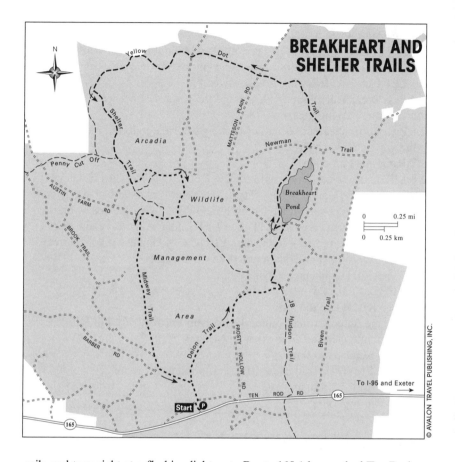

mile and turn right at a flashing light onto Route 165 (also marked Ten Rod Road). Supplies are available at the ice-cream stand and pizza store, which has soda and water machines outside. Drive 3.1 miles and turn right into the Arcadia Management Area and Midway parking lot. Another parking area .4 mile farther down the road, on the left, has an outhouse, picnic tables, and canoe launch. Parking is free. The nearest bike shop is in Wyoming, RI.

Route Directions for Breakheart and Shelter Trails

0.0 From the parking lot, go RIGHT onto the main dirt road.

0.2 RIGHT onto Deion Trail, marked by blue blazes. Ride around low red gate.

0.8 LEFT onto dirt road (unmarked Frosty Hollow Road).

1.0 RIGHT into parking area for Frosty Hollow Fishing Area. Trailhead is at far end of parking area; pass around a red gate to access trail. Go right at immediate fork.

1.3 LEFT at junction.

1.4 LEFT onto J. B. Hudson Trail, marked by double yellow blazes. Go LEFT again after about 500 yards, following yellow blazes.

1.6 LEFT at fork, following yellow blazes.

2.0 Pass Breakheart Pond. Ride around the southwest corner of the pond into the dirt parking area.

2.1 Pick up trailhead at far end of parking lot, riding around red gate. The pond will be on your right.

2.7 RIGHT at junction.

2.8 LEFT just before brook onto Yellow Dot Trail (also called Breakheart Trail) marked by double yellow blazes. Trailhead is marked by big boulders.

3.7 Make a dogleg turn, LEFT then RIGHT, following the yellow blazes.

4.3 Make a dogleg turn, RIGHT then LEFT, following the yellow blazes.

4.4 Cross bridge and take immediate LEFT, following the yellow blazes.

5.4 LEFT onto Shelter Trail, marked by white blazes.

6.0 STRAIGHT, staying on main trail.

6.2 LEFT at four-way intersection.

6.5 Bear RIGHT at the fork.

6.8 Emerge onto dirt road (unmarked Austin Farm Road). Go RIGHT.

7.1 LEFT into clearing. Join Arcadia Midway Trail. *There are a portable toilet and picnic table here.*

8.1 End of Midway Trail. Bear LEFT onto main dirt road.

8.2 STRAIGHT on main road.

8.7 Return to parking lot.

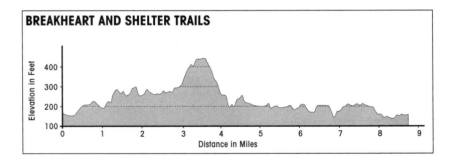

10 WORDEN POND LOOP

Great Swamp Wildlife Management Area, Kingston

dirt roads, bike path

Total distance: 8.7 miles

Difficulty: 2

Riding time: 1.5 hours

Elevation gain: 205 feet

An easy off-road ride through Great Swamp offers tranquil, pleasant scenery and an excellent chance to see lots of mammals and birds. This is a good place for someone who's new at riding off-road, with grassy and sandy stretches on mainly overgrown dirt roads with no technical riding.

Though you begin on the paved South County Bike Path, you quickly turn off to ride down a long dirt access road before entering Great Swamp. Low, scrubby vegetation lines the edges of the swamp, where lily pads float on the surface. You'll make a big loop around an L-shaped pond. Though the utility lines, which cut right through the middle, mar the view a bit, the wildlife doesn't seem to mind. Ospreys have nested on

top of the poles, turtles laze along the path, and wood ducks and mallards splash in the water.

As you leave the swamp, there's a very small incline to bring you into a series of fields as the trail becomes grassier. Take a right toward Worden Pond and enter a more wooded area. A tiny sandy beach is at the pond's edge, just to the left of the float plane hangar. It's not suitable for swimming but makes a good picnic spot. Take a left as you leave the pond to make a small loop, which goes up and down a small hill, before rejoining the path.

On the way back, you can always turn right and ride

Many birds and waterfowl nest in or near the swamp, and bird-watching is at its peak during the migration in May.

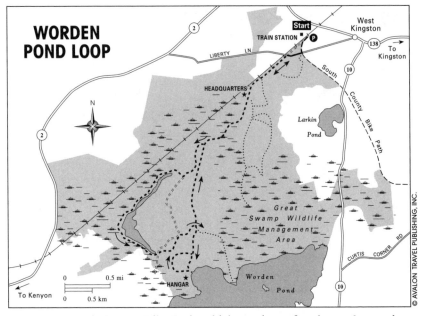

WORDEN POND LOOP

east along South County Bike Path, which continues for almost 6 smooth flat miles into Narragansett.

For more information, contact the Department of Environmental Management's Fish and Wildlife Division, Liberty Lane, West Kingston, RI 02891, 401/789-7481. Hunting and fishing are allowed here, so though most hunting seasons are in the winter, you should be aware of hunters.

Driving Directions

From points east or west, take Route 95 to Exit 3A. Drive about 8.3 miles on Route 138. Turn right, then left onto Railroad Avenue, following signs for the Amtrak train station. There are facilities at the train station and supplies available along Route 138 in West Kingston. The nearest bike shops are in North Kingstown and Narragansett.

Route Directions for Worden Pond Loop

0.0 Start on bike path.
0.2 RIGHT on Liberty Lane (unmarked).
0.4 Bear LEFT onto dirt road.
1.0 Pass Great Swamp Headquarters.
1.5 Go to end of large dirt parking area, ride around red gate next to information sign.
1.9 RIGHT at fork.
2.3 RIGHT onto grassy trail.

4.3 RIGHT at the fork into wooded area.

4.5 RIGHT at triangular intersection.

5.1 Pass floatplane hangar and arrive at Worden Pond. *A tiny sandy beach is just to the left.* TURN AROUND. Take immediate LEFT on narrow trail.

5.5 RIGHT at the junction and RIGHT again downhill.

5.7 LEFT on trail.

5.9 Bear RIGHT at the triangular intersection.

6.6 STRAIGHT under power lines.

6.8 Bear RIGHT at triangular intersection.

7.2 Return to dirt parking area. Go STRAIGHT on dirt road.

8.5 LEFT onto South County Bike Path.

8.7 Return to train station parking lot.

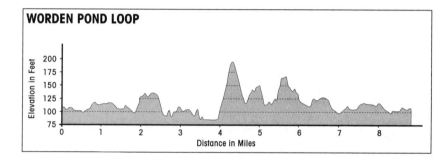

11 VIN GORMLEY TRAIL
Burlingame State Park, Charlestown

  single-track, paved roads, dirt roads

Total distance: 8 miles

Riding time: 2 hours

Difficulty: 4

Elevation gain: 315 feet

The wonderful 8-mile-long Vin Gormley Trail is primarily for hikers (and in places, it's even marked "Hikers Only"), but the state does allow mountain bikers as long as they remain courteous and low-impact riders, so make sure you respect those on foot, stay on the trail, and don't ride in weather or in a style that leads to trail erosion.

The trail goes through deep woodlands as it makes a big loop around Watchaug Pond in Burlingame State Park. For the most part, the trail is extremely well marked with yellow blazes and even, in some places, has special patterns to indicate a left or right turn. Check the trail maps, posted at the Burlingame Picnic Area and in the campground, or ask for a copy at the campground office, for general reference.

The northern section of the trail is extremely rocky and might be challenging for advanced beginners.

You'll leave the picnic area and head left, riding on paved roads for about 1 mile before turning into the woods. The next 2 miles, across the north end of the pond, are very technical and a little hilly, with some extremely rocky sections, some rooty, narrow bits, and a few rocky places where you might need to carry your bike (I definitely had to).

After a short stretch on another paved road, you'll head back into thick woods where marshy, wet areas have replaced rock ledges. There are several bridges, some quite long, and a sweet little covered bridge over the

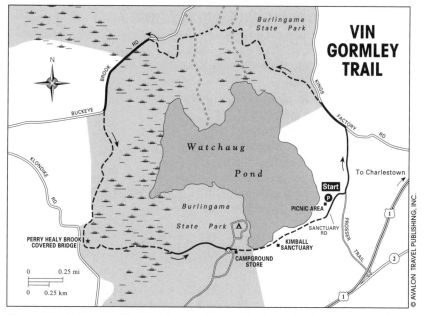

Perry Healy Brook. You'll ride on wide trails through pine forests and then some rooty single-track before you enter the Burlingame State Park campground area.

After the campground, you'll pass through a very short stretch through the Audubon Society of Rhode Island's Kimball Sanctuary, where you are required to walk your bike. Then there's a very bumpy gravel road to tackle before arriving back at the picnic area.

This is a popular place and the campground has more than 700 sites. Try visiting after Labor Day. For more information, contact Burlingame State Park, Route 1, Charlestown, RI 02813, 401/322-8910, website: www.riparks.com/burlinga.htm.

Driving Directions

From Westerley, drive about 5 miles on Route 1 north. Pass the exit for the Burlingame Picnic Area and make a left exit and U-turn from this divided highway. From Wakefield and points east, take Route 1 south and take the exit for the Burlingame Picnic Area. Drive .6 mile on Prosser Trail and turn left. The Burlingame Picnic Area has ample parking, picnic tables and shelters, seasonal restrooms, and a nice sandy swimming beach. The fee is $2 in summer. Supplies are available in Charlestown, at convenience stores on Route 1, and at the Burlingame State Park camp store in season. The closest bike shop is in Westerly.

Route Directions for Vin Gormley Trail

0.0 Exit the picnic area parking lot.

0.2 LEFT onto Prosser Trail.

0.7 Merge LEFT onto Kings Factory Road.

1.0 LEFT into woods.

2.2 Jog RIGHT then LEFT (cross a private camp road).

2.4 Cross a sandy gravelly road.

2.8 Bear LEFT following blazes.

3.0 Sharp RIGHT following blazes.

3.3 Emerge and go LEFT on the Buckeye Brook Road.

3.6 LEFT off Buckeye Brook Road into woods.

5.3 Arrive at stone wall and road. Follow trail LEFT back into woods.

5.4 Cross Perry Healy Brook covered bridge.

5.5 LEFT at the T.

5.8 Trail curves to right.

6.4 Enter campground.

6.6 STRAIGHT through rotary.

6.8 STRAIGHT through rotary. Follow the right-hand edge of the playground and take a RIGHT at the end, heading back into the woods. *The camp store is on the right, as are a pay phone and portable toilets. The camp store hours are limited off-season.*

7.0 Enter the Kimball Bird Sanctuary. Walk your bike in this section.

7.2 Resume riding on Sanctuary Road.

8.0 Return to Burlingame Picnic Area.

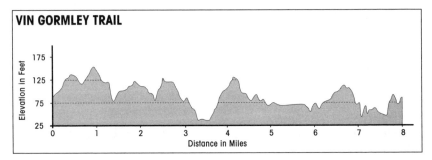

12 ISLAND LOOPS
Block Island

12A (South Island Loop)

 paved roads with some uneven pavement and minimal traffic

Total distance: 9.8 miles   **Riding time:** 2 hours

Difficulty: 2   **Elevation gain:** 480 feet

12B (North Island Loop)

 paved roads with some uneven pavement and minimal traffic

Total distance: 8.4 miles   **Riding time:** 1.5 hours

Difficulty: 3   **Elevation gain:** 315 feet

It's hard to overstate just how much fun you can have biking around Block Island. This small island off Rhode Island's southern coast is a popular destination for people attracted by the unspoiled rugged beauty of the beaches, cliffs, and ponds. Even the man-made features are lovely—the gray clapboard homes, a striking brick Victorian lighthouse, stone walls lining roads and fields. Unless you are willing to brave the summer crowds to swim and sunbathe on the beach after your ride, try visiting in spring or fall. It's breezier but you may have the back roads to yourself.

These routes travel on the island's main roads; it's easy to link the two. To explore the many dirt side roads, you'll want a hybrid or mountain bike. Ride A makes a counterclockwise loop around the southern half of the island. You'll encounter a few gentle hills and one very long downhill right at the end as you come back to the busy town of Old Harbor, but otherwise it's fairly flat. Several walking trails and nature preserves lie along the way if you feel like getting off the bike. A side trip down a bumpy dirt road to Black Rock Point is well worth the effort, as is a stop at Mohegan Bluffs. Even if you don't want to climb the 144 steps to and from the beach, you still get a fantastic view of the cliffs and the dramatic sweep of Crescent Beach.

Ride B heads north from Old Harbor, goes to Settler's Rock at the tip and comes back, with one steep hill at Sachem Pond to tackle. Three outstanding beaches on either side of the island are accessible by short rides along dirt roads, so leave plenty of time to poke around.

For more information, contact the Block Island Chamber of Commerce, 401/466-2982 or 800/383-BIRI (800/383-2474), website: www.blockislandchamber.com.

Driving Directions

Two main ferries go to Block Island, a year-round car and passenger ferry that takes 55 minutes and arrives in Old Harbor (www.blockisland ferry.com) and a high-speed catamaran, passengers only, that takes 30 minutes and arrives in New Harbor (www.islandhighspeedferry.com). Both leave from the main pier in Galilee. Ferries also travel from Newport, RI and New London, CT. On Block Island, you'll find several bike rental places, bike shops, supplies, public restrooms, bike racks, and lockers in Old Harbor.

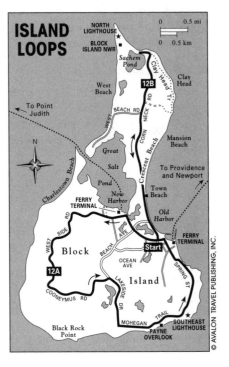

Route Directions for Island Loops 12A (South Island Loop)

0.0 From ferry terminal in Old Harbor, go RIGHT onto Ocean Avenue.

0.8 RIGHT onto Beach Avenue and immediate LEFT onto Ocean Avenue.

1.1 LEFT onto West Side Road. *Public restrooms, pay phones, and supplies are available in New Harbor.*

1.3 Bear RIGHT at triangle.

3.9 Curve LEFT. Road becomes Cooneymus Road.

5.4 RIGHT at stop sign onto Lakeside Drive.

6.5 LEFT onto Mohegan Trail. *Going straight onto Snake Hole Road will take you on an optional side trip. If you bear right after .1 mile and ride down the bumpy dirt road for about .5 mile to a dirt parking area, a trail will lead down the cliff to Black Rock Point Beach.*

7.8 Payne Overlook for Mohegan Bluffs. *Park at one of the bike racks and walk in to the observation area and stairs to beach.*

7.9 Pass Southeast Lighthouse and museum.

8.1 Road becomes Spring Street.

9.7 At stop sign, go STRAIGHT through rotary onto Ocean Avenue.

9.8 Return to ferry terminal in Old Harbor.

Route Directions for 12B (North Island Loop)

0.0 From ferry terminal in Old Harbor, go RIGHT on Ocean Avenue.

0.2 RIGHT onto Corn Neck Road.

1.0 Pass Town Beach. *Facilities available.*

2.6 *Mansion Road, a roughly paved road on the right, leads .5 mile to popular Mansion Beach.*

2.9 *West Beach Road, on the left, leads to the quiet West Beach.*

3.0 *For a side trip, you can take Clay Head Trail, a dirt trail on the right, for 1 mile, park at the bike rack, and take a 15-minute walk through a nature preserve to a stunning sandy beach.*

4.2 Paved road ends. *Leave your bike in the parking area and walk across the pebbly beach to North Light.* TURN AROUND.

8.2 LEFT onto Ocean Avenue

8.4 Return to ferry terminal in Old Harbor.

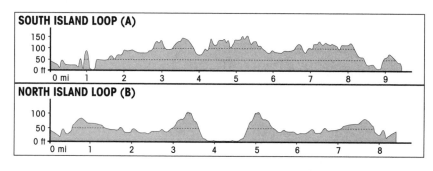

© ELLEN KANNER

Biking Organizations in New England

Below you'll find a list of selected organizations, clubs, and bicycle shops in New England. This is not a comprehensive list of clubs and shops, but you should be able to use this appendix to find a bike shop close to almost all of the routes described in this guidebook (several are too remote to have bike shops in the area).

Regional
NEMBA (New England Mountain Biking Association), P.O. Box 2221, Acton, MA 01720, 800/57-NEMBA (800/576-3622), website: www.nemba.org.

East Coast Greenway, 135 North Main Street, Wakefield, RI 02879, 401/789-4625, website: www.greenway.org.

Eastern Fat Tire Association, 15 Landing Drive, Methuen, MA 01844, website: www.efta.com.

Connecticut
Connecticut Department of Transportation, Bicycle and Pedestrian Coordinator, Bureau of Policy and Planning, P.O. Box 317546, Newington, CT 06131-7546, website: www.ct.gov/dot.

Connecticut State Parks and Forests, Bureau of Outdoor Recreation, Department of Environmental Protection, 79 Elm Street, Hartford, CT 06106-5127, 860/424-3200, website: www.dep.state.ct.us/stateparks.

Connecticut Chapter, New England Mountain Biking Association, website: www.ctnemba.org.

Connecticut Bicycle Coalition, 433 Chapel Street, 2nd Floor, New Haven, CT 06511-5830, 203/848-6491, website: www.ctbike.org.

Farmington Valley Greenway, website: http://fvgreenway.org.

Appalachian Mountain Club Connecticut Chapter, website: www.ct-amc.org/cycling.

Maine
Maine Department of Transportation, Child Street, 16 State House Station, Augusta, ME 04333-0016, 207/624-3000, website: www.exploremaine.org/bike.

Maine Bureau of Parks and Lands, Bureau of Parks and Lands, 286 Water Street, Key Bank Plaza, Augusta, ME 04333, 207/287-3821, website: www.state.me.us/doc/parks.

Bicycle Coalition of Maine, P.O. Box 5275, Augusta, ME 04332-5275, 207/623-4511, website: www.bikemaine.org.

Eastern Trail Alliance, P.O. Box 250, Saco, ME 04072, 207/284-9260, website: www.easterntrail.org.

Massachusetts

Massachusetts Department of Transportation, Bicycle and Pedestrian Program, 10 Park Plaza, Suite 3170, Boston, MA 02116, 617/973-7000, website: www.mass.gov/eotc/modes/modes_pedstrn.html.

Mass Bike, 20 Park Plaza, Suite 1028, Boston, MA 02116, 617/542-BIKE (617/542-2453), website: www.massbike.org.

Mass Parks, Division of State Parks and Recreation, 251 Causeway Street, Suite 600, Boston, MA 02114, 617/626-1250, website: www.massparks.org.

New Hampshire

New Hampshire Department of Transportation, Bicycle/Pedestrian Information Center, 7 Hazen Drive, Concord, NH 03302, 603/271-1668, website: www.nh.gov/dot/nhbikeped.

New Hampshire Division of Parks and Recreation, 172 Pembroke Road, Concord, NH 03302, (603) 271-3556, website: www.nhstateparks.org. Also, within the Division of Parks and Recreation:

New Hampshire Trails Bureau, website: www.nhtrails.org.

Bicycle Coalition of New Hampshire, P.O. Box 230, Stratham, NH 03885, website: www.bikenewhampshire.org.

Rhode Island

Bike Rhode Island, Rhode Island Department of Transportation, 2 Capitol Hill, Providence, RI 02903, 401/222-2481, Bicycle Program Coordinator, 401/222-4203, ext. 4042, website: www.dot.state.ri.us/WebTran/bikeri.html.

Rhode Island Parks and Recreation, 2321 Hartford Avenue, Johnston, RI 02919, 401/222-2632, website: www.riparks.com.

Greenways Alliance of Rhode Island, Rhode Island Affiliate of the East Coast Greenway Alliance, website: www.rigreenways.org.

Ocean State Bike Path Association, P.O. Box 548, Warren, RI 02885, 401/245-9755, website: http://members.cox.net/osbpa.

Bike Downtown Providence, Groundwork Providence, 69 Washington Street, Providence, RI 02903, 401/351-6440, website: www.bikedowntown.org.

Vermont

Vermont Bicycle/Pedestrian Coalition, P.O. Box 1234, Montpelier, VT 05601, 802/279-7545, website: www.vtbikeped.org.

Vermont Agency of Transportation, 1 National Life Drive, Drawer 33, Montpelier, VT 05633-0001, 802/828-2657, website: www.aot.state.vt.us.

Vermont Department of Forests, Parks, and Recreation, 103 South Main Street, Waterbury, VT 05671-0601, 802/241-3655, website: www.vtstateparks.com.

Vermont Mountain Biking Association, P.O. Box 563, Waterbury, VT 05676, website: www.vmba.org.

Local Motion, 1 Steele Street #103, Burlington, VT 05401, 802/652-BIKE (802/652-2453), website: www.localmotionvt.org.

Lake Champlain Bikeways Clearinghouse, 1 Steele Street #103, Burlington, VT 05401, 802/652-BIKE (802/652-2453), website: www.champlainbikeways.org.

Bike Clubs in New England

Connecticut

Hat City Cyclists, P.O. Box 1034, Bethel, CT 06801, website: www.hatcitycyclists.org.

Pequot Cyclists, website: www.pequotcyclists.com.

Sound Cyclists, P.O. Box 3323, Westport, CT 06880, 203/840-1757, website: www.soundcyclists.com.

Southern Connecticut Cycle Club, P.O. Box 51, New Haven, CT 06501, website: http://sccc.recol.net.

Yankee Pedalers, website: http://members.aol.com/yankpedal.

Maine

Casco Bay Bicycle Club, website: www.cascobaybicycleclub.org.

Maine Coast Cycling Club, Cape-Able Bike Shop, P.O. Box 581, Kennebunkport, ME 04046, 207/967-4382, website: www.portcycle.com.

Maine Cycling Club, Rainbow Bicycles, 1225 Center Street, Auburn, ME 04210, 207/784-7576, website: www.rainbowbike.com.

Maine Outdoor Adventure Club, P.O. Box 11251, Portland, ME 04104, 207/775-MOAC (207/775-6622), website: www.moac.org.

Merrymeeting Wheelers Bicycle Club, P.O. Box 233, Brunswick, ME 04011, 207/882-7206, website: www.merrymeetingwheelers.com.

Mount Agamenticus NEMBA, P.O. Box 40, Cape Neddick, ME 03902, 207/332 5497, website: www.mtanemba.org.

Portland Velo Club, P.O. Box 15093, Portland, ME 04112, website: www.portlandvelo.com.

Rage on Portland, website: http://mainiacs.ragemtb.com.

Southern Maine Cycling Club, Gorham Bike and Ski, 1440 Congress Street, Portland, ME 04102, 207/773-1700, website: www.gorhambike.com.

Western Maine Pedalers Bike Club, Chase Cyclery, 207/364-7946, website: www.angelfire.com/scary/chase/index.club.html.

Massachusetts

The state has too many to list, but here is a sampling of Massachusetts bike clubs. Check MassBike (under Biking Organizations) for a more complete listing.

Boston Bicycle Club, website: www.bostonbicycleclub.org.

Charles River Wheelmen, website: www.crw.org.

Essex County Velo, P.O. Box 2246, South Hamilton, MA 01982, website: www.ecvcycling.org.

Franklin-Hampshire Freewheelers, website: www.freewheelers.org.

Minuteman Road Club, website: www.minutemanroadclub.com.

Nashoba Valley Pedalers, website: www.nvpbike.org.

North Shore Cyclists, website: www.astseals.com/nsc.

Northampton Cycling Club, P.O. Box 886, Northampton, MA 01061, website: www.northamptoncyclingclub.org.

Rage on Boston, website: www.rageMTB.com.

Seven Hills Wheelmen, P.O. Box 20232, Worcester, MA 01602, website: www.sevenhillswheelmen.org.

New England Mountain Biking Association Massachusetts chapters: Berkshire, Greater Boston, Merrimack Valley, Pioneer Valley, North Shore, Cape Cod, Southeast MA, and Wachusett. For chapter details, contact NEMBA, P.O. Box 2221, Acton, MA 01720, 800/57-NEMBA (800/576-3622), website: www.nemba.org.

New Hampshire
Friends of Massabesic Bicycling Association, P.O. Box 155, Auburn, NH 03032, website: www.fomba.com.

Granite State Wheelmen, PMB 216, 215 South Broadway, Salem, NH 03079-3309, 603/898-5479, website: www.GraniteStateWheelmen.org.

New Hampshire Cycling Club, website: www.nhcyclingclub.com.

Seacoast NEMBA, website: www.snemba.org.

South Central New Hampshire NEMBA, website: www.scnhnemba.org.

Rhode Island
Aquidneck Bicycle Club, website: www.geocities.com/aquidneckbikeclub.

Narragansett Bay Wheelmen, P.O. Box 41177, Providence, RI 02940-1177, 401/351-3055, website: www.nbwclub.org.

Providence Velo Club, Providence Bicycle, 725 Branch Avenue, Providence, RI 02904, 401/331-6610, website: www.providencebicycle.com.

Rhode Island NEMBA, email: vcycles@mindspring.com, website: www.nemba.org.

Vermont

Green Mountain Bicycle Club, website: www.thegmbc.com.

Killington Pico Cycling Club, website: www.KPCCVT.org.

Montpelier Area Mountain Bike Association, email: info@bikemamba.org, website: www.bikemamba.org.

New England Bike Shops

Connecticut

Bethel
Bethel Cycles, 120 Greenwood Avenue, 203/792-4640, website: www.bethelcycle.com.

Bicycle Goodie Shop, 71 Stony Hill Road, 203/778-5431.

Bloomfield
Bloomfield Bicycle, 5 Seneca Road, 860/242-9884.

Branford
Branford Bike, 202 Main Street, 203/488-0482, website: www.branfordbike.com.

Bridgeport
Spoke and Wheel Bike Shop, 2355 East Main Street, 203/384-8779.

Canton
Benidorm Bikes and Boards, 247 Albany Turnpike (Route 44), 860/693-8891, website: www .benidormbikes.com.

Country Sports, 65A Albany Turnpike (Route 44), 860/693-2267, website:/www.countrysportsusa.com.

Clinton
Rock'n Road Cycles, 223 East Main Street, 860/669-7735, website: www.rocknroadcycles.com.

Colchester
Sunshine Cycle-Works, 467B South Main Street, 860/537-2788, website: www.sunshinecycleworks.com.

Danbury
Bike Express, 76 West Street, 203/792-5460, website: www.thebikeexpress.com.

Ski Market Underground, 61 Newtown Road, Plum Tree Plaza, 203/798-6616, website: www.skimarket.com.

Essex
Clarke Cycles, 4 Essex Plaza, 860/767-2405, website: www.clarkecycles.com.

Farmington
Central Wheel, 62 Farmington Avenue, 860/677-7010, website: www.centralwheel.com.

Glastonbury
Pig Iron Bike and Mountain Works, 2277 Main Street, 860/633-3444, website: www.pigironsports.com.

Granby
Valley Bicycle, Granby Village Shops, 10 Hartford Avenue (Route 189), 860/653-6545, website: www.valleybicycle.com.

Groton
Bicycle Barn, 1241 Poquonnock Road (Route 1), 860/448-4984, website: www.bicyclebarn.net.

Hebron
Cycle Escape, 50 Main Street, 860/228-2453.

Manchester
The Bike Shop, 681 Main Street, 860/647-1027, website: www.bikes-boards.net.

Monroe
Cycle Fitness, 612 Main Street, 203/261-8683.

Mystic
Mystic Cycle Center, 42 Williams Avenue (Route 1), 860/572-7433, website: www.mysticcycle.com.

New Milford
The Bike Express, 73 Bridge Street, 203/354-1466.

Putnam
Silver Bike Shop, 6 Livery Street, 860/928-7370.

Joe's Bike Shop, 33 Memorial Terrace, 860/928-6783 (repairs only).

Rocky Hill
Cycling Concepts, 825 Cromwell Avenue, 860/563-6667, website: www.cyclingconcepts.com.

Simsbury
Bicycle Cellar, 532 Hopmeadow Street, 860/658-1311.

South Glastonbury
Bicycles East, 2249 New London Turnpike, 860/659-0114, website: www.bicycleseast.com.

South Windsor
Bicycle South Windsor, 978 Sullivan Avenue, 860/644-0023, website: www.bicyclesouthwindsor.com.

Vernon
Vernon Cycle, 352 Hartford Turnpike, 860/872-7740, website: www.vernoncycle.com.

Maine
Augusta
Auclair Cycle and Ski, 64–66 Bangor Street, 207/623-4351 or 800/734-7171, website: www.auclair-cycle.com.

Bar Harbor
Acadia Bike, 48 Cottage Street, 207/288 9605 or 800/526 8615, website: www.acadiabike.com.

Acadia Outfitters, 106 Cottage Street, 207/288-8118.

Bar Harbor Bicycle Shop, 141 Cottage Street, 207/288-3886, website: www.barharborbike.com.

Camden
Ragged Mountain Sports, 46 Elm Street (Route 1), 207/236-6664, website: www.raggedmountain-sports.com.

Carrabassett Valley
Sugarloafer Shop at Sugarloaf USA, 5092 Access Road, 207/237-6718, website: www.sugarloaf.com (seasonal rentals only).

Ellsworth
Bar Harbor Bike, 193 Main Street, 207/667-6886, website: www.barharborbike.com.

Freeport
L. L. Bean, Route 1, bike shop 207/552-7834, store 877/552-3268, website: www.llbean.com.

National Bike and Ski, 308 Route 1, 207/865-0523, website: www.ski-market.com.

Greenville
North Woods Outfitters, Maine Street, 207/695-3288 or 866/223-1380, website: www.maineoutfitter.com.

Kennebunkport
Cape-Able Bike Shop, 83 Arundel Road, 207/967 4382.

North Windham
Sebago Outfitters, 100 Tandberg Trail (Route 115), 207/892-9228, website: www.sebagooutfitters.com.

Peaks Island
Brad's Recycled Bike Shop, 115 Island Avenue, 207/766-5631.

Portland
AllSpeed Bike and Ski, 1041 Washington Avenue, 207/878-8741, website: www.AllSpeed.com.

Back Bay Bicycle, 333 Forest Avenue, 207/773-6906, website: www.backbaybicycle.com.

CycleMania, 59 Federal Street, 207/774-2933, website: www.cyclemania1.com.

Gorham Bike and Ski, 1440 Congress Street, 207/773-1700, website: www.gorhambike.com.

Rangeley
Seasonal Cycles, 2593 Main Street, 207/864-2100.

Rockport
Maine Sport Outfitters, Route 1, 207/236-7120 or 888/236-8797, website: www.mainesport.com.

Rumford
Chase Cyclery, 485 Prospect Avenue (Route 2), 207/364-7946 or 800/834-7946, website: www.chasecyclery.com.

Westbrook
Ernie's Cycle Shop, 105 Conant Street, 207/854-4090.

Winthrop
Hilltop Ski and Bike, 2208 Route 202, 207/395 4010, website: www.hilltopskibike.com.

York
Berger's Bike Shop, 241 York Street, 207/363-4070.

Massachusetts
Amherst
The Laughing Dog Cyclery, 63 South Pleasant Street, 413/253-7722.

Valley Bicycles, 319 Main Street, 413/256-0880.

Barre
Country Bike and Sports, 12 Exchange Street, 978/355-2219.

Brewster
Barbara's Bike and Blade, Route 6A, 508/896-7231, website: www.barbsbikeshop.com.

Brewster Bike Rentals, 442 Underpass Road, 508/896-8149.

Rail Trails Bike Shop, 302 Underpass Road, 508/896-8200.

Chelmsford
Chelmsford Cyclery, 7 Summer Street, 978-256-1528.

Eastham
Little Capistrano Bike Shop, 341 Salt Pond Road, 508/255-6515.

Gardner
O'Neil's Bicycle Shop, 108 Main Street, 978/632-7200, website: www.oneilsbicycles.com.

Great Barrington
Berkshire Bike and Blade, 326 Stockbridge Road (Route 7), 413/528-5555, website: www.bike-andblade.com.

Greenfield
Bicycle World, 104 Federal Street, 413/774-3701.

Bicycles Unlimited, 322 High Street, 413-772-2700, website: www.bikes-unlimited.com.

Hadley
Valley Bicycle, 8 Railroad Street, 413/584-4466.

Hyannis
Bike Zone, 323 Barnstable Road, 508/775-3299, website: www.bike-zoneinc.com.

Lenox
Arcadian Shop, 91 Pittsfield Road, 413/637-3010, website: www.arcadian.com.

Mean Wheels Bike Shop, 57a Housatonic Street, 413/637-0644.

New Bedford
Cesar's Cyclery, 739 Ashley Boulevard, 508/998-8777, website: www.cesarscyclery.com.

Yesteryear Cyclery, 330 Hathaway Road, 508/993-2525, website: www.yesteryearcyclery.com.

Newburyport
Riverside Cycles, 50 Water Street, The Tannery, 888/465-BIKE (888/465-2453), website: www.riverside-cycle.com.

North Adams
The Sports Corner, 61 Main Street, 413/664-8654.

North Eastham
Idle Times Bike Shop, 4550 Route 6, 508/255-8281, website: www.idle-timesbike.com.

North Harwich
Bike Depot, 500 Depot Street, 508/430-4375, website: www.ccrail-trail.com.

Northampton
Northampton Bicycle, 319 Pleasant Street, 413/586-3810, website: www.nohobike.com.

Orleans
Orleans Cycles, 26 Main Street, 508/255-9115, website: www.cape-cod-orleans.com/orleanscycle.

Provincetown
Arnold's, 329 Commercial Street, 508/487 0844.

Gale Force Bikes, 144 Bradford Street Extension, 508/487-4849, website: www.galeforcebikes.com.

Nelson's Bike Shop, 43 Race Point Road, 508/487-8849.

Ptown Bikes, 42 Bradford Street, 508/487-8735.

South Dennis
Barbara's Bike and Blade, 430 Route 134, 508/760-4723, website: www.barbsbikeshop.com.

South Wellfleet
Black Duck Bike Shop, 1446 Route 6, 508/349-9801.

Idle Times Bike Shop, 2616-A Route 6, 508/349-9161.

Swansea
BikeWorks, 79 Swansea Mall Drive (Route 118), 508/677-0710, website: www.bikeworksma.com.

Westport
The Bike Shop, 1125 State Road (Route 6), 508/636-1266.

Williamstown
The Mountain Goat, 130 Water Street, 413/458-8445, website: www.themountaingoat.com.

The Spoke, 279 Main Street, 413/458-3456, website: www.spoke-bicycles.com.

Worcester
Bike Alley, 1067 Main Street, 508/752-2230, website: www.bike-alley.com.

Fritz's Bicycle Shop, 328 West Boylston Street, 508/853-1799, website: www.fritzsbikes.com.

New Hampshire
Berlin
Crooker's Cycle Sports, 240 Glen Avenue, 603/752-3632.

Concord
Banagan's, 67 South Main Street, 603/225-3330, website: www.banagans.com.

S and W Sports, South Main Street, 603/228-1441, website: www.swsports.net.

Dixville Notch
The Balsams, 800/255-0600, website: www.thebalsams.com.

Franconia Notch
Franconia Sports Shop, Main Street, 603/823-5241, website: www.franconiasports.com.

Hanover
Omer and Bob's Sport Shop, 7 Allen Street, 603/643-3525, website: www.omerandbobs.com.

Hooksett
Goodale's Bike Shop, 1197 Hooksett Road, 603/644-2111, website: www.goodalesbikeshop.com.

Keene
Andy's Cycle Shop, 165 Winchester Street, 603/352-3410.

Banagan's, 41 Central Square, 603/357-2331, website: www.banagans.com.

Norm's Ski and Bike Shop, 62 Martell Court, 603/352-1404.

Lebanon
Banagan's, 187 Mechanic Street, 603/448-5556, website: www.banagans.com.

Manchester
Alternative Bike, 616 Mast Road, 603/666-4527, website: www.alternativebike.com.

The Bike Barn, 33 South Commercial Street, 603/668-6555, website: www.bikebarnusa.com.

Jake's Bicycle Shop, 412 Kelley Street, 603/669-5422.

Nault's Cyclery, 30 Bridge Street, 603/669-7993, website: www.naults.com.

Milford
Souhegan Cycleworks, 227 Union Square, Unit 3, 603/673-1817, website: www.souhegancycleworks.com.

Newbury
Outspokin' Bicycle and Sport, Junction of Route 103 and 103A, 603/763-9500, website: www.outspokin.com.

North Conway
The Bike Shop, Mountain Valley Mall Boulevard, 603/356-6089, website: www.nhbikes.com.

Sports Outlet Shop, 2420 White
Mountain Highway, 603/356-3133,
website: www.sportsoutlet.org.

Peterborough
Ride 365, 109 Grove Street, 603/924-
9797, website: www.ride-365.com.

Plymouth
Rhino Bike Works, 1 Foster Street,
603/536-3919, website: www.rhino-
bikeworks.com.

Portsmouth
Bicycle Bob's Bicycle Outlet, 990
Lafayette Road, 603/436-2453, web-
site: www.bicyclebobs.com.

Papa Wheelies, 653 Islington
Street, 603/427-2060, website:
www.backbaybicycles.com.

Rindge
Pedalsnpacks, 222 Route 202,
603/899-5655, website: www.pedal-
snpacks.com.

Rochester
Tri-City Bicycles, 48 South Main
Street, 603/335-6440.

Rhode Island
Block Island
Block Island Bike and Car Rental,
Ocean Avenue, 401/466-2297.

Island Moped and Bike, P.O. Box
280, 401/466-2700.

Old Harbor Bike Shop, P.O. Box
2818, 401/466-2029, website:
www.oldharborbikeshop.com.

Coventry
Greenways Cycles, 585 Washington
Street (Route 117), 401/822 2080.

East Providence
East Providence Cycle, 414 Warren
Avenue, 401/434-3838, website:
www.eastprovidencecycle.com.

Newport
Newport Wheels, Brown and
Howard Wharf, Unit 2, 401/849-
4400, website: www.newportwheel-
sports.com.

Ten Speed Spokes, 18 Elm Street,
401/847-5609, website: www.ten-
speedspokes.com.

Narragansett
Narragansett Bikes, 1153 Boston
Neck Road, 401/782-4444.

North Kingstown
Bike Zone, 6322 Post Road,
401/885-8075.

Ron's Bicycle Shop, 7592 Post
Road, 401/294-2238.

Providence
Providence Bicycle, 725 Branch Avenue, 401/331-6610, website:
www.providencebicycle.com.

Riverside
East Providence Cycle, Riverside-
On Bike Path, 111 Crescent View
Avenue, 401/437-2453, website:
www.eastprovidencecycle.com.

Your Bike Shop, 459 Willett Avenue, 401/433-4491.

Warren
Your Bike Shop, 51 Cole Street, 401/245-9755.

Warwick
Caster's Bicycles and Fitness, 3480 Post Road, 401/739-0393, website: www.bikeri.com.

Westerly
Victory Cycles, 271 Post Road, 401/322-6005, website: www.victorycycles.net.

Wyoming
Victory Cycles, 1190 Main Street, 401/539-7540, website: www.victorycycles.net.

Vermont
Bennington
Eiger, 160 Benmont Avenue, 802/442-8664.

Bondville
The Startingate, Route 30, 802/297-1213, website: www.startingate.net.

Brattleboro
Brattleboro Bicycle Shop, 165 Main Street, 802/254-8644, www.bratbike.com.

Burrows/Specialized Sport Shop, 105 Main Street, 802/254-9430, www.sover.net/~specspor.

Burlington
North Star Cyclery, 100 Main Street, 802/863-3832.

Old Spokes Home, 324 North Winooski Ave, 802/863-4475.

Ski Rack, 85 Main Street, 802/658-3313 or 800/882-4530, website: www.skirack.com.

Craftsbury Common
Craftsbury Outdoor Center, 535 Lost Nation Road, 802/586-7767 or 800/729-7751, website: www. craftsbury.com.

East Burke
East Burke Sports, Route 114, 802/626-3215, website: www.eastburkesports.com.

Georgia
White's Green Mountain Bikes, 1008 Ethan Allen Highway, 802/524-4496, website: www.together.net/~wgmb.

Ludlow
Mountain Cycology, 3 Lamere Square, 802/228-2722.

Manchester
Battenkill Sports Bicycle Shop, 1240 Depot Street, 802/362-2734, website: www.battenkillsports.com.

Middlebury
The Alpine Shop, Merchants Row, 802/388-7547, website: www.alpineshopvt.com.

The Bike Center, 74 Main Street, 802/388-6666, website: www.bike-centermid.com.

Montpelier
Onion River Sports, 20 Langdon Street, 802/229-9409 or 800/894-7547, website: www.onionriver.com.

Rawsonville
Mountain Riders at Equipe Sports, Junction 30 and Route 100, 802/297-2847 or 800/282-6665, website: www.equipesport.com.

Rochester
Green Mountain Bicycles, 105 North Main Street, 802/767-4464, website: www.greenmountain-bikes.com.

Rutland
Great Outdoors Trading Company, 219 Woodstock Avenue, 802/775-9989.

Green Mountain Cyclery, 133 Strongs Avenue, 802/775-0869.

Sports Peddler, 162 North Main Street, 802/775-0101.

South Burlington
Earl's Cyclery, 2500 Williston Road, 802/864-9197 or 866/327-5725, website: www.earlsbikes.com.

The Alpine Shop, 1184 Williston Road, 802/862-2714, website: www.alpineshopvt.com.

Waitsfield
Fit Werx, 4312 Main Street, 802/496-7570, website: www.fitwerx.com.

Stark Mountain Bike Works, Route 17, 802/496-4800.

Winooski
Winooski Bike Shop, 12 West Canal Street, 802/655-3233.

Woodstock
Biscuit Hill Bike and Outdoor Shop, 490 Route 4, 802/457-3377, website: www.biscuithillbikes.com.

Woodstock Sports, 30 Central Street, 802/457-1568.

Campgrounds

Many of the routes in this book start at or pass by state park or other public campgrounds. You can ride out right from the campgrounds listed below.

Connecticut

Natchaug State Forest, c/o Mashamoquet Brook State Park, RFD #1, Wolf Den Road, Pomfret Center, CT 06259, 860/928-6121, website: www.dep.state.ct.us/ stateparks/forests/natchaug.htm.
Ride 5: Quiet Corner Loop; Eastford and Pomfret

Lake Waramaug State Park, 30 Lake Waramaug Road, New Preston, CT 06777, 860/868-0220, website: www.dep.state.ct.us/state parks/parks/lakewaramaug.htm.
Ride 6: Lake Waramaug Loops; New Preston

Devil's Hopyard State Park, 366 Hopyard Road, East Haddam, CT 06423, 860/873-8566, website: www .dep.state.ct.us/stateparks/parks/ devilshopyard.htm.
Ride 13: Devil's Hopyard Loop; East Haddam

Maine

Blackwoods Campground at Acadia National Park, 800/365-CAMP (800/365-2267), website: www.nps .gov/acad/pphtml/camping.html.
Ride 10: Carriage Roads; Acadia National Park, Mount Desert Island

Bradbury Mountain State Park, 528 Hallowell Road, Pownal, ME, 207/688-4712, website: www.state .me.us/doc/parks.
Ride 13: Bradbury Mountain; Bradbury Mountain State Park, Pownal

Massachusetts

Savoy Mountain State Forest, 260 Central Shaft Road, Savoy, MA 01247, 413/663-8469, website: www .state.ma.us/dem/parks/svym.htm.
Ride 3: Old Florida Road; Savoy Mountain State Forest, Florida

Otter River State Forest, New Winchendon Road, Baldwinville, MA 01436, 978/939-8962, website: www.state.ma.us/dem/parks/ottr.htm.
Ride 5: Beaver Pond Loop; Otter River State Forest, Winchendon

October Mountain State Forest, 317 Woodland Road, Lee, MA 01238, 413/243-1778, website: www.state .ma.us/dem/parks/octm.htm.
Ride 8: October Mountain Loop; October Mountain State Forest, Lee

Carroll A. Holmes Recreation Area, Lake Wyola State Park, Lakeview Road, Shutesbury, MA 01072, 413/367-0317.
Ride 9: Lake Wyola Loop; Shutesbury and Leverett

New Hampshire

Milan Hill State Park, Route 16, Milan, NH 03588, 603/466-3860, website: www.nhstateparks.org/Parks Pages/MilanHill/MilanHill.html.
Ride 2: Great North Woods Ride; Berlin

Lafayette Campground at Franconia Notch State Park, Franconia, NH, 603/823-9513 for information, 603/271-3628 for reservations, website: www.nhstateparks.org/Parks Pages/franconianotch/lafayette.html.
Ride 3: Franconia Recreational Trail; Franconia Notch State Park, Lincoln

Albany Covered Bridge Campground, c/o Saco Ranger Station, Kancamagus Highway, 33 Kancamagus Highway, Conway, NH 03818, 603/447-5448, website: www.fs.fed .us/r9/white/recreation/camping/ index.html.
Ride 4: Lower Nan Out and Back; North Conway

Pillsbury State Park, Route 31, Washington, NH 03280, 603/863-2860, website: www.nhstateparks .org/ParksPages/Pillsbury/Pillsbury.html.
Ride 11: Kittredge Hill Loop; Pillsbury State Park, Washington

Bear Brook State Park, Route 28, Allenstown, NH 03275, 603/485-9874, website: www.nhstateparks .org/ParksPages/BearBrook/Bear-Brk.html.
Ride 12: Kathy's Bear Brook Bounder; Bear Brook State Park, Allenstown

Rhode Island

George Washington Camping Area, 2185 Putnam Pike, Glocester, RI 02857, 401/568-2248.
Ride 1: Walkabout Trail; George Washington Management Area, Burrillville

Burlingame State Park, Charlestown, RI 02813, 401/322-7337, website: www.riparks.com/ burlgmcamp.htm.
Ride 11: Vin Gormley Trail; Burlingame State Park, Charlestown

Vermont

Grand Isle State Park, 36 East Shore South, Grand Isle, VT 05458, 802/372-4300, website: www.vtstateparks.com/htm/grand isle.cfm.
Ride 1: Grand Isle Getaway; Milton, Alburg, and North Hero

Brighton State Park, 102 State Park Road, Island Pond, VT 05846, 802/723-4360, website: www.vt-stateparks.com/htm/brighton.cfm.
Ride 4: Kingdom Trail Loop; East Burke

Ricker Pond State Park, 526 State Forest Road, Groton, VT 05046, 802/584-3821, website: www.vt-stateparks.com/htm/ricker.cfm.
Ride 6: Wells River Rail Trail; Groton

Branbury State Park, 3570 Lake Dunmore Road, Route 53, Salisbury, VT 05733, 802/247-5925, website: www.vtstateparks.com/ htm/branbury.cfm.
Ride 8: Leicester Hollow Trail; Goshen

Winhall Brook Camping Area, Winhall Station Road, South Londonderry, VT (mailing address c/o Ball Mountain Lake, 88 Ball Mountain Lane, Jamaica, VT 05343), 802/874-4881, for reservations call the National Recreation Reservation Service at 877/444-6777, website: www.nae.usace.army.mil/ recreati/bml/bmlres.htm. *Ride 16: West River Trail; South Londonderry*

Index

Wells River Rail Trail 33–34; West River Trail 58–61; Worden Pond Loop 335–337

Williamstown: **192,** 197–199, **198**

Winchendon: 206–208, **207**

Winchester: **113,** 113–114

Windham to Standish: **177,** 177–178

Winter Harbor: **130,** 163–165, **164**

Wolfe's Neck Woods State Park: 174

Wononskopomuc Lane: 258

Woodchuck Trail: 209

woodland trails: *See* forest/woodland trails

Woods Pond: 216

Woodstock: **16, 51,** 51–52, **74**

Woodstock-Ascutney Loop: **51,** 51–52

Worden Pond Loop: **306,** 335–337, **336**

Y

Yale-Toumey Forest: 113

Yellow Circle Trail: 293

Yellow Rectangle Trail: 293

York: 185–187, **186**

Acknowledgments

This book simply would not exist without the contributions of two people: Ellen Kanner and Penelope Kim.

Ellen Kanner contributed most of the chapters on New Hampshire and Vermont, and the book is as much hers as it is mine. She and I came up with the basic outline for the book, did the proposal together, made decisions about rides and regions, and swapped endless email about all aspects of biking in New England. A veteran outdoorswoman and photographer, Ellen has explored all the corners of the region and her contributions and perspective shape this book.

Ellen would like to acknowledge "my then-fiance, now-husband Ray Marcotte for riding so many rides with me and keeping me going when the going was tough; my parents, Werner and Gertie, for their support while living at their house so that I could get the book up and running; my sister Nancy and her husband, Dave, for allowing me to stay at their house numerous times when exploring the seacoast area for rides; special thanks to Melissa, for knowing what writing a book is all about and keeping us on course; and to those friends who said, 'Wow, that's so cool!' Hearing that was the juice to get me riding on those less than pleasant New England days."

Penelope Kim, my tireless mother, assisted me on rides in Massachusetts, Rhode Island, and Connecticut as she and my father, Richard Kim, let me make their western Massachusetts home my southern New England base. She served as my sag wagon, waiting patiently in deserted parking lots; guided me via cell phone when I got lost on more than one occasion; scouted countless rides with me, driving down dirt roads and dead-end streets; and never ran out of optimism.

Three mountain bikers contributed routes in Connecticut, sharing priceless insider information and perspective. John Isch contributed the Shenipsit, Bigelow Hollow, and Case Mountain routes, as well as the book's cover photo. Marc Fleisher contributed the West Hartford, Huntington, Pequonnock River Valley, and Westwoods routes. Steve Sands contributed the Bluff Point route. I got very valuable advice and cue sheets from Don Shildneck, a generous and enthusiastic trip leader for the Connecticut AMC biking chapter.

Dozens of other people gave me suggestions, advice, and encouragement. My late colleague, friend, and budding cyclist Zack Gaulkin gave me the push I needed to take on this project. Also in Maine, Ted Kerkam of Rage on Portland advised me on favorite mountain biking trails. The good folks at Back Bay Bikes, Gorham Bike and Ski, and Cyclemania all worked on my bikes. Johnny Field of Seasonal Cycles in Rangeley showed me the town's excellent mountain biking trails.

In Massachusetts, Mike Pappaconstantine at Belmont Wheelworks gave me excellent bike repair and maintenance advice. Becky at Valley Bicycles in Amherst suggested the West Stockbridge route. Tim and Sally Schrader helped me on Cape Cod. The late Minty Maloney gave me advice about biking in South Dartmouth. In Vermont, Steve Ovenden and Jeff Nugent with the Windham Regional Commission gave me scads of advice and wonderful maps. Francesca Dricot opened her home to me.

Finally, heartfelt thanks go to my husband, Blake Strack, a fellow cyclist who supported me through this entire project, rode with me on muddy mountain biking trails and in pouring rainstorms, helped me ride on a bike trainer in the basement to keep in shape through the long Maine winter, and rode a few routes for me when I was too pregnant to do it at the very, very end. This one's for you.

5

T.I.P.S.
(TELESEARCH Interview
"Prep" Session)

Some job hunters have been on so many interviews that they have given up trying—and don't even know it. They go through the motions. They will attempt to pick themselves up in the interviewer's office and crack a smile, but they have no idea what the company does, to whom they would report if they got the job, or anything about the department in which they wish to work. They are "professional interviewees" and can get through an application faster than the interviewer's assistant can return with the coffee. It is easy to see that they are completely out of touch with their barber or hairstylist; even their manner of dress suggests past glory rather than anticipation of future success. These "pros" are usually extremely impatient if the employer is running late. You get the feeling that they are more worried about missing the beginning of the "Three O'Clock Movie" on TV than being interviewed. Oh yes, they "won't take less than thirty-five K and have to be off a month next spring to help paint Mother's barn."

Absurd? Possibly, but I could write another book consisting of nothing but such anecdotes. I am not insensitive to the circumstances that may have led to such an attitude—rejection and frustration. The more rejections any job seeker receives, the more he begins to expect rejection. They eventually rationalize not trying hard because "it won't make any difference, anyway."

WE MAY NOT ALWAYS GET WHAT WE WANT, BUT WE INVARIABLY END UP WITH WHAT WE EXPECT.

Why? Because we have preconditioned ourselves to accept it.

If They Only Knew

The interview is what you have been working so hard to get. Yet people approach an interview as if it were the last place on earth they would choose to be: "I'd rather go to the dentist than interview for a job."

Each and every interview should be viewed for what it truly is—a golden opportunity to change your life for the better! Realize, once and for all, when you interview for the "right position," you will get it, and it will change your career forever. Even after you leave your next job, that most recent experience will take its place on your resume and another stepping stone in the career path of your life will have been permanently laid.

The annual salary for which you interview and finally accept will in turn grow to become the salary that future hiring authorities will compete against to obtain your services—for the rest of your life!

Believe me, the right interview will happen. No one who

diligently seeks work will stay unemployed forever. At some point, a prospective employer will come to terms and you will be employed again. This will be the "right interview."

We have no way of knowing in advance which one will be the right interview, because we cannot foretell the future. However, we do know this:

THE HARDER YOU WORK AT IT, THE SOONER
YOUR JOB SEARCH WILL BE OVER.

Commit yourself to concentrating upon making every interview a masterful performance, so that when the right one comes along you are sure to reap the maximum benefit.

YOU MUST MAKE EACH INTERVIEWER WANT
YOU BADLY ENOUGH TO LAY THE FULL SCOPE
OF THE OPPORTUNITY BEFORE YOU IN ITS
MOST ATTRACTIVE LIGHT SO YOU CAN MAKE
AN EDUCATED DECISION AS TO WHETHER YOU
WANT IT OR NOT.

When preparing sales professionals for interviews or applicants for a sales trainee-type position, I usually give them the following advice:

THE INTERVIEW ITSELF IS YOUR BIGGEST SALE
OF ALL. IT IS THE ONE SALE THAT WILL PAY
YOUR ENTIRE YEAR'S SALARY!

You do not have to be in sales to appreciate this kind of logic. It is the first interview with each company that we are most concerned with. If you make a suitable impression, you will be offered the position or invited back for another meeting. If, on the other hand, you goof in the first interview, well....

Let me remind you again that interviewers are only people.

Consequently, your experience and qualifications, though important, are not quite as important as you might think. What is most important is to convince the employer that you want the job and can handle it efficiently. Job interview situations are seldom clearly defined, all black or all white.

THE PERSON WHO STANDS TALLEST IN THE EYES OF THE EMPLOYER SHOWS A SINCERE INTEREST IN THE COMPANY; DEMONSTRATES CONFIDENCE THAT HIS EXPERIENCE AND INTELLIGENCE ARE SUFFICIENT TO HANDLE THE JOB SUCCESSFULLY; AND EXPRESSES A DEEP AND STRONG DESIRE FOR THE OPPORTUNITY WILL GET THE JOB OFFER.

Research

In your Company Contact Record list each firm that has agreed to an actual interview appointment. Before the interview, try to learn as much as possible about the company and the position being offered. Ask your librarian for any information available on the particular company granting you the interview and its industry in general. Ask for annual reports, product information, and brochures. If you are changing fields, read as much as you can about the new occupation you have chosen so that you can at least speak the language.

I discussed in Chapter Two the various means of checking out a small company. These methods are just as useful in researching a larger corporation if you cannot find printed material on it in your library. A friendly broker, banker or, even better, an aquaintance who is already employed by the firm can all be invaluable sources of information. You should not overlook the very real possibility of obtaining information from the company's public relations department with a simple phone call or visit.

As you read through annual reports, news clippings, advertisements, trade magazines, and other business articles, try to get the theme of the company's operations as well as its origin, accomplishments, and goals for the future. Study joint ventures and acquisitions in which the firm has participated and learn as much as you can about new products, services, and technologies it has developed. Pay attention to names, titles, and recent promotions in the news, particularly those of persons in that division of the company in which you wish to work. Your leading sources of information concerning your prospective company may be its customers, suppliers,and competitors, although information provided by competitors might not be trustworthy.

Write down any questions that come to mind about the company and the department and how you might best fit in.

THE VERY NATURE AND DEPTH OF YOUR QUESTIONS SHOULD REFLECT THE AMOUNT OF TIME AND EFFORT YOU HAVE INVESTED IN RESEARCHING THE COMPANY AND POSITION.

Researching the company and position is important. The effort required is well worth the big impression you can make with the interviewer, not to mention that it will help you better understand the situation you may be getting yourself into. You will immediately begin to impress the hiring authority that you are the best candidate for the position. Remember:

THE WAY TO GET OFFERS IS TO GO AFTER THEM.

Prepare For Tough Questions

While you are writing down the questions you wish to ask about the company, department, position, etc., consider some of the questions a prospective employer may ask you. Many

69

applicants have some questions that they would prefer the prospective employer not to ask. Nevertheless, you must be prepared to easily and confidently field any questions that might possibly be asked in an interview. Remember Truitt's Law from the previous chapter:

ANSWER QUESTIONS DIRECTED AT YOU TRUTHFULLY, BUT FINISH YOUR ANSWER WITH A QUESTION OF YOUR OWN—THEN FOLLOW WITH ANOTHER.

As I have no way of knowing what your "tough questions" are, the best advice is to prepare for the worst. Make a list of the ten worst possible questions an interviewer might ask. Then write down an honest answer to each question that presents your case in its most favorable light. Add a question of your own that might logically follow in the conversation, and regain control by implementing Truitt's Law in this way:

Yes, that was one of the biggest mistakes of my youth, but do you think that someone with the professional experience I have picked up since then could handle this job? What would you say is the most important skill one should possess to perform well in this position?

Have a response prepared for any tough questions you may expect. If answered easily, without great emphasis or evasiveness, then followed with a question of your own, the interviewer will probably not dwell upon those tough questions.

When You Must Have A Resume

Of course, there will be times when you must provide the employer with a copy of your resume. You do not, however, have to include your complete life history. Just a brief outline of your career highlights.

THE LESS YOU SAY IN YOUR RESUME, THE MORE FLEXIBLE YOU CAN BE IN THE INTERVIEW. THE MORE YOU CAN DIRECT THE CONTENTS OF YOUR RESUME TOWARD THE PARTICULAR PO-SITION YOU ARE APPLYING FOR, THE BETTER YOUR CHANCES OF ACHIEVING THE DESIRED RESULTS.

Whenever possible, rewrite your resume for the position for which you are applying. If time is against you, be sure to attach a cover letter pointing out the particular expertise in your background that qualifies you for the position.

The One-Page Resume

Judging from thousands of resumes I have personally re-viewed, the most difficult aspect of resume writing is con-densing a career into one page. Considering the volume of resumes in the mail these days, however, the value of a one-page resume cannot be overemphasized.

Many applicants seem to think that the more detailed job descriptions they include in their resumes, the more im-pressive they will be. Often, employers will require a resume to see how effectively you can express yourself in writing, using as few words as necessary. One or two lines listing your accomplishments with a particular employer would make for much more interesting and impressive reading than a "func-tional resume" that uses several pages to explain an appli-cant's capabilities.

Most companies and search firms deal with a tremendous volume of resumes. Personnel managers often end up read-ing resumes at home or in hotel rooms while on recruiting trips. Continuously faced with stacks of resumes on their desks, a foot deep or more, they will go through the stack separating the thickest, the sloppiest, and the most ornate from the others. These are the last to be read, if they get any attention at all. Most end up in the trash or paper shredder.

The one-page resume stands a much better chance of getting attention. The reader gets an overall picture of your background *at a glance*. If he has any interest at all, the brevity of your resume should arouse his curiosity. This is particularly important if you are answering a "blind-box ad" in the classifieds, or have to send an out-of-town employer a copy of your resume before he will agree to a meeting.

> THE OBJECT OF MAILING YOUR RESUME IN THE
> FIRST PLACE IS TO SECURE AN INTERVIEW.

Do not fret about being unable to include all the important details of your career on one page. You do not have to. Save them for the interview. When you think about it, you don't even know which "important details" an employer will be interested in.

Points to Include in Your Resume

> STATE YOUR NAME, HOW YOU MAY BE CON-
> TACTED, THE EXTENT OF YOUR FORMAL ED-
> UCATION, WHERE AND WHEN YOU HAVE
> WORKED (IN WHAT CAPACITY), AND WHAT YOU
> ACCOMPLISHED WITH EACH EMPLOYER.

These facts are all that any prospective employer will need to know before actually contacting you. Anything more will only bore someone who must go through thirty or forty resumes at a sitting.

What to Leave Out

Below is a list of things that should NOT be included in your resume:

~~~~~~

1. Age or date of birth
2. Religious affiliation
3. Career objective (Why limit yourself?)
4. Part-time jobs (except recent graduates)
5. Elementary and high schools attended
6. Position desired (cover letter)
7. Salary desired (*never*)
8. Salary history (even if requested in an ad)
9. References or letters of reference
10. Names of supervisors
11. Height, weight, and other physical descriptions
12. Photo, unless specifically requested
13. Hobbies or recreational activities
14. Detailed job descriptions or long lists of duties and responsibilities
15. Personal comments about failures, problems, or ideals

Avoid bound, typeset resumes and the use of expensive paper and inks (a sure way to let an employer know there are hundreds of copies of your resume floating around all over the country). You should not include college transcripts, performance reviews, clippings of articles about yourself, or any other bulky material with your resume. Artists and other creative people with a portfolio may include a sample of their work, but it should be small and easy to mail without defacing or damaging it. Otherwise, mention that you have a complete portfolio which you will bring to the interview.

The Best Resume

Use plain white, 8½″ X 11″ typing paper and black ink. Then, to get maximum results from your resume, follow this procedure and type it neatly:

> Beginning at the top of the page, center your name, address, and home phone number. Next, from the left-hand margin, state your marital status, number

of dependents, and your willingness to relocate or travel. Then include your degree(s), the name and location(s) of the college(s) or university(ies) you attended, and the date(s) of graduation. One line may be used to state your accomplishments in school.

Now, list in reverse chronological order (beginning with your present or last employer) names and addresses (city, not street) of previous employers, dates of employment, your last job title, and one or two lines explaining your accomplishments with each employer. Do the same for each period of employment going back through your career and finish with a statement that details salary history, and references will be furnished in an interview. (See Exhibit C.)

Employers Hire People, Not Paper

Risking redundancy, I feel compelled to emphasize that no resume at all is preferable to a bound, professionally typeset autobiography. If you can avoid sending a resume, don't.

If you have no real work experience, you do not need a resume. If, for instance, you are a housewife entering the job market for the first time, a recent college graduate, or a teenager without full-time work experience, a letter pointing out your educational background, grades, and career interests will accomplish more than a resume.

This same advice also holds true for someone who has had too many jobs in too few years. If you have changed employers more often than once every fifteen months to two years, a resume detailing all these job changes will do more harm than good. Just write a letter pointing out the experience you have without naming all of your previous employers. Get the interview appointment first. Believe me, you will get better results by explaining numerous job changes

74

Exhibit C

CONFIDENTIAL RESUME

William (Mac) MacDonald
1325 Red Bluff Rd. Dalton, Ga. 30621
Telephone: (404) 325-6777

Married, two children. Will relocate or travel.

BBA (1968) University of Georgia, Athens, Ga.

10–77 to Pres.	Sterling Mills, Inc.	Dalton, Ga.
	Marketing Manager	

Expanded sales force, new domestic markets. Opened foreign markets in Europe, Middle East, and China. Increased sales from $20MM to $70MM while corporate profits were almost quadrupled.

11–72 to 9–77	Johnny Carpetseed Ltd.	Charlotte, N.C.
	National Sales Manager	

Worked with founder to build company to an organization of nine stores spanning six southeastern states while consistently leading entire company in personal sales.

6–66 to 8–72	Hartford's Encyclopedia, Inc.	New York, N.Y.
	District Sales Manager	

Rose through six promotions from top Student Representative to number one District Manager in this $400MM worldwide conglomerate. Perfected many sales courses and training procedures still in use today.

DETAILS, SALARY HISTORY, AND REFERENCES WILL BE FURNISHED IN AN INTERVIEW.

75

or other problems in your past in the interview rather than in a resume and cover letter.

Many career books and counselors consider the resume the most important tool in your job search. Many even offer long lists of "action words" to use when describing your background and experience. These are supposed to make your resume sound as professional as every other applicant's. In reality, these action words end up making your resume look just like your competition's. Use your own words, and your resume will reflect the fact that you are unique. Keep it brief and it will be more professional.

Many of my critics will say this is only a matter of opinion. It is, in reality, much more important than that. If you must use a resume to secure an interview, then the impression made by your resume will make the difference in whether you are given an interview appointment or not. Stay with a simple, easy-to-read, one-page resume and you will get more interviews. That's what it's all about.

Sell Yourself in the Cover Letter

Once you have completed your resume, anything else of significance should be included in your cover letter. A cover letter addressed to the hiring authority should be attached to any resume submitted through the mail.

You may be more specific in the cover letter. Use it to detail your previous experience as it relates to the particular employer or position you are seeking. The cover letter provides a genuine opportunity to use salesmanship in written form. You should not oversell but do not pass up an opportunity to speak in your own behalf. Keep it brief. One-half to two-thirds of a single page is all that is necessary.

I have given two examples of cover letters that our friend Mac MacDonald (the person whose resume was used in Exhibit C) might attach to his resume. Exhibit D is an example of a letter to follow up a *TELESEARCH* call. Exhibit E would be used to answer a "blind-box ad" in the classifieds. A blind-box ad is an ad that gives no contact information other than

Exhibit D

1325 Red Bluff Road
Dalton, Georgia 30621
February 11, 198___

Paul Simmons, President
Worthington Industries, Inc.
711 Fifth Avenue
New York, New York 10012

Mr. Simmons:

Thank you for giving me so much of your valuable time during our telephone conversation this morning. As you can see from the enclosed resume, I have ten years' experience in the carpet industry, both retail and manufacturing. My track record with Sterling Mills over the last five years speaks for itself. I am particularly proud of our success overseas, and as you mentioned "familiarity with foreign markets", I may very well possess the qualifications and experience you are seeking.

In addition to sales and marketing skills, I have been fortunate in that I have gained expertise in negotiating joint ventures and acquisitions with firms in Europe and the Far East. A competitive team player, I thrive on challenges and responsibility.

Should you have any interest in discussing the position or my background in greater detail, feel free to contact me at my home by mail or phone. I realize how busy someone
in your position can be, so if I do not hear from you sooner,
I'll call your office in one week. I am very interested in discussing this opportunity with you and look forward to our meeting face to face in an interview soon.

Respectfully,

William MacDonald

encl.

Exhibit E

1325 Red Bluff Road
Dalton, Georgia 30621
February 11, 198___

P.O. Box 10001
THE NEW YORK CHRONICLE
1131 Third Avenue
New York, New York 10013

TO WHOM IT MAY CONCERN:

Your advertisement for a Vice President of Marketing is very appealing to me. As you can see from the enclosed resume, I have ten years' experience in the carpet industry, both in retail and manufacturing. My track record over the last five years with Sterling Mills will speak for itself, but I am particularly proud of our success overseas. As your ad mentioned "familiarity with foreign markets," I may well possess the qualifications and experience your firm is seeking.

A highly competitive, sales-oriented professional who thrives on challenge and responsibility, I have gained particular expertise in negotiating joint ventures and acquisitions with firms in Europe and the Far East.

Should your firm have any interest in meeting me to discuss this opportunity or my background in greater detail, feel free to contact me at my home by mail or telephone. I'll be more than happy to come to New York for an interview and look forward to meeting with you soon.

Respectfully,

William MacDonald

encl.

a P.O. box at the newspaper in which the ad appeared. (See Exhibits D and E.)

I do not like using resumes to arrange interviews but blind-box ads leave no alternative. Otherwise, carry your resume to interviews that are previously arranged by telephone.

Businesslike And Conservative

So much has been said and written about dressing for the interview that I truly hate to rehash the subject. Your manner of dress, however, is too important to pass over without comment.

YOU MUST MAKE SURE TO PRESENT YOUR "BEST SELF" IN EACH AND EVERY INTERVIEW.

Most of the professionals in my field agree that the proper style of dress for an interview is businesslike and conservative. We advise a conservative style because you have no way of knowing in advance the styles and tastes of all the people you may meet in your first interview. Some may even be ultra-conservative while others may be dressed in a golf shirt and sneakers. You may see full beards and long hair or the company may have a dress code against facial hair. The women in the office may wear jeans on Fridays, or there may be a ban against any kind of pants or pants suits being worn by women. The only thing we are certain of is that no one was ever turned down for a position because he or she dressed in a conservative, businesslike manner.

Men should wear a clean, neatly pressed, dark business suit. A new suit is definitely a worthwhile investment in your job search, if you want to look like the best candidate for the position. White shirt, conservative tie, matching dark socks, and *polished* shoes. No frayed cuffs or collars. Be sure your hair is clean and trimmed short, and clean and clip your fingernails. If you sport a beard or mustache, trim it neatly.

You may wish to call ahead and ask if there is a company policy concerning facial hair. When dressing for an interview try to impress, not dazzle.

Women should refrain from wearing pants or pants suits to their first interview. Wear something suitable such as a suit or businesslike dress with matching shoes and handbag. Makeup and jewelry should be worn sparingly. Stick to conservative colors in lipstick and nail polish, and be sure your hair is clean and neatly styled. Avoid loud or shimmering dresses that could be considered evening or cocktail wear. Dress sensibly, professionally, and carry a makeup kit, hair brush, and extra pair of stockings in an otherwise uncluttered purse in case a "quick fix" is necessary. Dazzle—don't decorate.

"Dress for the job" is poor, if perhaps not very costly, advice. Dress to make the finest impression you can. You can dress for the job after you have it. For the interview, dress to look better than anyone else applying for the same job.

FIRST INTERVIEW REALLY MEANS FIRST IMPRESSION. MOST OF THE INTERVIEWER'S OPINIONS CONCERNING YOUR CHARACTER, PROFESSIONALISM, CONFIDENCE, SELF-ESTEEM, AND WORTH TO HIS COMPANY WILL·BE FORMED DURING YOUR FIRST INTERVIEW.

Make sure you are attractively packaged. It will greatly influence the salary the employer will think you should receive. This is an easy way of presenting yourself as the best candidate and might significantly contribute to the amount of dollars that eventually end up in your pocket!

How Much Do You Care?

Another way of enhancing your first impression is by being punctual. It goes without saying, employers cannot help thinking that anyone who is late for an 11:00 A.M. interview may have serious problems getting to work on time at 8:00 A.M. or even 9:00 A.M. Leave early enough to allow yourself plenty of time to make the interview, and do not schedule appointments so closely together that if you end up being delayed in one, you will be late for the next. Allow from four to six hours between interviews.

> IF YOU DISCOVER THAT YOU WILL BE LATE FOR AN INTERVIEW, CALL THEIR OFFICE *BEFORE* YOUR SCHEDULED APPOINTMENT AND RE-SCHEDULE THE INTERVIEW. DON'T JUST SHOW UP LATE WITH A MOUTHFUL OF EXCUSES.

Plan your time so as not to arrive too early, either. An applicant with apparently a lot of time on his hands makes a poor impression indeed, cooling his heels in the outer office. Employees may interrupt their work to be nice and entertain you. This is sure to upset their supervisor, who may well be your interviewer. If you cause his department to miss an important deadline, you can forget about working for that company. If you arrive too early, wait in a nearby coffee shop, outside, or in your car.

> *NEVER* ARRIVE IN THE INTERVIEWER'S OFFICE MORE THAN FIVE MINUTES EARLY.

Cooperation Wins An Ally

Carry your neatly typed one-page resume to the interview, but keep it out of sight unless it is requested. Do not feel insulted if the interviewer's secretary asks you to fill out an application. Before you begin protesting that you have an accurate resume, think again.

> YOU ARE INTERVIEWING FOR A CAREER POSI-TION WITH THIS COMPANY. IF COMPANY POL-ICY REQUIRES YOU TO COMPLETE AN

APPLICATION, ARE YOU GOING TO START OUT
BY REJECTING COMPANY POLICY?

Are you too good or too lazy (too stupid?) to comply?
Everybody hates forms and applications. At least, in all my
years of experience I have never met anyone who told me
they enjoyed filling them out. If the position for which you
are interviewing has been open for any length of time, the
interviewer's secretary has already heard every excuse in the
book. Having given you the application along with the proper
instructions, the secretary does not care, personally, whether
you fill it out or make an airplane out of it.

Why not surprise him or her by asking if longhand is
acceptable or if you should print. Then, sit down quietly and
fill in *every line* neatly and completely, as if you cared about
getting the job. Do you know what a joy it is to find a cooperative person when you are instructed to require people
to do something that most of them detest?

MANY INTERVIEWERS SAY THEY JUDGE AN AP-
PLICANT'S SINCERITY AND DESIRE FOR THE PO-
SITION BY THE CARE AND EFFORT THE PERSON
PUTS INTO FILLING OUT THEIR COMPANY'S AP-
PLICATION.

Even if you think this logic is ridiculous, it is nevertheless
true of many employers. Be prepared by carrying notes with
dates of employment and schooling along with addresses,
phone numbers, supervisors' and references' names, and
contact information. This way you can complete forms quickly,
without using phone books, etc. Carry your own pen and a
spare.

NEVER WRITE "REFER TO RESUME" ON A COM-
PANY APPLICATION.

82

This indicates laziness and interrupts the interview as the employer shifts from one document to another in search of answers.

Three questions that normally appear on a company's application should be answered, if at all possible, with the single word, "Open." These are:

1. Salary desired?
2. Position desired?
3. Willing to relocate or travel?

Would you accept a different, possibly better job than the position advertised if offered to you? Would you relocate for a fantastic opportunity? If you do not indicate that you are at least open to discuss it, you may never even hear about it. Try to be objective, and do not "marry a piece of geography." Remaining open to salary will be discussed in detail in Chapter 6.

Answer questions on the application about your work record, salary history, and reasons for leaving former employers truthfully but briefly. Avoid vague terms like "personal reasons," "inter-office conflict," or "personality conflict." These terms normally suggest situations that may sound much worse than the actual occurrence. I advise you to be absolutely truthful. I have known people who got fired from positions they really liked because of some insignificant little lie they had put down on their application, a lie that had not affected the decision to hire them.

ONE FALSEHOOD MAKES THE ENTIRE APPLICATION SUSPECT.

If you were referred by an agency, be sure to write both the name of the agency and the counselor where the question "Referred by?" appears on the application. The same would apply if you were referred by a friend in the company. Otherwise, write "Self."

MAKE FRIENDS WITH THE INTERVIEWER'S SEC-
RETARY AND BE A MODEL OF COOPERATION.

Interviewers have been known to rely heavily upon their secretary's impressions of applicants during those "informal chats" in reception rooms. I would hate to count the times an interviewer has stepped out of his office after meeting with an applicant; looked over to his secretary (the only other company employee who has just met the same applicant the interviewer has); and asked, "What did you think of so and so?"

You should not give the interviewer's secretary or receptionist a hard time if the interviewer is running late. She is not to blame. You want her to like you and be on your side so that all of her answers, if her opinion is requested, are positive. Keep the conversation light in her office, and do not question her too closely about the company or the position. She may know very little about it or may well have been instructed not to discuss the position with applicants.

REMEMBER, THE ONE QUESTION ALL EMPLOY-
ERS MUST DETERMINE IS WHETHER YOU, THE
PROSPECTIVE EMPLOYEE, WILL GET ALONG
WELL WITH OTHER EMPLOYEES IN THE OF-
FICE.

Make friends with the interviewer's secretary and you will have someone pulling for you after you have left.

Do not go to any interview without preparing for it, or if you are not dressed properly. Postpone it to another day.

YOU GET ONLY ONE FIRST IMPRESSION WITH
EACH COMPANY. MAKE IT COUNT.

6

Interview For Offers

We have laid the groundwork to begin the interview on the right foot. As we come face to face with the interviewer, we realize:

WE MUST MAKE A FAVORABLE IMPRESSION UPON THE INTERVIEWER OR WE SHALL GO NO FURTHER.

This is essentially the same situation a sales representative is faced with on each cold call he makes. What are they taught? How does the professional sales representative ensure that his first impression is positive? In other words, how does the salesman persuade someone he has never met before to cast all misgivings and that old "invisible shield" of sales resistance aside and actually purchase his product for cash money?

The sales pro will first relax the prospect in order to gain his respect and trust. Then the client will actually listen to what the salesman is saying. He proceeds to present his product in such a way as to arouse the prospect's interest to the level where he wants to own it—at which point they both agree to write up the sale. You can do the same thing with a hiring authority except that instead of making him want to buy your product, you make him want to buy your services— to hire you. Like the sales pro, you must learn to be a *want creator*. Remember one of the most important principles in this text:

IF THE EMPLOYER REALLY WANTS YOU, HE WILL DO WHATEVER IS NECESSARY TO MAKE YOU WANT TO WORK FOR HIM.

This is a fundamental truth of interviewing for offers.

Melt That Old Invisible Shield

The first step is to break through that invisible shield most of us throw up when meeting someone for the first time. The interviewer is no different. The quickest and easiest way of accomplishing this is to smile. Sounds so obvious it could be considered ridiculous, does it not? You would be surprised how many applicants get so tense in an interview that they forget the obvious. Some even sit there in an interview with a pad on their knee and a scowl on their face taking notes, making demands, ready to fight over the terms of employment, expecting the worst. Who wants to be around this kind of person in an office all day?

A BIG SMILE CAN DO MORE TO "BREAK THE ICE" THAN ANY OTHER SINGLE TECHNIQUE YOU MIGHT EMPLOY.

It is almost impossible to avoid smiling back at someone sitting across a desk from you who has a big grin on his face. Smiling is easy if someone is smiling with you. You have to be the instigator and provide the spark. Once you notice the interviewer crack a big grin of his own, you know you are going to talk *to* each other, not *at* each other. That old invisible shield will begin to melt. It may be obvious, but do not get so balled up inside during the interview that you forget to smile and be pleasant.

> STAY FRIENDLY AND YOU WILL BEGIN TO RE-
> LAX THE EMPLOYER AND CONVINCE HIM THAT
> YOU ARE PLEASANT TO WORK WITH.

Are You A Truth-Teller?

Good eye contact will significantly aid you in gaining the interviewer's trust.

> IN THE EYES OF THE INTERVIEWER, GOOD EYE
> CONTACT LENDS TRUTH TO YOUR STATE-
> MENTS AND STRENGTH TO YOUR CHARACTER.

We have heard this advice since childhood, but during the conversation many applicants look out the window or at their hands, the interviewer's bald spot, or the pictures on the walls. They may not realize it, but this gives an impression of evasiveness or boredom.

If you have problems looking someone directly in the eye, try a technique that works for many sales professionals and actors.

> CONCENTRATE ON THE LITTLE SPACE BE-
> TWEEN THE INTERVIEWER'S EYES, JUST ABOVE
> THE NOSE.

This gives you a blank space upon which to focus your eyes while organizing your thoughts or formulating a response to a question. It gives the impression of a steady gaze. You may immediately evaluate the interviewer's reaction to your various statements or answers to his questions and act accordingly. Of course, he will be doing the same to you, so remember to maintain good eye contact when answering questions or reacting to his various comments—both the positive and the negative aspects.

WHEN YOU SMILE, LET YOUR EYES SMILE, TOO.

You will actually feel the tensions relax and trust begin to grow.

Physical Impression

As simple as it sounds, a firm handshake is another valuable means of improving the interviewer's first impression of you.

A FIRM HANDSHAKE PHYSICALLY DENOTES STRENGTH OF CHARACTER AND STRENGTH OF PURPOSE. ONE CAN ACTUALLY FEEL IT.

Unless you are seeking a position as a mistress or an instructor in the martial arts, this is probably the only time you and the interviewer will actually touch each other.

STAND UP STRAIGHT, INTRODUCE YOURSELF CLEARLY, SMILE, AND GRASP THE INTERVIEWER'S HAND IN A FIRM, SOLID HANDSHAKE.

Do not try to engage in a test of strength. Just a simple, firm handshake. Ladies, extend your hand first, as is customary according to proper etiquette, and you will significantly add to your professional image and self-confidence in the eyes of the employer.

A little thing? What kind of impression do you have of someone who gives you a weak or "cold fish" handshake? Makes you think of weakness or insecurity, does it not? If you will remember to shake hands firmly, the interviewer will actually feel your genuine warmth, inner strength, and confidence. These are the fundamental traits he is trying to find in the best candidate. If you can project yourself as having all these qualities while introducing yourself for the first time, the sailing will be much smoother as you proceed with the interview.

Your Professional Image

You may enhance your professional image even more with good posture, beginning as you get out of your car or a taxi and walk briskly into the building for the interview. I say this because you never know who may be watching you from a vantage point inside the building. It could be the employer, taking a break between interviews.

> STAND UP STRAIGHT AND WALK FAST. LOOK AS IF YOUR TIME IS VALUABLE AND YOU HAVE SOMEWHERE TO GO AND SOMETHING IMPORTANT TO DO.

You should not meander across the parking lot as if you were expecting the worst, or were down on your luck. You will have the appearance of carrying a heavy burden of problems, which no one wants because they have enough of their own. Walking briskly with your head up will actually help you outdistance your problems for the moment, and will give you the surge of energy that you need to clear your head and be alert in the interview.

When you, the professionally dressed candidate, stride purposefully into the employer's office, you will quickly gain respect and admiration from staff, not to mention the very real possibility of avoiding delays in the outer office. You may be immediately shown into the interviewer's office without having to fill out an application. Do not be too disappointed if you have to wait—another applicant may still be with the interviewer.

Good posture in an interview means more than walking fast. Remember to stand up straight and sit up straight in the interview. Leaning forward at times during the conversation will make you look more interested and more involved in the topic of conversation. Do not slouch or sit back and wait to be sold. Chances are that the interviewer has already been through the same conversation with several of your predecessors that morning and will have some difficulty arousing much enthusiasm on his own. Your attentiveness and appearance of strong interest may help develop his own interest in the discussion. Use this "body language" to emphasize both your sincerity and interest, and you may get a better presentation of the opportunity available from the interviewer.

Got A Light?

As a smoker, I tend to resent and want to rebel against those who advise people not to smoke in an interview. If the interviewer himself is puffing away and there are no non-smokers present, and you first ask the interviewer's permission, you may then light up.

> PROFESSIONALLY SPEAKING, HOWEVER, I MUST GO ALONG WITH THOSE ADVISERS WHO CAUTION AGAINST SMOKING IN ANY INTERVIEW; I DO NOT THINK A CIGARETTE IS WORTH TAKING THE CHANCE OF HAVING A GOOD OPPORTUNITY GO UP IN SMOKE.

Sorry fellow smokers, but don't you agree?

Parry And Thrust

> DECIDE NOW THAT YOU WILL BE A GOOD LISTENER IN EACH INTERVIEW.

90

Your mission, so to speak, is to learn all you can of the company, the department, and the position they have in mind for you. Encourage the interviewer to expound upon the qualities and experience he expects to find in the best candidate for the position. The areas of your experience that you will need to emphasize should be easily spotted along with the weaknesses you will wish to steer the conversation around. Try to nudge the interviewer to tell his story before you have to tell yours. If he starts firing questions at you, put something like the following into your own words and remember Truitt's Law from the previous chapter:

> Mr. Employer, I've researched your firm and I'm interested enough to want to tell you everything in my background that might influence you to offer this opportunity to me. If you will give me an overall picture of your department, the position, and kind of individual you think would be best for the job, I'll be able to answer your questions more accurately and in greater detail. Did you set this department up, yourself? How did you get started with the company?

Most people enjoy talking about themselves and their jobs. Make up your mind to be a good listener in the interview and the employer will think you are one of the best conversationalists he has ever met. And you will gain the information you seek.

Remember Truitt's Law and answer questions directed at you clearly, concisely, and honestly. Always remember that if you wish to take control of the conversation or if you feel the interviewer's questions heading down a track that you would prefer to avoid, answer the question as you have prepared to answer it, but finish your answer with a question of your own and follow with another. This bears repetition because conversations really are controlled by whoever is asking the questions. For instance:

"Yes, I worked there for four years. Have you ever hired someone from that firm? Have those people been successful? What would be the ideal experience you would really like to find in an applicant?

As you proceed in the interview,

LEARN A FEW FACTS YOU CAN SINK YOUR TEETH INTO AND THEN SELL YOUR STRONGEST POINTS IN THOSE AREAS.

Now that you know what the employer wants, you may begin to seriously sell your own background and particular skills. Try to cover as many of the skills the interviewer has told you he thinks are necessary to perform well in the position. Use your own enthusiasm to raise his interest in you.

Avoid asking questions about salary, benefits, vacation, sick leave, paid holidays, etc.—sounds like "gimmee, gimmee, gimmee." A company representative will go over all these things before your acceptance of a job offer. If not, ask that someone in personnel explain the entire benefit plan *after you have been formally offered the position.*

Negotiating Salary

People often ask if I have a formula for determining the amount of salary they should request in an interview. Where should they begin negotiations? How much should they expect to be offered?

THE BEST FORMULA TO GUARANTEE YOUR BEING PLACED IN THE STRONGEST NEGOTIATING POSITION, COME WHAT MAY, IS:

$$O + P + E + N = OPEN$$

Remain totally open to salary. The best interviewers and

92

negotiators will try more than once to get you to name an acceptable figure. Do not let them succeed. It is perfectly proper and even advisable to be honest and state your present or most recent earnings with your last or present employer. Do not, however, tell an interviewer how much you must have in order to accept a position with his firm.

NEVER ALLOW YOURSELF TO BE TRAPPED INTO NAMING A SALARY FIGURE FIRST.

You want the company to place its own estimate of your value, based upon your experience, ability, appearance, past earnings, interview skills, and the importance of the work to be performed. If you name an acceptable salary figure first, you might name a much lower figure than they are willing to pay. They will not offer more than you indicate you will accept. You could, on the other hand, name a figure that is much higher than the interviewer has authority to approve and be disqualified before meeting the real decision maker, who might very well be able and willing to authorize more than the sum you have in mind.

Why chance under-pricing or over-pricing yourself until after you have a formal offer? If you make a strong impression in the interview, the company will offer you a higher salary figure to be sure you will accept its offer. If the interviewer persists in asking:

A. How much will it take to get you?

B. What salary do you expect?

C. How much income do you need to support your family?

Just look him straight in the eye and say:

A. I'm interested enough to give any reasonable offer serious consideration.

B. You know what I've been earning and what the job is worth to your company. Make me an offer. I'll consider, seriously, anything reasonable.

(If they keep pushing)

C. Mr. Employer, let's see if I have the job first, then we can talk about money.

Keep your focus on what you want—a serious offer. If you can parry the prospective employer's inquiries and make him name a salary figure first, you have won!

WHEN THE EMPLOYER NAMES A SALARY FIGURE, IT WILL BE IN THE FORM OF A LEGITIMATE OFFER.

If you are not sure about or question the sincerity of the offer, ask:

Are you formally offering me this position at_____ thousand dollars per year?

If you like the figure, accept it. Do not negotiate for the sake of negotiating. If, on the other hand, the figure suggested is too low, you may then start negotiating a better offer or turn the company down, flat. You will at least have gotten a formal, if disappointing, offer and room to maneuver. Wouldn't you really prefer to be in a position like this where you hold all the cards? Here is where really selling yourself in the interview pays off.

SALARY OFFERS ARE DIRECTLY RELATED TO HOW IMPRESSIVE YOU ARE IN YOUR INTERVIEW. THE MORE YOU CAN MAKE AN EMPLOYER WANT YOU, THE MORE THE COMPANY WILL PAY TO GET YOU.

I stated in Chapter 2 that companies offer an average increase of ten percent over present earnings to those currently employed with a competitor. If you make a strong impression, you might be offered a fifteen or twenty percent salary increase. If you really "rock 'em," you could be offered an increase of twenty-five to thirty percent! If you expect more than this, you must be dreaming.

Disappointing Salary Offer

What if you really want the job but the salary offer is too low? Tell the employer exactly how you feel. You could say something like:

A. Jim, I really want this opportunity and would like very much to start work on _____(date) but I cannot afford to work for the salary you have suggested. We are really not that far apart and I believe we can get together on a figure that is satisfactory to both of us as reasonable adults. Can we work this out by ourselves or is there someone else that should participate?

B. Sue, this is the job I want and I can start work on _____. I can't support my family on the salary you have suggested but I am willing to negotiate. (Stand and prepare to leave.) We aren't that far apart and I think I can make a significant contribution to your department. You have my phone number. I'll be home this afternoon if you wish to discuss it further. Why don't you and your people give this some thought and call me this evening or tomorrow morning if you can improve your offer?

After a company makes a formal, though disappointing offer, you may be forced to name an acceptable figure to continue negotiations. Use your own judgment as to whether the company wants to "horse trade" or if you should name the actual amount that would be acceptable to you.

If you feel the company wants to horse trade, you might name a higher than acceptable figure—but not so high as to price yourself out of contention. You might even trade for a salary review in thirty days, seniority for benefits, performance raises every six months, or three weeks vacation. A company car and expenses are worth between six and eight thousand dollars a year, considering new-car prices, fuel costs, maintainance, insurance, interest, etc.

As you enter into these negotiations, enumerate all your strong points and what you believe you can do for the employer. Tick them off, one, two, three, etc.

YOU KNOW THE COMPANY WANTS YOU OR IT WOULD NOT HAVE PRESENTED YOU WITH A FORMAL OFFER.

Be enthusiastic and aggressive as you sell your strong points. The company wants what you are selling; you just need to encourage it to pay the full price.

7 TELESEARCH Closes

Towards the end of the first interview, you should have learned a great deal about the company, department, position, and type of employee it expects to find. Use your enthusiasm to seriously sell your background and particular skills in such a way as to emphasize your expertise in the areas the employer has indicated are important. Once you feel the interviewer is sold on you, stop selling and

ASK FOR THE JOB!

I cannot overemphasize the importance of your asking for the job in the first interview.

REGARDLESS OF HOW YOU FEEL THE INTERVIEW HAS GONE—WHETHER THE INTERVIEWER MENTIONS A DELAY IN THE HIRING PROCESS OR SOMEONE ELSE YOU MUST MEET,

EVEN IF YOU HAVE DOUBTS OF YOUR OWN—
MAKE ABSOLUTELY CERTAIN THE INTER-
VIEWER KNOWS YOU WANT THE JOB!

Why ask for a position you are not sure you want?

BECAUSE YOU DO WANT THE OFFER!

Remember, you will not hear the full story until the employer formally offers the opportunity to you. After he lays
out the duties, responsibilities, title, salary, benefits, bonus
plan, promotion and review schedule, you might very well
decide that you do want the opportunity. The fact remains
that you will never hear the full story until the position is
formally offered to you, and in order to stay in complete
control,

YOU MUST ASK FOR THE OPPORTUNITY YOUR-
SELF, BEFORE THE COMPANY WILL OFFER IT TO
YOU.

This is one way many employers evaluate your aggressiveness. More important to you, this is how you can make
something happen, now. Don't get "mealy-mouthed." Have
a definite starting date in mind and close the offer. You might
say:

A. Jim, I am very impressed with your company and I want
   to go to work for you. I could start work Monday morning. Is that agreeable with you?

B. Sue, I have spent a lot of time researching your company
   and I like what I've heard. I'm ready to work for you.
   When do I start?

C. Dick, you may need to give this some thought but I like
   what I see and I've made my decision. I can start next

Monday. Can you give me your decision now or should I call back this afternoon?

Sound too strong? What have you really got to lose? Use your own words but *do not leave an interview without asking for the job.* Believe me, this is the most important point in the entire text.

I recall the president of one of Houston's most successful independent oil companies telling me about one of my candidates he had just interviewed. He told me he was very impressed with my applicant and had spent several hours with her waiting for her to ask for the job, but she never did. He then very candidly explained to me that he would never offer anyone a position with his firm who did not want it badly enough to ask for it. I could not help agreeing with him, completely.

Surprisingly, when the applicant returned to my office for her debriefing, she told me that she wanted the position in the worst way. Luckily, we were able to save that opportunity for her by sending a Mailgram to the employer in which she made a point of declaring how much she wanted to work for his company. He phoned her the following day with an attractive offer, which she accepted on the spot. To my best knowledge, she still works for that firm.

Many employers feel the same way. They want you to ask for the job. They want to know that you are enthusiastic about their company. Sales managers have this to say about sales applicants asking for the job in the interview: "If they won't ask for the job in their first interview, they won't ask for the order in their sales calls."

EMPLOYERS WANT YOU TO BE AGGRESSIVE ENOUGH TO ASK FOR THE JOB IN NO UNCERTAIN TERMS.

Don't make them wait too long or you may miss your big chance. After all, the very worst the employer can say is no. You might save weeks of waiting and hoping. More often, they will either offer you the position on the spot, or invite you back for a second and possibly a third or even a fourth interview.

> BE SURE TO INDICATE A STRONG DESIRE FOR THE JOB TO EACH PERSON YOU MEET THROUGHOUT THE ENTIRE INTERVIEW PROCESS WITH EACH COMPANY.

When those people you have met get their heads together, you want to be certain they all know you want to work for their company. Often, employers will hire someone with less experience over another applicant with better credentials because he showed more aggressiveness, more interest, and a much stronger desire for the position than the candidate with all the credentials. It will be extremely difficult for an employer to turn someone down for a position who has performed as well as I have suggested in the interview and who really wants the job.

Do not fear committing yourself to a position you might not want. Once you have stated your desire for the opportunity, the employer will still have to offer you a package that you will accept, and you must, in fact, accept the offer before any kind of commitment is solidified. If the employer's offer is unsatisfactory, you may negotiate further, think about it, or simply turn the offer down. Even though you have told the employer that you want the opportunity, you still remain in complete control. You will hear the company's best offer before giving your final answer.

Debriefing

If your appointment was arranged by an agency or search firm, you should immediately see or call your counselor after the interview for debriefing. Your interview techniques will be reviewed and the counselor will want to contact the employer and review the interview while it is still fresh in everyone's mind. By reviewing quickly the counselor may clear up any misunderstandings before they become obstacles or problems. Your counselor will want to speak with you first so that he will be prepared for whatever the employer says. Here is your chance to learn the answers to all those questions you remembered just after leaving the interview. The counselor is trying to help you, so be courteous enough not to delay or forget calling him with the results of your interview.

The Follow-Up Call

Whether you are using a counselor or not, be sure to make a follow-up phone call of your own to the employer within a few hours after the interview or first thing the next morning. The best rule is:

> IF YOU FINISHED YOUR INTERVIEW BEFORE LUNCH, CALL BACK AROUND FOUR IN THE AFTERNOON.

> IF YOURS WAS AN AFTERNOON INTERVIEW, CALL THE INTERVIEWER BETWEEN EIGHT-THIRTY AND NINE-THIRTY THE FOLLOWING MORNING.

Your follow-up call could go like this:

> Jim, this is _____ _____. I wanted to personally thank you for spending so much of your time with me (when) and to tell you that I really want this opportunity. Can you give me your decision now, or is there someone else I need to see? May I see them tomorrow or would Friday be a better day for them?

Follow up your interview quickly for the same reasons a counselor would. Use the opportunity to ask any questions

101

that may still be on your mind about the company, department, or position. This may be your only opportunity to clear up any misunderstandings before they fester and become an insurmountable problem or obstacle to your being offered the position. It has happened much more often than I care to admit.

THE FOLLOW-UP PHONE CALL IS BETTER THAN A LETTER BECAUSE IT IS FASTER, MORE PERSONAL, AND ALLOWS FOR DISCUSSION.

A letter may take several days to over a week to reach the interviewer, depending upon the mail service and size of the corporation. As has happened frequently before, the employer could offer the position to someone else before hearing your own strong desire for the job. On the other hand, if you follow up your interview promptly with a phone call, the employer may offer you the position *before* meeting more applicants.

The follow-up call is nothing more than a simple courtesy call thanking the interviewer for his time and restating your strong interest in the opportunity. If the interviewer met with a large number of applicants, your call will remind him of you. The very worst that can happen is that the interviewer will have to search through that stack of applications and resumes on his desk to make a note of your call.

YOUR FOLLOW-UP PHONE CALL WILL HAVE THE EFFECT OF LIFTING YOU OUT OF THE CROWD FOR ADDITIONAL RECOGNITION.

Experience leads me to believe that you will be greeted warmly and either offered the position during the ensuing conversation or invited back for a second interview.

Tragically, most applicants do not take this very important step in the interview procedure. The interviewer indicates he will be meeting more applicants over the remainder of the week (month, sometimes) and advises the applicant to wait until he gets a call from the employer. The poor, mis-guided applicant then waits, and waits, and waits—some-times for weeks before finally getting up the nerve to call. By then, the interviewer has no idea to whom he is speaking because the position has been filled for weeks. Believe me, this is not uncommon.

> *REGARDLESS OF THE INTERVIEWER'S INSTRUC-TIONS*, FOLLOW UP YOUR INTERVIEW WITH A PERSONAL CALL WITHIN FIVE HOURS OF THE INTERVIEW OR FIRST THING THE NEXT MORN-ING UNLESS, OF COURSE, THE INTERVIEWER INSTRUCTS YOU TO CALL HIM SOONER.

Your follow-up call will make a *believer* out of your inter-viewer. He will be very impressed and appreciative of the fact that you were so excited about the opportunity you felt compelled to call and tell him of your desire for the job, again.

> THERE IS AN EXCELLENT CHANCE THAT YOU WILL BE THE FIRST AND/OR ONLY APPLICANT TO CALL BACK.

Talk about an edge over the competition, this little ma-neuver can set you head and shoulders above the entire field! If the interviewer likes you (by now, you may rest assured, he does), he will begin trying to bring you on board.

> YOUR FIRST INTERVIEWER WILL BECOME YOUR FIRST AND MOST IMPORTANT "SALE" WITHIN THE COMPANY.

The Mailgram

If, for some reason, the interviewer has not returned your phone calls, cannot be reached by phone, or is otherwise out

103

of pocket, send him a Mailgram from Western Union. This is the only technique I know of that might be a stronger follow-up than the phone call. A Mailgram will arrive on the interviewer's desk the following morning with the earliest mail. It is neat, brief, and very professional in appearance. Western Union charges only a couple of dollars to your phone bill for this service, and you may dictate your message over the phone without going to a Western Union office. Your Mailgram might read:

A. DEEPLY INDEBTED TO YOU FOR SHARING YOUR VALUABLE TIME WITH ME. I WANT THIS JOB. MAY I CALL YOU THURSDAY? RESPECTFULLY,

_____ _____ .

B. APPRECIATE YOUR SPENDING SO MUCH TIME WITH ME. VERY INTERESTED IN WORKING FOR YOUR FIRM. MAY I CALL YOU THURSDAY? THANK YOU,

_____ _____ .

C. THANKS FOR MEETING WITH ME TODAY. I'M SOLD; WHEN DO I START? WILL CALL THURSDAY. RESPECTS,

_____ _____ .

I highly recommend combining the Mailgram with a follow-up phone call. I have seen accountants, geologists, engineers, plant foremen, secretaries, and salesmen use the Mailgram with dynamic impact and impressive results. The Mailgram, telex, or telegram can be most effective for executives. Keep your message brief and to the point. The added recognition and impression made upon the employer is well worth the investment. Call the employer on the date specified in your Mailgram and ask for the job again. See what I mean by an "all-out offensive"?

Additional Interviews

You will meet the various other people in the company's hiring hierarchy as you return for more interviews. Your initial interviewer will probably remain your central contact throughout the process.

> THE VERY FACT THAT YOU HAVE BEEN IN-VITED BACK FOR ADDITIONAL MEETINGS IN-DICATES THEY ARE INTERESTED AND THAT YOUR FIRST INTERVIEWER (YOUR FIRST SALE) IS NOW ON YOUR SIDE.

Work with your first interviewer and do not be afraid to seek his guidance through the remainder of the hiring procedure. Ask him the names and titles of each person you will be required to meet as well as some background information on each individual. Memorize these names. As you meet with various people up the chain of command, ask each for additional brochures and printed material so that you may better prepare for the next meeting. As stated earlier, remember to ask for the job in all of your follow-up interviews.

Corporations sometimes seem to take forever to make up their minds. Delays occur due to budget timing or because certain key people may not be available for one reason or another. Put your very best efforts into each successive interview, be patient, maintain contact with your initial interviewer, and restate your interest and need to know the firm's intentions.

> WHEN THE COMPANY STARTS ASKING FOR YOUR REFERENCES, YOU KNOW IT IS SERIOUS.

Interview With Your Spouse

If you are requested to bring your spouse to an interview, meeting, or lunch, make sure he or she is dressed as neatly and professionally as you are. Your prospective employer may even invite himself to supper at your home. Take the time to brief your spouse beforehand so that he or she will know something about the company, position, and your previous discussions. The main reasons your prospective boss will want to meet your spouse are to make sure he or she will be supportive of your working with the firm and that you have a happy, stable home life.

Lunch Appointments And Meetings Over Drinks

Stick to coffee or some other non-alcoholic beverage during a lunch appointment with a prospective employer. Use your manners and do not speak with your mouth full of food. Try not to order anything messy or difficult to deal with. Make it a light lunch so that you will be able to speak clearly with the proper enthusiasm as you answer or ask questions during the meeting.

If you are meeting for a drink after work, stick to wine and sip it slowly. Some employers are really heavy drinkers and others are just plain crafty. Bear in mind the importance of this business meeting to your career and bank account; take care to keep a clear head and you will avoid slip-ups in these kinds of interviews.

Juggling Offers

What do you do if one firm offers you a position before another firm, which you feel may also offer you a position, has time to get back to you? If you do not really care which company employs you, accept the offer and call the other firm (a simple courtesy) to inform them of your decision. "A bird in hand...."

If, on the other hand, you receive an offer that is almost too good to refuse but not as attractive as the offer you believe you will receive shortly from a better company—ask to meet with co-workers or the personnel benefits expert in order to buy time. You may also simply ask for time to talk it over with your family. You may be given one or two weeks to reach a decision. You should not inform the employer of another offer pending until you have the formal offer in hand. Employers react differently to competition. Do not chance a big blunder until you definitely have the other offer. Use your own judgment as to whether you wish to accept "bids" from two competing employers *after both have made formal offers to you.*

After being granted time by one employer who has already extended a job offer to you while you await an offer from a better firm, immediately contact the manager or supervisor to whom you would report if you were employed by the better firm and set up a special meeting to discuss your situation. A sense of urgency in your voice should help you arrange the meeting. Remember to offer a choice of two time slots (as suggested in Chapter 4) for the meeting that are convenient to you, and let him choose the better for his schedule.

Explain your problem and go over, point by point, all the advantages and reasons you can think of for working for his firm rather than the company that has already extended the offer. Tell him why you believe you would be good at the job and how you feel the company would benefit from your services.

ASK THE EMPLOYER IF HE WOULD LIKE TO HAVE YOU ON HIS TEAM AND COULD HE HELP YOU GET A DECISION FROM HIS FIRM BY THE FOLLOWING DAY, OR NO LATER THAN THE DAY BEFORE YOU HAVE TO ANSWER THE OTHER FIRM.

Tell the employer that you want to work for his firm but you cannot wait any longer for an offer.

Job seekers have used an "imaginary offer"—with mixed success—to nudge a prospective employer into extending an offer. However, I prefer the use of one's wits and interview skills to overcome difficult situations and get offers, rather than allowing the relationship between candidate and employer to become anything less than honest.

Counter-Offers

After accepting an offer of employment from the firm of your choice, you will need to turn in your resignation to your present employer, unless you are unemployed. Two weeks notice is sufficient and proper. Sometimes an employer will ask for more time in hopes that you will change your mind or that the offer will be withdrawn. It is also possible that he may need you to see the company through a particularly tough time and request that you extend your term of notice. A couple of days to a week might be acceptable to your new employer, but you should not risk losing your new job to satisfy a former employer. If your former employer really needs you, he should be willing to employ you as a part-time consultant until the "crisis" has passed.

Some employers cannot stand for an employee to quit and will try almost anything to reverse the employee's decision. All of a sudden, executives, supervisors, and bigwigs you have only heard about before are now inviting you to lunch, patting you on the back, and reminding you of their big plans for your future with the old firm. You may be called into the manager's office and told how much you are admired and your work is appreciated. Then, you may even be offered that promotion you have always wanted or that raise you have been expecting for the past eighteen months. Simply write it off as too little, too late, and stick to your decision to leave. Why did you have to resign to get all the attention?

Acceptance of a counter-offer from your present employer can not only ruin your future but your credibility and reputation within your profession as well. You should not listen to those who say you can hold up your present employer for a raise by waving an offer from a competitor under his nose. Below are just a few good reasons to avoid counter-offers like the plague:

1. The loyalty tie is broken. Your old employer feels betrayed, and even if he comes through with the promised promotion, he will never place his complete trust and confidence in you again. You will be forgotten until you are eventually let go or quit of your own volition as the pressures of suspicion build.

2. Your honesty becomes suspect. The employer that offered you a new and better position will not react favorably to your telling him of your decision to accept a promotion with your present employer after you have formally accepted a job offer from him. You will never be able to seek employment with that firm again.

3. Your present employer may not be trusted. Once he feels you have broken the loyalty tie, he may no longer feel obligated to treat you fairly. He may speak glowingly of your continued success with his firm while his assistant is contacting his favorite head hunter about finding your replacement.

The easiest way to avoid problems or an emotional scene is:

TAKE ALL THE TIME YOU NEED TO CONSIDER AN OFFER AND ONCE YOU ACCEPT A JOB OFFER, STICK TO YOUR DECISION AND NEVER EVEN CONSIDER ACCEPTING A COUNTER-OFFER FROM YOUR PRESENT EMPLOYER.

You should not even discuss the possibility. Just work out your notice or, if possible, enjoy some vacation time between jobs. Taking a brief vacation will help you be fresh to start your new career position.

Your Attitude And Rejection

THE SECRET OF RECEIVING SEVERAL ATTRACTIVE OFFERS IS IN REMAINING OBJECTIVE ABOUT EACH FIRM WITH WHICH YOU INTERVIEW AND GIVING ALL OF THEM YOUR BEST EFFORT UNTIL YOU HAVE AN OFFER FROM EACH.

Try not to form opinions early and you will not be too disappointed if a firm turns you down. I realize this is sometimes easier said than done, but do not overreact to rejection.

THINGS USUALLY WORK OUT FOR THE BEST BECAUSE WE, AS HUMAN BEINGS, EVENTUALLY END UP MAKING THE BEST OF WHATEVER HAPPENS TO US.

The less time you spend dwelling upon past failures, the faster you will be on the road to recovery and your next interview. Go back to your library and make up another *TELESEARCH* List if you have exhausted the last. Five to ten interviews will be more than sufficient once you have mastered and practiced the guidelines in this text.

JOB HUNTING ITSELF IS A FULL-TIME JOB. IT IS ACTUALLY A QUEST FOR A BETTER LIFE. BELIEVE IT OR NOT, YOUR SUCCESS AND ULTIMATE REWARD WILL BE DIRECTLY RELATED TO THE AMOUNT OF REAL EFFORT YOU APPLY TO YOUR JOB SEARCH AND HOW CONSISTENTLY

YOU ARE ABLE TO DISCIPLINE YOURSELF TO
APPLY THAT EXTRA AMOUNT OF EFFORT.

There will be days when everything goes wrong. Nobody
listens, you have no good interviews, somebody hangs up on
you, shouts at you, or deceives you. There will be times when
you will hate to pick up the phone or go on another interview.
There may even be times when the only things you can see
ahead are failure and gloom. Faith in yourself, your God,
and these principles practiced with self-discipline will keep
you going through the bad days. It may help to remember:

THE ONLY PEOPLE WHO END UP FAILURES ARE
THOSE WHO STOP TRYING TO SUCCEED. AS
LONG AS WE KEEP TRYING, WE HAVE NOT
"ENDED UP" ANYTHING. THE FINAL TALLY HAS
NOT BEEN COMPLETED. YOU HAVE TO ACCEPT
FAILURE FOR IT TO BECOME A REALITY. IT
DOES NOT JUST HAPPEN. IN FACT, IF YOU RE-
FUSE TO ACCEPT IT, FAILURE WILL NOT OC-
CUR.

Positive Attitude

YOUR ATTITUDE IS YOUR MOST PRECIOUS POS-
SESSION. IF YOU LEARN TO CONTROL IT AND
KEEP IT POSITIVE, YOUR COMMUNICATION
SKILLS AND YOUR POWERS OF SELF-PROJEC-
TION AND PERSUASION WILL OPERATE AT FULL
STRENGTH.

When you place your *TELESEARCH* calls, interview for a
position, or meet additional corporate officers in follow-up
interviews, be as cheerful and positive as you can. Be the kind
of person that other people like to meet and associate with,
and they will want to have you working with them.

111

YOU SHOULD NEVER ALLOW ANYONE TO HAVE
A NEGATIVE EFFECT UPON YOUR POSITIVE AT-
TITUDE.

The negative influence of others, if allowed to affect your
own attitude, will cost you a lot of money, time, and heart-
ache. Stay positive, aggressive, and enthusiastic. No, you cannot change your experience or education but—

YOU CAN MAKE THE MOST OF YOUR BACK-
GROUND BY PRESENTING YOURSELF AS POSI-
TIVELY AND ENTHUSIASTICALLY AS YOU CAN
TO AS MANY PROSPECTIVE EMPLOYERS AS POS-
SIBLE.

To be sure that you have given each interview your very
best, use the Interview Checklist shown in Exhibit F to cri-
tique your techniques.

Practice & Improve

Exhibit F is an Interview Checklist you may use to review
each of your interviews and determine which areas you will
need to concentrate upon and improve. If, after your interview, you can answer "YES" to all of these questions, you
probably received an offer or will, shortly. If you answer
"NO" to any of these questions, then you may easily see where
you need to improve your interview skills. Use this interview
checklist before each interview and it will help you remember
all of the important little details during your interview.

Let's look at this Interview Checklist from another angle.
At the top, note the two words "DID YOU." Cover these with
a finger and substitute the words "CAN YOU" in your own
mind.

112

Exhibit F

Interview Checklist

(Answer YES or NO)

DID YOU:

1. Research the company and position?
2. Dress neatly, conservatively, professionally?
3. Arrive on time?
4. Make friends with the interviewer's secretary?
5. Fill out application forms neatly, completely?
6. Maintain good posture in the interview?
7. Shake hands firmly?
8. Smile during the interview?
9. Maintain good eye contact?
10. Speak with enthusiasm?
11. Sell your strong points?
12. Ignore your weak points?
13. Answer questions clearly, concisely, honestly?
14. Follow Truitt's Law in handling difficult questions?
15. Avoid asking about salary, hours, benefits, etc.?
16. Avoid naming an acceptable salary figure?
17. ASK FOR THE JOB?
18. Call your counselor for debriefing (if applicable)?
19. Make your follow-up call to the interviewer?
20. Send a Mailgram?

Now, is there anything on this list that you find impossible or even that difficult to do? I did not think so.

> THESE SIMPLE GUIDELINES ARE THINGS THAT YOU OR ANYONE ELSE CAN CONTROL BY PUTTING A LITTLE EXTRA EFFORT AND CONCENTRATION INTO EACH INTERVIEW. INDIVIDUALLY, THEY DO NOT APPEAR TO BE THAT EARTHSHAKING. WHEN COMBINED, HOWEVER, THEIR IMPACT IS POWERFUL INDEED. THEY LEAVE ABSOLUTELY NOTHING TO CHANCE.

Simply being aware of all of these principles is a good beginning. As you begin to practice and improve upon the basics of interviewing, these little things will become habitual. Then, you will be able to concentrate upon getting offers without being distracted by the little things. Good interview habits will handle them and enable you to concentrate upon larger issues.

Beating The Competition

As tough as today's job market is, if you can answer "YES" to all twenty questions on your Interview Checklist after each interview, you will not have any real competition! If you have difficulty believing this, let me illustrate from my own fifteen years of interviewing a myriad of applicants for positions.

Most people have a negative attitude about the whole job hunting scene. They find searching the classifieds, writing resumes, and filling out applications distasteful. Many view the interview process as something demeaning or depressing and refuse to take the time to learn about the company or position on their own; nor will they take extra care to dress properly for an interview. Quite a few cannot, or will not, attempt to control their emotions in interviews, while some arrive unnerved over or resentful of some small, imagined

114

slight by the interviewer's staff. Many job seekers are still bitter about being fired from their last position and the lengthy period of unemployment that has followed. Applicants will sit in an interviewer's office and demand this or that while stating they "won't take less than_____ dollars per year."

This kind of attitude really turns off a prospective employer and will probably ensure that such an individual's period of unemployment will last even longer.

A much larger number of your competitors will not have the right experience or education or the aggressiveness to actually ask for the job, much less follow up an interview with a phone call. I could go on and on.

> EVEN THOUGH THERE ARE A LOT OF UNEMPLOYED PEOPLE OUT THERE, THE COMPETITION IS REALLY NOT THAT BAD FOR THOSE WHO KNOW WHAT TO CONCENTRATE UPON AND PRACTICE AND PERFECT THEIR INTERVIEW SKILLS TO BEAT THE COMPETITION.

Think About it

If you research the company and position, dress impeccably, arrive on time, are friendly and cooperative with the interviewer and his staff, you will "outshine" most of your competition from the beginning. Maintain good posture, shake hands firmly, smile while looking the interviewer directly in the eyes, and speak with enthusiasm as you portray your background and interest in the opportunity. If, in addition, you sell your strong points and ignore your weaknesses, answer questions honestly while controlling the difficult ones, avoid a "gimmee gimmee" attitude, remain "open" to salary, ask for the job point blank, and then follow up your interview with a phone call or Mailgram, *you will have outdistanced the competition by a country mile*!

Get On The Horn

Well, there you have it—all the tools and information you need for a successful *TELESEARCH*. The telephone is your best friend in your job search. It is right at your fingertips, ready to help you find opportunities, set interview appointments, follow up interviews, win offers, and gain information. If we were born a century ago, the telephone would seem like a miracle. Two people (even more with conference calls, today) can actually communicate "brain to brain." Words spoken and ideas presented enter the other person's mind clearly and uninterrupted.

A friendly voice with a spark of excitement can alert the receiving mind, through combined impulses of pleasure and excitement, to stimulate an almost instantaneously favorable reaction. If you use these techniques to present a reasonable request (like requesting a convenient time for a meeting), the other party will try to fulfill your request. Herein lies the fundamental "magic" of *TELESEARCH*.

Follow these procedures and use your telephone for everything any "miracle" can be worth. Just because our generation has grown up surrounded with telephones, we have come to take for granted Ma Bell's microwaves, cablevision, satellite communications, and lasers; let's not forget the company's greatest contribution to our world—that instrument that allows us to communicate with almost anyone in the world by simply dialing the number.

Good luck in your *TELESEARCH* and I pray that you win the career position that you truly desire and that you sustain your faith in yourself and your goals until you attain them. If you follow your *TELESEARCH* Plan persistently, you will make it.

ROCK 'EM!

and

DON'T FORGET TO ASK FOR THE JOB.

Index

117